D0854292

THE ROAD TAKEN

THE ROAD TAKEN

MICHAEL BUERK

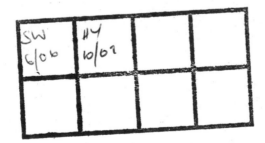
HUTCHINSON
LONDON

First published in the United Kingdom in 2004 by Hutchinson

1 3 5 7 9 10 8 6 4 2

Copyright © Michael Buerk 2004

Michael Buerk has asserted his right under the Copyright, Designs
and Patents Act, 1988, to be identified as the author of this work

Hutchinson
The Random House Group Limited
20 Vauxhall Bridge Road, London SW1V 2SA

Random House Australia (Pty) Limited
20 Alfred Street, Milsons Point, Sydney
New South Wales 2061, Australia

Random House New Zealand Limited
18 Poland Road, Glenfield
Auckland 10, New Zealand

Random House (Pty) Limited
Endulini, 5A Jubilee Road, Parktown 2193, South Africa

The Random House Group Limited Reg. No. 954009

www.randomhouse.co.uk

Lines from *Is That It?* by Bob Geldof (© 1986 Bob Geldof) reproduced by
permission of Sidgwick & Jackson, an imprint of Macmillan Publishers Limited.
Photograph on jacket back panel reproduced courtesy of Camerapix/Amin

A CIP catalogue record for this book is available from the British Library

Papers used by Random House are natural, recyclable products made from wood
grown in sustainable forests. The manufacturing processes conform to the
environmental regulations of the country of origin

ISBN 0 09 179967 8

Typeset by SX Composing DTP, Rayleigh, Essex
Printed and bound in Great Britain by
Clays Ltd, St Ives plc

For Christine, companion on the road, and Simon and Roland, now following roads of their own.

ILLUSTRATIONS

On the road with 999 (*BBC*)
The whiskers that never were
The Moral Maze (*Evening Standard/McTrusty*)
This Is Your Life (*FremantleMedia Ltd*)
Brothers who took different roads

Unless otherwise attributed, all the photographs are from the author's collection

ACKNOWLEDGEMENTS

I TOOK SOME convincing to write this book. Not, as you will quickly realise, through any lack of vanity, nor because of the effort involved; my natural idleness has always been usefully balanced by a nagging sense of insecurity. To be of any worth, an autobiography has to involve a degree of self-exposure that can, perhaps should, be uncomfortable. Journalists who spend their days opening up other people's lives are notoriously reluctant to open up their own, and I am no exception. I had to steel myself on occasions to tell what *really* happened, and what I *really* felt about it. There was plenty to write about, of course. I have had a lucky and more interesting life than I deserve. But the problem when I started to write about it was that it seemed such a jumble of horror and fun. It used to feel that way at the time, constantly stepping between tragedy and light comedy. I could have written a book entirely about war and suffering, about a world of terrible things and evil men. I could, equally, have written a light-hearted memoir, peopled by bizarre characters and funny incidents. I have tried to do both. If, occasionally, it might jar my only excuse is that it happened that way or, at any rate, that was how it seemed to me.

There are many to thank. My wife, Christine, of course, without whose love and support this life would not have been lived. She was also the most indefatigable of researchers, particularly into my rather complicated family history. Our sons, Simon and Roland, have been our pride and delight from the day they were born. I am indebted to Marjorie Buerk, my Aunt March, who has been a true friend since I was a baby and remains wise and tack-sharp into her nineties. Robert Anderson, my Uncle Bob, was kind to me as a child and went to great trouble to help me understand the family's troubled times during the Second World War. Nick Marcus, the head of the BBC News library and chief keeper of the archives, is an old friend who went to immense lengths to ensure the whole of my past life could pass in front of my eyes without the inconvenience of having to drown. I would like to thank all those who appear in these pages and particularly a long line of bosses who were also friends, Eric Belk, David Waine, Ron Evans, Peter Woon, Chris Cramer, John Mahoney, Ron Neil, Mark Thompson, Mark Damazer and Richard Sambrook. I am grateful to my agent, Sue Ayton, and my literary agent,

Felicity Bryan, for their shrewdness, their good company and their sweet ruthlessness. My editor at Hutchinson, Sue Freestone, gave me a long rein, wise advice and uproarious lunches. Lastly, of course, there is the BBC, by some way the finest and most infuriating broadcasting organisation in the world. It has often driven me to anger or despair but I have never once lost faith in what it stands for, and hope I never will.

Michael Buerk
London, 2004

'I shall be telling this with a sigh
Somewhere ages and ages hence:
Two roads diverged in a wood, and I –
I took the road less travelled by,
And that has made all the difference'

—'The Road Not Taken', Robert Frost

ONE

WE WERE RIGHT on top of it when it went up, but none of us heard the bang. None of us who survived, anyway.

It brought people out from their homes and their hiding places for twenty miles around, wondering if a nuclear bomb had gone off. That's what it looked like. A great tower of black smoke, a kilometre wide, rushing up from the southern suburbs of the city to smear itself across the bottom of the clouds. The blackness was lined with fire and shot through by a fountain of smaller explosions that arched up into the gloom and fell, miles away, in a crackling, golden rain.

They say what happened that morning in Addis Ababa was the biggest explosion in Africa in the history of man. We were only a couple of hundred yards away, four flimsy humans caught out in the open. Without warning, before our eyes could register, or our brains comprehend, what was happening, we were flung to our separate fates. We had been almost close enough to touch each other. One was killed instantly. One was terribly mutilated. One was blasted straight into unconsciousness.

I was the fourth. I had a brief moment of awareness; a sense of flying, or at any rate being airborne, in clouds of brown dust and singing metal. But, instead of hitting the ground, something very odd happened. My mind seemed to jettison the body, like the last stage of a space mission. I was suddenly in some parallel universe where time ran backwards, as well as forwards, in a jerky and random series of flashbacks. They made no overall sense, but they were vivid and overwhelming. They were like the closing credits of a film after the audience had left. Or how it is meant to be when you are drowning. To be honest, I thought: This is what it is to die.

I could tell the memories were authentic, though the unhappy ones, which had long been buried, seemed unfamiliar at first. They were all startlingly clear yet, at the same time, distant, out of reach. They were exactly like the early 3D slides I saw, much later, in a museum in Berlin. You look through eyepieces that shut out everything else, and a central European street scene from a hundred years ago leaps at you. It catches at your breath because it is so real, yet it's in a different dimension; somewhere halfway between the present and the past. There's a wheel at the side. Each time you turn it, it clicks you on, into a new scene and a new mood, entirely disconnected from the one before. One moment it's all sadness, then it's fearful, then it flicks you straight into a wild celebration. You instantly identify with what is both so near and yet so impossibly far away. It was just like that, that morning in Addis Ababa.

Click.

The first picture is almost all grey. Grey sky, the grey decks of a great grey liner as it ploughs the grey Atlantic on its way back, though I am far too young to know it, to a grey post-war Britain. The only splash of colour is the orange of a child's life jacket. It is far too large for me, for the three-year-old Michael Buerk who is fleeing with his mother from her doomed marriage in Vancouver. It was a marriage that had begun in bigamy and is ending in pain, recrimination, and legal fees neither can afford. My mother, seasick in our cabin below, is escaping back to her parents. My father, it turns out later, is looking for a more dramatic way out. He's flying north, to Yellowknife in the Northwest Territories, to a cheap hotel room where he's going to slash his wrists. It will be half-hearted and none too successful, rather like the rest of his life. He will marry the pretty nurse who pulls him round, and that's typical, too. He's the marrying kind.

That's not in this first picture, though. That's just a little boy in a big ship, alone and rather lost.

Click.

Now it's two small boys. My boys. This time the colours are vivid. Blond hair, small sweaters in stripes of primary yellows and greens, blue dungarees, surrounded by toys that are mostly cherry red. They are identical twins at that wonderful, staggery, eighteen-month stage. Pulling themselves up, collapsing down again, giggling and hooting into each other's faces, into the living mirror of themselves. Only their mother and father could possibly be happier than they are. After all, we can remember what they cannot, what is for them a lifetime away but, to us, seems only yesterday. The two of them, pink and plucked-looking, muffled and inert in the incubators of the intensive care unit. We had bent over them, racked with worry and surrounded by whispered concerns, day after day. First, they might not live. Then they might survive, but be damaged by the trauma of their birth. How could we have thought that, looking at them now?

There is no joy more complete and more selfless than the selfish joys of early parenthood.

Click.

A pale figure is trying to hide in the pools of darkness between the street lamps on a city centre pavement. Fat chance. Every few seconds he is swept by the headlights of a passing car. Some swerve and blow their horns. Some of the drivers lean out and yell at him, coarse or funny he cannot tell above the din of the traffic and his own rising sense of panic. It is not every night you see a man creeping, stark naked, through one of the smarter parts of even such a lively and liberal city as Bristol. Besides, isn't it that bloke off the telly? Oh, God, it is, it is . . .

Click.

Back in a childhood summer. Under a tree in the fields at Ravenscroft, sitting by my bike, trying to take in the news that my mother was going to die. I was sixteen that summer. I didn't know what to say or even how to feel. I had known she was ill but you never think your parents can die, especially when you only have one.

I was there again the day she died, rather than with her. They had thought it best I shouldn't go. They thought it best I shouldn't go to the funeral either. I still don't know why I agreed, except that I was dazed and uncertain, and stayed that way for months. Later I would sometimes feel I traded in death. Odd I should have had so little connection with the death that meant most of all to me.

Click.

A nuclear landscape around the flaming ruins of the chemical plant. The smoke is blotting out what remains of the daylight and is being flayed by the rotor blades of the helicopter that brought us. The air we are breathing is stiff with phenyls. And the image you can never forget, that was bound to come to the top of the shuffled cards of memory: a steaming lake of chemicals, brewed up by the explosion, and, out of the middle, a man's leg. It's bent at the knee and the boot points like a signpost to what's left of the Nypro plant at Flixborough.

Click.

Faster now.

The pub was blown apart by the IRA earlier in the evening. The walls are pocked with debris, and spattered with blood and human remains. They had pushed the bomb under a table in the bar. When it went off it blasted the sixties tubular furniture through the soft flesh of the laughing crowd. What is left now looks like a stage set from hell. I am seeing it through the window of a taxi, suddenly aware that my hand, on the door handle, is sticky with blood. The taxi, like many others in Birmingham that night, had been used as a makeshift ambulance to take the dead and the dying away from the Tavern in the Town.

Click.

The light is blinding. It is midday and the African sun, shining out of a dry, blue Highveld winter, casts no shadows from the shacks that line the dirt road. There is nothing to shade or cover the puddle that once was a human being. The 'necklace' is a cruel way to kill; it is meant to terrify. This is exemplary punishment for a young man caught informing on the township 'comrades' to the white policemen.

An hour ago, he was a frightened teenager at the centre of a crowd that mocked and prodded him. Then they pushed a tyre over his head and his shoulders. They filled it with petrol and set it alight. He jerked and screamed a full minute before he died and, quite literally, began to melt. Now the comrades, his schoolmates, laugh and dance, pointing at the unrecognisable mess spreading across the dirt. Some wave tyres at the white reporter who has just been violently sick in the scrub at the side of the road.

Click.

Faster still and, though the fleeting images have no theme, there are connections, short-circuits in the subconscious.

A local radio studio. Four of us round the familiar green baize table and its old-fashioned BBC microphone. The first news programme I ever presented. The first disaster. Two minutes in, and the tickle at the back of my throat has become a full-scale nose bleed. At first, it only covers the typewritten scripts in front of me, but as I continue talking it sprays everywhere, splattering a fellow reporter and two local worthies on the other side of the table.

Click.

A bigger radio studio, thirty years on. The panel of the Moral Maze have worked themselves into a terrible state over the iniquities of modern sexual ethics. The 'lively debate' has turned into a pretty vicious quarrel the chairman can do little to moderate and less to bring to an end, which is a problem with only fifty-five seconds to go. The studio door has banged open and the veteran producer stands in front of us, impressively tall and distinguished with his natty suiting and trademark silver hair. Slowly he is unzipping his fly. The quarrel dies away in a second. The problem now is that everybody has stopped speaking, the women in horror, the men choking with unseemly, schoolboy mirth. The silence goes on so long Radio Four is worried the transmitter has failed.

Click.

The television studio is a flurry of banging doors, with the main news programme of the evening only seconds away and the big breaking story only five minutes old. Is it the night the Chancellor resigns, or an airliner's exploded over Lockerbie, or maybe the evening the Israeli Prime Minister is assassinated? It is a rare night – perhaps two or three times a year – when one of the easiest jobs in the world, basically a matter of reading out loud, becomes a great deal more difficult. Very little is known, but the quick rumours have solidified into one doubly confirmed fact. Reporters and cameramen are being scrambled in all directions, producers are working on library material, graphics and maps. Potential interviewees are being tracked down. But there's not much to go on, and not much to go to. The plastic in your ear begins to count: five, four, three, two, one . . .

Click

Back in Africa. A room with a dirt floor opening out on to the road, the main spinal highway that runs north from Addis towards Tigre and Eritrea. This is Korem, little more than a village straggling along the road, and the epicentre of the twentieth century's worst famine. We had been filming all morning, among the dead and the dying camped out on the plain beyond the town, and had come searching for water to the house that was used as a sort of primitive café. We had not expected food here in the land of starving, but they offered to sell us a couple of pieces of bread that they pushed across the makeshift counter.

There was a rustling behind us. Somebody coughed. While we had been talking a crowd had gathered at the doorway. Emaciated men and women and children – so many of them that they are filling up the road outside. As I reach for the bread a ragged old man in the doorway, at the front of the crowd, sinks to his knees and shuffles across the beaten dirt floor. He raises his hands high above his pleading eyes in the most abject beggary.

Is this what life amounts to, once it has been lived? A jumble of disconnected memories, mere snapshots of fun and fear, embarrassment and other people's pain. Where's the continuity and the context that made sense of it all? A worrying thought. Perhaps it never did.

Click.

This is recent. Only two days ago. One of the sidebar tragedies of war. The tide of fighting had ebbed back from this part of the outskirts of Addis and left nobody to guard the ammunition depot that stood there.

The local people were poor and hungry. They had broken into the factory looking for things to steal, first in ones and twos, then in dozens, finally in hundreds. When somebody inadvertently struck a spark that blew the place to bits there were 800 people inside and they were all killed. It had happened several days before. They are still lying all around now, blown inside out by the force of the explosion, pale entrails ballooning outside blackened skins. The stench of death hits you in the face. We've copied the few locals who are picking in the ruins and pushed grass and coarse brown herbs up our nostrils to try to keep it out. It's probably the most awful thing I have ever seen.

Only 48 hours ago, and now it has happened to me.

Click.

My eyes open. I am back in the real world, and it is worse.

TWO

IT HAD BEGUN well before dawn that morning in June, 1991, with a pulsing, yellow light that shone through the heavy curtains of my room on the fifth floor of the Addis Hilton. Even through closed eyelids I could see it like a Belisha Beacon flashing on and off every couple of seconds. I'd had a restless night anyway. It had been a difficult and dangerous week reporting on the tail end of Ethiopia's civil war: the final triumph of the rebel coalition, led by the little Tigrayan Highlanders, over the Stalinist military government known as the *Derg*.

Ten days earlier, I had talked my way out of the *Nine O'Clock News* studio to report on the last moments of one of Africa's longest running and most bloody conflicts. I had wanted badly to go. I still pretended to myself that I was a reporter, not just a newsreader who spent all his days smug and safe in the Television Centre, wondering if the make-up girl's latest foundation made him look rugged enough (I swear there are some that do) or how high his name was ranked on some celebrity B-list. Besides, over the years, I had developed a deep emotional attachment to Ethiopia and its long-suffering people that I couldn't fully explain, least of all to myself.

Like many wars, the endgame seemed to drag on for ever, but then came with a rush. By the time I joined up in Nairobi with the BBC's East Africa radio correspondent, Colin Blane, the rebels were in the suburbs of Addis and were fighting for control of the airport. It took a brave pilot to agree to take us, in a little charter plane, on the four-hour flight to an airport in the middle of war. It might already be wrecked or, worse still, be surrounded by scared African soldiers who would shoot down anybody who tried to land. Ted Watts, the chief pilot of Bosky Air Charters at Wilson Airport, was a brave man. He had flown us to dangerous places before and would do so one more time, though not without some sharply expressed reservations about the whole exercise.

Colin and I were catching up – always a depressing and uncomfortable position for a reporter to be in. Others were already there, including a very able team from Channel 4 News. Now the story had grown so big, they were filing reports for all the ITN programmes, including the arch enemy, *News at Ten*. Television News is, or at least was, ridiculously competitive, a battle to be won and lost each night. Fortunately for the

9

BBC, my friend and companion from dozens of African assignments, Mohamed Amin, was already in Addis. By that time, and mainly because of what we had already done together, Mo was probably the most famous news cameraman in the world. He was also a ruthless operator (the man from *The Times*, whose restrained and elegant prose brought quiet pleasure to maiden aunts in the Home Counties, wrote that Mo 'wouldn't piss on a competitor if he was on fire'). Mo ran the African operations of Visnews, now Reuters TV, an international television news agency then partly owned by the BBC. The footage he managed to get out was keeping the BBC in the game, but as he himself put it when I finally got through on the phone to him in Addis, it would be good to have 'a gob on a stick'. I said I was surprised he could work out who was doing what to whom without me being there to tell him. Mutual respect was the key to our relationship.

We weren't shot down, and the rebels moved the buses they had used to block the runway at the last moment to let us land. It was mainly thanks to Mo, who had brought food and drink for the soldiers who hadn't had a meal for days, and was there waiting for us outside the damaged terminal building. He was keen to see us, and even keener to send his latest pictures back to Nairobi with the returning plane. I wrote and recorded a commentary and piece to camera in the ten minutes Ted took to refuel. It wasn't ideal, writing to pictures I had not seen of incidents I had not witnessed, but it was a start. We were in business.

For a week, it had been marvellous. The rebel tanks had swept up the street past the Hilton and crushed fierce resistance from the government forces dug in at the old Menelik Palace at the top of the hill. I had got into the palace with the rebel soldiers, right into the magnificent office of the leader of the *Derg*. Colonel Haile-Mariam Mengistu was an outstandingly evil bastard, even for a continent stiff with vicious dictators. He had escaped the fate he richly deserved – he had, after all, presided over a regime that had killed millions of its people – and was on his way to a luxurious exile in Zimbabwe.

Some of what he left behind was fascinating. There was a collection of books about that other murderous East African madman, Idi Amin. And every drawer of his giant desk was packed with contraceptive pills. Why he had them, what he did with them, are mysteries nobody has been able to explain.

In my report that night, I also made passing reference to a moth-eaten old lion that was kept in a cage out in the courtyard. He was the last survivor of the pride that had been established there by the old Emperor Haile Selassie, a tiny man who liked to style himself the 'Lion of Judah', who was murdered out of hand by the hard-eyed young men of the *Derg*. The lion had looked rather sorry for himself, licking his sores as the rebel soldiers poked at him with their AK47s to see if they could get him to snarl.

Predictably enough, the plight of the old lion engaged the viewers of the *Nine O'Clock News* more closely than the fate of some 50 million Ethiopian human beings who had spent decades being ridden over by all four Horsemen of the Apocalypse. I should have known better and ignored the poor old lion. Not for the first time, I wondered what we were risking our lives for.

We cleaned up as the rebels mopped up. Mo and I knew many of the rebel leaders from previous assignments during the war. We had sat round camp fires together in the bleak Tigrayan Highlands arguing about Communism (they were Marxists and, after the collapse of the Soviet Union, regarded Albania, of all places, as the promised land). Mo also knew the people at the television station. With nobody else foolhardy enough to attempt to land at the airport, the only way pictures of what was happening could reach the outside world was via the fragile satellite link from the station, over which Mo soon established a stranglehold. He used a mixture of charm, bullying and bribery to such effect that all our reports reached London with no more than the usual African difficulties. But those of our competitors, particularly ITN, were struck by endless 'technical problems'. Their producer, Chris Shaw, and reporter, Lindsay Taylor, two of the most experienced and effective television journalists in the business, knew exactly what was happening and complained to me in the lobby of the Hilton. I am too embarrassed to remember how I brushed aside their perfectly justified resentment. I feel ashamed now, after what happened at the high point of our hubris.

When I went to bed that night, we had agreed to pursue what was left of the war out into the east of the country where the rebels had not yet imposed their authority and there was heavily armed anarchy. Dreadful stories were starting to come out. We had decided we ought to go and see for ourselves. It was a particularly dangerous idea, I thought, but did not want to sound as windy as I felt and, when I could not find a reason any more convincing than we might very well get killed (always a clincher for me), reluctantly agreed.

11

MICHAEL BUERK

My first though, as I drew back the curtains just after 4.30 that morning and saw that the pulsing lights were a chain reaction of explosions out on the southern horizon was: Good – a perfect excuse not to go on that mad trip.

Soon, the whole hotel was awake. It was almost entirely occupied by the world's media. Everywhere, cameras were being set up, phone calls were being booked. The Hilton had already provided a grandstand view of the war, albeit a dangerous one. Those unlucky enough to have a room on the exposed side were liable to have their windows shattered by shrapnel and generally took to sleeping in the bath. That morning it was again a vantage point. More to the point, the rebels imposed a curfew and were cheerfully shooting anybody who ventured out on the streets before seven o'clock.

Bit by bit, and by a process of journalistic osmosis, we found out what was happening. An ammunition dump, by far the biggest in Africa, was on fire. It had been well camouflaged and not many people had even known it was there. To this day, nobody knows for sure what set if off. A stray bullet, perhaps, sabotage, most likely, or just the squatters and refugees that swarmed all over Addis, getting too close with their little oil fires. The official version was that soldiers still loyal to the old regime had attacked lorries, parked near the dump, with grenades. The lorries were themselves packed with ammunition, and when they blew up, they set off the dump.

It did not matter. Tens of millions of pounds' worth of shells, missiles, rockets and bombs were going up like the devil's bonfire party. The background noise was a dull, crumping roar, with, every so often, a whoosh and a crack when the flames reached some particularly virile piece of Soviet ordnance. Everywhere, skinny dogs howled at a sky on fire.

Dawn came up, unnoticed at first behind the blazing horizon. With it came rumours of terrible death and destruction out on the Debra Zeit road. When the night-time curfew came to an end, and with it the high possibility of being shot out of hand by the rebel patrols, we started arguing about the wisdom of venturing out to find out what was going on. Some felt they could see quite enough from the hotel coffee shop and headed off there for an early breakfast, knowing they would be able to pad out their reports with details gathered later from their more daring colleagues. Many would have gone but for the almost total lack of transport; those vehicles that hadn't been hidden away during the fighting had been commandeered by the rebels.

12

Mo had found a car, of course, a black 1960s Mercedes, battered but serviceable and, in that place and at that time, worth its not inconsiderable weight in gold. Four of us packed into it, with all the camera gear, including the three stills cameras that Mo, the eternal freelance, always wore round his neck. He drove. I reluctantly took the other front seat (very much the short straw whenever Mo was driving). Colin was in the back, along with John Mathai, a gentle and friendly video technician who hailed from a village on the slopes of Mount Kenya. Mo had brought him up from Nairobi to edit the video material in the relative safety of the hotel. Now, he was being pressed into service as Mo's soundman so that Nick Hughes, a strapping Englishman who had been working with Mo, could operate separately with another camera and double our coverage.

We headed for the dump, past hundreds of peasants who were running for their lives with shells and missiles howling overhead. What we wanted was a place of relative safety, close to the explosions, where we could see what was going on. What we didn't know was that only 200 metres from the world's biggest fireworks display was a fuel storage depot – huge tanks full of hundreds of thousands of gallons of high-octane aviation fuel. A typically African piece of planning; the safety and welfare of the people put first, as always.

We parked the car behind a high stone wall, a few hundred metres from the epicentre of the explosions. It seemed a good place to film what was going on. The wall felt reassuringly thick, and we were close enough to see the individual missiles as the fire reached them. They whooshed off in all directions. A few skimmed over our wall, but we seemed to have time to duck. Some of the shells were armour-piercing tank rounds and it was only a matter of time before one of them hit the giant fuel depot. We didn't know that. There was a lot we didn't know that morning.

While we were filming, a ragged and terrified man ran up to us. It wasn't easy to make out what he was saying, but the gist of it was that there had been a squatter camp, shacks built of mud and sticks with corrugated iron roofs, on the rough land beyond the fence of the arms dump. The initial explosions had wrecked it, and wiped out dozens, if not hundreds, of people. We asked him to show us where it was, but he was too frightened. He just pointed down to the left, beyond the wall, to the other side of a little valley which had the remains of a stream running through it. Then he ran away.

Unusually, it was me who suggested we go and see what had happened.

I was normally the nervous one urging caution, the one saying loudest that he wasn't going to get killed for the BBC. It was obvious there was risk, but it seemed minimal. There was something of a lull in the thunder of explosions. Shells and missiles were still going off but, it seemed to us, fewer than before. We would be exposed when we came out from the shelter of the wall, but once we were across the valley, which was only 50 metres or so wide, there would be more cover in the wreckage of the squatter camp.

Three of us had been in plenty of these kinds of situations. We were experienced. We thought it was a calculated risk.

We were complete fools, of course.

As we came out from behind the wall and edged down into the creek, it seemed OK. The odd bullet and shell came whining down the valley, but it was too random to seem dangerous. We were more concerned about what we were stepping in. The squatters had used the creek as an open-air sewer; it was covered in small piles of human excrement.

John was a few paces ahead. Mo had edged out slightly into the valley for a better view of the dump. And then it happened.

Now, I understand why we never saw or heard the explosion. The blast wave travelled faster than sound and plucked us up like dust. Other journalists, much further away in side streets, said their cars were picked up by the force of the blast and flung into buildings. Nick Hughes was behind a wall on the other side of the dump. He would have been killed outright if he had still been filming over it. But that very moment he had ducked down and put his camera on the ground to get a steady shot of two fire engines parked in a gap in the wall. The camera was actually running when it happened and filmed the two fire engines being picked up like toys and blown to bits in an instant whirlwind. Nick was senseless for a while, but escaped with only a burst eardrum.

Eye-witnesses described pieces of concrete the size of dining-room tables raining down in the seconds after the explosion. Enormous chunks of the roof of a reinforced underground bunker were thrown more than a mile. That single explosion obliterated an entire suburb. Even though nearly everybody had fled from the area by that time, it still killed more than 100 men, women and children.

Those journalists who'd thought they had taken the safe option, and were still breakfasting in the Hilton a couple of miles away, said the whole sky suddenly went an incandescent silver. They just had time to dive under the tables before the plate-glass windows of the coffee shop on the ground floor shattered into tiny pieces. The mushroom cloud spread across the sky. The city was silent but for the bursting ammunition. By now, the dogs were too terrified to howl.

I don't know how long I lay unconscious in the dust and shit of that hellish valley. When I came to, I gradually became aware of a dozen different cuts and bruises. I tried my arms, and then my legs, with my eyes still closed, trying to find out how much of me was left. I remember now being surprised that it all seemed to be working.

I still did not open my eyes. With consciousness had come fear. There was the constant whizz of bullets overhead, punctuated by the whang of bigger shells. I squirmed into the dirt and tried to hide, tried to pretend none of this was happening. Something must have shaken me out of this funk, some special fright like a bullet slicing through the dirt alongside me, or so close overhead that fear jerked my eyes open as a reflex, rather than a conscious decision.

I was facing back up the valley. The world was grey with the dust that still hung heavily in the air, lit by streaks of white and gold from the exploding ammunition. I could see John, about thirty yards away. He had no obvious injury that I could see, but I knew he was dead. A corpse lies differently from an injured man, in more of a heap, a bundle ready for the wash. John lay in the careless tangle of death.

I was looking at him, remembering the life in his eyes and the way he never stopped smiling even when the report we were editing looked like missing its satellite and the hotel room crackled with tension, when Colin came slowly into my line of sight. He was crawling, belly down, like a snake. His prematurely white hair stood out in the sombre half-light. His bony face was full of purpose, fixed on something away to my left.

I only had to turn my head a fraction to see Mo, surprisingly close to me, but a bit further out where a trickle of water flowed through the gravel, and where the shit was particularly thick. I could see the blood over his chest and arms. He was conscious, moaning a bit, and saying 'fuck' a lot.

Just at that moment a fusillade of explosions and shells sprayed down the valley, just over our heads. A bullet clanged off one of Mo's cameras. Then a rocket fizzed past and buried itself in the slope of the valley behind me. Colin pressed down in the dirt. I closed my eyes.

When I opened them, Colin was crawling again. It takes a coward to know what bravery really means, and he was truly brave that day. For a long time, I didn't move. I lay there wrestling with fear and guilt. Guilt, or perhaps a kind of shame, won in the end, though it was a very close thing. So much of me just wanted to curl up and wait for the world to come to its senses.

I got to Mo as Colin was trying to see how badly he was injured. He had been hit in the right arm by seven bullets or fragments of metal. His chest was bloodied and bruised. There was a bullet in his shoulder and the bruising was from the flying metal hitting the equipment he was holding in front of him. But it was his left arm that caught my eye and wouldn't let it go.

There was nothing but a strip of bloody sinew between a point just below his shoulder to his wrist. The hand was still there, apparently undamaged. So was his watch. But his forearm and elbow had just been blown away and all that remained connecting his hand to his body was gristle. His blood pumped weakly out into the dirt. It would have been flooding out of that kind of wound, in fact it would probably have killed him already, were it not for the stills cameras he had been carrying over his left shoulder. When the explosion hurled him through the air, the cameras were blown round in a tangle and the straps became a tourniquet.

We had two immediate problems. The first was staying alive, for the bullets and shards of flying metal were still whizzing around us, and we would have to get off our stomachs to pull him away. The second was his arm. I really thought that as soon as we lifted him, his hand would just drop off. Colin and I muttered to each other about what we should do – in my case, through chattering teeth. Mo started bleating about his cameras. How he would never forgive us if we left them behind. And, you know, he never did.

Saving ourselves was difficult enough. We put what was left of his arm, and the hand, on his chest and started to drag him, on our knees, towards the shelter of the wall. He was a big man, thick-chested and heavy-boned, and it was agonisingly slow. We had to get on to our feet to get any real purchase on him. The shrapnel came so close I could feel the wind of it as it passed. Mo cursed us when we dragged his injured body across some rocks but I didn't care. I just wanted to save myself.

Just then, Nick Hughes arrived from nowhere and ran, crouching, over to John. He looked at him for a moment, apparently oblivious to the explosions around him, and then lifted the corpse of his friend – they'd been very close – and carried him up past us and out of sight.

Hours seemed to go by before we reached the relative safety of the wall and I almost collapsed with relief. We found the car keys in the pocket of Mo's jeans and Colin went to try and find it. While he was gone, Mo kept on about his cameras. The idea of going back out into that random battleground made my stomach turn to jelly. I tried to lie, to say we had his equipment and it was all safe, but he knew that wasn't true. In the end I just told him to shut up. It was a miracle that I had nerved myself to risk my life for my friend. I was damned if I was going to lay it down for his Sony Betacam.

The car, when it came, was nothing like the Mercedes we had left only an hour or so before. We had parked it behind a wall but, even so, its back windows had been blown out, the roof was stoved in, the doors were hanging off their hinges. As gently as we could, we slid Mo across the broken glass on the back seat. His face was like putty and his breathing had become laboured. Colin was unnaturally pale and wide-eyed. I caught sight of myself in the car mirror. I looked like a bloodstained ghost.

Colin drove like a maniac back into town. He barely stopped to let me out as we passed the Hilton. I wanted to alert the others and try to get a rescue operation in from Nairobi. Addis was in such turmoil, the medical services were so poor, we knew if we didn't manage to fly Mo out that day he would die.

Word of what had happened to us had already reached the Hilton by the time I got there. Colleagues, friends, competitors gathered round me as I tried to tell them the full story. Before I could stammer it out, there was a shout from the reception desk that I had a call from the BBC in London. Calls in and out of Ethiopia then took hours, when they came at all. Without thinking, I picked up the phone and had a surreal conversation with the foreign desk. I was trying to tell them what had happened to us. The line was bad and it was somehow not registering at their end. They kept asking me when I was going to file a piece on this tremendous fire they had been reading about on the agency wires. I lost it then, swearing and cursing at the top of my voice down the phone in all the confusion of grief, relief and shattered nerves. It was several minutes before I calmed down enough to tell them what messages to pass on and how we would have to be evacuated if Mo was to stand a chance.

It was the other reporters and cameramen there in the Hilton who saved his life. They went out and queued to give blood – at that time, without the clean needles we routinely carry around with us these days, a very dangerous thing to do. They even joked, as they waited in the stinking and insanitary hospital, that giving blood to Amin was nothing new. The Reuters team, who had the most secure communications links with Nairobi, set about trying to organise an air ambulance to make the perilous flight to Addis. Others tracked down the rebel leaders to persuade them to open up the airport to let our plane in and to clear the roadblocks they had set up all over the city to let us through.

There were times during that long day when I cried with gratitude for the selfless generosity of those who, only yesterday, had been competitors. Chris and Lindsay from ITN, whom we had been so smug about doing down, were the most supportive of the lot. It made me feel very small.

The hospital where Mo was taken had no drugs, it was filthy and cockroaches ran across the floor of the operating theatre. The Ethiopian doctor wanted to amputate straight away. The arm would have to come off at the shoulder, he said, or else Mo would die, maybe within the hour. Colin had said no. It was a terrible decision to have to take. But we had both persuaded ourselves in the car, racing back along the Debra Zeit road, that microsurgery in Nairobi might just be able to put him back together again. In fact, there was no possibility of saving his arm, but the decision was probably right anyway. His chances of surviving a major operation in those conditions would have been slim.

By mid-afternoon, the Hilton press corps had worked a miracle. Not one, but two small planes were on their way from Nairobi. The first was an air ambulance operated by Amref, the charity that, among other things, runs the famous East African flying doctor service. The second was our friend Ted Watts in the Bosky plane that had brought us in.

They had found an ambulance to take Mo to the airport and a nurse to go with him. The rebels had agreed to open up the airport for the two planes and let us through the roadblocks to get there.

We all went to the airport, in a big convoy of commandeered cars. It was touching the way they formed a kind of guard of honour for us when we got there, lining up on the tarmac between the terminal and the plane to wish us well. There were many who thought that Mo would not survive the four-hour trip. He was conscious again, shouting weakly: 'Get a fucking move on! Not upside down – fucking hell!' as they carried him up the steps of the Amref plane.

Nick Hughes carried the body of John Mathai in a green canvas bag up into the Bosky Cessna. He was gentle, as if he might bruise him. As if he wasn't now beyond hurt. Colin and I followed along with a pregnant Kenyan woman with complications that could only be treated in Nairobi.

That was how we took off. One friend, close to death, his blood pressure falling despite the drip the nurse was holding over his stretcher. Another, already dead, going home in a bag strapped into the seat behind me.

The two planes flew in convoy through banks of white clouds, across the Ethiopian Highlands, across the great Rift Valley, down over the plains of northern Kenya, and we had eyes for none of it.

Mo would not find out John was dead until he reached Nairobi; we had kept it from him. He would never know that the Visnews executives who would come and sympathise and pay a fortune for a state-of-the-art artificial arm had been planning to sack him on his return from Addis. The agency had decided it could no longer afford such an expensive and unmanageable employee, however famous a cameraman he was. But you can't sack a crippled hero and the decision was quietly shelved.

John would be buried in the rich earth near his *shamba* on Mount Kenya, mourned by his wife and three young children and everyone who knew him. The post-mortem in Nairobi showed he'd died of a fractured skull; the explosion had apparently thrown him, with massive violence, into a wall.

I was going back to the Television Centre in West London and the newscaster's life of sedentary celebrity. And, not for the first time, I was wondering what my life had been all about. It could so easily have ended back in Addis and, if it had, what would it have amounted to, what difference had I made to anything or anybody? I had a lot of time to think, as we bumped along across Africa on the thermals of a dying day. However had I got here? That was the big question. The answer was complicated and difficult and started with my father.

THREE

THE CURTAINS WERE drawn even though it was early afternoon and a watery sun was shining on the slush in the road outside. My father looked smaller than I imagined. He seemed to shrink into the shadows of the big armchair so that only his face and his constantly moving hands had any life. 'I have waited a long time for this, my boy,' he said.

It was a lie and we both knew it. He had not even wanted to see me when I had phoned him in Vancouver out of the blue that January in 1972. He'd tried to make excuses but he had nowhere to run any more. He was old and sick with the cancer that was halfway through killing him. I had come a long way for this, in every sense, and was not going to be fobbed off. I could not fill the hole in my childhood where my father should have been but I wanted that gap to have a face and a voice. And, yes, a reason.

'Maybe you could have written,' I said, finally. 'Just once. A letter. A Christmas card. A phone call even. Any sort of contact would have been better than none.'

He held his hands out, palms slanting upward with the salesman's practised sincerity: 'I thought it would be better this way. I only ever did what was best for you.'

I wanted to ask him why, if that was the case, he had never paid a cent to support me. Why he had constantly changed houses and jobs to stay ahead of the private detectives trying to enforce the maintenance order made by the divorce court when I was a toddler. Their reports made up boxfuls of disappointment and contempt. In them, he was always called 'subject' and their failure to pin him down was shrouded in moral condemnation. 'Subject appears feckless', 'subject simply disappears when an order is made to garnishee his wages', 'subject is a plausible liar, a ne'er-do-well who will not face up to his responsibilities'. Subject was my father and I did not know what to say, or how to be, with this stranger.

There were so many things I had wanted to know.

I had wanted to ask him why he had committed bigamy, and risked a long jail sentence, to marry my mother. How they had the nerve to go through two marriages, in the same register office, with the same registrar and even the same witnesses, in order to make me legitimate. I wanted to

20

know what had gone so catastrophically wrong with their passionate, but ill-starred, love affair. I wanted to know how easy it had been for him to write two wives and a child so firmly out of his life that his present family did not even know we existed. Most of all, I wanted to know whether he had ever missed me, whether he had ever felt guilty about me, whether he had ever thought about me at all.

I did not ask any of these things and it was only partly because I knew he would not tell me the truth. The strangeness of the occasion was overwhelming. I kept telling myself that this portly little old man, with the cad's moustache nailed to a fading face like a flag still flying even though the battle had been lost, was the father I had not seen since I was three and would never see again. I caught sight of my young wife looking at us both as we talked of lesser things. The meeting had really been her idea. I had either been trained, or trained myself, to suppress all curiosity about my father, as thoroughly as he had put me out of his mind. Now we were face to face, son and father in a darkened room, we were both preoccupied. He was worried that his family would come home and find us. I was shocked by my total lack of feelings about him. I kept ransacking myself for appropriate emotions and finding nothing, nothing at all. After half an hour or so, everything had been left unsaid but there seemed nothing left to talk about.

'You only just got here in time, my boy,' he said, 'I'm dying.' It was an appeal for sympathy, but I could not find words to express feelings I did not have. He got painfully to his feet and ushered us both to the door with obvious relief. As we walked out of his life his last words to me were: 'Your wife's a doll.'

The charm was a reflex by then, thin and insincere; like him, a sad shadow of what it must once have been. I drove away waiting to feel something – sorrow, anger, regret – anything would have been better than the big blank I was left with. But there was nothing then, nothing when he died, nothing now. It worries me sometimes.

We are all the result of infinitely random choice, of chance meetings, unpredictable attractions and zygotic roulette down thousands of generations. Even by those standards, it was unlikely that my parents should ever have met and fallen so disastrously in love. There is something fateful about how the descendants of a German watchmaker, an American rebel, a Scottish mercenary soldier and a Birmingham silversmith came to their tragic flashpoint. It took a world war to do it and the story has two themes that, curiously, have recurred in my life – time, and hunger.

*

There was famine across the land and revolution in the air. The price of basic foods had doubled almost overnight. Peasants were reduced to eating grass, clover and old potato peelings. Crowds of starving beggars roamed the country roads and there were bread riots in the towns. Small businesses went bust, large firms laid off hundreds of thousands of workers. Banks closed their doors. The old rulers dithered and did nothing, but the movements that took to the streets had no effective leaders, no plan and, after the heady days of spring had gone, no chance of success.

Jakob looked at the chaos around him and the ruin of his own hopes and made the biggest decision of his life. My great-great-grandfather decided to emigrate to America.

He was born Jakob Eduard Bürk in 1823, the third son of a shoemaker, also called Jakob, in Schwenningen-am-Neckar, then a small town of some 2,000 inhabitants in the Kingdom of Württemberg. It was one of several German states, sandwiched uncomfortably between the Hapsburg Empire and Prussia, whose rulers bred exclusively amongst themselves. 'Of all those utterly petty princes,' says a leading historian of the time, 'hardly one was sane.' It was a feudal society with the future breathing down its neck. The railway and the telegraph were coming. The industrial age was spreading across Europe and with it new ideas of emancipation and workers' rights. It all reached a crisis in the turmoil of 1848, but it was to prove a disastrous year for rebellion, as for so much else.

Jakob turned 25 in April of that year. He was neither a peasant nor a revolutionary. He was a shoemaker, like his father, clever with his hands, as shoemakers have to be, and with a flair for mechanics. He could see how machines worked, how to pull them apart and put them back together again. He had an instinct for how they could be improved. Above all, he had ambition. He did not want to be a little shoemaker in a small town in the corner of a mini-kingdom for ever. He would talk and plan with his clever oldest brother Johannes long into the night. Johannes was an official at Schwenningen Town Hall, a steady job but not an exciting one. He had ambitions, too, but 1848 seemed to have put paid to both their dreams.

It was the last major famine in Europe. Hunger killed thousands right across the continent and reduced many more to beggary and destitution. There had been widespread crop failure over the previous three years because of extraordinarily wet weather, and the same potato blight that devastated Ireland. Starvation laid siege to the towns, where food prices rose even faster and higher than in the countryside. Poverty spread from the peasants, to the craftsmen, the industrial workers and the businessmen of the towns and cities. There was no money to buy produce or products, not even shoes. In the small states of Germany, three-quarters of the labour force was idle. Rebellion was fomenting from Palermo to Paris. Revolution broke out in Sicily, civil war in Switzerland. In February, King Louis-Philippe of France was forced to flee, sparking a huge upheaval across the continent. In Württemberg and the other German states the old order tottered but did not fall. In the middle of that year of crisis, with the revolution stalled, with troops confronting armies of the hungry, and with every street corner of his small town thronged with unemployed, Jakob booked his ticket to the New World.

America must have sounded like paradise. The agents of the shipping companies touted passages across the Atlantic with wildly exaggerated promises of what life there had to offer. Many Germans had already gone and their letters home were read out in public, in Schwenningen as everywhere else in the German Federation. Whole populations would turn out in the villages to hear about a new life across the sea. In truth, the America of 1848 was a land of opportunity that did not need exaggerating. It was in the middle of a dramatic westward expansion of white settlement. There was no conscription, no censorship, no political police. There was no legalised class distinction; employers ate at the same table as their men. There were fewer taxes; no tithes because there was no state church; no poor rate because there were hardly any poor. Wages were enormous by European standards. The thousands of Germans escaping a continent hungry for land were finding they could buy the finest agricultural countryside for almost nothing in the newly opened mid-West. One of Jakob's friends had written that he could save enough from his wages to buy an acre and a half of good land every week. Another said he had bought a big farm for just $160. Jakob was not a farmer but he worked out that the richest land would create the most wealthy communities where everyone, including a shoemaker, could prosper. Indiana was where many Germans were settling. Jakob was determined to be one of them.

We know little of how he got there. As summer turned to autumn in 1848, he left Schwenningen by cart, waved off by a family who must have thought they would never see him again. He had paid around £5 for a passage by ship from Hamburg; he was too poor to buy himself out of the appalling conditions in the steerage section of the ships that plied the Atlantic in those days. He left no record of his feelings on arrival in New York after two rough weeks at sea, probably relief mixed – though he was said to have been a confident young man – with some apprehension. He was processed, like more than a million other Germans who emigrated to America in the years between 1845 and 1855 – by the United States immigration service and then took ship again, up the Hudson river, across the Great Lakes and the Erie Canal and down to the burgeoning new towns of the mid-West.

Jakob settled in Paoli, a small town in Orange County, Indiana. Many of the 500 people there were Germans, attracted by some of the most fertile farmland on earth. The new settlers called it Canaan, 'God's country'. The railroad was on its way to Paoli, construction was in full swing and the new court house was nearly finished. Jakob seems to have prospered there from the start. He set up business making shoes and found a wife, Millicent Garrison Vail, seven years younger than himself.

In 1852, he became an American citizen. He anglicised his name – Jacob, instead of Jakob, Edward for Eduard, Buerk instead of Bürk, presumably hoping the additional 'e' would give his surname the attenuated German vowel sound. The Americans didn't bother. He and his descendants could spell it how they liked, but from that time on it was pronounced Burke like an Irishman, whether they liked it or not. Later that year he moved into a brick house, north of the new railroad, where their first child, Theodora, was born. Five more children would follow, a new baby every two years, regular as clockwork.

It was clocks that would change Jacob's life, make him mildly rich and give him a small, if rather specialised place in history. Back in Schwenningen, his brother Johannes was the official in charge of the town's nightwatchmen. His biggest problem was making sure the men did their jobs properly, that they patrolled the town at regular intervals and did not stay huddled over the brazier in the relative comfort of their hut. Jacob and Johannes had wrestled with this problem and, before Jacob left for America, had come up with the basis of the idea that would make their name. Johannes continued to work on it in the early 1850s and in 1855 patented the result, the world's first portable watchman's clock.

The idea was simple, but required considerable ingenuity. The clock was about the size of an old-fashioned alarm, but made of heavy brass. There was a drum inside it rather than a face with hands. Every afternoon the boss wound the clock up, locked a paper strip round the drum inside and gave it to the watchman. There was a different key, fixed by a chain, at a number of particular points on his round. At each place the watchman put the key into the keyhole cover on the clock and turned it, which produced a mark on the paper strip. At the end of his duty the following morning, there was a complete record of where he had been and when. It was an immediate success with managers everywhere. Less so with nightwatchmen, presumably.

Soon the royal household in Stuttgart was using them and they were being exported from Württemberg across Europe. The Black Forest had long been famous for clocks, but the Bürk device would eventually help make Schwenningen the world's largest clock town.

By 1860, demand for the Bürk watchman's clock had outgrown the capacity of the master clockmaker, Michael Vossler, where it was being made. Johannes founded his own firm, which Vossler and his entire workforce joined. (The factory, the *Württembergische Uhrenfabrik Bürk Söhne*, still exists as the Clock Museum, in Bürkstrasse, Schwenningen.) The time had come to export the clock to America and that was when my great-great-grandfather comes back into the story. The brothers applied for an American patent, which was assigned to Jacob, who set up his business in Boston.

It was slow at first. The American Civil War had just begun. My great-great-grandfather was the drill sergeant in the local militia back in Paoli and his shoemaker's business was selling boots to the Union Army. He seems to have been constantly on the move between the two places, a thousand miles apart.

As soon as the Civil War ended, Jacob took his first trip back to Germany and made his own particular contribution to clockmaking history. He rearranged the insides of the clock so that the watchman's movements were recorded on a simple paper disc, rather than a strip of paper that wound round a heavy brass drum. It greatly simplified manufacture and became the standard for most portable clocks of the type to this day.

The new watchman's clock, manufactured in his brother's factory, was a big success for Jacob in America. So much so that it attracted competitors and imitators. He fought those who infringed his patents through the American legal system, right up to the Supreme Court. There he won a rather Pyrrhic victory, being declared the inventor of the dial watchclock two years before his patent ran out anyway. The Bürk factory moved to industrial timeclocks and clocks for railway stations and institutions. The company survived Johannes' death in 1872 and a falling out with his nephews who took over the German end of the business. It made Jacob enough money to return to Schwenningen every two years where, his relatives recalled, he never lost the local dialect. Jacob E. Buerk may have become a successful American entrepreneur – indeed the *History of Orange County* describes him as one of the state's leading businessmen – but his heart never really left his homeland. He died in Boston in 1896. His daughters, Theodora and Flora, were still running the firm in the 1930s, when they were both in their eighties. It finally closed in 1955 and part of it was absorbed into what was to become IBM.

My great-grandfather could not have been more American. Harry Archibald Buerk was Jacob's fifth and most successful child. He was something of a sports star but even better in the classroom, to the extent that he never really left it. He went to Harvard University but came straight back to his native Indiana, where he was principal of a high school by the time he was 25. He was a lawyer as well as a teacher and was admitted to the bar of the United States circuit court where, it is said, he could have made a fortune if he had not chosen to run schools instead. For 28 years he was superintendent of schools in New Albany, Indiana, where the family had moved when he was a child. He used to buy football strip for the students out of his own pocket when their families could not afford it. He was evidently a warm and generous man, much admired and well remembered. The football pitch at the New Albany High School is called the Buerk Field to this day.

He named his first son after his father. Jacob Edward II, my grandfather, was a civil engineer who played a major part in the development of Western Canada. He moved to Winnipeg towards the end of one of the most extraordinary building booms in north American history. Forty years before, it had been little more than a village of fur trappers and buffalo hunters. The arrival of the Canadian Pacific Railway in 1882, and its strategic position on the eastern perimeter of the great wheat belt of the prairies, sparked off a frenzy of construction that turned it into Canada's third largest city in just a few years. The population tripled, tripled again and kept on tripling. Building lots were sold in mad periods of land speculation that made fortunes for the nimble and unscrupulous who celebrated by soaking themselves in baths filled with $300 worth of champagne.

The wilder excesses were over by the time my grandfather arrived, a

26-year-old with a wife and two children, in the early months of 1914. The boom was past its peak, but there was still enough work, building grain elevators and marshalling yards, public buildings and company headquarters, for a young civil engineer to cut his teeth. He and his family became Canadian citizens. My grandfather had decided to put down roots. He thought the boom in Winnipeg would go on indefinitely, but he was wrong. The war stopped the flow of British money that had underpinned the huge spurts of development. Wheat prices tumbled and with them the price of land and real estate. Labour problems grew worse and worse and culminated in the Winnipeg general strike of 1919, the worst labour dispute in Canadian history. Above all, Winnipeg had lost its stranglehold on the prairies that had made it the greatest grain trading centre in the world. Other cities on the plains were shipping wheat and, with the opening of the Panama Canal in 1914, much of it was going west, to ships on the Pacific Coast, rather than east through Winnipeg. Vancouver was the place now for an ambitious construction engineer. In 1925, my grandfather packed up his family again and crossed the Rockies, to a new town, full, he thought, of opportunity. This time he was right.

Vancouver has one of the most majestic locations in the world, spreading out from the flat land between the arms of the Frazer river and the Burrard Inlet, with snow-crowned mountains behind and the indigo blue Pacific at its feet. It must have been a relief after the ferocious winters and achingly flat plains of eastern Manitoba.

Over the next twenty years, Vancouver expanded into a major city and my grandfather put up many of its most important buildings. The company he ran built the City Hall, a strikingly angular 1930s building that stands with its statue of Captain George Vancouver, RN, looking down on the city that took his name. It was a prestige project of which he was duly proud. But he actually made more money out of a single fountain he built in the middle of Lost Lagoon, the lake in Vancouver's Stanley Park. 'I made $35,000 out of that piddling fountain,' he would say, 'but hardly a damn buck out of the City Hall.'

He built banks and hotels, including much of the work on two of the most famous in the country, Chateau Lake Louise in the Rockies, and the Empress in Victoria on Vancouver Island. 'Jake' Buerk hobnobbed, as builders have to, with the movers and shakers of the city and seems to have been widely liked. Nobody who remembers him has a bad word to say for him, or a good one to say for his wife.

My grandmother, Julia, was, by all accounts, a cold, ruthless, mean, two faced, ill-educated snob. She had eloped with my grandfather, which her enemies said was the only warm and impulsive act of her life. In fact, it might have had something to do with the inconveniently early arrival of their first child, Elizabeth. Certainly the precise dates of her birth, and their wedding, have always been something of a family secret.

Julia was a Daughter of the American Revolution, a descendant of one of the rebels who fought in the War of Independence against the British. It might have gone down well in Indiana, but in British Columbia, the most English of Canadian provinces, such a tenuous link with treachery was less likely to command respect. Julia spent most of her life trying to break into what high society Vancouver had to offer but, as one of her surviving relatives told me, 'failed as soon as she opened her mouth. She just mangled the King's English'. Her few friends called her 'Jule' but even her daughters-in-law called her 'Mrs Buerk' to the end of her days.

My grandfather had a heart attack in the middle of the Second World War, at the age of 55. It was not a particularly serious one and he wanted to go back to work. But my grandmother forced him to retire so they could start drawing on his pension, which was generous for the time. Thereafter he survived life at close quarters with 'Jule' by hiding bottles of Scotch in every room and inviting lady golfers in from the course at the back of the house for a 'toot' when she was not looking.

My father, then, came from a long line of inventive, hard-working, successful family men. He was none of those things.

My father was a phoney. Everything about him was false, right down to his name. At one time or another he lied about his age, his height, his education, his job, his women and his prospects. He pretended to be a war hero but was really a glorified army clerk. He claimed he was a widower when his wife was well enough unwittingly to buy presents for his girlfriend. He was not even a straightforward rogue. He spent the last half of his life as a loyal husband and a loving father which, for me, somehow makes it worse. My brothers remember him with love and affection. He gave me nothing at all, not even memories.

He was born shortly after his parents had arrived in Winnipeg, the family's first Canadian. He was christened Gordon Carl. As a gesture of respect for the family's German ancestry it was particularly badly timed. It was 1914 and Canada, along with the rest of the British Empire, had just declared war on Germany.

He was ten when the family moved out west to Vancouver. The house they moved to, in the network of suburban streets that stretch towards the university out at Point Gray, was comfortable rather than grand. There was a tulip tree that shaded the steps up to the front door and his father built a conservatory beyond the bedrooms, into the back yard.

He went to Magee High School and was, by all accounts, popular there with both sexes. He played football and hockey for the teams and did a lot of dating. He was short, dark and handsome, already an apprentice charmer. It was not long before he was going steady with an attractive, uncomplicated brunette at Magee called Helen Teasdale. The school's motto was *esse quam videre* ('to be, rather than to seem'), the ultimate Latin distinction between substance and appearance. It was a motto he would spend much of his life turning upside down.

His friends certainly thought he was smart and his parents were comfortably off, but there seems to have been no question of him going to college. He worked as a clerk in a hardware store for a couple of years, earning $16 a week, before moving into his father's civil engineering firm. He was employed there as a timekeeper. His job was to keep track of the hours worked by the labourers and sub-contractors and arrange for them to be paid accordingly. There was a neat historical resonance in all this, but the family had moved far and fast and he was probably unaware of it.

On 23 June 1937, at the age of 22, he married Helen Teasdale at the local church, St Mary's, Kerrisdale. It was a sunny summer's day and the church was packed with their families and friends. Outside, they kept a space open for the bridal car on West 37th Avenue with twee little signs that said 'Thou shalt not park'. Inside, the little church smelled of wood. It had been built just before the First World War in the British Arts and Crafts style, but was unmistakably Canadian with its timber frame and shingle cladding, topped by a squat wooden steeple. The two fathers were the witnesses. Bride and groom both had to affirm they could read and write. The Anglican minister, the Rev. James H. Craig, asked if anybody knew of any just cause or impediment to the marriage, but barely paused for a reply.

Helen's father, Ralph, was a retired pharmacist and by no means rich but Helen was an only child and the reception was held in the grandest place in town. The Hotel Vancouver was the last link in the chain of great railway hotels that followed the railroad across continental Canada. It was an extravagant affair, especially for a young couple in a country still emerging from the Depression. But then, as Ralph Teasdale said, it was a once-in-a-lifetime event.

After a honeymoon spent house-sitting for family friends round the corner from his parents, the newlyweds settled into the pleasant, if humdrum, routine of young married couples in pre-war Vancouver. Several evenings a week they had friends around to their small apartment over towards English Bay. They went to the Commodore most Saturday nights to dance to the thirties big bands. The Art Deco concert hall on Granville and Smithe was already a city landmark. The hard wooden floor had been built on a layer of old tyres and horse hair so it sometimes felt like you were dancing on a stiff trampoline. They were friends with Johny and Nick, the Greeks who owned it, and knew how to get round the licensing laws by smuggling in their own hooch and being ready to pour it out on to the carpets under the tables if there was a police raid.

It was not long before my father was feeling bored and stifled. If he had married for sex, as many young men did in those unliberated times, then the novelty may soon have worn off. Not so for Helen, who confessed to her friends that sex was 'a revelation'. He probably also got married to get away from his ghastly mother but, although he had moved from home, he had not escaped. Attendance at her precious Sunday evening dinners was compulsory and at all other times 'Jule' cast a long shadow. The couple moved across to Victoria on Vancouver Island where again he worked as a timekeeper on another of his father's projects. Even that was not far enough. When war broke out, he started calling himself Charles rather than Carl and was one of the first to volunteer.

His initial army medical describes him as 'aged 25, 5ft 6½in tall, 10st 9lbs, black hair, brown eyes, good development. Category A'. He was fit to fight but not obviously keen to do so. When he got to the transit centre at Camp Debert in Nova Scotia he wangled himself a job as a map-reading instructor. It was unusual for recruits to spend more than a fortnight there before being shipped off to England. He strung it out for seven months. The H-shaped huts built around a central ablutions block were not very homely, but they were warm. The entertainment was good and the food was outstanding. Most Canadian soldiers had dreams about Camp Debert's big one-pound blocks of ice cream and quarts of chocolate milk when they got across to Britain where such things were not even a memory.

Most soldiers in most armies want a cushy number with the maximum of comfort and minimum of effort and risk. My father was particularly skilled at it.

He eventually sailed for England from Halifax to Liverpool in August,

1941. He was posted straight to Aldershot where he soon fixed himself up with another job as a basic training instructor, teaching the drivers and mechanics of the Royal Canadian Army Service Corps how to read maps. It must have suited him. By the time of the next interview on his army record in April, 1942, he had put on a stone in weight, despite wartime rations. He claimed to be 5ft 8ins tall and to have trained as both an accountant and a structural engineer, all of which was, to say the least, an exaggeration. He had certainly caught somebody's eye. He is described on his record as 'highly proficient, very bright and a hard worker' and was recommended for a commission.

The officer training unit was impressed, too. Their report on his file talks of his 'considerable personality. He is careful in appearance and is an interesting and easy person to talk to'. He pushed hard for a job as a paymaster and was commissioned as a lieutenant in the Royal Canadian Army Pay Corps by the end of the year. His first posting as a paymaster was to an artillery detachment with headquarters in a requisitioned preparatory school in Bexhill-on-Sea. After so long in England without any action the Canadian 3rd Field Regiment was bored to distraction. An entry in the regimental war diary at the time describes a talk on 'enemy identification' by the intelligence officer. 'We are rather handicapped at the moment', the diary notes sadly, 'by not having met the enemy in three years of war and therefore having not much idea of what to expect in terms of his detailed appearance'.

But no sooner had my father joined the unit and issued a flurry of orders to make the issuing of pay more convenient to him and less so to those being paid, than change was in the air. The 1st Canadian Division was mobilised and sent to Scotland to join a convoy bound for the Mediterranean. My father's regiment found itself billeted in Stewarton, a town where pubs were banned. Not even the officers were allowed to visit Glasgow, with one exception. 'The luckiest man in the unit', the war diary says, 'was undoubtedly Lt. G. C. Buerk, our paymaster, who had just discovered that the field cashier was located in the heart of Glasgow and who no doubt visualised many necessary official conferences with him'.

He always landed on his feet. Not for him Operation Wetshod where the Canadians practised storming Sicily by wading ashore, fully armed, at Inverary on the nastiest of nights. Even the journey to the Mediterranean was comfortable. He left from Gourock on the *Jersey Hart*, a brand-new, 10,000-ton cargo ship with luxurious accommodation for officers. Their first meal was turkey and pork, and the standard never slipped. The sun shone all across the Bay of Biscay and they were soon ordered into shorts.

The *Jersey Hart* was in convoy EE10 which had a safe and uneventful journey to Sicily. A second Canadian convoy, BB3, was attacked by U-boats off the coast of North Africa and several vessels were torpedoed. My father later claimed to have been on one of the ships that were sunk and to have survived a long period in the water. It is clear from Canadian army war records that this was untrue. He even claimed for the complete loss of all his kit in this incident more than a year later, explaining away the lack of confirmation from his commanding officer by saying the CO was 'still on active service'. He swore to it all in front of a notary public back in Nova Scotia and was reimbursed to the tune of £22 10s 6d.

The Canadians' landing was largely unopposed. The assault troops were put ashore on 'false' beaches, jumping out into two feet of water and stepping smartly into depths that were over their heads. The paymaster, though, did not get his feet wet this time either. He landed five days later, on a jeep. The regimental diary reports his arrival, along with the padre, just before breakfast – 'they must have smelt it' – on D-Day+6.

For the next nine months he followed first the 3rd Field Regiment and then the Carleton and Yorks at a safe distance as they fought their way across Sicily and on into southern Italy. The conditions, and the fighting, got tougher as the winter drew on. But the pay parades were held well out of range of enemy fire and in lulls in the overall battle. My father, a captain now, would sit at a table with his clerk. The troops would go up with their brown pay books and their personal records which they carried at all times. They drew a bit out or saved it up and it was recorded in the pay book. My father would then head back to the rear and the fighting soldiers returned to the front line.

There is no indication in the regimental records that my father ran any kind of risk other than food poisoning and possibly malaria. But it was an unpleasant war, even for those well out of the fighting. It was cold and wet that winter and the Canadians were taking a hammering. By the spring, my father was looking for a way out. He tried to get home on compassionate leave after his father had his heart attack early in the year, but was turned down. An officer from the Family Welfare Bureau interviewed his mother and reported: 'although they are naturally anxious to have their son home on leave, Mrs Buerk states that his presence would make no appreciable difference to them'. Jule, true to form.

Instead, he wangled himself out of Italy as a prisoner-of-war escort. It was the cushiest way back to Britain and there was a long list of people with pressing reasons to go, but he pushed himself to the head of the queue. He even got back on leave to Canada, which took some doing in the late summer of 1944, with the war reaching its climax.

He did not return to England until December. He was posted to be paymaster for 19 Canadian General Hospital at Marston Green, five miles east of Birmingham and even closer to my mother's home in Solihull. Fate had it in for both of them and seemed to be in a hurry.

My mother was 26 then, four years younger than my father. She was a tall woman with striking dark looks and a vivid personality. Her spirit undoubtedly came from my grandfather's side. According to family legend, the Andersons were Scots mercenaries who fought in Flanders for whoever would pay them. My great-grandfather, Robert Muir Anderson, started his working life as an engineman, operating the winding gear at a coal mine south of Glasgow. He taught himself mathematics and enrolled, part time, to study engineering at Glasgow Technical College, now Strathclyde University, where he seems to have carried off most of the prizes. He became a university lecturer in Manchester and, according to his obituary, was the first academic in Britain to teach the workings of the internal combustion engine.

My grandfather was one of five brothers who all followed in his footsteps. Duncan Anderson was an experimental mechanical engineer who worked with many of the early giants of the motor and aircraft industries, during and after the First World War. They were a much more driven and formidable breed than my grandmother's family. The Goulds were Birmingham silversmiths, as wispy and indistinct in reality as they now appear in the fading photographs that are left to record their uneventful lives.

The war meant liberation for my mother. The dull routines of middle-class suburbia were blown away by the first bombing raids, one of which resulted in a spent shell cap coming through the sitting room window. She started doing war work assembling carburettors at the S.U. factory, but became ill and had to give it up. It did not stop her having the time of her life. My grandfather had that peculiarly Scottish mixture of grumpiness and sociability and had thrown the house open to trainee naval pilots being taught at Elmdon airport which was just down the road. Her life was a constant round of parties, many at the house around the old upright piano and the gramophone, both of which were soon revarnished with spilt beer and gin and scarred by ranks of cigarette ends.

33

At Christmas 1944 my mother was invited to a dance at the Canadian hospital at Marston Green by one of her friends who was a nurse. She met my father there; the attraction was mutual and explosive. She was a vibrant, passionate woman ready for a good time. He was a good-looking Canadian with plenty of money and charm, not to mention, or so he implied, an heroic war record. He talked of being torpedoed, of hand-to-hand fighting on the Gothic line in Italy and the stomach wound he got there. He told her about his successful pre-war career as a civil engineer. He promised her a wonderful future after the war back in Canada or maybe even South America or Australia. He did not talk much of his first wife, except to say she was, sadly, dead.

Not only was she alive, but my father soon had her using up her army wife's allowance buying presents which he gave to my mother and her family. His sister, too, was roped in to buy my mother stylish shoes which were unobtainable in Britain. My father was soon a regular visitor at the house, drinking with the navy flyers round the piano and squiring my mother to the weekly dances at the Solihull Council House and the George Hotel. The George, an old coaching inn opposite the church, was the centre of the village's social life and the war was its greatest hour. The passageway bar was crammed every evening and the owners ran a horse-drawn bus service to carry the drunks home. My father fitted in perfectly. My mother was besotted and everybody seemed to like him. Only my grandfather had his doubts. He reckoned the Canadian captain was 'shifty'. But he was famously uncharitable where boyfriends were concerned and my mother was nothing if not headstrong. His reservations were ignored.

Within four months, my parents were married. We will probably never know what persuaded my father to commit bigamy. There is no doubt the two of them were passionately in love but it seems out of character for such a calculating chancer. It would have been more understandable if my mother had been pregnant, but that is unlikely as I was born exactly nine and a half months later. Maybe he thought he could get away with it. Maybe he just got carried away by his own fantasies and, with the war clearly coming to an end, found himself marooned in a cul-de-sac of lies. The marriage took place at Solihull Register Office on 27 April 1945. The registrar had a flowing, old-fashioned hand and the writing is still clear on the fading green certificate in front of me. My father gave his name as Gordon Charles Buerk, his profession as Captain, Canadian Army (civil engineer), and his condition as 'widower'. It was a quiet wedding, just the family and a couple of witnesses. The registrar asked if anybody knew of a reason why the marriage should not take place, as he was required to do. Nobody said anything because everybody who knew the truth was half a world away. Everybody except my father, of course. I wonder what he was thinking at that moment.

There does not appear to have been much of a honeymoon. If he had applied for wedding leave somebody might have checked his army record and seen he was already married. Instead, he moved into our family home and pretended to be a carefree newlywed.

The bigamy was still undiscovered when I was born, on 18 February 1946, at St Philomena's nursing home in Solihull. My head was wetted in the passage bar of the George but war had given way to austerity and these were more sober times. My father was said to have looked pleased but preoccupied which, if true, would not be surprising. He was still with the Canadian Army but it was being disbanded fast and there were difficult decisions he could not put off much longer.

Back in Canada, Helen had got wind that her husband was planning to be discharged from the army in Britain. She got her local MP to write to the Department of National Defense asking that he should not be allowed to do so. The department reassured the MP that army head-quarters would not approve Captain Buerk's release in the UK 'unless Mrs Buerk's written concurrence had been obtained together with a statement from her to the effect that satisfactory financial arrangements had been made for her support'.

Shortly after this my father sent a melancholy letter to Helen full of self-pity. It began: 'I would rather cut off my right arm than write this letter to you'. It went on to say that he had found somebody else in England and they had fallen in love, despite all his efforts and his better judgement. He was still very fond of her and did not want to cause her pain but it would be best if they parted. He begged her for a divorce. She'd obviously had her suspicions that all was not well, so it may not have been too great a shock. Had she known what was really going on, it certainly would have been. My father returned to Canada to be demobbed in January, 1947, on the liner *Aquitania*. He went back to his parents' house in Vancouver and that was where it all came out.

It was his mother who checked the post box that morning and found the blue Basildon Bond envelope. The front was addressed to Captain Gordon Buerk and had an English stamp. The bombshell was on the back. It was customary in those days for letters overseas to have the sender's name on the outside of the flap. In my mother's clear handwriting it read: FROM – MRS GORDON CHARLES BUERK.

In the consternation that followed, only one person was thinking clearly. My grandmother, Julia, never one to allow sentiment or loyalty to get in her way, put an overseas call through to England that morning. As soon as she got hold of my mother, she welcomed her into the family as if her son did not already have a wife, a woman now living round the corner even as she was speaking, who had also been told she was 'part of the family'.

If she thought she could hush it up and sort it out before my mother had a chance to find out, she was mistaken. I don't know how the Andersons got to know the truth. My grandfather had a vicious temper and my mother was tempestuous. The scenes were so terrible nobody would ever talk about them.

Everything depended on Helen. She was a good-natured woman and when she was told there was a child involved, decided not to bring charges of bigamy. She agreed to a divorce on grounds of adultery. My father's youngest brother, Robert, who had been an officer in the Canadian Navy, perjured himself in court by saying he had seen him with my mother in a hotel in London, and the divorce was granted.

Back in England my mother was in a terrible position. She was discovering that everything Gordon had told her was a lie. Canadian military records even have a letter from her solicitor in Birmingham asking about the 'serious stomach wound' he claimed to have received in May, 1944, and asking for more information. Perhaps he was using the wound as an excuse for not returning to Britain. The records office replied that he had never appeared on any casualty list. The war wound was entirely fictitious. He had a scar all right, but it turned out it was from a hernia operation in his early 20s.

All her instincts must have been to turn her back on the man who had betrayed her. I was the problem. There would have been a huge stigma then about her being an unmarried mother and me being illegitimate. Despite everything, she agreed to marry him again. He came back to Solihull in the middle of 1947. He tried to see my mother but my grandfather ordered him out of the house. He rang my grandfather from the George, asking to meet him in the local park. My grandfather was warned that he was desperate, and had a gun. The local police superintendent was a drinking chum at the George and sent two detectives to conceal themselves in the bushes near their rendezvous. I don't know what happened when they met on that park bench under the shelter in Malvern Park, but some sort of deal was done.

Their second wedding was on 27 August 1947. It was performed in the same register office, in front of the same registrar and with the same witnesses as the illegal ceremony 16 months before. This time, my father had reverted to his original middle name, Carl, and described himself as the 'divorced husband of Helen Margaret Buerk, formerly Teasdale, spinster'. My grandfather was an influential man in a small community, but how he persuaded officialdom to turn a blind eye to bigamy, and even to put their names to a record of doing so, is a mystery to this day.

What is almost as mysterious is how my father managed to re-establish himself with my mother's family and their circle of friends to such an extent that they were prepared to lend him quite large amounts of money. My grandfather was a hard-headed man with every reason to be suspicious of his son-in-law but still gave him a slice of his savings to invest in a new business in Canada. Other regulars at the George lent him smaller amounts. When my father left Solihull for the last time in the autumn of 1947 to go and set up a home for us in Vancouver he was well off, as well as forgiven. He had got away with bigamy and even profited from it.

My mother and I left England as the bitterest winter for decades settled on a country where fuel and food rationing were stricter than they had been in the war. We arrived in Vancouver by air and almost the whole Buerk family turned up at the little airport to greet us. The matriarch, Julia, had convinced herself that my mother was a more socially upmarket and financially attractive daughter-in-law than poor Helen, whose reputation she tried to blacken with stories about a bathroom abortion and 'flushing Gordon's baby down the lavatory'.

I like to think we were happy for a while in Vancouver. My father set up a business to import luxury sporting goods from England, expensive fishing rods and Purdey shotguns. The Buerk Agency (G. Buerk, Prop.) had its offices on Water Street just across the railway line from the harbour front. It was really a self-indulgence. He was a keen hunter and fisherman and it gave him an excuse to enjoy himself.

We lived in an apartment in the best part of town; they called it a 'suite' in those days. It was on the ground floor of a big old building on Robson Street, where the city centre butts up against Stanley Park and the Lions Gate Bridge across to the North Shore. Lost Lagoon was only a couple of hundred yards away from our front door and the little black and white photographs my mother brought back show us walking under the willows and the blossom trees that line the water's edge. A little boy, barely able to walk, waves at the ducks and swans and feeds the big lead-coloured Canadian squirrels. In some of the shots you can see my grandfather's fountain, the falling water caught by the afternoon breeze. Slightly older, I sit on the dock with a miniature fishing rod, looking hopeful. Across the railroad line, my father was shoring up his failing business with borrowed money and a barrage of lies.

It could not last. The dam wall of deceit broke as my grandparents set out to visit us in the autumn of 1949. The level of betrayal must have been unbearable because my mother at once decided their marriage was over, however unpalatable the alternatives. She invited the family around to the apartment, ostensibly for a party to welcome her parents. The real purpose, as she confided to my aunt Marjorie, her only real friend amongst the Buerks, was to tell the family they could have their treacherous son back. Nobody who was at that showdown would talk about it afterwards and now they are all dead. Only Aunt Marjorie is still alive. She did not go because her torn loyalties would have made it too difficult for her afterwards. Her husband, my father's older brother, Bud, did go but never said a word to her about what had happened.

My grandparents had booked their return passages and left before us. My mother and I got the train out of Vancouver on a dark and wintry night at the end of 1949. Aunt Marjorie had been baby-sitting when we had arrived and was the only member of the family not to welcome us. Now she was the only Buerk to see us off. She says we made a lonely pair with our small mountain of luggage on the station platform; the woman who had been betrayed once too often and the child who did not understand and would not remember.

By then, my father had fled to Yellowknife, way up in the Northwest Territories, on the shores of the Great Slave Lake. The only way to get there was in a small plane. It was a God-forsaken place then, a building site on top of two gold mines. The joke at the time was that Yellowknife was the only city where the gold was paved with streets. In his hotel room he filled out an application form to re-join the army. Almost everything in it was a lie. He claimed to have been born in 1920, rather than 1914. He said he was single and had no children. He invented a totally false employment record after the war and claimed to have lived for years in America.

He must have been desperate. Even so, it is difficult to see how he thought he would get away with it. The army wrote back: 'In reviewing previous documents held on file here several discrepancies appear, notably your marital status and the date of your birth. Further information including a birth certificate will be required.'

My father tried to commit suicide by half-heartedly slicing his wrists. Recovering in hospital, he met a senior nurse called Fern Teed who would become his third wife at his fourth marriage and who was the making of him.

He eventually settled down in Vancouver with her and a black Labrador he called Michael. He was inordinately fond of it, apparently. He became a car salesman, moving from firm to firm. Perhaps it was to stay ahead of his creditors, perhaps because charm was not enough and his brief moments of success were eclipsed by failure when he was given responsibility.

They had two sons and moved to a cheaper house in the eastern suburbs of Vancouver. He still showed signs of the old 'flash' Gordon. My cousins say he always paid them more than twice the going rate for babysitting, however poor he was, and he would lend out his car for a hot date with lots of advice on how to pull off the perfect seduction in it without damaging the upholstery.

He was overtaken by a heart attack and then by lymphatic cancer. His final years were painful and difficult. He worked as a nightwatchman though he did not want his children to know and tried to hide the uniform. Night after night he punched the time clock and did his rounds, oblivious of the historical symmetry involved.

On his deathbed, he was befriended by a Unitarian minister who he impressed with his war record. It was all in the eulogy at his funeral. The minister was particularly moved by his account of how, sickened by all he had been through, he had kicked his medals into the dock at Liverpool. It was the story of a shy hero. It was not true, but it was very moving. His obituary described him as a major, a posthumous promotion and my phoney father's last throw.

FOUR

THE LIFE HAD gone out of the house my mother and I returned to in the last, freezing cold weeks of the 1940s. The cigarette burns still lined the top of the ebony piano, but it was never played again. The big old gramophone had become just another piece of furniture. Its steel needles rusted in their packets and the brake on the turntable had already seized up. The dance music 78s were still stacked in the corner, but they stayed in their plain brown sleeves and soon began a slow retreat, with many casualties, to the attic. The disappointment and the recriminations were, for the most part, suppressed, at least when I was around. But I was aware of the undercurrents and my earliest memories are tinged with unease.

The fifties are a lifetime away now. Their discomforts and small pleasures, their stuffiness and their innocence, are halfway into history. It was a resolutely middle-class life. My grandparents' home was in a cul-de-sac, a four-bedroomed red-brick house that was theoretically detached but stood, shoulder-to-shoulder, so close to its neighbours even a toddler could hardly squeeze between them. My earliest nightmares were of being stuck down the side of the house and nobody ever finding me.

It was nearly always cold. There was a coal range in the breakfast room but it would only warm one person at a time and then only if you pressed yourself against it. The lounge, a modest room with incongruous baronial panelling, had a coal fire which we lit in the evenings with a gas poker. The overstuffed furniture was pulled tightly around it, backed by an elaborate system of bolsters, rugs and screens deployed in a hopeless attempt to keep the swirling draughts at bay. There were no fires anywhere else in the house; central heating then was only a rumour. My normal childhood reluctance to go to bed was reinforced by the distinct possibility of being struck down by hypothermia halfway up the stairs. Except in high summer, we spent our lives scurrying between little islands of warmth. Fitted carpets were unheard of and nobody had a shower. The bathroom was particularly cold. We only bathed once a week. It was more than enough; I dreaded it.

The fifties knew a lot about nutrition, but nothing about food. Every morning, my mother would greet me at the bottom of the stairs with a tablespoon of cod liver oil, a grim start to the day. Breakfast was always the same – fried egg, bacon and sausage with a dollop of HP sauce, which

I thought at the time was terribly exotic. It was not just the sledgehammer spices dropped on to otherwise bland fare. Part of the label was written, for no obvious reason, in French. I can still remember every word: '*Cette sauce de haute qualité*' . . . it was one of the few hints of a wider world that penetrated our small lives.

You could tell which day it was by lunch. Sunday was roast lamb – always lamb, never beef or pork. Monday the meat was reheated, Tuesday it was cold, Wednesday it was minced down into Shepherd's Pie, Thursday was sausages, Friday was fish and Saturday was one of three tinned meats, a tantalising touch of unpredictability. A lot of food seemed to come from tins, especially peas which we had every day. Cabbage made an unwelcome appearance from time to time, but only after it had been boiled for several hours to make it safe. Sprouts were even worse, but they only turned up at Christmas. We had tea in the early evening. It was mainly sandwiches or something else out of a tin. Dinner and supper might just as well never have been invented.

It was a narrow and, in retrospect, monotonous diet. I was 18 before I knew that spaghetti did not have to come in tins of tomato sauce and was not always eaten on toast. I was even older before I tasted proper cream. I had only ever had something called evaporated milk or, a rare treat, the condensed stuff, which was sickly sweet and glutinous enough to weatherproof flat roofs. I had to ask a friend's mother what a cheese knife was for because I didn't see what use it could be getting the silver paper off the Kraft triangles. I don't think I was particularly deprived; it was part of the general experience of living through the fifties and is now inexplicable to our pampered, worldly children.

Nearly all our food was delivered. The groceries came in a rickety old black van twice a week. The butcher's vehicle, which might once have been white but had had a tough war, came on Fridays. Jack the milkman delivered every day. He distrusted all motors and reckoned they turned the milk. He had a flatbed cart pulled by a horse that was big, bony and bored. It always seemed to be in a bad mood, which I suppose was not very surprising. It would never look at you, turning its blinkered head away if you went near it. But, if you got too close, it would very deliberately try to step on your foot. Jack was as cheerful as his horse was disagreeable. We could hear him whistling from the top of the street, long before he would swing up the front path in his flat cap and leather apron. He would crash the metal basket full of big milk bottles down on the step and whip out his greasy ledger, licking his thumb to riffle through its

41

pages and pulling the pencil out from behind his ear. His conversation was mainly a heavy-handed kind of banter, full of innuendo that was lost on me and, probably, on the housewives to whom it was directed. I am not totally sure of that, though. He had a very knowing look and on the frequent occasions when he was later than usual, looked particularly pleased with himself.

In those days, Solihull was halfway between the village backwater it had been for most of its history and the upmarket (at least for the Midlands) garden suburb it was to become. It resisted the gravitational pull of Birmingham, either with a kind of lofty desperation or by pretending it did not exist. Birmingham was then an unlovely place. It was a metal-bashing metropolis in swift decline from the days when it was the world's manufactory and the second city of Empire. Brummies were sharp and cheerful, but rarely stylish. Other industrial cities, Liverpool, Manchester, Glasgow, might go through phases of being fashionable and their accents trendy. To come from Birmingham has always seemed common and speaking Brummie always made you sound thick.

Even then, Solihull thought a lot of itself and resented its social status being dragged down by its noisy neighbour, the more so as most of the people who lived there were Brummies who had made good. Many of the men in our road ran factories in Birmingham, like my grandfather, and felt they had earned their home in more salubrious surroundings.

It was still a small place. A disproportionately large church stood at the top of the muddy slope that gave it its name ('soily-hill'). Anglo-Saxon peasants from Acocks Green and Yardley used to have to push their carts up the hill to get to the Solihull market and it has specialised in social climbing ever since. There were six pubs as well as the George hotel and a café called the White Cat where ladies in hats spent the morning fencing with their little fingers. The cinema was known locally as the 'bugpit' and was nearly always full. People went to see every film as a matter of course. Everybody smoked and the products of Hollywood and Ealing were all filtered through a soupy blue haze. The only exception was Saturday morning when we children went to watch black and white cowboy films and American cartoons. If the film was boring, fights would break out between the boys from private schools in the balcony and those from council schools in the stalls. It was never very serious and mainly consisted of throwing Kia-ora orange cartons at each other and leering. The private schoolboys held the advantage, not just because we were above our foes, but because we nearly always seemed to leave more juice in our cartons.

My first school was called Cedarhurst, which occupied a big old house surrounded by huge cedar trees on the edge of the local park. I can still feel the scratchy grey-flannel shorts which we had to wear. The school blazer and cap, which we were trained to lift sharply on encountering any adult, were strawberry coloured and exactly matched the headmaster's nose. He was a thick-set and rather flamboyant character who drove a huge black Mark V Jaguar with flowing wings and running boards. He always wore orange suede shoes, known at the time as 'brothel creepers'. None of us had the remotest idea what a brothel was, of course, and I remember wondering why soft shoes should be named after a kind of soup. The two male teachers both had handlebar moustaches, hoping, I imagine, to be mistaken for Spitfire pilots. They said 'wizard' a lot, too.

I loved Cedarhurst, but have few clear memories of it. I can remember buying sweets in the tuck shop. You could get four chews, each so big you could barely push them into your mouth, for an old penny, a coin that now seems as large as a dishplate compared with today's tiddly money. I was also addicted to Barratt's sweet cigarettes, sickly white sticks with red ends, that I used to hang from the corner of my mouth in what I felt sure was a convincing imitation of Humphrey Bogart.

The lowest branches of one of the cedar trees came down close enough to the ground for us to be able to sit on them. I fell in love for the first time, sitting in the cedar tree. Hilary Wood had the dark hair and high cheekbones of a very superior Red Indian, which was probably why I fancied her; I was going through my Roy Rogers phase at the time. I gave her my sweet cigarettes but would not let her hold my toy revolver. You can't be too careful with Indians.

Like a lot of people, we got our first television in time to see the Coronation in 1953. As far as I can remember, the cabinet was the same size as the sideboard and yet the screen was no bigger than a postcard. The picture was just fuzzy shades of grey and much prone to interference, but you could just about make out what was going on. It seemed a miracle at the time.

I was actually a bit old for *Muffin the Mule, Andy Pandy* and *The Flowerpot Men,* and my strongest memories are of radio. The Home Service had a serial on Sunday evenings called Journey into Space. I felt compelled to listen to it, even though it terrified me. I used to listen on my own because the radiogram was in the breakfast room and the rest of the family were in the lounge, jostling for position round the fire. Unspeakable evil lay just outside the airlock of Jet and Lemmy's spacecraft and every time the doors were opened, with an extraordinarily sinister hiss and clunk, I almost wet myself. My grandfather came in once and found me under the table with my hands over my ears. Radio punctuated many of the days of my childhood with programmes like Mrs Dale's Diary and Workers' Playtime. It continued to be the backdrop to every Sunday. We always listened to Two-way Family Favourites – when I got older, in the forlorn hope of hearing some pop music. Then we would sit down to Sunday lunch with comedies like The Navy Lark and Round the Horne and I was grateful for them, because mealtimes were potential flashpoints in a family with much unresolved resentment and tension.

My mother was effectively trapped by her circumstances – me, in other words. Her health was already failing, though I was unaware of it. Her heart had been damaged by a near-fatal bout of scarlet fever when she was a child. Early on in the war, she developed pleurisy and then pneumonia and a Belgian doctor had to perform an emergency operation in the front room of our house. He tapped into her lung and drew off the fluid using an electric pump. It saved her life, but weakened her heart still further. By the 1950s there was no question of her getting a job, or ever having any kind of independence with a child in tow.

Most of the time it was reasonably harmonious. My grandparents were decent people who, I am sure, loved their daughter and me. But my grandfather could be cantankerous and, particularly when he came back from the George, would needle my mother about the marriage he had tried hard to prevent. He would take some delight in pointing out how dependent she and I were on him. My grandfather was not normally unkind but, on these occasions, seemed to me to be malignant and cruel. My mother was a spirited woman and would stick up for herself and me, but he would play with her until, presumably, the effects of the drink wore off.

It was all made worse by complicated family dynamics that were a mystery to me then and I am not very clear about now. They revolved around my mother's younger brother, Bob, who lived with us while recovering from a long history of tuberculosis. My grandmother had doted on him as a child and my grandfather had become terribly jealous. Certainly, he often seemed to hate my uncle. He would take every opportunity to be nasty to him and put the worst possible interpretation on what he said and did. My mother would defend him, as she had all through their childhood, and so, apparently, would my grandmother.

But, somehow, everything she said only made things worse. She seemed to have a genius for stirring up the situation while appearing to try to calm it down. She may just have been clumsy but I think she rather enjoyed his jealousy and the power it gave her. In any event it was another inflammatory ingredient thrown into already explosive family rows. Crockery would get smashed, the yelling would rattle the windows. My mother would be left shaking. She had given up smoking long before, but I would see her drawing hard on a cigarette held between trembling fingers.

I dreaded these occasions to the extent that they overshadowed my childhood. I would see them coming and try, nearly always unsuccessfully, to steer the conversation away from the danger areas. When that did not work I would plead with them to stop, but they rarely did. I tried to get away, but they could be heard in every corner of the house and, however far I went, I could still hear them in my head. My imagination was probably worse than the real thing.

I was relieved when I got a scholarship to the local public school. Anything that reduced our indebtedness to my grandfather was a great weight off my mind. To be fair, he was often very generous to me and never quibbled at the expense of going to that kind of school, which was still heavy, even though the fees were all being paid. There was a lot of uniform to buy. We wore grey herringbone tweed suits (short trousers for the younger boys of course) with a cap during the winter and a blazer and flannels with a straw boater during the summer. There were uniforms for the Scouts and endless different kit for all the sports that were played there. I got all the basic stuff, but when I turned up for the first afternoon of rugby it was not enough. As well as the shirt I was wearing, which was my house colour, black, I needed a white one so they could easily make two sides. It was not a serious telling off, but it was made pretty clear I must not turn up again without it. Somehow, I just could not ask for anything else. Every Tuesday and Saturday afternoon, when the other boys set off for the sports fields, I would lock myself in the lavatories and sit, very still, in one of the cubicles, praying that nobody would notice I was missing. Inevitably, they did, and a search of the school did not take long to find me. I could not explain what I was doing, or why I was doing it. I made up some story about being afraid I would get hurt which led to a lot of mockery from the other boys. I would rather be despised than tell the truth.

All the other boys had fathers. I never let on I did not. When I was asked what my father did, I would talk about my grandfather's job, running a gear grinding factory on the southern fringes of Birmingham. Later, I gave my non-existent father my uncle's job because 'aeronautical engineer' sounded more glamorous. Nobody noticed the career change. I rarely, if ever, invited other boys home in case this pretence was discovered.

Solihull School was not Winchester or Eton but it was a good school with a fine reputation and long history. It was, perhaps, unfortunate that one of its main claims to fame was in turning down Dr Samuel Johnson when he applied to be master (a 'haughty and ill-natured gent' who was so ugly he might frighten 'some young ladds'). It was then approaching its four hundredth anniversary. It had trained a dozen generations of boys to take their places in the industrial squirearchy of the West Midlands. Most of my friends were the sons of local businessmen, but not all. There was quite a large proportion of scholarship boys like me, from a wider range of backgrounds, and the boarding house had boys from much further afield.

Leadership was the quality they were trying to instil. It was taken for granted we would soon be running something, the family ball-bearing business, perhaps, or a battalion in the army; the school had a strong military tradition. It was still suffused with the public school ethos of Empire, some lingering traces of the idea that the school's purpose, and our destiny, lay in civilising the natives in some benighted corner of Britain's dominions. The maps in our geography lessons were mostly red when I went there but, by the time I left, the Empire had been given back. Nonetheless, the message was still that we were special and our privileges carried duties towards those less fortunate. This attitude arguably worked well in the Malayan rubber plantations, but was proving less effective in the Longbridge car factory, flagship of a British motor industry then in even sharper decline than the Empire.

Respect and obedience were instilled by a bookful of regulations which dictated our behaviour. We were not allowed to chew in public, have our hands in our pockets or our jackets undone, wear shoes without laces or walk across a bewildering number of lawns and quadrangles that were in some way sacred. Deference to all adults at all times was obligatory. Failure to offer your seat on a bus to any female, or any man past his prime, was practically a capital offence. It was all policed enthusiastically by ranks of monitors and prefects who were called, for reasons that were never explained to me, 'benchers'. They wore tassels on their caps and rosettes in their button holes. They enforced the school statutes with detentions and an inventive range of beatings.

We learned the techniques of leadership in a dozen different hierarchies. On the sports field, of course; we spent a lot of time playing sport, learning to win but not crow about it. Sporting achievement was reflected in the clothes you wore. Each team awarded colours which entitled you to a different tie. If you got into the senior teams you were entitled to a special, candy-striped blazer, which you could festoon with a gold school badge and gold numerals underneath. There were special scarves and bands for your boater, track suits and medals. We paid as much attention to uniforms and accoutrements as they did in Hitler's SS. The school outfitter was easily the most prosperous business in the town.

There were two troops of Scouts, run on soldierly lines. I rose to be patrol leader of the Peewits, my first opportunity to boss rather than be bossed. It was intoxicating. I learned to cook on cow pats and won badges for everything except my narrow victory in the masturbation race at the annual Scout Camp. Solihull had a paramilitary organisation called the Terriers, who spent all their time swinging around on ropes, to bridge the gap between the Scouts and the Cadets. The school's Combined Cadet Force was large, ferociously disciplined and heavily armed. There were enough antique Lee Enfield rifles in the armoury to take over a small African country. Something quite similar was practised at regular intervals. It could all be rather alarming for parents of prospective pupils who would sometimes turn up in the middle of what looked like a re-run of D-Day. Khaki-clad boys would be abseiling down from the Big School roof with knives in their teeth. Platoons of Cadets in battledress and camouflage would be staging 'section in attack' across the car park, with real weapons, smoke and – though it was not immediately obvious – blanks. Overhead, the school air force mounted patrol. It was only a glider on a ski, it did have to be launched by a small army of boys pulling what were, in effect, two large elastic bands, and it could only stay in the air for about 20 seconds, but, once launched, it was completely out of control and more frightening than anything else.

The masters were a mixed bunch. Most of them were good men, fine and dedicated teachers. The staff room had more than its fair share of oddities. One of the German teachers was strange enough in the lessons, investing the language with such gobby enthusiasm that every class he took was hosed down as if it was on fire. This was nothing to what happened when he put on his lieutenant's uniform and led his platoon of cadets out on night exercises. He was found in a local churchyard one night, hurling thunderflashes in all directions and baying at the moon. The chemistry teachers seemed uniformly loony – the best of them, a truly inspirational man called Arculus, seemed as unstable as one of the rarer elements he described in such loving detail. In the laboratory he would foam over faster than a beaker on his Bunsen burner. He was riveting and got spectacular results, but would have made far more money playing mad professors in Hollywood. We had a rather porky paedophile on the teaching staff but this was regarded by the boys as no more than an eccentricity. His groping could largely be avoided and his little favourites were ribbed rather than bullied.

All the teachers, indeed the whole school, lived in the long shadow of the headmaster, H. B. Hitchens. Only Field Marshal Montgomery had ever called him Harry, for he had a formidable war record. At one time he was said to have been the youngest Brigadier in the army. His physical presence was totally intimidating. He was very tall, slim and erect. He had hair like patent leather and a high-boned, mahogany-coloured face with glittering eyes. He looked like a cross between the Duke of Wellington and Count Dracula, an impression reinforced by his habit of striding around the school in a floor-length grey cloak fastened at the neck with a gold chain. He was a figure of awe to masters as well as boys, until the day he was caught in the public lavatories at Banbury soliciting young men. There had never been a hint of this at the school. He committed suicide before the news broke and was replaced by a mild-mannered son of a bishop with five children.

Sex was something of a pre-occupation to all of us. I had learned all about it from a boy called Peter Bragg as we played Dan Dare on a building site in our road. He had imaginative explanations for how girls were made which fitted the few facts available to us at the time, but were wildly wide of the mark. I was particularly intrigued with his ideas of where girls kept their willies. It seemed inconvenient, if not rather painful, but I knew very few girls at the time and they did do a lot of complaining.

This changed around about the time I got my first pair of long trousers, a rite of passage then as important as the circumcision ceremony for Xhosa warriors. James Bond had just gone into paperback and I was amazed how interested he was in girls and the strange-sounding things he seemed to get up to with them. Around about the same time I got hold of a magazine called *Health and Efficiency*, a blameless title for a publication then considered the height of salaciousness. It mostly showed black and white pictures of wholesome girls playing with a beach ball. They had no clothes on and, I was astonished to see, no willies. The words were all about the joys of exposing yourself to the English weather, but the pictures were strangely exciting. I became very popular indeed at school.

My attempts to get to know real girls were disappointingly unsuccessful. There was a playground in the local park which the girls from Malvern Hall grammar school had to pass on their way home. It had swings and a conical shaped structure that revolved around a pole and was called, I think, a Witch's Hat. With my quasi-military training and lots of practice, I became adept at climbing all over these swings. I could hang from the highest bars and leap, daringly, from one to another. For a long time, I would race across to the park at four o'clock and be there, showing off madly, as the girls went past. They were probably very impressed, but they pretended to take no notice. As a sexual strategy it was a failure. It was like a field course in evolution.

All this time, my mother's health had been deteriorating. She had been getting thinner and out of breath more often. I did not know it, but my grandfather had been called in by the local hospital after mother had been examined, to be told that her heart was fatally damaged and she had less than a year to live. He kept the news to himself.

My mother and I were very close. The previous summer she had borrowed my uncle's red Morgan sports car to take me to Borth, the little village on the Welsh coast where we (and most of the Midlands) took all our holidays. I remember coming back, very early in the morning, with the hood down at what seemed like a hundred miles an hour. She was a vivid woman, revelling in that rare moment of freedom.

She went into hospital the summer I took my 'O' levels. I hated the place and I hated going there and seeing her get steadily worse. I had no idea she might die until I went one Sunday and found her barely conscious and in an oxygen tent. I had just been getting to the age when we might have had proper conversations about important things. I didn't speak to her again. She died that September and I never said goodbye.

The rest of that year is just a blur. I didn't go to her funeral, whether because I thought I could not face it, or my grandparents wanted to protect me from hurt, I don't know, but I am desperately ashamed about it now. I know I went for long rides on my bike and spent hours and hours in lonely places staring into space. I was unprepared for her death and emotionally too immature to cope. My grandparents were old now and dealing with their own grief. The teachers were concerned but their kindness was unobtrusive, giving me space rather than any sort of comfort. My schoolfriends did not know what to say. After a week or so of awkwardness, the subject was never mentioned.

It took years to get over it. In some ways, I feel I never really have. It had an immediate and profound effect on my school career. I was reasonably bright, with an aptitude for the arts subjects and some talent at English and history. The events of that summer, though, made me decide to become a doctor. The teachers advised me strongly against it but I would not listen and, as I had comfortably passed all the science 'O' level subjects, there was very little they could do.

The sciences soon bored me. I found physics in particular both tedious and incomprehensible. It is odd to be descended on all sides from fine engineers and yet be unable to grasp a theorem or change a plug. It did not help that I made no effort at all. The stuffing was knocked out of me and I drifted.

I stopped chasing butterflies and beetles with my friend, John Badmin. He and I had been collecting them for years and had become reasonably expert entomologists. He went on to make a distinguished career out of it; I turned to drink and sex, or rather tried to. I picked up with a lad called David McNally, who was as close to a dissolute wastrel as Solihull School could get at the time. Together, we would scour the hottest night spots in the town, like the Congregational Church Junior Youth Club, looking for talent. There was no such thing as fashion in those days. The trick was to dress as much as possible like your father, if you had one, of course. I wore a sports jacket, cavalry twill trousers, highly polished brogues and a cravat, I remember, and felt I looked very dashing. Dave dressed much the same but was blond and rather more handsome. I thought my tweed pork pie hat more than compensated for his advantages.

The famous sixties sexual revolution passed me by. To be more precise, I was a very keen revolutionary but could find nobody to be revolting with. Sex was as slippery a concept as the girls I tried to corner and seduce. Progress was measured by which part of their anatomy they allowed you to touch before slapping you away or bursting into tears. Every evening we would compare notes about how far we'd got. Dave always seem to be several steps ahead in this until one evening when he came round and said he had gone 'all the way', a mythical destination far beyond the bra strap fumblings that were the height of my ambitions. Dave was a notorious liar and I was sure he was a virgin until he started looking smug and saying nothing.

My biggest problem was my glasses. The lenses were thick and not very flattering so I used to take them off when moving in for the *coup de grâce*. I was devastatingly intense at close quarters but was so blind otherwise I had to move around mostly by intuition. A promising relationship with a lovely girl called Brenda came to an end at a bus stop outside the Land Rover factory. I was waiting for her to get back from school and, as soon as I had checked it was the right bus, whipped off my glasses and stood, blinking in a light drizzle, ready to give her an affectionate welcome. It was my bad luck that two brunettes in her school uniform stepped off the bus at roughly the same time. I lunged at the nearest and was already committed to a passionate clinch before I realised I had guessed wrong. It was difficult to tell who screamed the loudest. I backed away and fell over a rubbish bin I would not have spotted even if I was looking that way. By the time I'd picked myself up and found my glasses they were both far away, backs bristling with different kinds of rage. I knew if I could get into bed with a girl I would have no trouble telling who she was, but it was proving remarkably difficult.

Cricket was some consolation. I was a reasonably skilled batsman, good enough to play occasionally for the Warwickshire Nursery as well as the school first eleven. The summers were spent practising at the nets in the easy comradeship of friends I had grown up with for a decade. Boys were much less complicated. It would have been far less stressful to be homosexual, I suppose, but there weren't any in those days, at any rate the subject was never mentioned. They were golden afternoons, playing on the school team's little green jewel of a ground, flanked by the old wooden pavilion and the tuck shop which was run by the cricket pro's indulgent wife.

I also made something of a mark in the school cadet force. I was naturally pompous and liked ordering people around. By then, I had got the knack of lining the serge trousers with glue to get a sharp crease, and shining the toecaps of my boots with melted polish and the back of a hot spoon. It was clear by then that no medical school would have me and joining the services seemed to be the answer.

I went along to the officer selection course with a considerable degree of confidence. By then I was the Solihull School CCF under-officer, a teenage Napoleon, entitled to carry a leather-covered cane, rather than an antique rifle, and stand out in front, barking orders. I could do all those things they test you on. I could get the supposed nuclear bomb across the bottomless chasm marked out on the gym floor, using only three ropes, a stick and five fellow candidates, no problem. I was glib. I looked good in a uniform. And I felt the right sort of person to have a servant.

I had already left school, in a welter of suppressed emotions, when the rejection slip came through. They had not turned me down on the perfectly reasonable grounds that I was an insufferable little jerk. My eyesight was simply not good enough to be considered for Her Majesty's Forces.

It was all too much. My eyes seemed to be condemning me to a life as an unemployed virgin. I was devastated and, frankly, lost.

I could no longer live off my aging grandparents and went and got a job on a building site while I worked out what to do. I became a hod carrier, carrying bricks in a three-sided box on a stick up the sides of a half-built block of flats. The team of brickies I served were on piecework. They got paid £12 for every 1,000 bricks they laid and their trowels flew all day. I thought I was pretty fit and sneered at the other hod carrier, a pot-bellied old slob of a bloke called Alf, when we met at 6.30 the first morning. He ignored me and wiped the mud off his shovel so that he could use it to fry sausages and eggs over the brazier. He managed to eat it all without removing the cigarette end from the corner of his mouth. It was finally dislodged by the third of three shattering belches he let out, before we picked up our hods and got to work.

I was exhausted by 9 a.m. and stayed that way for three months. Alf never broke sweat as far as I could see. I sweated so much I used to stop in the Malt Shovel on my way home every night for three pints of bitter, drunk straight off, and I can't remember any need to pee for weeks.

It was tough and I never really got used to it. The gang were pleasant enough, but the conversations were rather limited, the money was not very good and it was getting cold and dark out on the site. Besides, it wasn't doing much for my sex life. A half-blind hod carrier hadn't much chance of pulling the more glamorous of Solihull's mini-skirted dolly birds. Even the dogs were turning up their noses. I couldn't see them most of the time, but I still got the message.

I needed a different job. Something raffish to impress the girls and my schoolfriends who would soon be coming back from their colleges for Christmas. Something glamorous, well-paid and trendy.

I know, I thought. I'll be a reporter.

FIVE

'SHORTHAND?' It was more of a bark than a question. The editor cocked a bloodshot eye in my direction.

'Erm, no,' I said, thoughtfully.

'Can yuh type?' Both bloodshot eyes were now fixed on the ceiling.

'Not exactly.' I had never touched a typewriter in my life.

'Courts, councils – how much d'ye know about 'em?'

'A little,' I said. I did not mention my criminal record, the result of an under-aged motorbike jaunt that had ended when rain smothered my glasses and I had crashed into a policeman. It didn't seem the right time.

'A little's no good to me, son,' he said.

He wrestled with the papers in front of him for a moment and suddenly leaned forward so that he was staring up at me from just under my chin.

'Football?'

'I'm afraid not. We played rugger at school.'

The editor let out a shuddering moan and wiped a meaty hand down his big red face. He dragged a pencil from behind his ear and started writing on my application letter, underlining it a lot.

'You're not much use at all, are you?' he said. It was not going quite as well as I had hoped.

After a long silence, he tried his last shot. 'What about cricket?'

'Oh, yes,' I said brightly. 'In fact, I didn't do too badly against your town team last season.' There was a crash as he pushed himself back from the table and lurched over to the corner of room, where back copies of the year's papers were stacked on a large lectern. He ripped through them until he found the match report. 'Fifty-nine,' he said. 'Not bad. Not bad at all.'

His face suddenly broke into a smile and he stretched his arms out wide. 'Welcome to the *Bromsgrove Messenger*, Mr Buerk. You are just the sort of young man we need.'

I was a journalist at last.

The *Bromsgrove Weekly Messenger* was not top of the list of the newspapers I wrote to in that winter of 1965; I was thinking more in terms of the *Sunday Times*. I hedged my bets, though, by going to the library and copying the names and addresses of 149 newspapers out of *Willings Press*

Guide. I wrote the same letter to them all, wondering how I would be able to choose between them, in the unlikely event of the *Sunday Times* turning me down.

I got eight replies, all brisk rejections. The *Grimsby Evening Telegraph* said it would keep my letter on file. It's probably still there, awaiting a suitable vacancy. The *Sunday Times* was one of the 141 who did not bother to write back.

I was wondering how to dress up 'hod carrier' so it would look a bit better in the *Where are they now?* section of the school magazine, when the letter from the *Messenger* arrived and rescued me from a life of manual labour. My letter to the evening paper in the group had somehow filtered down to the weekly just when they were looking for somebody young, enthusiastic and cheap. I was indentured for three years, like an apprentice to a medieval guild, at a starting salary of £9 10s 6d a week.

The editor's name was Eric Belk. He had worked for the paper for 40 years and been editor since the week before D-Day. He seemed to have come barrelling into the 1960s from another era; there was something of a whiff of the Edwardian ostler about him. The *Messenger* was made in his image. The Bromsgrove it described, the social order it endorsed and the attitudes it reflected were already rapidly fading into the past. Belk himself was a bucolic figure who took life at the charge. He came into every room with a crash, staring short-sightedly around and sniffing the air like a buffalo breaking through into a jungle clearing. His face was florid and fringed with purple. It framed an heroic nose, broad and bulbous, a memorial to a lifetime's devotion to cider. He was a bulky man. His trousers were often held up with an old tie and he hadn't been able to button his blazer since the end of rationing. His big feet were horribly misshapen; the bunions threatened to break out of his shoes like tree roots pushing up through a pavement. He stamped around on them all day long, both beefy hands held out in front of him as if shooing cattle down a lane. He was a force of nature, noisy, irascible and blunt often to the point of being appallingly rude. He would have been a tyrant, but for a schoolboy sense of mischief and a thick streak of kindness he did his best to hide.

His editorial empire consisted of two rooms up a rickety staircase behind a shop on the High Street. The ground floor was occupied by the *Messenger's* advertisement department. Winnie took the classifieds; nobody knew her last name. Mr Bradley was responsible for the display ads; nobody seemed to know his first one. The shop had been the

Messenger stationery store until a couple of years before, but was now a bookshop. Like all the little independent weeklies with wonderful names round there – the *Redditch Indicator*, the *Kidderminster Shuttle* (it was a carpet town), and the *Smethwick News-Telephone* – it had been snapped up by a bigger newspaper firm. The *Messenger* was now printed at the group's head office in Worcester and the ultimate owner of this most staid of country papers was the *News of the World*.

Upstairs, in the *Messenger* news headquarters, Belk had the gloomier room while the reporters shared the other. Ours was little more than an attic. There were three or four battered tables and half a dozen hard wooden chairs. The typewriters were all pre-war and no more than half were ever working. Even with those that were operational, you had to punch the keys viciously to produce any kind of mark on the paper, the mechanism was so worn out and the ribbon so old. There were only two reference books. The *Who's Who* was dated 1954 and a *Wisden* cricket almanac was even older.

Life had not been kind to my fellow reporters, wary, middle-aged men with an air of defeat about them. Ray was a balding Welshman with somebody else's teeth. He would sit, gurning, at his typewriter trying to wrestle them into position and when he started speaking they would rattle like castanets. Ray had been the editor of the *Abergavenny Chronicle*, another weekly in the group, but had found it an intolerable strain. He was a decent man who worried too much. He worried about filling the paper. He worried about his daughter going on a diet and making herself infertile (last time I heard, she had five children). And he worried about sheep.

Then, as now, the hills above Abergavenny swarmed with sheep and the Magistrates' Court in the town, which Ray covered, had regularly to deal with those farmers whose affection for their animals crossed the limits laid down by the law. What got to Ray was not so much having to deal with furtive shepherds trying to keep their names out of the paper – though that was tricky enough – but the fate meted out to the sheep, who were routinely taken aside and shot. He would inveigh against this double injustice from the sheep's point of view, his eyes rolling and his teeth clacking in sympathy. It has only occurred to me now that he might have been winding me up. I was very gullible and he could be quite droll when he was in the mood.

George was a beaky little Scotsman with bad feet. He, too, had edited local newspapers in his day but did not like the responsibility. George smoked all the time, mostly the same cigarette. He would stub it out after a couple of puffs and put it behind his ear. He could keep going like that for hours, right down to the last couple of shreds of tobacco, which he would still be sucking even though we could hear his lips sizzling. George was one of life's pessimists. He would shuffle around with a raincoat neatly folded over his arm whatever the weather, even indoors.

Ted was the chief reporter but as diffident as the others. He was tall and thin with rather ragged grey hair and a tubercular cough. He would read his copy out loud as he typed, punctuating each sentence with the dry bark of a chain-smoking consumptive.

The *Messenger* newsroom was long on long-suffering decency, but short on vigour and confidence. There was no doubt who was the boss. We all flinched when Belk banged in from next door, waving sheets of copy and demanding to know: 'Who wrote this rubbish?'

It was not exactly the *Sunday Times*. Journalism was meant to be about covering major crimes, racing off to disasters, passing judgment on the powerful. There did not seem to be very much of that kind of thing though, to be fair, I did play a small part in a major crime story that led the front page the first week I was there. A criminal, or maybe even a gang, had stolen a shepherd from the nativity tableau under the arch of the lychgate at All Saints Church. It was a well-planned operation, according to the police. The anchoring bricks had been removed from the wooden container and the tallest of the shepherds had been taken from behind the crib. I thought this fell rather short of the international terrorist outrage I felt I ought to be cutting my journalistic teeth on. I said so and was severely slapped down. The snatched shepherd story, it seemed, had *everything*. It was a ruthless crime, a kidnapping really. The motive was a mystery, the criminal was still at large and the police were baffled. The congregation prayed for the thief to repent and bring the shepherd back. The town was agog. Ray made £3 17s 6d lineage out of it, selling paragraphs to the dailies. All were agreed this was the big time, in Bromsgrove terms, at least. I was allowed to make a few inquiries but the story had to be written by more experienced hands.

The excitement eventually died down and I settled to more humdrum stories and people like Bessie Nickless, stalwart of the local Women's Institutes. Bessie's fame arose from her skill in making hats out of crêpe paper and she would demonstrate it at several WIs a week, all of which had to be reported. 'A new hat for one shilling and sixpence?' I wrote. 'No, Dodford WI didn't believe it either . . .' In another: 'Wonderful creations came to life in Bessie's shapely hands'. Belk's headlines were equally imaginative. 'Glamorous "Tiles" at Wildmoor'; 'Bessie's Hats Charm Dodford'.

Belk sometime used his headlines to settle old scores, or parade a remarkably long list of prejudices. Because of some half-remembered slight back in his youth, he had it in for the Scots and everything to do with Scotland. He ruined a rather evocative report I did on the Burns Night celebration in Droitwich Spa with the headline: 'Spa Scots Sup, Swill, Speechify and Sing'. The Scots of Droitwich took themselves extremely seriously and their national poet even more so. They got pretty shirty about this and naturally blamed me. I got several nasty letters and one of the most respectable members of the Spa's Burns Club threatened to give me what I think is known as a 'Glasgow kiss' in the middle of the High Street. Belk treated it all as a huge joke and said he had the headline 'Spa Scots Slay Snide Sassenach' set up in print, just in case.

The list of Belk's likes was somewhat shorter. Their activities were always described in the most flattering terms and at considerable length. A pensioners' party at the Stoke Brush Works, organised by one of his cronies, was made to sound like a Hollywood movie premiere.

'After a delectable and delightfully served meal, an entertainment began with a film taken by Mr L. G. Harris while on a recent holiday tour of Europe. Mr Harris's subdued commentary contrasted oddly with the film's exquisitely colourful record of a tour which was evidently chosen for its scenery. The largely stay-at-home audience thrilled at the views of France, Switzerland and Germany. A scene on a mountain top, reached after a spine-chilling ascent by a hazardous-looking chair lift, was made still more thrilling by the appearance of a sinister-looking vulture. The bird seemed aggressively anxious to regard climbers as a welcome addition to its menu. The only fault that could be found with this engrossing film was that it was short, much too short.'

That wasn't all.

'Later, George Lucas, a local artiste, brought down the house with his inimitable offering of at least a dozen of the well-known "Albert" monologues'. You had to wonder how the pensioners, most of whom looked in the accompanying photograph to have only the most tenuous hold on life, survived all that excitement. As it happened, they were not so mad with joy that they overlooked a small spelling error I made in the list of the 150 or so old crones who were there. The fact that I had reduced Mrs Anne Higgins to Mrs Ann Higgins was, she wrote, 'part of an appalling collapse of standards on the *Messenger* and in society as a whole'.

People did get terribly upset if you got their names even slightly wrong. It was an early, and often repeated, lesson in accuracy. The biggest crime was to make a Mrs into a Miss, an unendurable slander for any woman over 25 in those days. It required a grovelling apology that drove Belk into full blast. The *Messenger*, like most weeklies of the day, was full of names. It worked on the principle that every name mentioned sold at least two papers. The junior reporter's job was endlessly to make lists at fêtes and flower shows, at sports days and Lions' meetings.

Funerals were the worst. You had to get everybody's name or there would be hell to pay. This required advance planning and a very thick skin. First, you had to close off all the other entrances to the church, if necessary by dragging a pew or even the font against any side door. Once you had ensured nobody could get in without you noticing, you stood squarely in the doorway and did not let anybody past, however grief-stricken, until they had given you their name. Every name had to be spelled out (Smith could be Smythe, after all). A surprising number had difficulty with their own names. Many would insist they were representing others, sometimes large numbers of people, and they all had to be spelled out, too. It took a long time. For a big funeral this would sometimes mean the queue of mourners would stretch out of the graveyard and down the road.

I was so scared of missing somebody out I used to stop the coffin to get the names of the pallbearers until, one afternoon, the Vicar of Hanbury gave me a dressing down in language quite unsuited to his cloth and the sombre gravity of the occasion. The job wasn't over even when the funeral was under way. I had to go round noting down the names on the wreaths. They weren't very legible at the best of times and, if it was raining, quickly became completely undecipherable. I hated funerals.

My main role, though, was to be Belk's private secretary. I spent long hours in his room, hammering away at one of the antique typewriters, while he stumped up and down, dictating copy in orotund Edwardian sentences, punctuated from time to time with a snarled footnote.

'At a meeting of the Lickey Hills Rotary Club, the President, silly old fool's been sleeping with the Vicar's sister for fifteen years and thinks nobody knows about it – don't type that you damned fool!' It was a nerve-racking business. I was not a very good typist but I got a lot of practice.

Shorthand was more difficult. I went twice a week to a crippled old lady who taught shorthand in a sprawling house where she kept 23 cats permanently incarcerated. The stench hit you at the front door like a cosh across the nose. The loathsome creatures were everywhere. They took turns to stroll across my notebook as I tried to practise my outlines. They deliberately held their tails up like flagpoles so they brushed across my face. I am allergic to cats and ten minutes into every lesson my eyes were streaming, my nose was flooded and I was finding it difficult to breathe. The ringleader was a particularly arrogant tabby called Desmond who specialised in backing across the table until his rear end was inches away from my face. I found myself fantasising about how to discourage Desmond with a pencil I sharpened specially for the purpose. A 2H up to the rubber in his rectum would take some of the swagger out of Desmond, I thought, but I never summoned up the nerve. Progress with shorthand was slow.

I quickly discovered that journalism is largely routine. The weeks had a pattern to them. Five types of law courts and four different levels of local councils had to be covered. Meetings and proceedings of all kinds had to be reported, almost verbatim. The reporter's job was mostly to record what everybody said, rather than come to premature conclusions about what was going on. The *Messenger*'s readers could be trusted to make up their own minds, with the odd nudge from one of Belk's idiosyncratic editorials. Thursdays were quiet because Belk spent the day in Worcester putting the paper to bed. We took it in turns to answer the phone, mostly Belk barking queries and instructions, but otherwise spent the day larking around like schoolboys, playing mini-cricket in the back yard or seeing if we could throw paper darts as far as the bus station.

It was Fridays that were exhausting. Shortly after half past nine Belk would barge through the door, yelling: 'Are ye coming?' It was not really a question and he would be halfway down the stairs before I could answer anyway. We were off to look for news 'wherever it's to be found', as he put it.

News, it seemed, was to be found, almost exclusively, in pubs. The quest was really a day-long pub crawl from the Country Girl to the Bowling Green, on to the Raven, the Kings Head, the Swan, the Plough . . . after pub number six I generally lost track. Belk judged a pub by its cider and its barmaid. He liked the one rough and the other buxom. Once he had a pint of what often looked – and smelled – like raw sewage in his hand he would launch into provocative, heavy-handed banter. This was effective in winkling out a surprising amount of local gossip, some of which was even printable. I don't expect the *Daily Express* ever lashed itself for missing these stories, but they filled up acres of the paper. He would dictate them as he careered around the country lanes for me to take down in my apprentice shorthand. This would have been difficult enough if I had been sober and seated at a desk, rather than seeing double and being driven down the wrong side of the road by a roaring drunk. He always had to dictate them again when we got back to the office late in the evening. As he was banging off the walls by then and I could barely see the typewriter, let alone the keys, the odd mistake did creep in.

Belk was not the best of drivers even when sober. His company Austin 1100 was not so much driven as bullied. He sat hunched over the wheel as if he thought it might escape. He wrenched so hard on the gear lever it ended up like stirring a vat of porridge. He always parked by banging into the cars in front and behind and often didn't bother to close the door, let alone lock it, when he got out.

It was all an ordeal for the other people we sometimes carried on these expeditions. John Webb, the *Messenger*'s gooseberry-eyed photographer, bred Pekinese dogs and so was impervious to fear. The paper's star writer was not and would sit, shivering, in the corner of the back seat. F. Fincher was the only byline name that ever appeared in the *Bromsgrove Messenger* (though I did achieve a 'writes Michael Buerk' at the end of the third paragraph on a village art exhibition when Belk was on holiday). Fred, a gaunt and bearded man, was the *Messenger*'s tame naturalist and his column Field, Wood and Hedgerow had been a regular feature of the paper for many years. Fred was a true science enthusiast and was wholly unsuited to the compromises of popular journalism. Not for him the obvious glories of the English countryside or the sentimental charm of its furry animals. What Fred found sexy was Cuckoo Spit. When it appeared at Burcot a full month before not only Fred, but 'Prime in his well-known monograph on the subject', expected it to, he was almost orgasmic with excitement.

Fred got even more worked up about Fungus Gnats and could not understand anybody who failed to share his passion. These microscopic insects, he acknowledged, had been unfairly overlooked, even by entomologists. The *Messenger* corrected this situation by devoting almost an entire column to these elusive creatures and the difficulty, even under a microscope, of discerning the particular humped thorax of *Dynotosoma Fuscicorn* that distinguished it from its more common fellows.

Belk would sometimes grumble at Fred's arcane subject matter and rather dry style. Indeed, from time to time, I was instructed to 'ginger it up a bit' and my very first appearance in print was as Fred Fincher's ghost writer on Field, Wood and Hedgerow. By and large, though, change was not encouraged at the *Bromsgrove Messenger*. F. Fincher remained the only named writer on the paper. All the other columnists – Farming Notes by 'Countryman', Bowling Notes by 'Stryker' – laboured on under their pseudonyms. My favourite was the anonymous author of Hunting Talk, known to his readers only as 'Loppylugs'. Loppylugs did more than chronicle the weekly war for supremacy between 'Brother Reynard' and the Worcestershire hunts. He saw centuries of tradition under threat and a world gone soft-hearted and spineless. Every week, some new evidence of this would drive him into a frenzy. However harmless it might appear, he would see the sinister implications. He was horrified when he spotted children out beagling in Wellingtons. 'Why can't mothers turn them out in running pumps like they used to?' he demanded. 'It is all a stupid modern idea that wet feet give you colds. Good, fast running with wet feet will soon see a cold off!'

In the mid-sixties the world *was* changing. The Empire had gone, the class system was crumbling, the young were no longer content to be junior old people. There was a slow-motion social revolution going on, even in Bromsgrove. Not everybody saw it as clearly as 'Loppylugs'. No one fought so hard to stop it.

After a year on the *Messenger*, I was sent on a training course that changed my life. All apprentice journalists had to go for two 'block release' courses during their indenture period. It was eight weeks away at some run-down college in an industrial city to grapple with the theory of our craft and the rudiments of law and constitutional government. We looked forward keenly to these courses, not out of a thirst for knowledge or the desire to widen our skills base, but because it was a break from routine. Besides, there was the certainty of being sloshed on an almost daily basis and the outside chance of getting laid.

Wolverhampton College of Art, through the sleet of that January day, was some way short of *Brideshead Revisited*. It was a dingy place in what was then a dirty and depressing town. My fellow students were all from local papers in the Midlands and Wales. The lads were boisterous and the girls distracting. This was my first experience of co-education since being wrenched away from Hilary Wood to go to senior school at the age of nine. The *Messenger* was a totally babe-free zone as well. I was not used to girls in the workplace and unsure how to react, particularly as they were all attractive. I found one particularly disturbing. Christine came from a daily in Newport. The *South Wales Argus* was not the most sophisticated of evening papers, but it was a lot higher up the journalistic food chain than the *Bromsgrove Messenger* and sounded impossibly glamorous to me at the time. She was much the same. She was dark and beautiful, with a wide smile and a way of arching one eyebrow that made me very excited. I made sure I got as close to her as I could, telling myself I was being subtle and biding my time. The truth was I fancied her rotten but was too nervous to make a move. She made me laugh a lot and we quickly became good friends, which was not quite what I had in mind.

My sex appeal had been pushed up several notches, or so I hoped, by swapping my thick glasses for a pair of contact lenses. I was meant to wear them only for short periods until I got used to them, but I was so vain I kept them in until the pain became unbearable. I spent most of the day crying, which gave me a totally unwarranted reputation for sensitivity. Or I wandered blindly around with eyes so bloodshot it looked as though I had been on a record-breaking binge, even on the rare occasions when I had not.

From that point of view, the course had started badly when I got thrown out of the best pub in Wolverhampton, not perhaps the highest accolade in the licensed victualling world, which I think was called the Criterion. I was wrestling with my lenses, sobbing and cursing, when the waitress came up with our sausage and mash lunches. She was a large lady who wore her name badge – 'Deirdre' – on her pinafore over the left side of what was a quite remarkable chest. As she arrived, I leaned short-sightedly towards her and asked: 'What's the other one called?' The response was little short of nuclear. I was out on the street before I had time to snicker at my own wit. I think the plate of sausage and mash came too, slashing through the air over my head like a discus. Deirdre was a powerful woman, and proud.

The two teachers were complete opposites. The senior lecturer, who ran the course, was so full of shit you could smell him in Shropshire. He was a particular journalistic type, a bumptious fantasist. In no particular order we were quickly told he had been (a) a war hero with the 8th Army, (b) a fighter pilot, (c) tortured by the Gestapo, (d) he was closely related to the Royal Family and had turned down a front seat at the Coronation. His newspaper career was something of a mystery. He hinted at great things in Fleet Street but the truth seemed to be a succession of mundane jobs on out-of-the-way papers before washing up in Wolverhampton. He was a great believer in the virtues of clean typing and an accurate note. He himself claimed to be able to do 'quadrilateral' shorthand, taking verbatim notes of four conversations at once. We were keen to put this to the test but, somehow, the time never seemed right.

John Hilton, the other lecturer, was resting before setting off round the world again, sub-editing on big city papers in America and the Commonwealth. He had worked on the *Plain Dealer* in Cleveland, Ohio, I remember, newspapers in the Far East and Australia and the *Rand Daily Mail* in Johannesburg. He was the first journalist I had met who wasn't shabby or socially on the back foot. He was friendly and funny and opened up a world of exciting opportunities. Until then, my career horizons had been limited to the *Bromsgrove Messenger* and the likelihood of a glacial progression through provincial newspapers towards a job on a big daily, impossibly far in the future. Half the students on the course were already on daily papers and were no better than I was; in my conceit, I thought *I* was more talented than *them*. The idea of spending three years on the *Messenger* seemed more and more like a prison sentence. As I circled longingly, but hopelessly, round Christine, my life seemed full of unrequited ambition. I might have wept with the frustration of it all, if I hadn't been crying already. Those contact lenses take some getting used to.

It could so easily have stayed that way but, in the last week of the course, we were all invited to a party out in Shropshire. Charlotte, one of the girls on the course, worked for the *Shropshire Star* and so, I discovered, did a school friend of mine called John Perkins. He had been flung out of college and spent a long time as a tramp before starting a journalistic career that eventually led him to become Editor of Independent Radio News. We compared career trajectories for a while, but my mind was elsewhere. It was a good party but I don't remember much about it. The record player, it must have been a Dansette, kept playing a Donovan record I had never heard before (and have never heard since) that was all about buying a Chevrolet. Christine was looking especially gorgeous that night in a short brown sweater dress and those white plastic Courrèges-style boots that were high fashion in the sixties. We talked and joked for a while but something seemed different. I looked at her and she looked at me and, well, you read all about it, God knows, but it still seems like a collision with a truck when it happens. We spent most of the night driving around the border country in my Mini, rather than a Chevrolet, in my case in a state of high level ecstasy.

Belk was pleased to see me when I got back to the *Messenger*. He had had to do without a PA for nearly two months; I think he also missed my company. I tried to get enthusiastic about the local stories but they seemed even more mundane than they had done before. I remember sitting in a meeting of the Alvechurch Parish Council, listening to a bunch of village harridans whining on about how the ash that had been laid on the pavements in the frosty weather was treading into their houses, thinking, There has to be more to life than this. I did my best to hype it up – 'Angry grannies of Latimer Road storm the annual parish meeting – their vacuum cleaners are still pinging with the ash brought in on the kids' shoes', but not even the Messenger was holding the front page. When I looked at my notes I saw I had written the shorthand outline for 'Christine' over and over again.

By this time I had been invited around to Sunday lunch at her parents' house in Hereford. Her dad was a butcher in the town, a good-natured, sturdy and decent man, an embodiment of the virtues of a way of life now gone. Her mother was jolly and fat and always snorting with laughter about the cast list of eccentrics who came to the shop. It was a welcoming place, and lunch – a joint of pork *and* a chicken, vegetables that didn't come out of a tin and real gravy – was a revelation. I would not say it made me even more fond of Christine – actually, I would. I was lovestruck anyway and the combination of heart and stomach was irresistible.

I had already decided to move out of my grandparents' home into a flat in Droitwich. It was behind the front office of the *Droitwich Guardian*, a weekly in the same group as the *Messenger* with a full-time staff of one. His name was Alex Collinson and he was about my age, but had packed in far more experience of life and journalism. Nominally at least, he was editor of the paper and had the master bedroom. The engine of his A40 car occupied most of the rest of the flat. He let what would now be called the utility room to me for £3 10s a week. There was just enough space for a single camp bed between the lawn mower and the wall on which an unknown hand had scrawled a limerick:

A vice both obscene and unsavoury,
Held the Bishop of Worcester in slavery.
Amid bestial howls,
He deflowered young owls,
In a crypt fitted out as an aviary.

It would give me the shudders now but, at the time, it was a kind of liberation. For part of the week I played at bachelorhood with Alex, drinking in the country pubs when not covering council meetings. At the weekends I pursued Christine across five counties. On one perfect weekend I had Sunday lunch – a mountain of roast beef and Yorkshire pudding, I can taste it now – in Hereford and managed to lure her back to my 'flat'. It was all too much for me and presumably for her, because we were both still asleep at ten the following morning. We were woken by crashing noises, as if a rhino had got loose in the kitchen. I knew instantly who it was, but was still frozen in horror when the door was flung open. Belk stood for a moment, goggle-eyed and breathing heavily, before turning on his heel and slamming out of the house. It was difficult to know who was more shocked. It was tricky going into the office after that. I prepared some joke about knowing we all ultimately worked for the *News of the World* these days but wasn't this going too far? Shouldn't he have made an excuse before he left?

I did not get a chance to come out with either; the subject was never mentioned. After a slightly uncomfortable week or two he began to give me coded warnings about 'bits of fluff' turning young reporters' heads. I was keener and keener on my bit of fluff and took no notice. My head was turned. I disposed of my tweed jacket with the leather patches, and the cavalry twills. I never wore a cravat again and my trilby became a holder for Alex's sparkplugs. Instead, I got myself a cape slashed with gold, and a crimson kaftan. The electric blue jeans chimed with it all, I thought, rather than matching any of it too slavishly. Orange suede ankle boots set the new ensemble off pretty well, particularly when I had the ManTan on. These were the early days of tanning lotion and it produced a kind of patchy orange effect across the face and the palms of the hands, by happy chance exactly the same shade as the shoes. A friendly junior photographer called Stuart Roper had just joined the paper and he took some pictures of me in my new gear. In his photographs, I certainly look colourful, even in black and white, and even if I do seem to be suffering from a terminal skin disease.

I was desperate to move on to a bigger paper but there seemed to be two insuperable obstacles. I had to find a newspaper that would take me on, half trained and without much experience of any kind. Even if I did, I was still legally indentured to the *Messenger* and weekly papers were famous for treating their reporter apprentices like galley slaves, chained to their tasks until the very last day.

I got *Willings Press Guide* again and wrote a very different kind of letter from the one I sent before, gambling on catching someone's eye by being outrageous.

Dear Sir (I wrote, 67 times)

I am about to cross a private Rubicon by leaving my first newspaper after fifteen months. The trouble is that my amazing and ever-growing talents are allowed little (or to be more precise, no) scope on the *Bromsgrove Weekly Messenger.*

I have a car, boundless talent, astounding intelligence, a high standard of education, shimmeringly attractive personality, some conceit and quite a capacity for self-delusion.

It went on in this vein for several more paragraphs about my brilliance at everything except, I remember, ice-skating (neat touch that). It concluded:

In short, I would be an asset to any paper if it were not for my one obvious weakness – my modesty.

If you are not already drafting a sternly-worded document to the National Council for the Training of Journalists, or my present employers (which would be embarrassing), could you at least give me the opportunity of exerting my spell-binding personality in your presence?

Yours in hope and desperation,

Michael Buerk

This time I got ten rejections, though one, from an editor in Bristol who Christine would later work for, did commend my 'enterprising audacity'. I was about to give up and go into the men's fashion trade, for which I thought I might have a rare talent, when an eleventh letter arrived at the flat. It was from Thomson House, Cardiff.

Dear Sir,

I feel after reading your letter that I should offer you my job forthwith. However, this is a cruel and hard world, so I would ask you to complete the attached pro-forma . . .

Yours faithfully,
John H. Wiggins,
Editor, *South Wales Echo*

Jack Wiggins himself looked like a retired general with his silver hair and moustache, immaculate charcoal grey suit, with a white linen handkerchief in the breast pocket. I went in to see him as the great presses started to roll out the *Echo*'s fifth edition of the day in the bowels of the building. He was a bit stiff, but there was a twinkle about him. For my part, I tried not to seem the juvenile lunatic the letter had made me sound. A week later, he sent me a letter saying he would take me on, but only if the *Messenger* agreed to release me. He warned me this was unlikely to happen and suggested I contacted him again at the end of my indentures.

It was the most difficult of afternoons with Belk. I broached the subject on a Friday over a liquid lunch at the Country Girl. He talked again about 'bits of fluff' turning young men's heads, about learning to walk before I could run. Back at his office, both of us rather more sober than usual, he held out the prospect of the *Messenger*'s district office, up in baleful Northfield on the southern fringes of Birmingham. It was not an inviting prospect, but it was the best he had to offer. He wanted to persuade me, rather than force me, to stay.

I was desperate and I dare say it showed. We ended the afternoon both rather sad. Early the following week he said the group management had agreed to let me go. He must have argued long and hard on my behalf because they had turned down everybody else who had tried to move in the past. I think he was really fond of me. I never did thank him enough. I tried, but he got very gruff and crashed out of his office to go hunting news on his own.

My last piece for the *Messenger* was an apocalyptic report on the Barnt Green Horticultural Society's Flower Show & Fête headlined 'Russian Roulette in the Rain'. 'Thunder rolled like a heavenly fanfare', I wrote 'and all afternoon the rains came down on Fiery Hill.' It seemed appropriate. I got every name right, too.

I pretended to have regrets, but I felt as if life was getting started at last.

The *Echo* was a real newspaper and, what's more, it was only fifteen miles away from Christine and the *Argus*. Who says there's no such thing as fate?

SIX

THOMSON HOUSE is a big, gimcrack building sandwiched between the heart and the soul of Cardiff. It is only a step away from the shopping streets that are the beating heart of the Welsh capital. Its soul, the rugby ground then known as Cardiff Arms Park, is just around the corner. On international days Thomson House would be submerged in scarlet as the fans from the valleys washed out of the railway station, through the city's pubs, to the match. The *Echo*'s sub-editors, embittered men by and large, would take a break from their full-time job of disparaging the reporters to pour scorn on the crowds. They regarded themselves as cosmopolitan scholars and people from the valleys as primitives. For ten minutes or so they would have a competition to see who could spot the most evidence of inbreeding and then they would go back to their big horseshoe desk to rip apart another carefully crafted story and poke it into the paper. Journalism is a lifetime course in misplaced superiority. Sub-editors, who sit in a little world of their own passing judgment on grammar, punctuation and style, have it more than most. I sat on that desk for six months so I know. I also know that nearly all the subs came from the valleys themselves. More knuckles brushed the ground in the newsroom, more squints and limps and Quasimodo look-alikes were gathered round the *Echo* subs' table than there ever were on the streets of Cardiff, even on international days.

The hundred-years war between reporters and sub-editors was just one of the things about big-time journalism I had to learn. By provincial standards, the *Echo* was a big paper. It had the largest circulation in Wales, selling 150,000 copies, in half a dozen editions, every afternoon. Its heartland was Cardiff and the Glamorgan valleys. To the east, it competed with my new lover's paper, the smudgy *South Wales Argus*, which had a loyal following in what was still called Monmouthshire. Far to the west, it took on the *Evening Post* around Swansea. The *Echo* was better as well as bigger than both of them. With its sister paper the *Western Mail*, a morning paper that claimed to cover the whole country, it was owned by the Canadian press baron, Roy Thomson. The Thomson Organisation also had *The Times* and the *Sunday Times* so I had some notional connection with the paper I thought I should be on. More to the point, Thomson had the best graduate training scheme for journalists in the country. I had backed into it without realising and without a degree – a stroke of luck I did not deserve.

The other trainees were far more impressive. Sue Lawley was obviously just making a pit stop on the racetrack to stardom. She was a striking and dynamic girl, with legs up to her eyebrows. She would walk up the newsroom like a supermodel and the subs' table would give a collective sigh as she sashayed past. Sue was clever and determined, as well as glamorous. She came from Dudley and had apparently had a strong Midlands accent before she went to university. She became President of the Union at Bristol and, it's said, practically ran the place. Her best line was that she had come to the *Echo* with a low second in English and a first in Received Pronunciation. She was kind and nice, but had a way of wrinkling her upper lip when she wasn't pleased that frightened almost everybody in the newsroom, including me. Giles Smith was tall, thin and haughty and would go on to be industrial editor at ITN. Glyn Mathias was short and boyish; he looked far too young already to have a politics MA from Southampton as well as an Oxford degree. He ended up as ITN's chief political correspondent. Geraint Talfan Davies was gold-standard Tafia. His family did run Wales, or large slices of it, and he dressed like an off-duty Guards officer. We had every reason to dislike him, but didn't because he was always pleasant and obviously very capable. He went on to be Managing Director of Tyne-Tees Television and Controller of BBC Wales. Alun Michael, with his ginger toothbrush moustache and battered corduroy jacket, was a rather Pooterish character for the sixties. He did not stay in journalism, which was no surprise, but went into politics, which certainly was. He was a Home Office minister in the first Blair government and, for a time, leader of the Welsh Assembly, effectively Prime Minister of a devolved Wales. Chris Potter was easily the brightest of us all. Kip looked like a pixie and had considerable charm. He gave off the air of somebody who saw all the subtleties in a complex world and knew every button to press. For reasons that were never clear to me he went straight from the *Echo* to the *Sun* and stayed there. He was political correspondent when he died, as elegantly as he had lived, from cancer at a tragically early age.

The newsroom was a busy, exciting place after the *Messenger*. The reporters sat in rows nearest to the door behind big typewriters that were still old-fashioned, but at least post-war. By each one there was a 'spike', a sharply pointed metal rod for skewering unused copy, that made any newsroom horseplay potentially fatal. The desks were rimmed with cigarette burns and crowded with half-full coffee cups. The subs sat in similar squalor round their horseshoe at the other end. The room was divided by a row of copytakers, middle-aged women in headphones who typed stories dictated down the telephone to them by reporters in the field. Most were fast and accurate and motherly with it. 'Oh, that's sad,' they would say as you spelled out the details of yet another low-level crime '. . . at capital "C", Cardiff, capital "M", Magistrates' – s-pos there – capital "C" Court, comma, today point par'. Some were cranky or deaf. The occasional babe was much cherished but never stopped long.

Below the newsroom were the printers, the Morlocks to we Eloi. One room was full of clattering Linotype machines which had a look of the Industrial Revolution about them. Half-sheets of badly typed copy covered in illegible scribbles were propped up in front of them like the score of a symphony on a grand piano. They played it in hot metal; each machine had a vat of liquid lead and the operator on his giant typewriter cast the stories line by line. I watched the process all through once, following a story I had been proud of being hacked down into something nondescript, and thought, in my conceit, it was the opposite of alchemy; they had turned pure gold into lead.

The 'sticks' of stories were lined up in their page frames, fitted round the advertisements and topped off by headlines on a table called the 'stone'. This was the preserve of people with arcane skills, like reading upside down and finding their way round the most complex, illogical and dishonest set of restrictive practices ever invented. The great presses waited nearby for the touch of a button to set them thundering. They shook the whole building as they turned a corner of a Scandinavian forest into journalism and fed the delivery vans waiting patiently in the alley outside.

My boss was the news editor, who sat on a big desk in the middle of the room with his deputy, marshalling the reporters, checking their work and trying to feed the ravenous maw of a fast-changing evening paper. Graham Bailey was tall and dark and looked like Gregory Peck would look if his only suit came from C&A ten years ago and he was on the verge of a nervous breakdown. His deputy, Peter O'Connell, had been built to last. He was pugnacious and so stocky he seemed to rock down the newsroom rather than walk. They were good at their jobs and easy to work for except when a big story broke at edition time when everybody within range risked a bollocking. Except Sue, of course. Everybody was polite to Sue.

Our work was largely dictated by the diary, a big book on the newsdesk where all the routine jobs were written up. Much of it was similar to the *Messenger*'s, only on a bigger scale. But an evening paper cannot wait for news to come down the grapevine. Two reporters were detailed to do 'office duty' every day, one in the morning, one in the afternoon. It meant being stuck in the newsroom, calling all the fire, police and ambulance information rooms across the region every hour. It was a tedious job, I thought, constantly asking: 'Anything for us?' and 99 per cent of the time getting the answer 'no'. Once, a real reporter took over from me at lunchtime who was more imaginative and persistent. Suddenly, all those sergeants who had been telling me: 'No, not a thing' started coming up with all sorts of stuff that filled half a page of that afternoon's paper with plenty left for the following day. There was clearly more to the job than met my eye.

We had to work two or three nights every week. It was mostly the rural and urban district councils out in the valleys, but occasionally we would have to stand in at concerts and plays for the man who thought he knew about music or the woman who really did know about the theatre.

The main difference was that a big city paper had breaking news. The phones were always ringing in the newsroom. Most of the calls were querulous or mundane but one in a hundred was a real and urgent story. These had a rhythm of their own. The first call would be no more than a rumour, a busybody or a passer-by who 'thought we might like to know' that 'something big seems to be happening out at Rhiwbina'. Then there would be another from a bored housewife who could see smoke rising from behind the council estate and hear 'hundreds of sirens'. The police were never helpful, at least not straight away, but their reticence sent out its own message that something serious was up. The firemen were a little better. They did not tell you much about what was happening on the phone, but you could get some idea from how many appliances they had sent. The ambulance service was the most forthcoming. You did not get many facts, but you got a lot of colour, most of it red. 'Blood all over the place, boy. The lads have got a few out. One stiff, another's pretty far gone – really buggered, they say. Bloody clear off, I've got work to do.'

By now, we would have the electoral register and the telephone directories out, looking for the numbers of people living nearby. We would all be trying to catch the news editor's eye at the same time, performing small miracles of body language to show how keen we were to get out and cover it on the ground.

Few things are as exciting as being in on a big breaking news story, and most of them are illegal. The race to the car, with the photographer, clumsy under all his gear, trying to keep up; the high speed slalom through the side streets because the main roads would always be jammed. The trick was to be there before the police had the tapes up, to get in close, to be your own eye-witness. It wasn't always possible and sometimes you wished you had kept your distance. I was sent one lunchtime to a bad road smash on the dual carriageway at St Mellons. A lad who was better at tuning his car than controlling it had tried to drive through an articulated lorry. The highway was strewn with big bits of truck and small bits of car. The firemen had levered what was left of the boy's vehicle from under the lorry and stood around, the lamps from the police cars turning the shadows under their helmets blue, the urgency gone and the clearing up still to do. I rushed across to them, conscious of the deadlines stacking up behind me. 'How's the driver?' I said. The fireman looked me up and down and didn't seem to like what he saw. He had had a tough half-hour. 'See for yourself,' he said, very offhand, and turned away.

I did. The boy's body was still at the wheel. His head was on the back seat. The severed neck still seemed to pump blood, but it was very weak and I might have imagined it. The face wore a look of mild surprise, though I might have imagined that, too. I was sick over one of the lorry's wheels. The firemen raised their eyebrows at each other, but said nothing. They spat, significantly, on the kerbstones and went back to work.

The nastiest job, which I seemed to get more than anybody else, was to be sent round to the house where somebody had died in that sort of way to get a photograph for the paper. I don't know why they picked on me. They said it was my public school manners, but I think they were winding me up. If they thought I was thick-skinned, they were wrong. I used to go through agonies in the car outside, trying to work up the courage to knock on the door. Invariably, when I did, I would be made welcome, given tea, told to make myself at home. Tragedy isolates the families it visits. Friends and neighbours don't know what to say and stay away, just when the bereaved need to talk, need to go over the dreadful thing that has happened with someone, anyone, again and again. The difficulty was seldom getting into the house, it was always getting away.

There was rarely any need for them to search for the photograph I wanted. They would usually be spread out on the kitchen table when I arrived with the family trying to piece together the life that had gone, out of the random snaps that were left, a jigsaw of memories with most of the pieces missing. Usually, they welcomed the idea of a report in the *Echo*. They wanted a public record, however brief, that the dead person had existed, something tangible in the vacuum of nothingness they had been left with. Occasionally, it would go the other way. The family would have turned inwards; my arrival would be a terrible intrusion into grief that was determinedly private. I would be left on the doorstep, still hearing the slam reverberating down the hall and the harsh words that had gone before; it was a moment of pure wretchedness.

The *Echo* was my first introduction to journalistic rivalry which, one way or another, would rule my life from then on. There had never been much competition for the sort of stories the *Messenger* covered but South Wales was quite a battleground. Four local dailies, countless weeklies, two local television stations and staff correspondents from the Fleet Street papers were all trawling for stories. There was a scrum at anything really big and a notable absence of any sense of brotherhood amongst the bloodhounds. It was an apprenticeship in dirty tricks. It became second nature in the pub to let the opposition overhear a snatch of conversation that would send them haring off in the wrong direction. I never let their tyres down, but I know many who did, and mine were flat more than once. Certainly, we would all try to block each other's cars in, so that we would be the first to get away.

In those days, before mobile phones and computers, the main thing was to establish secure contact with the office to send the story back. If you could ruin the opposition's chances of doing so at the same time, so much the better. Big court cases gave ample opportunity for sabotage. There were normally only a couple of public phones in the court building. It was the work of a moment to unscrew the mouthpiece and slip the diaphragm into your pocket. If that was not possible you could always jam button 'A' in the old-fashioned call boxes with the thin piece of wood we carried for the purpose. Sometimes the violence amongst the reporters out in the corridor was worse than what was being alleged in the courtroom.

The fiercest competition was with the sister paper, the *Western Mail*. Although it had highbrow pretensions and a reassuringly dull layout, it also had a news editor who was legendarily deranged. He ran his newsroom like an eighteenth-century sugar plantation and used the phone as a whip. He had a battery of them and always seemed to be yelling down two at once. The cords tethered him to his newsdesk, but he was always on the move, rolling his eyes and punching the air with exasperation. It was exhausting to watch; what it was like to work for him does not bear thinking about. At head office, the two reporting teams were separate but the district men worked for both papers and nervous breakdowns were common. The Newport reporter, a witty and bird-like man called Russell Lyne, got so desperate trying to drum up pieces for two demanding newsdesks every day that he made one up. He chose the longest road in Newport and invented a story about the occupants of one of the houses, that he was careful not to identify. The trouble was that he got more and more pleased with his invention and kept embellishing it with more details. The girl involved became younger and more beautiful with each draft, the predicament more dangerous, the animal more appealing, the outcome more heartwarming. The *Western Mail*'s volcanic news editor was delighted and Russell sloped off to the pub with the pressure, for once, off his shoulders.

It was the following morning that he realised his mistake. The *Echo*'s news editor wanted a follow-up and was sending a photographer. When the two of them got to the street they found two television crews already there. There was a queue of frustrated reporters at the phone box at the end of the road, while the more persistent photographers were still banging on the doors searching for the plucky, but elusive family whose experiences had been so graphically described on the front page of the *Western Mail*. Russell broke down and confessed. It was a lesson. Don't make stories up or, if you do, don't make them too good.

It was 1967; work was fun and life was good, if not exactly stylish. I was earning £17 a week and living in a ground-floor bedsit in Cathedral Road. It was gloomy, smelt of long-dead rodents and had an open drain in the corner. The landlord was a city councillor, then on trial for corruption along with several of his colleagues. I sensed a scoop and tried to pump him when he came round every week for the exorbitant rent. He fended off my inquiries with irritating ease. I had a lot to learn, about investigative journalism and flat-hunting.

Most of my salary went on my long-distance love affair. Christine was sharing a slightly better flat in Newport, sleeping under a sign that said 'Repent, for we are all sinners'. It was difficult enough sneaking in without being seen by the lynx-eyed shrew who owned the place. This baleful warning, I felt, cast something of a shadow over proceedings. I tried to prise it off the wall with a kitchen knife but it was firmly fixed, nailed and glued, I imagine, in case someone liked it so much they tried to steal it. Newport landladies were a suspicious lot, with no great reputation for generosity.

I was smitten and would race off to see Christine whenever I did not have a night job for the *Echo*. The rhythm of life was slower on the *Argus*. Most of the reporters were girls. They came in all shapes and sizes, from the willowy and decidedly upmarket Daniella to a notorious trio called Kate, Merle and Sally who were guaranteed to make any party go with a bang. As well as being partial to young women journalists, the editor of the *Argus* was obsessed with music. Everybody who so much as picked up a trumpet within fifty miles of Newport got full coverage. Christine had music 'O' level and so was regularly sent over to Bristol to review concerts at the Colston Hall. I would go too, out of love and loyalty, for most of the concerts bored me senseless. The fun bit was trying to cudgel a high-falutin', if deeply suspect, review out of the programme notes on the way home. Actually, of course, the really fun bit came later still when we tried to find something meatier to be repentant about than cod music criticism.

Slowly, I began to pick up a few craft skills. Nicholas Tomalin was right when he said all a reporter needed was 'a little literary ability and rat-like cunning' but there was a bagful of tricks and accessories that came in useful. We had a training day, once a week, when we were lectured by grizzled old supernumeraries from the subs' desk and learned shorthand from a delightful blonde with a very satisfactory outline herself. She called me 'the Duke' for some unaccountable reason. She was quite an incentive and, with Desmond's whiskered arse no longer standing between me and the genius that is Pitman, I made swift progress. I ended up with a certificate for 150 words per minute, which was no more of a lie than most diplomas.

I also learned how to angle for scoops. It was mostly a matter of working out the fault lines in an organisation, or finding the cross-grained character who might leak the secrets ahead of time. There was a lot of concern then about what were called 'long-stay' hospitals in Wales after scandalous conditions were uncovered at Ely hospital, and 24 women patients had died in a fire at a mental institution in Shrewsbury, on the Welsh border. The country's hospital board ordered an inquiry into all its long-stay hospitals and the report was keenly awaited. One of the members of the board was a local councillor with something of a reputation as a maverick and I set out to cultivate him over a period of several months. I knew that the board members would be given copies of the report ahead of publication and, if I could persuade him to let me have a look at it, I would have a great exclusive. He was a self-regarding crank, like a lot of local politicians, but good company and we got on pretty well. There was no great trick to it. It was partly flattery, partly making a case that the premature disclosure would illuminate the hospitals' shortcomings more effectively, but mostly building trust and reassuring him he would not be found out.

It worked a treat in the end. He swithered for weeks, but then the Chairman of the Hospital Board announced the report would not be published for fear of 'damaging morale and recruitment'. He slipped it to me that evening and it was gratifyingly damning. It painted a grim picture of administrative failure and bad management. Twenty-four hospitals for the chronically sick had no fire alarms at all; the ones that were installed were not maintained properly and most of the staff did not know how to use them. There were wider problems over cleanliness, training and poor conditions. The most vulnerable in society were living in filthy slums, run by incompetents, with every chance of being fried alive. Great story.

It led the paper and filled a couple of pages inside, backed up by a thundering editorial. The furore led to major changes in the way the hospitals were run and might have saved quite a few lives. The really important thing, though, was that my name was at the top of the front page and in *capital* letters. Bylines were a vexed issue on the *Echo*. The reporters regarded them as a reward for their investigative skills and fine writing. The subs, who laboured in thoroughly deserved anonymity, thought we were all posturing ponces and automatically crossed out the 'By MICHAEL BUERK' I put at the top of every story and replaced it with '*Echo* reporter'. They did it to everybody. Except for Sue Lawley, of course. She would get her name on a one-paragraph filler about road-works in Pontyclun. It was very odd.

There is a formula to writing news. You start with a pithy, two-line 'intro' that gives the gist of the story with as much impact as possible without straying too far from the truth. Then a series of crisp paragraphs with the supplementary facts in declining order of importance, so the sub can cut it from the bottom to fit the available space. It's a knack, rather than a talent. Some reporters are barely literate after all.

I also learned to produce readable features. It was slightly more difficult, particularly when you had to start with unpromising material. I used to do a big feature called In the Spotlight which, as the title implies, was a regular interview with some South Walian who had caught our eye. We had long ago run out of truly noteworthy people and the job was now to find something interesting in frankly rather ordinary lives. There always was something, though it sometimes took a lot of finding.

A rather unpromising interview with a Rumney man who had just retired after 45 years as a steward on the railways perked up when we worked out between us how far he had travelled while he was serving the food and drink. He was an active, restless character, so it made a neat intro: 'The man who had walked four million miles shuffled from foot to foot and said: "The trouble with me is that I can't sit down." ' The rest – how the railway staff were now riff-raff 'but then so are the passengers', how he used to serve pheasant lunches for 2s 6d (12½p) and now they had to pay an exorbitant 16s 6d (82½p) for lamb – fell into place. A part-time magician from Tylagarw told me how business was picking up so his life story started: 'Success to Uncle Eric the magician means buying a second white rabbit. "I was working the other to death," he says.' In the Spotlight became a parade of blind physiotherapists, rat catchers, credit sleuths, water diviners, who I turned into local celebrities for an afternoon. It was fun doing features and, besides, you always got your name on them and that was the main thing.

My love life was becoming a bit more manageable at this stage. Christine and I had moved in together. We joined a houseshare with some of the other Cardiff reporters, which meant more time for canoodling and less time spent driving, which was thoroughly satis-factory. Sue Lawley had the master bedroom and drew up the washing-up, dusting, vacuum-cleaning and putting-out-the-dustbin rotas, sorted out the bills and made sure the overall tone of the place was not ruined by any adolescent slackness. We had the back bedroom and painted it purple. That's what you did in the sixties.

One day, the *Echo* was offered a giant sturgeon, an ugly-looking fish that had been dredged up in Cardiff Bay. For some quaint historical reason to do with the possibility of it being packed with caviare, sturgeons have to be offered to the reigning monarch. There was no caviare in this one and the Queen, quite sensibly and very promptly, turned it down. So did everybody else and the fishermonger, clearly years ahead of his time, decided to retrieve the situation by turning it into a publicity stunt. It ended up, a little past its best, at our house and Sue turned it into a banquet for the benefit of the feature pages. There is a picture of us, buried somewhere in the files, with me in my kaftan, Sue looking impossibly glamorous and everybody else looking glum. For, despite Sue's best efforts (she was a very good cook) and, if I remember right, a last-minute douche of cheap brandy, it tasted like Tracey Emin's bedclothes. Sue glossed over this in her piece. She included the recipe, even though there was little chance of even the most fish-loving *Echo* reader trying it out, thank goodness. We all felt very sophisticated, but rather ill.

The houseshare did not last long. Christine was sent off to the Chepstow office of the *Argus*, a pleasant little town where the Wye meets the Severn, but a long way the other side of Newport from Cardiff. I became a long-distance, love-hungry commuter again and stepped up my campaign for her to marry me. I even wrote messages in her diary of the 'When are you going to marry me? This week? Next week? What about Xmas?' variety. Eventually she agreed, to shut me up probably, and the date was set for September in 1968 when her sister could get back to England from Kenya where she was living at the time.

The wedding itself had a magical quality about it. It had to be on a Monday, because that was the only day Christine's father could shut the shop. It was bright and clear, Holy Trinity church was packed with beaming people and Christine looked utterly gorgeous. The reception was held in the medieval upstairs room of the Booth Hall Hotel that was owned by my new brother-in-law's family and everybody got charmingly squiffy. Alex Collinson from Droitwich was my best man and gave me some fatherly advice, though God knows why, as he was only a year older than me and his own love life was in tatters at the time.

At the end of a golden afternoon, in a state of high happiness, we left for our honeymoon from Hereford railway station. Most of the town seemed to have turned up to see us off. It was a steam engine, of course, and the driver blew his whistle in our honour as we got on board.

Things did not go quite so well after that. We had to change four times to get to London and the room I had booked at White's hotel, overlooking Hyde Park, turned out to have two single beds and be too narrow to push them together. Sheekey's, the fish restaurant we wanted to go to, turned out to be closed on Mondays so we went to a pretentious dive called Chez Solange I had seen advertised in a magazine, where we were both violently ill. We recovered on honeymoon in Majorca, then an exotic foreign destination, and I spent the afternoons writing passionate letters for a lovesick Spanish waiter to keep my hand in.

*

We moved into a bright, modern flat in Lakeside, taking over the lease from Sue Lawley, who was moving on. It was £5 a week but we could afford it. We might have stayed in Cardiff for years. We were happy there. I had the *Echo* job taped with more than my share of the good stories and the chance to slide off and do features when things got slow. But I was ambitious and conceited, a fatal combination. I was 22, my indentures with the *Echo* would soon be coming to an end. I thought I could handle much bigger stories and was getting impatient to try. The truth is, of course, that the big stories are easier. It's simple to find something to say about a war; spinning out half a page on a parish hall magician from the backside of nowhere takes real skill.

As it happens, in 1968 I got a sniff of one of the biggest news stories of the age and a foretaste of what was to come for me in the seventies, when I was sent to Northern Ireland with the Royal Regiment of Wales. The army had just been ordered in, with the province on the brink of civil war. I went on patrol with them down the Falls Road, which was littered with barricades of torn-up paving stones, burned cars and barbed wire. Huge slogans had been painted on the walls about the hated Protestant police auxiliaries – 'B Specials Child Killers Keep Out' – and Loyalist politicians – 'Chichester-Clarke the Mad Major'. The Catholics treated us like heroes who had come to rescue them. They brought the patrol cups of tea and sandwiches made with dripping.

It was in the side streets, the no-man's-land between the two communities, that our patrol ran into trouble. Gangs of young men threw petrol bombs at us and somebody, somewhere fired a gun. It was not really dangerous, but it was the first time I had been under fire. Churchill's line about there being 'nothing so exhilarating in life as to be shot at with no result' came to mind and I began to wonder if the grand old man was sane. It was terrifying. I learned to walk backwards very fast with my buttocks clenched. We retreated to a Catholic enclave called Bombay Street, or what was left of it. A Protestant mob had destroyed it in three hours of energetic petrol-bombing. The pavements were mostly rubble and each tiny house was just a smoking shell. Here and there, Catholic families looked around for something of their lives to retrieve, mostly without success. They melted away as we left. The street was not safe for them without armed soldiers nearby.

We spent that night in a park off the Falls Road. We all slept in our clothes, the soldiers with their rifles alongside them and the company commander, a major, cuddling a radio. It was a quiet night. We were put on half-hour standby when a police van was shot at a few streets away. Next morning, the Colonel, an extravagantly courteous man, told me it was all 'extremely ticklish'. 'We are hoping we can cool everybody down and hand over to the police. We'll be tolerated for just so long and then they'll get mad with us and we'll end up getting shot at by everybody.' You could tell the idea of spending the rest of his career in the back streets of Belfast, rather than the sunny, servanted outpost of Empire which was promised him at Sandhurst, didn't exactly appeal to him.

The following night I got sloshed in the Royal Avenue Hotel with one of the subalterns, as a platinum-blonde singer in a scarlet sheath dress rotated round a white grand piano belting out Sinatra songs. She looked like a cream sundae swimming round an ice floe, or at least she did after half a dozen Jameson's. The lieutenant, who at 23 was a year older than me, started talking about a nightmare evening he had spent with his platoon being attacked and wondering whether he should give the order to open fire. He had discussed it beforehand with his sergeant and decided that they would shoot back if they were petrol bombed. But, just as he was about to give the order, he had a mental image of the street being full of dead bodies and kept his mouth shut. Instead, he called for reinforcements, but none came. He was drinking a lot faster than I was, I noticed. It was a strange feeling then, being in a part of your country that was more like Beirut than Birmingham. It was obvious, even to somebody as raw and ignorant as me, that this was not going to be resolved and was only going to get worse. I wondered if I would be coming back. I got a really big byline on that piece and felt I deserved it.

I wanted a job on the nationals, and the more I saw of the high-octane lifestyle of the Fleet Street reporters I bumped into, the keener I got. I had seen quite a bit of it covering Prince Charles' investiture at Caernarvon Castle and the royal tour of Wales that followed. At the end of a long day's driving, stopping off to bellow rather vapid copy down the phone to Cardiff, I would get invited to dinner by a gang from London. The *Daily Mirror* men were always the best dressed, the man from *The Times* was inevitably the scruffiest. They all had what seemed to me bottomless expense accounts, apart from the man from the *Guardian* who always brought sandwiches. I suppose I was a good contact for I was wined and dined until I nearly burst, and regaled with stories of skulduggery and misbehaviour of a hundred different kinds. It was all very attractive.

I had some second thoughts after an incident one day in Cardiff that

81

pointed to an altogether more glittering future. I was sent, hotfoot, to the site of a gas explosion, which had blown up a terraced house and killed two of its occupants. I turned up in my scruffy raincoat with my dog-eared old notebook and started to look for eye-witnesses. I had just found one and had started questioning her, when a voice cut across our conversation like a whiplash. 'Do shut up, won't you, I am just recording my piece.'

I can't think why I had not noticed him before. He was standing on top of the rubble in a shiny, shark-skin suit, holding a microphone and a clipboard. A camera crew was standing around their tripod, level with his feet. From behind they looked like worshippers. The bystanders who had come to see a tragedy had something far more interesting and important to gawp at. Chastened, I asked – in a whisper – who it was. 'That's John Humphrys from the television,' they said. We all stood around respectfully until he had finished. I wanted to be like him. I wanted to wear a smart suit and be treated like minor royalty rather than a mangy hack. I wanted a clipboard, it looked so much more important than a notebook, which would have ruined the cut of his jacket. I am sure he had somebody to carry it for him, in any case.

Fired up by this, I applied for a junior job in the newsroom of BBC Wales. All of us on the *Echo* and the *Mail* filled in the astonishingly long application form. Not only was broadcasting posher than newspapers, it also paid twice as much. They could have had their pick of a dozen future media stars, but none of us got so much as an interview. They chose a teenager from a newspaper in Aberystwyth because he could speak Welsh. Fewer than one in five Welsh people spoke the language, but the BBC insisted on it, which explained quite a lot about their output at the time.

For the first, but definitely not the last, time in my life I was deeply offended by the BBC. The following week I saw an advertisement for a reporter in the Manchester office of the *Daily Mail*, which was astonishing because the nationals hardly ever advertised for staff. Even more astonishing, I got it.

There was a farewell drink in the Queen's Vaults, the *Echo*'s local, a spectacularly squalid place but a second home. It would have been sad, but there was a sense of everybody moving on, a kind of seasonal change for all of us. One last famous Queen's Vaults onion roll, the taste guaranteed to last a week; one last pint of Brains (it's a kind of beer, or at least claims to be) and it was farewell Cardiff.

SEVEN

Manchester was a dump. It was a grimy, rain-sodden, post-industrial graveyard of a place where everybody looked depressed, with very good reason, it seemed to me. They spoke in a gloomy, self-pitying whine, the men only of football, the women mostly about chilblains, whatever they are. We were constantly told how friendly it was and never felt so friendless. They kept saying it took time to appreciate Manchester and I kept saying I would be dead first and it might be preferable. The people were sour, the city was bleak, the moors to the east were barren, the plain to the north was boring and the commuterland to the south, banal.

I didn't like it much.

We had driven north in the Austin Healey Sprite which had replaced the trusty Mini. The hood ripped and unpeeled itself on Christine's side just south of Birmingham. It began raining somewhere near Nantwich and didn't stop until we left the North a year later. We arrived soaking wet, half the hood still in place, thanks to three clothes pegs and Christine clinging on with both hands. It wasn't a good start.

We rented a one-bedroom flat in a housing development outside Stockport, which was one of Manchester's mongrel pups and, if anything, even more loathsome. Christine had got a job on the *Stockport Advertiser* and, as everywhere looked drab, if not actually derelict, we thought it was as good a place as any. Our new home was just off the main road to nowhere, or Macclesfield which is roughly the same thing. We rarely met any neighbours. They never spoke, but you could hear them sobbing sometimes in the downstairs flat.

The Manchester newsroom of the *Daily Mail* was in Deansgate. It had a shell-shocked atmosphere about it. My arrival coincided with the departure of a megalomaniac news editor called Ken Donlan, an intensely dynamic little man who had ruled by fear. The reporters looked as if Genghis Khan had just left town and all they could do was see who was still standing and count how many times they had been raped. He had gone off to be a news editor in London. Everybody said he was brilliant, everybody seemed glad to see the back of him. They told me I was lucky and I believed them.

Bill Dickson had been his deputy. He was a tall, lean man and rather careworn which, by all accounts, was understandable. As far as I could see, he never went home. Bill was a driven man, but kind and reasonable. Mind you, after the dreaded Donlan, he could have been Caligula and still be thought a blessed relief.

The *Mail* was a hard-edged and professional paper, with old-fashioned virtues. It was still a broadsheet then and not as pre-eminent as it is now. It was full of news, rather than features, and did not flaunt its politics quite so much. The *Mail* was tough to work for; you were good or you were gone. After all, they were paying you £35 a week. The other reporters looked like they had come to rub out a rival Mafia boss. They wore dark blue Crombie overcoats all the time, in the office and throughout what was laughingly called the summer. A few wore dark glasses a lot, even though the sun hadn't been seen in Manchester since 1951. They sucked on the ends of their Zapata moustaches on the rare occasions they weren't smoking, and paid a lot of attention to looking hard. There were a few girls, definitely not the squishy kind. Those that weren't actually armour-piercing were very, very complicated.

It wasn't what you would call a family-friendly place. On the rare occasions when there was a party and Christine came along I would be despised and pitied. 'You've brought your *wife*?' they'd say in tones that indicated I had committed a social gaffe on a par with piddling on the Pope.

As the newest, and by a long way the youngest, of the reporters I got the worst shifts. The real killer was the last one, from nine at night to four in the morning. It wasn't so much the work, which mainly consisted of following up stories in other papers and trying to reason with furious people you had just dragged out of bed; it was the socialising. There would be one break just before the pubs shut, when you had to administer the last rites to reporters on the day shift who had been 'unwinding'. There were two more breaks up the road at the Manchester Press Club, which never shut, and it was compulsory to go there after the shift was over.

Even Hogarth would have had difficulty doing full justice to the Manchester Press Club at four in the morning. Nobody had ever tried to open the windows and, as far as anybody could remember, it had never been cleaned. The furniture looked as though it had been rescued from a disastrous fire in a railway waiting room. It was impossible to tell what colour, or even shape, the couch was when it was new. It was covered in archaeological stains. Each one was a testimony to some heroic binge or the unlikely achievement of two drunks copulating in a crowded room.

There was not much food, which was regarded as a distraction for both the barman, a gloomy sod even by Manchester standards, and the drinkers, who were generally past caring. They did, occasionally, have a luke-warm 'pie' which looked like a hand-grenade and tasted like gravel wrapped in nappies. Some nights you would go there and wonder if there was anyone left alive. It had all the hallmarks of a casualty clearing station after anybody with a chance of survival had been triaged down the line. Those left conscious would be confiding or belligerent, often both. You had to watch your step, particularly if you were a limp-wristed southerner who not only still had a wife but even liked her.

'Thisha great place. Izznit a great place?'

'Unique atmosphere, certainly.'

'Where wudwebeee without it?'

'Home?'

The custom was to carry on drinking through the night and then lurch round to the Midland, the old railway hotel. There, in surroundings that can only be described as moth-eaten Manchester Baroque, we would order a massive fried breakfast, with black pudding, naturally, and Champagne if we could afford it. Then we would go straight into work again. Now do you see what I mean when I say it was tough?

I was soon sucked into the mainstream of the paper and began to enjoy the professionalism, if not the surroundings. We spent a lot of time in the office, rewriting stories from local freelances. Every town had a freelance agency in those days and, as many local newspaper reporters supplemented their thin incomes by selling stories to the nationals, there was a constant flow of half-baked news items to choose from. They nearly always needed a lot more work. Partly, this was deliberate. Bloodsucker of Barnsley could charge more if we asked him to make more inquiries. Even when the story had most of the facts and quotes from all the people involved, it still needed the *Daily Mail* touch. Bloodsucker would undoubtedly have tried to sell the same thing to all the other papers and it was a point of pride to add a bit of value. It was good to sneer at the *Daily Express* the next morning if its version showed any resemblance at all to the original.

The master at this was a wonderful old boy called Harold Pendlebury. He looked like a knobbly, northern Mr Pickwick, and was even more benign. He sat in the corner of the newsroom, beaming at everybody and nodding a lot as if everything met with his full approval. He had an extraordinary capacity for attracting affection; you couldn't help liking him the moment you met him. What's more, he had this effect on the phone. Flint-hearted policemen and the most hardened of harpies would melt after about three sentences. I sat next to him for several months, in total admiration and never saw him fail. It wasn't contrived, it wasn't manipulative, it was pure good nature, rare enough in any workplace let alone the vipers' nest of a national newsroom.

After about a month I got my name at the top of the front page of a national newspaper for the first time. The weather had been even worse than usual, but when it snowed in the middle of winter it came as a complete surprise to everybody. The authorities we pay to prepare for these eventualities had, apparently, forgotten that it was a possibility at all. Motorists seemed to think it didn't apply to them, and when the fog came down as well, hurried on home a bit faster, rather than slowing down. The result was a series of spectacular crashes across the North that killed half a dozen people and injured another fifty. I was only one of several reporters who had spent the day and half the night badgering the emergency services and local freelances. It was my name that had been chosen, largely for typographical reasons it turned out, to be used as the by-line on the lead story. I stared for a full five minutes at it in the local newsagent the following morning, ballooning with self-satisfaction. I bought a dozen copies and would have taken more if the shop had not run out. I settled down to read it out loud to myself in the car and, right away, it sounded unfamiliar. After a close, textual study of the piece I did find a sentence, just the one, that I had written. It was the second from the end. I was very modest about it in the office. Not for the first time, I had a lot to be modest about.

National newspapers were different in those days. They were more serious, on the whole better written and with not so much crumpet. Less tat and no tit, in fact. These days the *Mail* is what marketing men call a 'category buster'. It has swamped the middle market. A succession of brilliant editors have got into the heart, and sometimes the less attractive soul, of Middle England. They also discovered at least half the readers were women. Most national newspapers have stepped smartly down-market. *The Times*, which in those days had only just stopped having advertisements all over its front page and whose sub-editors were better on Greek declensions than league division one, now goes big on stories the *Mail* of my day would have thought too tacky. The *Daily Mirror* of that time was making a brave attempt to analyse important international issues for mass-market readers. The *Sun* was an unsuccessful experiment in finding a middlebrow successor to the old socialist *Daily Herald*, awaiting the genius of Rupert Murdoch to give it its full flowering.

Maybe I am being po-faced. The truth, and not everybody saw it at the time, is that television was rapidly becoming the public's main source of news, usurping the newspaper's primary role. Fleet Street had to find things television wasn't good at, was too lofty to stoop to, or was specifically forbidden to do by government regulation. All newspapers got more gossipy. They became star-struck. They were increasingly opinionated and less respectful. They ushered in a more egalitarian and prurient age, or maybe they just reflected a zeitgeist in full flight.

Mind you, even then I had to cover a naked lady, so to speak. A young man who owned a bathroom shop in Liverpool had the bright idea of putting a young woman in a bubble bath in the window. What's more, he knew a girl stupid enough to do it. Marianne's breasts were much larger than her brain (37-23-36, according to my notes, I was a stickler for the details). She hadn't realised that bubbles burst, or maybe she had. An hour after she stepped in there was nothing but a plate-glass window between the Venus of Bury Street and a crowd of, by now, 200 people. The *Daily Mail* photographer insisted on the bath being filled with bubbles again before he took the picture, which shows you how times have changed. Marianne played her part in every way and only needed a little coaching to come up with some arch quote about the nice policeman who 'took down her particulars'. This kind of journalism takes a lot of skill.

I also did some early celebrity gumshoeing. George Best was the prototype of the modern celebrity, except that he had talent, of course. He was the most brilliant footballer of the day, possibly of all time. He looked like a Beatle and acted like a prat. When he should have been wrapped up in bed, guarded by his landlady and with only his hot water bottle for entertainment, he would be out clubbing. He had an awesome capacity for drink and girls – mainly, but not exclusively, blondes. My job was to track him at a safe distance and chronicle his Cresta Run to self-destruction. This was not difficult as he created a huge hubbub wherever he went. Girls threw themselves at him, sometimes literally. He was not very clever at slipping away quietly with the one he fancied, partly because he was so much the centre of attention, but mostly because, by then, he couldn't walk.

I got to be sorry for some of them, particularly a Danish girl called Eva Haraldsted. She had met him when he was signing books in her home town and she lasted longer than most. She was sweet and did not seem to understand what was going on. When she found she did not have an exclusive hold on George's affections, not the most surprising of discoveries you would have thought, she sued him for breach of promise and said all she had ever wanted was peace. Funny way of going about finding it, but there you are. I was sorry for George, who seemed a nice enough bloke. He was driven by demons he did not even try to wrestle with but embraced with a great deal of enthusiasm, as far as I could see.

Most of all I was sorry for myself. Trailing George around had a certain zoological attraction. I got to ogle some nice-looking girls (even Manchester girls can look attractive in that kind of light). And I had a lot to talk about with the men who thought only of football and women who would forget their chilblains to gossip about George. Looking back, it is interesting how sanitised my stories about him were when they appeared in print. Given that David Beckham, a footballer with a boringly blameless life, can fill most papers just by changing his hairstyle, you have to wonder if George was in his heyday now whether there would be room for anything else at all.

I had two great slices of luck while I was at the *Mail*. The paper found it had been contributing for years to the Printing and Publishing Industry Training Board but had never got anything out of it, because it didn't do any training. The *Mail* was a sharp newspaper and promptly invented a course for its less experienced journalists. It consisted entirely of sending the youngest reporter in Manchester, me, to London and the youngest reporter in London to Manchester. The second slice of luck was that the news editor from hell was on holiday.

Expense, as the board would be paying, was no object. This was wonderful for me but no consolation at all to the poor devil who had to come North. He would later be a colleague at the BBC and never lost the look of someone who just knew fate was waiting round the corner with a sockful of sand.

The *Mail* booked me into the Waldorf, a grandly snazzy hotel in Aldwych at the top of Fleet Street. I was positively encouraged to be profligate and felt like James Bond. One night, I even ordered a Vodka Martini, shaken not stirred, in the bar off the Palm Court and got a pitying look from the barman. At the time, I interpreted it as respect. Old friends were invited round to dinner. We worked our way through the menu and ransacked the wine list to make sure the *Mail* got full value. I was 23 and felt remarkably sophisticated. I have grown up a little since, but I have never lost the quiet joy of putting a strenuous evening of self-indulgence down to somebody else's expense.

The London reporters did not seem to do very much. The second morning I was in the newsroom just off Fleet Street, a tall, breezy man came over and asked me if I was new. Before I could answer, he said: 'Look here, it's nearly ten o'clock. Time for my first bottle of Champagne. Care to join me?' This was Vincent Mulchrone, a giant of the last days of Fleet Street and one of the kindest, nicest people you could meet. He was white-haired, red-faced and wore an extremely expensive light tan suit. He looked like the kind of gentleman farmer who can spend most of the year in the South of France. For reasons that will shortly become obvious, I cannot remember which of the Fleet Street hostelries he took me to, El Vino's probably. He asked me about myself which, conceited though I was, only lasted for one bottle. Then he launched into an extremely funny description of his own career, which could have accounted for half the cellars in Rheims and, the way I felt later that day, probably did.

Mulchrone was a wonderful raconteur, talking almost as well as he wrote. He did all the big events for the *Mail*; he had a sense of the sweep of a great occasion, he was good at colour and had an eye for the telling detail. He also had a thirst which, as he cheerfully confessed, sometimes put him in debt to the hard-working, but anonymous, hacks from the Press Association news agency. He told of one big royal day, a wedding perhaps, or a funeral, which dragged on so long that Vincent had been able to finish the case of Champagne he had taken with him to his vantage point. The front page had been cleared for the great writer's take on the event the whole nation was talking about. Unfortunately, Vincent was so drunk he couldn't find his typewriter, let alone compose the magisterial piece the whole paper was waiting for with increasing anxiety as the deadline drew near. At the last moment, some old newspaperman's sense of self-preservation led him to a phone box. He called the *Mail* and loudly, to cover up the slurring in his voice, bellowed out his story. 'What a day!' he said. 'Oh, what a day! Take in PA. Goodbye.'

I went out on a murder story in South London, which seemed quite important at the time, but did not come to much in the end. I did get to meet some of the other Fleet Street characters of the day. The most striking was a *Daily Express* reporter, universally known as the Prince of Darkness. I did not know his real name and, anyway, nobody used it, even to his face. We all called him Darkness for short and he did not seem to mind. Whenever I hear the first line of the Simon and Garfunkel song, 'The Sound of Silence', I think of him. He looked like the sixties comic Max Wall. His face was a skull and his mane of greasy black hair was in full flight off his head, heading for safety between his shoulders. He wore a black cape all the time which made him look even more sinister. Children would whimper as he walked past and even the Murder Squad detectives went pale in his presence.

The *Daily Telegraph* chief reporter was quite the opposite, as you might imagine. He was called Guy and looked like an East Grinstead bank manager, with a toothbrush moustache and regimental tie, but was chronically insecure. He went round the pub, where we would all gather to agree what the story was, asking everybody: 'What's your intro?' He even pinned down the teenage apprentice of the local weekly behind the cigarette machine to find out how he was planning to start his story. It seemed a peculiar weakness for the top reporter on one of the greatest newspapers in the world, but it seemed to work. He must have had more front-page leads than anybody else in Fleet Street, even if he wasn't ever sure how to write them.

I was promised a job in Fleet Street, but told I might have to wait. Manchester seemed even worse when I got back there. We had just had a winter in which the government had experimented with the clocks. Everybody had to put up with a kind of double wintertime. Dawn broke about 11 a.m. as far as we could gather; with Manchester forever buried under ten-tenths grubby grey cloud it was difficult to tell. The city was benighted in every way.

Christine's Morris Minor was stolen twice. It was probably about as much excitement as a Manchester joyrider could handle. We got it back, unharmed, the first time. But the second thief, giddy with the power under his right foot, rammed it into a parked car. It was taken to a garage where the owner, a malignant man with the brain of a whelk, kept it for nearly six months.

I began to look at the job advertisements again. The BBC was offering a post in Bristol. It was for local radio, which I thought was a bit beneath me. They wanted a programme assistant, which sounded like somebody to empty the ashtrays. But they were paying twice as much as I was getting on the *Daily Mail* and anything was better than Manchester.

We sang as I pointed the car south. The rain stopped just below Crewe. We sang harder and did not stop until we got to Bristol.

EIGHT

THE BANGING WOULD not stop. I had tried to ignore it but it was getting steadily worse and threatening to ruin everything. I was in a phonebox on the outskirts of Chippenham doing a live broadcast for the Radio Bristol lunchtime news. There had been a demonstration against cuts in the rural bus services by a huge crowd of housewives (well, 18 at least) and it was the biggest story of the day. I was the lead and had only just started my graphic account of the morning's events when the town drunk appeared. He moved so slowly that even the most elderly of Chippenham's residents were normally able to avoid him, but someone in a phone box was a sitting target. The second sentence of my carefully crafted report was interrupted by the swooshing noise of the door being wrenched open and an imperious, if barely intelligible, demand for 'a few punnies forra coopa tea'.

'Fuck off,' I said, in a useful gap between paragraphs, just failing, as I later discovered, to get my hand over the microphone in time. I managed to push him out of the box, while moving, reasonably smoothly in the circumstances, into a detailed breakdown of how the wilds of Wiltshire were about to get wilder. But the drunk's general rage and frustration had something to focus on for a change and the banging reached a crescendo that all but drowned me out. There is no recording of this, one of the station's most memorable broadcasts, but those few who heard it have remarkably clear recollections to this day. It was not just the inadvertent f-word, then thought to be unknown to most of the public. Nor was it the unequal contest between my ever-rising voice and what came to sound like an artillery barrage. It was more the indefinable sense of strain that comes from someone trying to look murderous while reading out loud. And the rather unfortunate ending to the piece, of course. The station assistant who should have closed the fader on the control panel to cut me off was on the floor, sobbing with laughter. My report, which should have finished with a dignified: 'Now back to the studio in Bristol' in fact ended: 'Right, you bastard', followed by an eerie scream. It was a good job hardly anybody was listening.

They hadn't taught us about that kind of thing on the training course. Apart from a few lessons in knob twiddling, they hadn't taught us very much about anything at all. It was mostly about coping with the BBC – a brief introduction, needless to say, as it takes a lifetime's study to get the hang of it.

We were rather smug when we gathered that first morning at the Langham, at the bottom of Portland Place. The ten producers on the new station had, after all, been chosen from nearly 3,000 applicants. It sounded good but the truth was that the BBC had decided it needed to widen its intake of staff and this new local radio business would be a painless way of doing it. The jobs had accordingly been advertised everywhere, with heavy stress on talent rather than experience. A small army of fantasising no-hopers had seen it as their golden moment; the bottom rung on the ladder to stardom. To be picked out from among their number was no great distinction, though we felt very special at the time.

The Langham proved a useful antidote to self-satisfaction. It had been a very grand hotel (and is again now) but at the time was a kind of giant box room for Broadcasting House, the BBC's headquarters across the road. It was, effectively, an eight-storey filing cabinet, housing the administrative overflow of a corporation whose main purpose has always seemed to be paperwork rather than programmes. We had a front-row vantage point for observing the mysterious workings of the BBC and to see how marginal we were to them.

The little stations were Auntie's bastard children. Their pioneers thought it would take the corporation back to its cat's-whiskered roots and bring it closer to its audience. A fair slice of the BBC shuddered at the very idea. It was all very *de haut en bas* at the time and the feeling was that the licence payer should be kept at a respectful distance. Besides, if the idea got round that anybody off the street could do the job (a fair description of the local radio recruitment process), the game was up. In public, there was a lot of talk of maintaining standards. In private, they called us Toytown Radio.

They weren't far wrong. The group in the Langham that morning were mostly very young or very inexperienced; most of us were both. The education producer was a tubby young teacher from Yorkshire, called Ken Blakeson, whose catchphrase was 'don't ask me, squire' which seemed to sum things up rather. The women's producer sat in the corner muttering to herself and emitting the occasional shriek. Her name was Kathryn Adie, though we called her Kate when we found she wasn't quite as strange as she appeared. The religious producer was an unlikely

Methodist minister and was only there in spirit, as the BBC was still wrestling with the unions over his appointment. Frank Topping was a raffish young actor who had been studio manager for the comedy series *Bootsie and Snudge* before his ordination and presumably felt there was more Godlessness in broadcasting than anywhere else.

I was one of four news producers under a BBC regional freelance who had been made news editor. His long blond hair looked as though his mother had brushed it a lot. He wore cravats, pushed his polka dot handkerchief up his sleeve and said 'ahem' at the beginning of every sentence. The *Mail* newsdesk would have had him for elevenses, but he was good-natured and energetic, before lunch at any rate.

The station manager, who had handpicked this lot, was only 25 himself. David Waine had made some interesting choices. Ken went on to be an award-winning playwright and one of the main writers on *Coronation Street*. Frank made a terrific career on radio and television out of not being sanctimonious. Jonty Fulford, another of the 'programme assistants', became one of BBC television's leading arts producers. Roger Bennett, who was with me in the newsroom, stayed with the station and became Britain's best-loved local broadcaster, showered with awards. David himself always refused to work in London and ended up running the BBC in the Midlands. I am not sure what happened to Kate but she must have made her mark somewhere.

The course was good fun. I struggled a bit with the practical side, being mechanically inept. Eventually I got the hang of the chunky German tape recorder called the Uher and how to edit with a razor blade and some sticky stuff; it was finicky but at least you could understand how it worked. The technology lost me a bit after that, but I could just about get by on a small corner of the control desk that we newshounds needed, after it was explained to me no more than a hundred times.

We practised on each other to start with. My first project was to interview Sheila Young, an attractive station assistant. By the time I had worked out how to get the Uher going, I had forgotten the questions I was going to ask. All the tape actually recorded was embarrassed silence. It might have had something to do with Sheila wearing the shortest skirt in West London, but it wasn't an auspicious start to my broadcasting career. We were sent out to interview people in the street on a wide variety of current issues. Local radio was keen on these 'vox pops'; they had the demotic touch that was meant to be its defining characteristic. It has always seemed to me a rather dubious way to survey public opinion, unless you want some entertaining answers to questions like: 'Does this carrot look like a penis?' But Esther Rantzen hadn't been invented then and the British public hadn't yet developed a taste for exhibitionism. Nine times out of ten, I would get the answer: 'Not today, thank you' no matter if I asked them about nuclear disarmament or neutering cats.

The main importance of the Langham was that it housed the BBC Club, or at least a couple of its bars, as the corporation's collective thirst required a lot of them. They were freely scattered among the BBC's own buildings and several pubs nearby had been co-opted for those who didn't mind mixing with the general public from a position of strength. There were clubs within clubs, really. The announcers sat in one corner, Woman's Hour in another. The suits did their backstabbing, appropriately enough, in an upstairs watering hole. News, which tended to regard everybody else as effete, took themselves off to the Crown and Sceptre, aka the Hat and Stick, to protect their impurity. We recruits went to an institution in the Langham called the Salad Bar, which never had any; salad, that is. There were plenty of fruits, certainly, but the only thing green was our faces after a typical BBC day.

Everybody drank most of the time. Work stopped on the dot of one for an hour and a half's energetic elbow exercise if your programme wasn't actually on the air at the time, and sometimes even if it was. The same thing happened at half past five. Some departments even had their own booze trolley that came round to rescue the desperate in the long dry afternoons. It was all very civilised. Sodden, surreal, but civilised.

I loved it from the start. It was a very middle-class place and I felt at home. There were carpets on the floor and good things to eat whereas my last memory of the *Mail* was the slap of the canteen lady's bare feet as she paddled through the grease with my sausage and chips. People were unfailingly courteous. However ruthless or devious they were it all took place behind at least a mask of civility. People could, and frequently did, spend half their careers at the BBC before finding out they were regarded as hopeless. If you were on the staff it did not really matter. Your job was safe until you collected your generous pension at 60 unless you did something really outrageous, like serial killing or forgetting to pay the licence fee.

For all its idiosyncrasies and its self-indulgence, the BBC did have an ethos I felt I could sign up to, and have felt comfortable with ever since. At the core of it all was a sense of purpose that seemed genuinely high-minded. It was clearer then than it is now but it survives in at least parts of the BBC and sustains those of us who care for the place. Listeners and viewers were there to be informed, educated and entertained, not patronised and exploited. The inviolability of truth and the slippery notion of quality were at the heart of it all. Both were difficult ideals, but we had to try, because if the BBC didn't strive for them, who would?

There was a remarkable sense of democracy then. We were the lowest of the low, junior plankton in the BBC food chain, and yet a stream of bigwigs came down to talk to us, and, even more impressive, argue with us. The intellectual freedom seemed remarkable; the executives cheerfully rubbished each other's cherished projects while, in true BBC style, remaining respectful about them personally. It was intoxicating if rather chaotic and, doubtless, not very efficient. It would not happen these days. Under John Birt, and even, in a rather more human way, under Greg Dyke, there was a more totalitarian atmosphere. Dissent was discouraged. As one of the most senior of the corporation's news executives put it to me (before departing to CNN): 'The motto of the BBC used to be "Nation Shall Speak Peace Unto Nation". Now it's "Fit in or Fuck off".'

BBC Bristol was like BBC London but more so. It was a laager of Georgian and Victorian houses drawn up in a defensive circle in the middle of Clifton, itself an upmarket Regency district that looks down on the smellier bits of Bristol and does not like what it sees. The BBC was a cosy place, populated by nest-building females who would have been pleased to have been described as middle-aged and seemed to regard their jobs as akin to selling flags for the Red Cross. The men wore woolly socks and sandals, even in mid-winter. The more glamorous of them had handlebar moustaches. They went for tea and buns every hour or so until the club opened. Then they had two or three gins, and perhaps a little half-hearted groping, before heading home to their sedate suppers.

It wasn't clear what they did. Just, whatever it was, it would probably take a year or more to do it. A gentle retreat then, something like a cross between a bowling club and the teachers' common room at a second-rate public school.

They hated us and had every reason to do so. Many of them were having to go to make way for a brash gang of kids who did not know what they were doing. The BBC bridge club was losing half its members, redeployed to the ends of the earth or worse, Manchester.

We had our own Victorian house in Tyndalls Park Road and the first job was to build the furniture, or at least screw it together as it had arrived in flat-pack boxes and been left in the car park. We tried to spread the word amongst the newsier of the local institutions, the police and the other emergency services, the motoring organisations and sports clubs. We didn't just need their news; we needed them. There were a lot of hours to fill and we had to have a lot of voices to fill them. We went out on training exercises with the Hillman Hunter radio car, an eccentric vehicle which even Kate, who was already cultivating a brisk military style, described as a 'bloody-minded bit of kit'. The idea was to drive to the location and then erect the mast which was meant to shoot up from somewhere around the back bumper. Ours seemed impotent, or at least only spasmodically interested in performing. Worse, once we had got it up, it was reluctant to come down. This left you with the choice of bedding down in the back while you waited for the engineer, or short-circuiting the mechanism that normally prevented you driving a 20-foot erection around the countryside and risk demolishing half the bridges in Somerset. It didn't matter much. Everybody thought it was a detector van anyway and rushed home as soon as it appeared to make sure their TV was switched off.

While on one of these practice runs, I vox popped an extremely glamorous young teacher who batted her eyes at me and asked for a job. I put her on to the news editor. She must have batted much more than her eyes at him because she had been taken on as a freelance before I had even got back to the station and their affair became the worst-kept secret in Bristol.

Their trysting place was a little cubbyhole behind the reception desk which was known officially as the 'unattended studio'. They took this rather too literally and counted on not being disturbed. One day when I was on duty something went wrong with studio one, where we normally did the news bulletins, and, with a matter of seconds to go, I raced down to the unattended studio. I knew something was wrong when I flung the door open and there was a squashy noise followed by a high-pitched 'Oooh!' as a descant to a low, but urgent, groan. I was already on the air as the door closed again, revealing my boss and the dark-haired lovely *in flagrante* very *delicto*. Or at least it would have done if I had lifted my eyes from my script. It was tricky not to do so, even trickier to back out through the door without catching their eye or any more interesting part of their conjoined anatomy. I managed, though. Local radio develops very special skills.

*

We were on the air before we knew it. I said the very first words ever uttered on the station, to wit: 'Good morning, this is BBC Radio Bristol. It's eight o'clock. Here's someone else.' This might not sound the most stressful of broadcasts but I had been worrying about it for days. Think of all the possibilities for error. If I said 'good afternoon', for instance, or got the name of the station wrong at the very moment of its launch, I would condemn the whole enterprise to decades of ridicule, as well as destroying my broadcasting career at birth. I was not, perhaps, the most natural of broadcasters. It was *live*, for goodness' sake, and, besides, there must have been a couple of dozen people listening.

Between them, the BBC and the government had made it as difficult as possible for the new local radio stations with a series of crass decisions and messy compromises. The worst was that we were only on FM (or VHF as it was known then) and hardly anybody had a radio that could hear us. Having no listeners might be a point almost of pride in some of the more stuck-up corners of the corporation, but it made it tricky for us. The whole point of local radio was to involve the community, to be its village hall, its notice board, its next-door neighbour – we had foldersful of corporation clichés about all this. When most people had never even heard of you and those that had thought Radio Bristol was an electrical repair shop in the Gloucester Road, it was discouraging to say the least. The biggest problem was the phone-ins and record request programmes. We had a lot of these, partly because they were cheap, but also because they were a way of involving the community and turning us into the local notice-board, village hall, etc.

Nobody called. We had to line up friends, landladies, Ron from the Coach and Horses, Christine's brother-in-law, anybody we could lay our hands on, in fact. Most of them were just doing it as a favour and had no burning urge to sound off about whatever topic was under discussion, which made the phone-ins sound rather passionless and reasonable. Sometimes we were so desperate we had to phone up ourselves, covering the mouthpiece with a handkerchief even though there wasn't the remotest chance our voices would be recognised. You always knew it was one of the station staff, in vocal disguise, because we nearly always claimed to be phoning from Nempnett Thrubwell. How this blameless Somerset village came to represent for us the epicentre of yokeldom I cannot now remember but in the early days of Radio Bristol we made it famous. Or certainly would have done if anybody had been listening.

As we gradually acquired an audience, the very tight restrictions on what music we could play became increasingly irksome. We were only allowed to broadcast a couple of hours a week of records anybody in their right mind might want to hear. That was the limit on so-called 'needle time' that had been agreed between the BBC and the Musicians' Union. We did have stacks of records that didn't count and the BBC hierarchy kept telling us the 'non-needle-time' discs were just as good. But these were the glory days of the Beatles and the Rolling Stones. The Silesian Strings' haunting version of 'The Moon over Bratislava' could not compete. It does explain, though, the curious popularity of Bulgarian dance music in some south Somerset villages which, until then, had only been enthusiastic about incest.

Radio Bristol was very serious about news. We had four main news programmes, imaginatively named Morning West, West to One (it went out at 12.45), West Tonight and Late Night West; there was never much doubt which point of the compass we were coming from. It was pretty hand-to-mouth stuff after working on a big newspaper. There were only four reporters, sorry Programme Assistants (News), to cover all the hours in the day and to fill all those bulletins. There was not much time for analysis or fine writing. We lived life at a pelt, squabbling over the tape recorders (there were never enough), interviewing anything that moved, hacking at tapes with our razor blades, back to back, like it was the last stand on the Little Big Horn, and finally racing into the studio, just in time. Or not.

We goofed a lot. Most of our mistakes were stupid or embarrassing, but we had some laughs as well. One evening a major part of West Tonight was to be a live interview with the local British Rail manager about some crisis or other on the railways. He was a nice man with an unfortunate name and we were given strict warnings that, on no account, should Mr Richard Titball occasion unseemly mirth. The task was given to Richard Talbot, who was presenting the programme. Richard was an almost painfully upright young man, the son of the BBC's royal correspondent at the time, and he took these warnings very seriously. He did not flinch when Mr Titball said: 'Call me Dick', even though the rest of us – children that we were – struggled to suppress our sniggers. He almost lost it when the railman complained about all the trouble he had with his frozen points. Richard got through it all and wrapped up the interview with obvious satisfaction in a difficult task, impeccably discharged. The momentary loss of concentration was fatal. He turned away from his interviewee and said: 'Mr Titball, thank you. Now football.'

The tricky programme was Late Night West. You did it on your own and it went out at 10.30 when there was nobody else in the station. The most important thing was not to lock yourself out, which I managed to do one night and the programme was never broadcast at all. The second most important thing was to stay out of the BBC Club. Broadcasting is very difficult when you have had a few, about which more later. But this was what was called in the jargon a 'self-op' programme. You had to do everything yourself, opting out of Radio 2 which the station broadcast in the mid-evening, reading all the links, playing in the tapes and opting back in again; one whiff of alcohol and the whole elaborate process would collapse in chaos.

The worst moment was at the end. We had to switch back into the middle of Late Night Extra on Radio 2 which was a mixture of records and chat. This was a difficult junction to pull off smoothly. It was considered to be an almost capital offence to drop back in while people were talking. We had to wait until they played a record so we could gently fade into it and then go home. We had a stack of discs of Mongolian municipal brass band selections to tide us over; we rarely had to wait more than a minute or so. Until that Friday. I was blathering my goodbyes and when I pressed down the prefade button they were talking in a rather excitable way for Late Night Extra, which could normally be guaranteed to put you to sleep in about 30 seconds and most people thought was part of a covert government energy-saving campaign. I pressed the button again and they were still talking. Not just talking, it dawned on me, but *commentating*, which is not like human speech at all. Late Night Extra had been given over to a football match. And it had just started.

The Mongolians got more air time that night than they ever did in Ulan Bator. So did the Kronstadt Chorale's vivacious medleys, and I bet the Youth Orchestra of Minsk never thought their grand symphony glorifying the achievement of the 1961 industrial production targets would ever be heard in Midsomer Norton. I played them all. I also read out large sections of the *Radio Times*, telling my puzzled listeners about every programme they could hear the following day on six networks, very slowly. Finally, after the closing whistle and the post-match analysis and the weather and the shipping forecast, I faded back into 'Sailing By'. I was shaking and badly needed a drink. But I was proud, too. A BBC Sacred Rule had not been broken.

That first year on a new local radio station was a golden time. We were all, or nearly all, very young. The job was new and exciting; we were making it up as we went along. David was the perfect boss, energetic and enthusiastic, terrific fun without losing his grip on what constantly threatened to dissolve into anarchy. We played as hard as we worked and, as the station's roots grew down into the subsoil of Bristol life, we swept others up into our hectic socialising. A gay local restaurateur started doing cooking spots on the afternoon show and we went in for a lot of subsidised carousing down at his restaurant. We went dog racing with Jerry the Greengrocer who became the Radio Bristol tipster. We had parties round the battered old station piano on which an old boy called Arthur Parkman did a daily request programme called Call a Tune – he only had the one, as it happened. It wouldn't matter if you asked for 'Jesu, Joy of Man's Desiring' or 'Brown Sugar', it would be impossible to tell the difference. We teased Kate, who ran a programme called Womenwise and was going through a social realism phase, trying to get her to do features about stripagram girls, then a charming novelty. We were a whoopee cushion under the bland backside of BBC Bristol. We loved it.

Christine and I were very happy. We bought a detached, three-bedroomed house in a pleasant village just outside the city. It cost only a little more than twice my annual salary, I remember, and inflation was whittling away the real cost of the mortgage. Christine had a features sub-editor's job on the city's morning paper, the *Western Daily Press*, which had been rescued from oblivion by a frankly terrifying editor called Eric Price. He had a habit of throwing typewriters out of the windows and had got through hundreds of sub-editors in his time on the paper. The record stay in the job was half an hour, though it was said there were dozens who hadn't lasted more than a day. Christine was the first woman he had allowed to sub on his paper and prospered there. When I was doing the early shift on Radio Bristol, we would pass each other at lunchtime on Brunel's Suspension Bridge high over Clifton Gorge. I remember thinking how lucky I was to have a gorgeous wife, a fun job, and to live in such a beautiful city.

Of course Radio Bristol was parochial. That was the point. There wasn't much in the way of money, or resources, or help, and we were working ridiculously hard. But there was a great sense of ownership of what we were doing. You did it all yourself, researching, interviewing, editing and broadcasting. There was no team of technicians to cajole into doing what you wanted. There was no producer with a different slant on what the story was and how it should be told. There were no suits, hurrying off to meetings to chunter over whether your report would fit the template of the BBC's editorial policy guidelines. You were on your own.

Most of what we produced was unremarkable. Some was no doubt crass. There were, though, programmes of extraordinary quality, considering the circumstances in which they were made. Frank, our not-so-tame vicar, wrote and produced a passion play called On the Hill. Roger, a jazz clarinettist in his rare moments away from the newsroom, did a blues score. The whole thing was hugely ambitious, an intricate weaving of sounds and themes, shifting periods to underline the timelessness of Christ's sacrifice, and a cast of hundreds, all played by the station staff. Ken the education man was Jesus, cast rather against type, we thought. I was the centurion, two Pharisees, an unidentified apostle, man in the crowd and, nice touch, the donkey. Kate was a tart, maybe even Mary Magdalene; at any rate her best line was: 'Want a nice time, dearie?'

On the Hill went out on Radio Bristol at Easter and later was broadcast on Radio 3. It won a sheaf of awards in this country and abroad.

A couple of months later, I was covering a murder trial, a bleak affair in which a lad was killed by a skinhead of about the same age down in Weston-super-Mare. I managed to speak to the mother of the murderer. She was crushed by what had happened, but thoughtful and articulate about what it meant from her perspective. She would be losing her son, too, at least for many years to come. She and her family would have to live with obloquy for the rest of their lives. Worst of all was the endless worrying about how her son had turned out the way he did and the part she had played in moulding him and so in the events of that tragic night.

Roger managed to interview the mother of the victim. Her feelings were, of course, less complicated, her grief was more straightforward. But she was a reflective woman and she described the everyday realities of her loss in ways that brought tears to harder eyes than mine. At the end of the trial, when the verdict of guilty had been delivered and the sentence passed, Roger and I cut the two interviews together into a half-hour special programme. The interviews fitted perfectly together into a counterpoint of consequences that flowed from one brutal moment in a seaside back street. It was probably clumsily edited by today's standards, but it was extraordinarily moving. It was re-broadcast on Radio 4 and made as big an impact nationally as it did in Bristol.

The head of the BBC in Bristol, Stuart Wyton, had a hand in making sure the murder programme reached a wider audience. He had been kind to me since hearing a string of reports I had done for national radio on the crash of two RAF Red Arrows jets at Fairford, their base then in Gloucestershire. Stuart was an old-fashioned kind of BBC boss with an impressive career that stretched back to the Second World War. He was cultured and intelligent, supportive in a dozen different ways. He was an enabler; he made you feel you were capable of big things, that big things were expected of you. He took Christine and me out to dinner and urged me to set my ambitions high. When BBC mandarins are good, they are very good indeed, and Stuart was one of the best.

Many of the others in Bristol at the time were pretty hopeless. The regional television unit that, amongst other things, produced the nightly news magazine *Points West*, was one of broadcasting's backwaters, stagnant at that. The magazine itself was dull. Dreary stories, sloppily reported for the most part and presented by a succession of ex-army officers. There were a couple of good reporters but they struggled with a badly run and complacent newsroom. There was a great determination to have nothing to do with Radio Bristol, just next door. They were scarcely at the top of the tree, but we were far beneath their notice.

Regional television was the obvious next step for me so, after a year at Radio Bristol, I pushed for a job on *Points West*. With some reluctance they eventually gave me an audition, which consisted of reading a script from the previous night's programme into the camera. It took about 45 seconds. I passed the testy little man who ran regional television several times a day for the next fortnight but he did not speak. Instead, he sent me a formal letter saying the audition showed I had no possibility whatsoever of an onscreen career in television and I was best advised to stick to radio. I was told he had been equally discouraging with Jonathan Dimbleby and he subsequently rejected Kate Adie out of hand. Perhaps he just had very high standards, though few of those he did take on troubled the scorers, as my cricketing friends would say.

It was a blow, and it hurt. I had become unused to rejection, particularly in such categorical terms. But fate was playing jokes again. That same week in 1971 Christine and I went to a dinner the Lord Mayor gave at the Mansion House for 'members of the press'. I sat next to a news executive from the local commercial station, HTV, who said they had a vacancy for a television reporter. They had heard my stuff on Radio Bristol and wanted me to apply. I had, understandably, fallen out of love with the BBC and grabbed the chance with both hands.

NINE

'BACK A BIT,' said Graham the cameraman. I shuffled backwards, obediently. I had a lot on my mind. It was my first television report. The camera crew had filmed the story about flood defences on the Avon without much reference to me. I had done a couple of quick interviews and they had moved us around like chess pieces, making it obvious the background was more important than anything that was likely to be said. Now was the biggest hurdle, the 'piece to camera', the bit where the reporter delivers a few lines straight into the screen. The glory moment, we call it.

'Back a bit more.' It looks easy, but let me tell you it isn't. I had to remember the words I had written out on my clipboard (got one at last) a few moments before. Besides, the wind was blowing my hair around in what I was sure was an unflattering way. The soundman was astonished I had not brought some hair spray like a proper television reporter.

'Bit more still.' I ran through it again, trying to get the facial expression right. I was aiming for gravitas, leavened by a pinch of boyish charm.

'Gnat's more.'

It was a full second before I realised I was up to my waist in the river.

I had been concentrating so hard on my lines that the reality of stepping backwards into first nothingness, then the sludgy waters of the Avon, dawned only as the cold clamped on to my crutch. I blinked at the crew who were slapping each other as if they had just scored a goal in the World Cup final. They had not had anybody this raw to practise on for a very long time. I would have burst into tears if they hadn't still been filming.

The HTV film crews were famous practical jokers and often put a lot more effort into it than the job they were being paid to do, quite royally as it happened. You had to be on your guard all the time. They would take you into a prissy tea room in Bath and suddenly disappear. You'd be alone at the table amongst all the maiden aunts and retired colonels, when the tape recorder they had hidden underneath started belting out a song about the joys of anal sex. If you were going to an old folks' home, they would ring up beforehand and say it was your birthday so you would arrive to a cake covered in candles and a drooping choir of octogenarians. One New Year's Eve, Ken Rees, the newsreader, later to be Washington correspondent for ITN and head of HTV news, was broadcasting the evening bulletin when the door of the studio was flung open and one of the station's more flamboyant reporters lurched in, horribly drunk. The studio manager tried to intercept him but it turned into a brawl that swept right in front of all the cameras and ended with the two of them trying to strangle each other across the newsdesk. Ken kept going as long as he could but was a matter of seconds away from nervous collapse when they both leapt up and cried: 'Gotcha!'

It turned out there had been a vast crew conspiracy and all the clocks in the building had been advanced five minutes. Everybody had been in on the joke. There was no time for Ken to recover his composure. The studio manager straightened his tie and started chanting the real countdown: 'Thirty seconds to on-air . . . twenty . . . ten, nine, eight . . .' It kept you on your toes.

HTV was full of surprises right from the start. I arrived for the interview and was rather flattered to be greeted by Stan Hazell, the newsroom number two, out in the car park. We walked round the side of the building straight into a camera crew who were all set up, ready to shoot. I was looking keenly around to see what it was they were filming when Stan said: 'Just talk to the camera.'

'What about?' I said

'Anything you like,' he said. 'Until I tell you to stop.'

The trapdoor at the bottom of my mind opened and everything I have ever thought about anything emptied out on to the tarmac. I mumbled about myself eventually, but the crew didn't seem very impressed. I didn't realise at the time they never do. If I had announced the Second Coming they would probably have said it was too late, they were off shift in half an hour.

Stan's boss, Ron Evans, was one of the great figures in ITV. He practically invented the regional news magazine, as we see it today. He was a bluff Yorkshireman who had come from national newspapers and had a real flair for television. Ron's basic idea was simple: television is about pictures. His talent was in knowing how to bring the serious stories visually to life, and spotting the human interest items that would make good television. The station had gone into colour the year before and the programme *Report West* had really taken off. It was filled with film packages and was presented with warmth by Bruce Hockin, who never seemed to age, and dewy glamour by Jan Leeming, who never seemed to stop marrying people.

There were only three full-time film reporters and *Report West* was often a forty-minute programme. We turned up at nine and Ron would brief us closely on the day. He knew exactly what he wanted. He would tell us what sequences to film, what questions to ask (he had often already told the interviewees what to answer) and the line to take in the piece to camera.

We were expected to do two, or even three, film reports a day. What made it more difficult was the crews' restrictive union agreements. They did not start until 9.30. Even then, you could not ask them to move until after their protected half-hour 'loading up time'. They normally insisted on a full three-course lunch. If there was any industrial tension in the air, which was most of the time because the union was bloody-minded and the management slippery, they would break on the dot even if you were halfway through an interview. But they were decent people and the cameramen were outstanding. They were proper lighting cameramen who shot network dramas as well as news. One later filmed the Bond movie *Goldeneye*.

With my four skilled, and only intermittently truculent, technicians I would spend the day roaring round the West Country in the big Volvo estate, knocking out news reports to Ron's recipe. This required some versatility. A bad road crash in the morning might be bracketed with a vox pop on whether oysters really are an aphrodisiac in the afternoon. (Sample Ron Evans' briefing: 'See this new report on oysters. Not now, read it on the way. Here's a silver tray. Buy two dozen oysters and a couple of bottles of Champagne. Go down to Bedminster where the real people live. Stick to attractive girls and unattractive old men. Give 'em an oyster each and a glass of bubbly and ask them if they feel sexy. Do a piece to camera with the last one. Remember – twinkle, don't leer, it's a family programme.')

It was film, not video, in those days. Each 400ft roll only lasted about 11 minutes and it took ages for the camera assistant, fumbling blindly around in his black cloth bag, to load up another magazine. You could not waste a frame. It wasn't just that it was expensive; the real problem was that it all had to queue up to be processed at the end of the afternoon and if you wasted a lot of film you threatened the whole programme. These days, you can go on shooting an interview on video for hours to get the clip that you want, out of sheer exhaustion if necessary. Back then, if the interviewee did not deliver in the first couple of answers, you had to fight down the urge to put a knife to his throat and dictate it to him. Film, though, did give you a breathing space when you got back to the studio. Each roll took about forty minutes to go through the bath. It was just enough time to get your thoughts in order before the chaos of the edit room.

The film editors had high blood pressure and wore white gloves, which made them look like Minnie Mouse with apoplexy. Theirs was not a healthy life. They spent their time in dedicated patronage of the HTV bar, broken only by a couple of hours' frenzied hacking in the late afternoon. It was gloriously mechanical and even I could follow what was going on. They sliced each shot out of the roll and hung them up on pegs over a bin. When they had cut them all out and put them in order, and if they hadn't inadvertently kicked the bin and reduced it all to unidentifiable spaghetti at the bottom, they slammed them together and spliced them into the finished item. We always wrote the commentary after the pictures had been assembled so we had to make sure there were enough pictures in the right places to tell the story; it was important not to be left with five seconds to explain the pros and cons of the latest White Paper on local government reorganisation. You knew how long each shot lasted. You knew that you spoke three words a second. Most of all, you knew the programme was on the air in fourteen minutes.

The commentaries were always broadcast live. We reporters would rush into the studio at one minute to six and stand in a queue behind the commentary desk, still scribbling the lines for one or other of our reports. You just had to hope you had got the timings right. The commentary could be a bit short; with luck, it would sound like an intentional pause for effect. But if it was too long and you began talking over the Lord Mayor, it was a disaster and the wrath of Ron was waiting at the studio door. Big Dennis, the floor manager, was meant to stop this happening. He stood right in front of you, listening to the timings from the studio gallery in his headphones and throwing fingers into your face to count you down. This only made it even more terrifying, particularly when you had only just launched into that florid sentence you were so proud of and Big Dennis was already down to two fingers. At zero he drew his finger across his throat, which summed up the situation, and the consequences, all too well. It was good experience but they probably said that about being burnt at the stake.

The other reporters were, in their different ways, fascinating. Richard Cottrell had a misleading air of piety about him. He looked down on the world with a sort of benign contempt. He did not so much walk as glide around the place with his hands steepled prayerfully in front of him as if looking for a rich supplicant to bless. Richard was an efficient reporter who delivered his films, and his rather more creative expenses, without breaking sweat. He was good company and his distinctly irreligious approach to life meant he was dogged by thoroughly entertaining scandals.

Richard was on a curious political journey. When I first met him, he seemed so left-wing he was almost a revolutionary, albeit of the kind that would urge on the *sans culottes* from the rear and end up, when the heads had all rolled, in the château, probably in bed with the Vicomtesse. But after a surprise Conservative election victory in the early seventies he shocked us all by coming into the newsroom and saying: 'Well, we won.' It turned out he had identified the potential of the European Parliament earlier than anyone else and, being a railway buff, could spot a gravy train when he saw one. He set out to cultivate the West Country's Tories and impress them with his knowledge of European affairs. He did so with such good effect he ended up as an MEP. He would probably be in Strasbourg still were it not for two unfortunate incidents. One was a lunch, spectacular even by the pantophagous standards of Europe's law makers. The main dish was pigs' trotters, appropriately enough. It included enough vintage Cognac to anaesthetise a battalion of the Irish Guards and cost something akin to the gross national product of Gambia. When news of it reached the ears of the *Daily Mirror*, which is not noted for its love of high-living Tories, they spread it across the whole front page.

Sometime later, and perhaps after a lunch of similar proportions, Richard decided it was beneath the dignity of an MEP to fasten his seatbelt when coming in to land on a return trip from his parliamentary duties. He insisted on pointing out the reasons why to the pilot, personally, as he was on finals. His dignity came under further pressure as a result and soon after that he lost his seat.

Jon Pepper lived in that narrow strip of country that divides genius from insanity. He was an intensely imaginative reporter who really lived the stories he covered. He illustrated one about the economic problems of the West Country by emerging from a pawnbroker's shop wearing only a barrel.

Jon finally went too far when reporting on a child judo prodigy. Even in those days, the sight of Pepper in a posing pouch rolling on the floor with a ten-year-old was unseemly, and Ron, a puritan at heart, went berserk. The last I heard Jon had changed sex and was living as a woman in a caravan in mid-Wales.

Sex was quite a preoccupation at HTV. There was a traffic jam at the gate on to Bath Road most lunchtimes as the producers and directors took their PAs out for trysts in the woods around Chew Lake, or somewhere more comfortable if the weather was inclement. They used to describe it as 'location research' on their expenses.

The cameramen were famous swivers, but were not always very clever at hiding it from their wives. One of my favourite cameramen had his comeuppance, so to speak, when he told his wife he was going away filming for the weekend and settled down to 48 hours' horizontal jogging with a PA in her cottage. At ten o'clock on the Sunday morning the doorbell rang and, thinking it was the paperboy, he opened the front door wearing only a tea towel extolling the grandeur that is Minehead. Imagine his surprise when he realised it wasn't the paperboy but his wife, and not in a good mood at that.

This became public remarkably quickly. The following day, the cameraman's wife barged through the newsroom door and threw a suitcase at her rival, which broke open scattering shirts and murky-looking underwear over the desks. 'You can have him AND his bloody washing,' she yelled, with some satisfaction, it seemed to us. It was a lively place to work.

Television in the West proved even more prone to error and embarrassment than radio. It was not long before that a live, three-handed interview had proved to be something of an exaggeration. It was a debate about what these days would be called the right to roam, between a man from the Ramblers' Association, a landowner and some environmentalist, though the word had not yet been invented. After a few minutes, the director noticed that the rambler had not made much of a contribution, indeed seemed to be asleep. He told the floor manager to creep across on all fours to give him a poke. The control room was still happily cutting between the more vigorous participants when they were stopped short by an electrifying whisper: 'I . . . think . . . he's . . . DEAD.'

TV directors were proud of their ability to cope with these things. The camera shots were tightened to exclude the corpse as much as possible. In any case it was caught in some breeze from the air conditioning and seemed to be nodding sagely at the points being made. His name was removed from the closing credits before he had been removed from the studio. Television fame can be very fleeting.

My most difficult moment in the HTV studio was caused by entirely the opposite problem. I was interviewing a contingent from the Sealed Knot, who had turned up in their Civil War fig and were grouped picturesquely in the corner of the studio around an extraordinarily large and apparently somnolent Wolfhound. I was talking to their leader, Count Tolstoy, about the Sealed Knot's strange purposes, when, out of the corner of my eye, I saw the dog languorously open its hind legs to reveal a truly magnificent erection. It must have been the studio lights, I suppose. The dog seemed to have a real instinct for television, because he timed these displays perfectly. Whenever the director cut to a wide shot, where the Wolfhound was, of course, centre stage, the dog opened his legs and his tackle sprang up like a pink Roman catapult. Something of the anxiety amongst the crew must have communicated itself to the Count because, without pausing for a moment in his description of the joys of being a Cavalier, he raised a shining boot and brought it crashing down on the beast's haunches. The West Country winced. The dog yowled piteously. The interview came to a halt in the confusion. The dog's grief could still be heard ten minutes later over the weather forecast, even though it had been removed to the car park and was being fed sausage rolls off the hospitality trolley.

HTV was enormous fun but I fell out with the management before long, as most people did. I had gone there for less than I was getting paid at Radio Bristol. The deal was that if I adapted to the new medium I would get a 'substantial' rise after six months. No precise figure was mentioned, but this was the HTV way. When the time came, Ron gave me a warm review. The details were out of his hands, but he had sent the strongest of recommendations that the management should be generous. I waited several months for an interview with the accountant who handled these things. He read out Ron's glowing report, added a few gratuitous remarks of his own and said I would be getting another £50 a year. Even in those days it was pretty insulting. I packed my bags, with genuine regret and went back to the BBC.

The job I had landed was with the BBC in Southampton and should have been much the same sort of thing. It was to work primarily on the local television news magazine which was (and still is) called *South Today*. I had seen the post advertised and was impressed enough by the size of the salary – half as much again as HTV – to put in a speculative application. There was not much of an audition, but I did make a lengthy appearance in front of an appointment board, a dull-looking quartet who, as far as I can remember, did not ask me a single relevant question; but that might have been their skill. I was surprised to get the job, particularly as there were better qualified internal candidates. I did not know the BBC that well in those days.

BBC Southampton was a big disappointment. It was a cave in the hills compared with HTV. It was housed on a couple of floors of the old Cunard building just over the road from the docks and smelt of decay. The place was primitive and the programme was hopeless. Worse, it was still in black and white, in every sense stuck in the dark ages of television.

South Today was presided over by the baleful figure of the news editor, Michael Harman. He knew almost nothing about television and precisely zero about news, but did not see either of these things as a disadvantage. Quite the opposite, in fact. To him, journalism was a dirty word and he waged a constant war to keep its practices from soiling *South Today*. He would not pander to the vile popular taste by having anything vaguely interesting on the programme and he regarded pictures as a diabolical distraction from his holy purpose of boring the pants off the South of England.

Harman had only one love and that was music. He had been a choral scholar at Cambridge and music remained a passion that blotted out everything else, with the possible exception of squash. It was unfortunate that the rehearsal schedule of the Winchester Cathedral choir, where he was a lay clerk, should clash so frequently with the transmission of his programme. His madrigal group could not do without him either. After all his musical commitments, he had to maintain his position at the top of the ladder at his squash club, and that soaked up the remaining weekday evenings. He was not the only BBC editor I have known who was never around when his programme went out; but nobody slipped away early with such a light heart. He was a melancholy, rather lowering man but he would whistle a thrilling little arpeggio as he put on his bicycle clips at about four o'clock each day. He was always pleased to be gone; almost as pleased as we were to be rid of him.

His idea of a story was a conference being held somewhere in the South. It did not really matter who they were, or what they were discussing. Fortunately for him, there were always plenty going on in Bournemouth and Brighton to choose from. His instructions were simple. All he wanted was an interview with the keynote speaker at the Corset Manufacturers' Association of Great Britain annual conference about the issues currently facing the world of supportive underwear. He wanted you to do a piece to camera to go on the front saying no more than that the conference opened today in the Winter Gardens and how you had spoken to the *fundi* of foundation garments. Occasionally, the odd shot of corset industry movers and shakers walking in through the Winter Gardens' doors might be laid over the top of this worthy conversation but that was regarded as dangerously subversive. The programme was as exciting as second-hand chewing gum.

Until I arrived, nobody tried to stand up to Michael Harman. We had some dreadful rows. He was not a nasty person but insecurity made him obstinate and dogmatic. The newsroom people mostly wanted a quiet life and all the reporters, apart from me, were freelances and so dependent on him for their daily bread and butter. Actually, it was pure jam. They made an extremely good living out of a system that went out of its way to reward inefficiency and bad journalism. The reporters were paid by the length of the item when it was broadcast, in guineas of course. Up to two minutes paid six guineas, three minutes was seven guineas, four minutes eight guineas, and so on. The secret of this kind of journalism is brevity but the reporters had every incentive to pad out what they were doing and, because they were astute enough to buy a lot of drinks in the bar, the technicians were happy to oblige. No report was ever just under the round minute. An astonishing number were 3'01" or 4'01".

The same regime applied to the late-night newsreader. It was a dreadful job. You had to type the bulletin yourself on what resembled a toilet roll which you then inserted into a primitive autocue. You controlled the speed by foot with an accelerator pedal under the newsdesk. On the rare occasions I did it, I was so nervous my foot clenched over the pedal and kept driving it faster and faster. I finished the five-minute bulletin at a breathless gallop in 2 minutes and 15 seconds. The regular newsreader, Peter McCann, on the other hand, wanted to spin it out, because he got an extra five guineas if it went on beyond midnight. This became a challenge and when there was no more news he invented a completely fictitious newsroom cat and described its doings in ever more fanciful detail. This became cult viewing for insomniacs and he got away with it long enough to buy a rather charming beamed cottage in Buckinghamshire, at least partly on the proceeds.

After Harman left at tea-time, there would be half-hearted efforts to pump a bit of life into the programme, though by then it was like trying to resurrect a corpse. These normally consisted of arranging for a light-hearted studio interview to try to lift things at the end. For some reason – I am convinced it was the mournful shade of Michael Harman that still lay across us all – these efforts nearly always ended in failure, or even outright disaster. We had high hopes of a Mynah bird which was famous locally for its linguistic skills, particularly its ability to sing 'Land of Hope and Glory', admittedly somewhat off-key. But when we opened its cage it flew straight into the studio lights and incinerated itself. *South Today* was left, not with the performance of a remarkably gifted bird, but a powerful smell of roast chicken which lingered for weeks.

Plant life fared little better. A local gardener produced an extraordinary Amaryllis plant, the tallest ever grown according to its owner, who had contacted the *Guinness Book of Records* for its pre-eminence to be recorded. It was a shame this had not been officially registered before he brought it in for a colourful end to our programme. George, the studio manager, was known for his clumsiness but on this occasion he surpassed himself. Carrying the record-breaking plant into the studio, he failed to notice it was taller than the door and snapped it in half. The interview took place with the Amaryllis in a splint made up of two pencils and half a roll of Sellotape and failed, not surprisingly, to be as upbeat as we had hoped.

The *South Today* studio did seem to be blighted. The Indian round-the-world cyclist who was passing through Southampton did everything right. He rode his bicycle dramatically into the studio and pulled up with a flourish beside the presenter's desk for the closing interview of the programme. It was just unfortunate that he did not speak a word of English.

Nothing mechanical ever worked. The experimental robot that was meant to walk into the studio in front of the presenter came to a halt right in the middle of the doorway. The opening half of the programme had to be introduced from the corridor with the presenter hopping up and down so as to be seen over the robot's shoulder. An inquest into this regrettable incident found that the newsroom had been so fascinated with this gadget they'd had it marching up and down most of the afternoon. When it got to its big moment the batteries were flat. Exactly the same happened with a Christmas novelty called Talking Fruit but, well, you get the picture . . .

*

Christine and I were not impressed by Southampton, especially after Bristol. The heart of the city had been destroyed in the war. It had the double misfortune of being rebuilt in the sixties and it was difficult to say whether the Luftwaffe or the developers had done the most damage. There was little in the way of theatre or concerts and when we arrived there seemed to be only one restaurant you would want to eat in for fun. It was a pizza place that the deprived people of Southampton regarded as a thrilling novelty and was packed day and night.

We found a charming little house in an enclave that had been developed in the thirties by an oxymoron, a philanthropist builder. The houses were mostly arranged around little village greens and their gardens were comparatively large. Best of all, the council had never adopted the roads, so nobody ever used it as a short cut and it had the quiet calm of another age.

Christine was a skilled daily paper sub-editor by now and had no difficulty getting a job on the local evening, the *Southern Evening Echo*. That, too, was dull by comparison with the *Western Daily Press* but the people were friendly and we both had the sense that we would be moving on. We began to think about children. I really could not stand much longer on *South Today*. I'd had five jobs in less than five years but was already planning another career move. Soon I would be 27 and felt it was time for London and network news.

I was very lucky that year. There were a series of big news stories on our doorstep that had to be covered for the national BBC News and, as I was the staff reporter, it was my job to do them. I was lucky in the type of story, too. That year there were three sensational trials at Winchester Crown Court and I covered them all. There is nothing better than a big court case for a television reporter who wants to get noticed. They go on for weeks and, because there are very few other things to film, the reporter gets to spend a lot of time telling the camera what has been going on in court. You get your face on television a lot, in other words.

The Great Hall of Winchester Castle was the most dramatic setting for the machinery of justice to go through its motions. There, amongst the columns of Purbeck stone, the pointed arches and plate tracery windows, where Henry II held his banquets, the accused had to face a judge who sat under what looked like a giant medieval dartboard and was long thought to have been King Arthur's round table. (Carbon dating finally established that the 18-feet-diameter circular table, divided into 25 white and green segments, was made around 1270. It was painted with a likeness of Henry VIII and a Tudor rose in 1522. The legend of King Arthur places him in the sixth century.)

Noel Jenkinson did not look a particularly evil man to me, watching him in the dock from my vantage point on the press bench. He was 42 at the time and probably thought of himself as a soldier on a mission of vengeance. He was actually an unemployed painter, and an amateur terrorist. It was three weeks after Bloody Sunday, when soldiers of the Parachute Regiment had killed 13 civilians in Londonderry, that he dressed up as a paratrooper and drove a hired Ford Cortina with 50 lbs of explosive packing the boot into the regiment's base in Aldershot.

He parked the car outside the three-storey Officers' Mess and walked away. The explosion practically demolished the building and was clearly heard in Aldershot town centre, a mile away. If he had hoped to wipe out the 16th Parachute Brigade's officers as they eased their Sam Browne belts around the mess lunch he must have been disappointed. He was too eager and the bomb went off at 12.40, twenty minutes too early. He killed seven people: a Catholic padre, five women who worked in the mess kitchen, and a middle-aged gardener.

I used to watch him sitting in the dock and wonder what had gone through his mind when he drove into the base with his bomb; whether he was scared or excited, whether he ever thought about what explosives did to the human body, how he felt when he found out that he had murdered a priest and some mothers rather than 'enemy' soldiers. There were no clues to any of this in his face, which remained totally impassive throughout the month of the trial in November, 1972.

The reports were difficult to do, and quite stressful. I had to memorise long passages of evidence to repeat to the camera crew waiting outside. There was, perhaps, more concern then about not making mistakes, particularly in court cases where the consequences could be very damaging. There was no question of a relaxed interview with the newscaster. It had to be a straight three-minute report each time. It could not be edited, so if I made a mistake, I had to start all over again. There was always a distracting crowd, and the BBC dispatch rider waiting to whisk it off to London would always be looking meaningfully at his watch.

The case against Noel Jenkinson seemed conclusive enough. Though he had lived in London for several years, he had been born in County Meath and was a member of the Official IRA. He was traced through the number on the car's cylinder block and betrayed by one of the two other Irishmen who stood trial with him and received lesser sentences. The police found two more bombs and some Parachute Regiment uniforms in a lock-up garage he was renting in London. He did not even blink when the jury pronounced him guilty on seven charges of murder and the judge sentenced him to life imprisonment, a minimum of 30 years. He just clicked his heels in a rather pathetic mock-military style and turned away. Life proved to be a surprisingly short sentence in the end. He died of a heart attack in prison less than four years later. He was only 46.

Although £54 million has been spent on judicial inquiries into Bloody Sunday, and the names of those civilians killed that day are cherished by the Nationalist community and regarded by many as martyrs, Jenkinson's victims have been largely forgotten.

For the record, the padre was Captain Gerry Weston, aged 38, who had spent the 2nd Battalion's tour of duty in Belfast working for reconciliation, unarmed and alone on the Catholic Ballymurphy Estates. He had been awarded the MBE for it the week before he died. The kitchen workers were Jill Mansfield, 34, Margaret Grant, 32, Thelma Bosley, 44, Cherie Munton, 20, and Joan Lunn, 39. Between them they had eight children, most of whom heard the explosion that killed their mothers. The gardener was John Haslan, aged 58.

The Bingham case was like a two-part television spy thriller, only a bit more far-fetched. The first trial concentrated on the husband, but the most interesting character in the drama was always his wife. Sub-Lieutenant David Bingham was a weapons electronics officer in the Royal Navy. He was 31 and had been commissioned from the ranks, which explained why he was so old to be such a relatively junior officer. He was not very well paid and he had a costly family. There were four children, aged between five and eleven, for a start, but his wife, Maureen, was by far the biggest expense. She was what would now be called a 'shopaholic' and was also addicted to gambling. She got a job as a part-time cleaner and he drove taxis in the evenings, but they got ever deeper in debt. One day, when he was in hospital recovering from a slipped disc, she simply went and knocked on the door of the Russian Embassy in London and offered her husband's services.

Over 18 months they passed on information that ranged from Navy battle plans to details about nuclear depth charges. They were paid a total of £2,810 for secrets that were later described as 'almost beyond price'. It was never really clear which of them was the driving force behind this cut-price treachery. The Russians got a bargain but their two spies were both too flaky for it to last very long.

Eventually Bingham confessed – at a second attempt. He had tried to admit it all to a fellow officer who thought he was such a good chap it could not be true. The police were less trusting. His confession, it was said, read like a 'lurid melodrama full of secret assignations, signals that involved empty cigarette packets in rural phone boxes and posting church notices to addresses in Kensington'.

David Bingham was tried on his own. He was a tall, handsome man who looked totally shell-shocked. We felt rather sorry for him as his crimes were catalogued and the judge talked of 'incalculable harm' and 'monstrous betrayal'. He was sentenced to a total of 126 years in jail and the Prime Minister of the day, Edward Heath, expelled 105 Soviet diplomats in the wake of the verdict.

Maureen Bingham, a dark bird-like woman, had been around at her husband's trial and we all speculated about her role in the affair. I sat next to a misanthropic old bore from the *Daily Telegraph* who found it impossible to believe that any serving naval officer would betray his country, or that any depth of wickedness was beyond womankind. She certainly struck me as seriously unhinged. Within a few weeks of the end of her husband's trial she held what amounted to a press conference outside the Russian Embassy saying it was all her fault and that the Russians had treated them far better than the Navy. She was promptly charged under the Official Secrets Act and we all went through round two.

I remember feeling even more sorry for David Bingham as the story emerged of their life together after she had proposed to him on Leap Year Day and the poor devil had said 'yes'. It was not just her extravagances – the outfits that had to be bought for the Commander-in-Chief's parties on HMS *Victory* even though they were thousands of pounds in debt – it was the way she obviously lied nearly all the time. Even the judge said she was a 'woman almost incapable of telling the truth'. There were so many lies that it was impossible to tell whether she had been the main mover in the plot and, after five hours, the jury gave up trying. They convicted her of paving the way for her husband's betrayal, but not of passing on secrets herself. On the evidence, she got off lightly. The judge talked of her 'disastrous loquacity' and sentenced her to two and a half years in prison. I had a surreal conversation with one of the editors in London about whether the viewers would understand what the word 'loquacity' meant and whether 'talkative' carried quite the same nuanced meaning, missing one of the bulletins as a result.

The trials captured the public's imagination at the time. Until recently Maureen Bingham was complaining she was still shouted at in the street and having excrement pushed through her letter box. She still insists that MI5 were in on it from the start. The last I heard she had been convicted for falsely claiming more than £13,000 worth of housing benefits and income support.

After he was released, David Bingham remarried and rebuilt his life under an assumed name. He ran a hotel in Bournemouth for a time and was Vice-president of the local Conservative Club until his real identity was discovered. He changed his name again and moved to Stratford to manage an alternative lifestyle centre. The hypnotherapist 'David Brough', who was once David Bingham 'the most despicable traitor in the history of post-war espionage', died in 1995 when his car hit a tree near his home and burst into flames.

I was very grateful to the BBC South cameraman who covered these stories with me. Ron Longman was, to put it mildly, a local character. As his soundman, Ian Killian, used to say, if there was any justice in the world Ron should have been in the dock rather than across the road filming. Ron was thirty years too late. If he had been born at the right time he would have made his fortune out of wartime nylons and black market food coupons. As it was, he did his best with a dozen different jobs and wheezes. At the time, he had just given up a parallel career as an undertaker. The last straw had been an old lady who had died in her rocking chair in a cottage in the New Forest and not been discovered for several days. Rigor mortis had locked her into the sitting position and, try as hard as he might, Ron could not straighten her out to fit her in the coffin. The way Ron told it, he tried everything, even to the extent of jumping up and down on the corpse, but even that didn't work. Eventually, with the lateral thinking that was his trademark, he dressed her up in his undertaker's black jacket and bowler hat and put her in the front seat of the hearse. He lay down in the coffin for the journey back to the parlour. 'Surprisingly comfortable, Mike,' he told me. 'You could spend for ever in one of those things.'

Ron conspired to make me look good to the bosses in London. These long and detailed pieces to camera, done on the run, were difficult and I often needed several goes to get it right. When I messed up the third take Ron would simply throw the film away and start a new magazine. 'Never mind, Mike,' he'd say, tapping the side of his nose. 'If I can't lose that in the paperwork, my name's not Ron Longman.'

The most sensational trial that year was over a rather trivial affair. It amounted to a question of who was driving a car when it went the wrong way round a roundabout at Totton, just outside Southampton. The car's owner was a flamboyant Tory MP called Sir Gerald Nabarro who was a colourful ingredient in Britain's public life at the time. Sir Gerald was an English character of a kind that seems to have died out. He was a bald, blustering rogue with an enormous handlebar moustache. His origins, which he made no attempt to disguise, were humble. His father was a failed shopkeeper. Nabarro ran away to sea at 14 and later became a sergeant in the army. He made his money out of timber, working his way from yard labourer to tycoon, and thereafter devoted his life to right-wing politics and showing off. He was a hanger and a flogger, and his predictable views on anything you cared to mention were in continual demand. There was no mincing prevarication about Sir Gerald. He was a preposterous old rogue really but the public loved him.

Sir Gerald cultivated eccentricity, from his pet prawn (called Simon) to his eight cars which all had similar number plates. It was the Daimler, NAB 1, that went the wrong way round the roundabout. That was never disputed. The prosecution witnesses said Sir Gerald was driving. He said he wasn't. According to him, the driver was his company secretary, Mrs Margaret Mason.

The jury at the first trial took one look at Sir Gerald's big whiskered face and bald head and decided it would be difficult for anybody to confuse him with his very feminine, blonde secretary. They speedily found him guilty and he was fined £250.

Sir Gerald thundered at the injustice of it all. That he, a baronet and, above all, a Member of Parliament, should be called a liar was not to be borne. He harrumphed on to the airwaves and used words like 'Calumny, sir!' His honour was at stake, he said, and whatever it cost he was going to prove his innocence.

Sure enough, his expensive legal team came up with witnesses of their own who said they thought they saw Sir Gerald sleeping in the passenger seat on that day. The Court of Appeal ordered a retrial in Winchester and the press licked their lips.

In the interval between the two trials, Sir Gerald, who was then 59, had a stroke, but he looked healthy enough when he turned up on the first day. He was ideal for television. There was no danger of him slipping unnoticed into the court. He came marching up to the Guildhall, whiskers at the high port and nostrils flaring. He denounced his accusers in the fruitiest of terms at every opportunity. There was always a crowd and they nearly always clapped. Television News in London wanted every detail and I did my best to give it to them. I did pieces to camera three and four minutes long with all the twists and turns in the evidence. It sometimes felt like learning *Hamlet* to a stopwatch.

None of us could see how Sir Gerald hoped to win. His new witnesses were not very convincing, I felt, certainly not compared with the certainty of those for the prosecution. Most damning of all was the non-appearance of Mrs Mason, who had gone to ground. When I taxed him with this on the court steps, Sir Gerald fixed me with his beady eyes, moustache positively fluttering with disdain. He made out it was a deliberate choice of his legal team whereas, in fact, Mrs Mason had refused to give evidence for him. She had actually resigned a fortnight before the retrial began and had disappeared.

Sir Gerald and his lawyers argued that it was easy to mistake him for his secretary, who, they said, was wearing a wig that might have somehow looked similar to his magnificent facial hair. I remember trying to describe this passage in the evidence without cracking up and wasting a lot of film before I managed to keep a straight face.

It was an open and shut case. The judge, in his summing up, practically told the jury to convict him. He was particularly scathing about the absence of Mrs Mason, whom he described as the key to the case. While we were waiting for the jury to come back I wrote a strong story about the downfall and disgrace of Middle England's most notable knight and speculated on the chances of him now being tried for perjury. Then, blow me, the jury came back and declared him not guilty.

I don't think he could believe it himself. He looked for a moment as if he was going to cry then he raised his right hand and clenched it in a salute towards the jury, all men as it happens. How they had come to that verdict beggars belief. Perhaps they felt sorry for the old boy, particularly as he had been so seriously ill. Perhaps they just could not believe that it was possible for a Member of Parliament to behave dishonourably or tell a lie. Behind him, his new private secretary, an attractive 22-year-old blonde called Christine Holman, burst into tears and Lady Nabarro passed her a handkerchief. Christine Holman would later marry a young

Tory politician called Neil Hamilton and have the misfortune of facing scandal in less trusting times.

I had scuttled out of court and was waiting with Ron and his crew for what was bound to be some vintage grandstanding. We were not disappointed. Sir Gerald came out on to the steps and the mob surged towards him. I was right in the centre of the crush and practically had my nose pressed into his waistcoat, which was not very dignified. Ron, who had lethal elbows, and Ian, an accomplished all-round thug, were good at that kind of thing and got a clear shot of Sir Gerald at the moment of his triumph. Nab was soon at full throttle. 'When a gentleman and a Member of Par-lee-agh-ment is called in court a liar, sir, and a perjurer, sir, it does the cause of justice a great deal of good, sir, to have the traducers properly dealt with!'

It wasn't justice but it was wonderful television. Sir Gerald was not only vindicated but the judge made an order that his costs of around £10,000 should be paid out of the public purse. Sir Gerald even had the gall to complain about the legal system; about how 'if a man can afford to pay for justice he will secure it, sir, if he cannot afford to pay he rarely secures it'. I thought it was a bit thick because, as far as I could see, he had just paid a lot of money to escape justice and then had it handed back to him.

As it happens, Margaret Mason later became a secretary at the BBC in Birmingham and made no secret of the fact that Sir Gerald was driving and had perjured himself in the most high-handed and shameless way. His motto, by the way, was *audax et fidelis*. Audacious hardly begins to describe him.

I cannot complain. Sir Gerald did me a good turn. I was all over the national television news again and in line for a network reporter's job. By then I was working in the London newsroom every weekend, waiting and hoping for an opening. In those days there were only a dozen or so network television reporters and there was a lot of competition on the rare occasions a job came up. I was lucky. They had a vacancy before memories of my court reporting started to fade, I did all right at another of those strange BBC appointment boards, and they chose me. I just pipped Angela Rippon but they were keen on the novel idea of having a woman reporter and gave her a short-term contract. I also edged in ahead of Michael Cole, who was doing the same job as me in Norwich. He got the next post that came up. It was a small world, but I felt I was on top of it at last.

I had other reasons for feeling on top of the world. Christine was pregnant and everything was changing for the better. It was one of those moments of undiluted happiness in life.

I was even nice to Michael Harman when I went to say goodbye to him and he was so pleasant to me I felt I might have misjudged him entirely. Besides, my successor would be Kate Adie. That would teach him.

TEN

JOINING BBC TELEVISION NEWS as a national reporter in those days was a bit like becoming a secret agent. You had to go through the same lengthy bureaucracy that was tedious but had exciting overtones of secrecy and danger. I had to sign the Official Secrets Act (God knows why) and I was told that my background had been checked by 'The Investigator' for any links with subversive political organisations. There were ominous forms to be filled in about my final wishes and my next of kin. I was given a brochure about special war insurance, codenamed 'Spaggis', which put alarmingly precise valuations on the bits of me that might get shot away. Two thousand pounds for a hand, for instance, three thousand for a foot, five thousand for a leg. There was the same sense of stepping into a job where you might be sent anywhere in the world at any moment of the day or night. My arm was peppered with injections and inoculations. I was given advice on what to do about every conceivable threat from Tsetse fly to Soviet bloc tarts. I had to buy a new wallet for the fistful of credit and travel cards that are commonplace now, but then seemed like entrance tickets to the big wide world.

The BBC got me a second passport and issued me with its own identity document, which looked far more impressive with its shields and stamps and its peremptory demand that I be given all the assistance I required in six languages. I was amused to see the German title of my new boss, a languid Oxbridge lush, was *Geschäftsführender Direktor BBC Fernsehen.*

We even had our equivalent of 'Q' department. I was issued with a special Ministry of Defence watch which had knobs on it for timing things but, alas, no lethal devices. I got a box, promisingly labelled 'Protective Clothing', but that proved to be the trade name for cheap blue anoraks, manufactured in Manchester. They gave me two pairs of Wellington boots, an *A to Z* of London and, after a month of prevarication, a car. It was not, I have to say, an Aston Martin. It was the cheapest Ford Escort and rathered battered at that, but it did have a two-way radio that worked reasonably well if you could actually see the Television Centre and the wind was blowing the right way.

No matter. I was equipped to quarter the world for danger and excitement; ready to cover the toughest stories, anywhere on earth. It was a shame that for a month the furthest I got was Wandsworth.

My fellow television reporters were an extraordinary bunch of tough extroverts who would have made a wonderful study of the psycho-analytical roots of machismo. Only a short while before, the BBC had decided that its reporters should specialise in either television or radio. The ugly ones, and those considered insufficiently bombastic for TV, were packed off to Broadcasting House and most of them never got over it. Those that were left mostly dated from a period of expansion at BBC News when they had gone on a recruiting spree for hard-bitten beasts in Fleet Street.

A silver-haired slugger called Peter Stewart was the unconscious author of one of the most famous lines in journalism. He had arrived at Kinshasa airport to find the survivors of massacres in the then Belgian Congo, up against a deadline and, anyway, not the sort of man to let mealy-mouthed sensitivity get in the way of a good story. He marched around the airport, which was filled with shell-shocked nuns, bellowing, 'Anybody here been raped and speaks English?' He got the story and the line was picked up by an American magazine writer who was there at the time for the title of his book. A strange route to immortality, when you come to think about it.

Keith Graves had come from the *Express*. He was tall and bearded and was rather like Saladin except that he wore horn-rimmed spectacles and took no prisoners. Keith was a fine reporter with a personality that could charitably be described as overwhelming. He had an air of barely suppressed violence about him and was widely feared. We were on a directors' course together at another BBC building in West London when a commissionaire, who did not know Keith's reputation, attempted to stop him parking his Escort. Keith simply drove over him, breaking bones in his leg, and got away with it. The BBC can be curiously tolerant of the odd ruffian, or spineless, I am not sure which. I took care to stay on the right side of Keith and actually rather liked him. I sometimes used to help him buy white mice in Shepherd's Bush market for the python he kept in his spare bedroom.

They were all odd in their way. There was another ex-*Express* man, who seemed to have been a former Special Forces officer and who radiated virility and ill temper. He was involved in some scandal involving young boys and a sailing school on the south coast and never appeared again.

The reporter I had replaced was a rather upper-crust character called Michael Clayton who had insisted on covering the Vietnam War with a gaily coloured parasol and constantly described the Viet Cong as 'those fellows over there'. He left to become editor of *Horse and Hound* and, at his leaving party, came up with the rather amusing line that what was different about the BBC was that when you retired *you* gave *them* the watch.

Martin Bell was the best reporter and I think we all secretly knew it. He was slim, dark and dedicated, holding himself apart from the stag-like rivalries of the rest. He sometimes seemed a man after his time. He had the clipped reticence and high sense of duty that would have been more at home playing the Great Game on the fringes of the British Empire at its zenith. His reports were always 1 minute 42 seconds long, intricate, parenthetical and impossible to cut. Most of us unconsciously aped his style, with varying degrees of success.

We inhabited a tiny room in the Television Centre, presided over by our secretary, Lydia, a disappointed ballerina of refined sensibility. Not surprisingly, her eyebrows were nearly always hoisted to her hairline and she spoke in a series of tuts. Because we were always being sent off to places, the junior executive who was supposed to make up the reporters' roster could never get it right. It was not too bad when there was just one reporter on duty to cover the world, though hard work for the man himself, of course. Trouble came when nine of us turned up. There were only four desks for a start. It swiftly became a day-long testosterone tournament, with mayhem spreading through the building. The news editor, a delightful, mild-mannered character, would appeal to our better nature, but it only made things worse. By midday, the newsdesk would start to invent stories just to get us out of their hair.

The newsroom, where our reports were handled and slotted into the daily bulletins on BBC1 and BBC2, was populated by gentler, shyer souls in the main, though there were a smattering of untamed egos there too. They were mostly middle-aged men of slovenly appearance who got through the day by dint of frequent trips to the BBC Club bar, two floors below.

In between was the viewing theatre where they tried to spend as much of the day as possible, on benches in the quiet semi-darkness, watching the rushes of all the stories as they came out of the processing bath. The pace of events was much slower then and it was possible for the assistant editors in charge of the programmes to see almost everything that had been shot that day and know exactly what would be in their programmes. Now, the huge volume of video from every corner of the world is overwhelming and editors have to delegate and take bigger risks.

It was all technically very primitive in those days. The newsroom journalists, still known in the newspaper style as sub-editors, wrote their introductions to our reports and the shorter items in the programme in longhand on their clipboards. They dictated them to a row of middle-aged typists. The system at least guaranteed that the script could be read out loud and was legible. As a further precaution, the BBC only recruited mature and motherly ladies for the job; some said they even required a medical certificate that they had successfully negotiated the menopause, but I don't think even the 1970s BBC would have gone that far. The autocue girls, on the other hand, were not BBC employees and were quite ravishing. It was a joy to watch them typing away on their toilet rolls and tossing their long blonde hair as they tried to keep up with the changes by cutting and pasting the long curls of paper. One of my newsroom friends liked them so much he married two of them, though not at the same time.

There were three newsreaders, handsome, well-groomed ex-actors with impeccable received pronunciation. They had no say and no interest in what was in the programme, only in how it should be pronounced. They made a point of not appearing in the newsroom until ten minutes before the bulletin. They would settle down in the chair next to the editor, flick imaginary dust off their pinstripes and, in the one case, tether a pair of West Highland Terriers to the newsdesk. Their preparation consisted of flicking through carbons of the stories, referring occasionally to the *BBC Pronouncing Dictionary* or checking more vexed questions with the special pronunciation department at Broadcasting House which was the last word in these matters. They were now household names, or rather faces, but their salaries were modest and their status low. They were pleasant and cultured people but they only had a walk-on part. None of the reporters would have dreamt of trying to become a newsreader, except for the poor fellow who kept having panic attacks whenever he got into a plane, a serious disadvantage for a globetrotting correspondent.

It was all a lot shabbier and less sophisticated then. The graphics were done with little more than Letraset and a few razor blades. The artists had an alarming habit of moving whole cities around the country. I remember an early piece of mine from Scotland was preceded by a map that put Glasgow in the precise location of a place most people know as Aberdeen.

The newsroom floor was covered in linoleum, the air was blue with cigarette smoke, windows were grey and grimy, but so was Shepherd's Bush, which you could just see through them. Everywhere was buried under piles of yellowing paper and the detritus of untidy men. They were the Dickensian days of television.

We reporters were supposed to cover anything, anywhere, at a moment's notice. There were far fewer television reporters then. There were only a handful of specialists and hardly any were based abroad. We were expected to be knowledgeable, even authoritative, about everything from the latest constitutional crisis in Sarawak to the vital statistics of Miss World. It was an apprenticeship in bluff really and the truth is we relied heavily on the hard-pressed clerks in the news information library next door. However urgent the story, however much the newsdesk might be panicking or the crew revving up their big green Vauxhall saloon down in the underground garage, if you left without that wad of newspaper cuttings you were sunk.

I started on the small change of bigtime news. A Ford strike at Dagenham after an assembly line worker took a swing at a foreman, the hunt for an arsonist at Heathrow airport, a background piece on how to fake audio tapes to go with the American coverage of Nixon's Watergate downfall, a reunion of Colditz veterans, the opening of a new motorway (the M3), the hunt for Lord Lucan. With so few reporters there was not so much of a pecking order as there is today when the stars and the specialists have a monopoly of the important assignments. It was a taxi rank with not enough taxis. Actually, it was much more exciting than that – a lottery, say, with a new ticket every day.

The crews were a lottery, too. They divided neatly into two groups. Half of them were superb to work with, committed professionals who were brilliant at their jobs and good company afterwards. The other half were dickheads who didn't appear to know one end of the camera from another, were always complaining and were a total embarrassment to be with. The BBC didn't seem to be able to tell the difference.

I remember Michael Cole just after he had come back from an exotic royal tour that he had tried to cover with one of the more difficult crews. 'You know,' he said, 'in this job you get to go to the world's nicest places with the world's nastiest people.'

Most of the time I was lucky and worked with the good cameramen and rarely had to put up with one of the ex-minicab drivers who seemed to have got the job through some mate in the Masons. Not long after I joined the London newsroom, though, I ended up at what was probably the most expensive restaurant table in Scotland with the soundman from hell.

We had been covering a firemen's strike, chasing the army's green goddesses around and I suppose, if I am honest, hoping for a really big fire that would put the issues into a sharper moral context (i.e. be a rattling good story). The S from H had been bleating all day. He moaned about getting up early, he was upset at missing meals, he didn't really like getting out of the car when it was raining. To placate the crew, after a difficult day, I took them off to the Malmaison, then the poshest restaurant in Glasgow. It was over the top in a *Belle Epoque* way, all crimson banquettes, damask napery and waiters, if memory serves me right, in tailcoats. The head waiter was unctuous in a comically exaggerated French accent. He had barely started describing the sophisticated dishes on his menu when the soundman from hell cut right across him.

'Never mind the foreign muck,' he said. 'You gotta steak?'

The head waiter sighed. Steak barely began to describe what he could offer. 'Ah yes, *monsieur*, and what a dish! *Boeuf en croûte*, the finest beef with, *comment s'appelle*, a golden robe of pastry.' And much too good for the likes of you, his profile seemed to say as he retreated, with immense dignity, to the kitchens.

It seemed to me he made a special effort with the presentation of this dish, out of wounded professional pride, perhaps. Another waiter brought it in on a silver salver. In a series of dramatic gestures, the head waiter removed the cover, lifted a shining cleaver and split the *boeuf en croûte* into precise halves, the meat pink and succulent and the pastry, indeed, golden. '*Voilà!*' he said.

'Wass this then?' said the S from H.

'*Boeuf en croûte, monsieur*. Perfect, *n'est ce pas?*'

Perfect it might have been but it did not suit the soundman from hell.

'Look here, cock,' he said, 'if I had wanted a Cornish pasty, I would have asked for a Cornish pasty – now fuck off and get me a steak.'

The big story in the seventies was Northern Ireland. These were the bloodiest years of the Troubles, with more dead and wounded than in most of the fringe wars we were sent off to for light relief. Between 1972 and 1976 nearly 1,600 people were killed out of a population no larger than an English county. Many more were blinded and maimed in a hundred horrible ways.

The province had been close to all-out civil war in 1972 when the devolved government at Stormont was suspended and direct rule imposed from Westminster. The army saturated the Catholic areas. When they went into the Bogside in Londonderry in July with 26,000 men, tanks, helicopters and bulldozers it was the biggest British military operation since Suez. It was a time of terrible communal violence and nightly confrontations across the sectarian fault lines. The IRA bombing campaign was at its height; the record was 22 bombs going off in less than an hour in Belfast. Equally sinister, and even more shadowy, Protestant gangs were murdering Catholics indiscriminately. Their drinking dens had so-called 'romper rooms' where they tortured their victims. The Shankill Butchers were the worst and got their name from the way they hacked at the poor devils they caught with big butchers' knives. It was an awful place and an awful time.

Television News had a permanent parallel operation in Northern Ireland and we reporters were rostered through Belfast and Derry on eight-day tours every couple of months, more if it was particularly hectic. It was a strange feeling, coming in to land at Belfast Aldergrove airport and stepping into a low-intensity war in your own country. There were roadblocks everywhere, police in green uniforms with bullet-proof vests and sub-machine guns. Grey armoured Land Rovers crept around the streets in pairs. What made it all surreal was the juxtaposition between the familiar and the shocking. The streetscapes were homely and recognisable, all the same names as any other town in the United Kingdom, and the shoppers as dowdy and ordinary as in Rotherham, say, or Swindon. But the biggest queues were at the police search points, not the check-outs. An army foot patrol would scuttle past the shop windows, scanning the rooftops for snipers. It was such a usual part of their lives the pedestrians barely seemed to notice them. Saracen armoured cars cruised the streets with their hatches battened down, machine guns traversing the pavements, and got no more than the odd casual glance. Parts of the towns would be untouched and appeared almost normal, but you would turn round a corner and the bomb damage made it look like part of the Russian sector in 1945 Berlin. Out of 150 shops in Derry at the time, only 20 were still trading.

I was very raw at this kind of thing. There was a lot to learn and the penalties for getting it wrong were severe. The lessons in street wisdom came from the local freelance crew we used in tandem with our own units from London. Cyril Cave was a piratical Protestant with a hooked nose and black hair understandably streaked with grey. Jim Deaney, his soundman, was a chirpy young Catholic. Between them, they seemed to know every street corner in the province and all the horrible things that had happened on it. A drive round Belfast with them was a Cook's Tour of death and destruction.

'That's where the car bomb took off the policeman's leg and killed that poor old lady,' said Cyril. 'Isn't that right, Jim boy?'

'Just the other side of that building is where the squaddies cornered Big Joe McCann – do you remember that night, Cyril?'

It became a kind of competition and just went on and on. Ligoniel, where three off-duty soldiers were lured out of a pub and executed by the IRA. Donegal Street, where they blew up a small crowd and killed seven people. Every other bar seemed to have been bombed. They drove me past the Abercorn in the centre where the IRA only managed to kill two people but injured more than 130. We went to see McGurk's up in the north of the city where the loyalist UVF managed to bring the whole building down. Cyril and Jim had filmed people scrabbling in the ruins with their bare hands searching for survivors and not finding any, just 15 corpses. It was surprising the whole province wasn't teetotal by now.

I was thoroughly frightened by the time we got back to the BBC's headquarters in Ormeau Avenue. That wasn't very reassuring, either. The entrance was sandbagged and the windows were shuttered with steel. The newsroom itself was the same sort of tip as every other place that journalists work. Like all of them, it had maps of the area around the walls. Unlike the others, their maps were a patchwork of orange and green, right down to individual streets. Knowing which side of the sectarian divide you were on could save your life.

The people who worked there were remarkably cheerful considering what they had to live with every day. They didn't seem at all resentful of young and ignorant reporters breezing in from London and began patiently explaining the subtleties and the sensitivities all over again.

Even what you called the bloody place seemed a problem. The Protestants wanted to call it Ulster but that was anathema to the Catholics because historic Ulster included Cavan, Monaghan and Donegal, which were now in the Irish Republic. Northern Ireland didn't suit many Protestants because it made them sound like an adjunct of Dublin, 'province' didn't wash with the Catholics because it sounded too much a part of the British imperium. The people were just as bad. You had to be careful about Catholic and Protestant; they weren't interchangeable with 'Republican' and 'Nationalist' on the one hand and 'Unionist' and 'Loyalist' on the other. And don't even start on Londonderry – sorry, Derry. The BBC rule was to call it Londonderry on first mention and Derry thereafter, which was probably the best that could be done when people were killing each other over the name of where they lived.

That first night we ended up at a riot in the Ardoyne and Cyril and Jim gave me a lesson on how to cover violent confrontation without getting hurt. It was a matter of careful positioning and looking in six directions at once. The housewives' call to arms, a rolling thunder of dustbin lids, had brought them out, hissing and spitting at the army who had been trampling through their houses all day. Hatred made them look ugly. They were pasty and slack-jawed but their collective sense of resentment gave them a primitive energy. They worked themselves into a frenzy and the abuse was foul. Their urchin kids ran out from behind their skirts to hurl bricks at the line of soldiers and join in the chants of 'Fuck the Brits'. I had never thought it before but I realised then that I had led a very sheltered life. If you've been brought up without sisters in a middle-class suburb and, still more, if you go to an all-boys school, women become identified with respectability, femininity, refinement. These women, who had lived harder lives by other rules, seemed to be a different species entirely. And that was before one of them threw a shovel full of particularly slimy dog shit over me. Welcome to Belfast, Mr BBC man.

There was a ritual to these events. The women were replaced by older lads who threw bigger rocks and even paving stones at the troops. Then there was a sploosh and a sheet of flame from the first petrol bomb. The troops took it for a while, then opened up with rubber bullets. Three or four of the youths were carried away by their mates and there was a brief lull. But soon more petrol bombs landed right at the feet of several of the soldiers and one in particular seemed to have been badly burned before they could get to him with a fire extinguisher. The soldiers charged the mob a couple of times but it didn't disperse.

Cyril and Jim were watching the crowd to see if the younger children and the women were starting to melt away – apparently a sure sign the Provo gunmen were around – but that night they stayed away and the riot, like the petrol bombs, fizzled out. I did not have time to change and had to sit in an editing room in my stinking clothes. The editor put one of the pegs for hanging up the film clips rather histrionically on his nose. I was past caring.

We were called out early next morning to check one of the endless stream of tips that flowed into the Belfast newsroom. An anonymous caller had phoned to say there was a body out on the Lisburn road. We got there just ahead of the police. He was a Catholic who had been shot in the back of the neck. The entry wound was neat, the exit wound was not. As far as we could find out later, he had been kidnapped at random, taken off the streets in a Catholic area and probably shot by the side of the ditch where his body had fallen.

There was a lot more to think about than to film. How much did you have to hate to kill someone you had never met so cold-bloodedly? Were they nervous as they cruised the streets on the other side of the sectarian divide? Did they just pick the first person walking on his own or did they look for something special about their target? And why is it that the people who carry out these execution-style killings can never face their victims when they do it, even when, as in this case, they are blindfolded?

That night I had to go off down the Falls Road with one of the less experienced London crews and between us we got into real trouble. We found ourselves in the pitch dark between the army and a serious crowd of rioters. We were backed up against the railings of a small triangular park near the Royal Victoria Hospital with nowhere to hide and nowhere to run to. The rubber bullets whanged into the metalwork around us and screamed off into the trees. From the other side there was a steady hail of bricks and petrol bombs. All of us got hit by some missile or other, resulting in bad bruises but no broken bones. We were all very scared. It seemed a very long time before we could convince the army who we were and they let us retreat down the Falls Road. We were in the middle of a deserted crossroads, thinking how lucky we had been, when there were a series of cracks and the classic *peeyong* sound of a ricochet. All around us there were puffs of dirt and dust from the tarmac and we realised we were being shot at by a sniper. We crawled on our bellies all the way back to the car mainly to present as small a target as possible, though in my case I was so terrified I don't think my sphincter would have coped if I had tried to stand up.

Every day in Belfast seemed to be like that. My diaries of the time are full of riots and bombings and we spent our lives racing from one bloody incident to another. One day I rushed up North to cover the attempted murder of a county court judge, who had been shot in the neck and back. We had hardly got there and begun filming the bullet holes in his car and the blood on the back seat than we got a message to head off to a bomb at Newtown Butler. It contained 800 lbs of explosive, they decided later, and it practically blew the little town apart. This time, though, there was a warning and only two people were hurt.

In some ways the saddest story I covered over that period was the killing of one of the army's *charwallahs*. The IRA had ambushed a Pakistani tea boy called Mohamed Abdul Khalid whose only crime, even in their eyes, can have been serving soldiers with hot drinks and sweets. I gave up wondering what kind of men would go to such trouble to extinguish such an inoffensive life as finally beyond my comprehension. He was the second tea boy they had killed; perhaps they were the easiest target. You wondered what the *charwallahs* made of it, far from home in a ferocious and hate-filled land not even their British masters could understand.

I did try. To start with, my sympathies were entirely with the army, though I did my best not to let it show. Given my own background that was understandable, particularly as I would regularly bump into old school friends who now led patrols into Ballymurphy or the Bogside. But the more I drove around Northern Ireland and saw how ancient resentments had solidified into a bloody sectarian standoff, the more I came to realise what deep forces were at work. Cyril and Jim were ideal teachers. Though they were both as cynical as journalists who've seen so much of human cruelty can be, they could still see the world through the eyes of their different communities.

Through Cyril, I got a sense of the stability and cohesion of the Protestants, descended in the main from the original Scots planted on the low and fertile land in the seventeenth century. Though he laughed at it, he could explain the Protestant neuroses, the fear of their ascendancy being overwhelmed, the fear of being betrayed by those whose identity they clung to, the British.

From Jim, I learnt of the Catholics' ancient sense of dispossession after the Gaels of the north were pushed out to the mountain lands of the west or the marshes round Lough Neagh. How that resentment was given a new focus after partition in the 1920s as the Protestant Unionist majority in the north gerrymandered their way to continual power. They controlled the allocation of public housing to corral the Catholics into certain constituencies and rigged the boundaries to give themselves control even in places like Derry where Catholics were in the majority.

Protestants used their political power to ensure they got the best jobs. A survey before the Troubles began showed the Civil Service was almost entirely Protestant, certainly in anything other than the lowest grades. Not a single one of the top 55 jobs in the public service was held by a Catholic. It was the same in every public body, notably in the police. But it was also true in the private sector and the big industries like shipbuilding and heavy engineering. Not surprisingly, Catholics turned their backs on the state. There were some reforms in the sixties, some attempt to entice Catholics into the Unionist enterprise, but the campaign for civil rights seemed as much to discredit the government as to reform it.

The biggest lesson, the unplumbable depth of the divide between the two communities, dawned more slowly because the two of them were good friends who spent most of the time in mutual chaffing. Nothing has happened to bridge it. There's been very little migration into Northern Ireland since the 1600s and hardly any mixing between the communities. Only 5 per cent married across the religious divide and even then one partner had to jump the barrier into the other community; the barrier never came down. To me, though not to them, they all looked and sounded pretty much the same. But the reality was that Cyril and Jim came from discrete societies that lived cheek by jowl but had totally different traditions, aspirations and senses of identity. The two communities had never really been at peace with each other. They were incompatible, uncomprehending and, when I was there, murderous.

The descent into violence was swift and badly handled at almost every stage. The IRA had been close to fading into history when the authorities allowed the Protestants to burn 50,000 Catholics out of mixed areas in Belfast and push them back into their ghettos. The IRA were caught out but emerged as what many in their communities saw as their only protectors against Loyalist attacks and, later, against the army. When the violence in Catholic areas threatened to get out of hand, the army decided to take a strong grip on them. Constant highly intrusive patrolling amounted to a policy of repression. In 1973 when I started going there on a regular basis there were 75,000 house searches, and 4 million – yes, million – vehicles were stopped and searched. Some of this looked pretty rough. The patrols we followed around the Catholic estates had been on the receiving end for a long time. They weren't polite and sometimes seemed to take pleasure in doing as much damage as they could to the houses they searched. The resentment promoted the re-emergence of the IRA which, in turn, gave the army a recognisable quasi-military target to focus on. Both sides were settling into what looked very much like an unwinnable war.

The government was always ambiguous about the IRA. When you interviewed ministers they would call them gangsters and ridicule the military trappings they had copied out of army manuals. But, even then, we heard whispers of secret negotiations with them at Laneside, a large government house in County Down. They treated them as captured prisoners-of-war in the Long Kesh internment camp, down to letting them drill with wooden guns. And later, when the IRA agreed to a short-lived 'truce' in 1975, we found the government had supplied the Provos with green Ford Cortinas in which to patrol the Catholic estates.

We would occasionally catch glimpses of IRA men, the odd shadowy figure in the middle of a riot or an honour guard at a Republican funeral in Milltown cemetery. I found it difficult to see them as anything other than murderers. As long as they took on the army, or the Loyalist killers who were, if anything, even more vicious, they could argue some kind of moral justification, I suppose. But when they took to deliberately killing ordinary people to terrify the population, they lost all claim to it, whatever injustices might have motivated them. It is difficult to look at a child's entrails spread across a blackened pavement and regard the man who did it, who *wanted* to do it, as anything other than evil.

I remember trying to explain this point of view to a couple of rather attractive girls at the Andersonstown Social Club one night and not making any headway. It wasn't surprising as the place was a real Republican hangout and we had probably been unwise to go there. But it had been a quiet few days and a Catholic journalist I had met felt it would do a couple of BBC reporters good to soak up the atmosphere. We had sat through 'Cromwell's Men Are Here Again' and 'My Little Armalite' and I was only gently suggesting that killing innocent people wasn't the best way of advancing any cause when the girls got up and flounced out. Ten minutes later one of them came back and gave me a rubber bullet and a look that was more frightening than any riot. We didn't make an excuse, we just left. Very quickly.

Our tours in Northern Ireland could be very sociable. I have found the most violent parts of the world often seem to contain lots of kind, friendly and hospitable people. It's true of Northern Ireland, of South Africa, of Israel, right down to the smaller countries riven by hatred and bloodshed like El Salvador and Sri Lanka. They might be blowing each other to pieces out on the streets but they can be extremely chatty in the bar over a hot Powers whiskey. When they are not trying to kill you, they can't do enough for you.

We used to stay in the Europa, a big modern hotel in the centre of Belfast with, for a time, a charmed life as far as the bombers were concerned. It was always a nasty moment after the *Nine O'Clock News*, when you had just sent a report you knew might rub one set of gunmen or another up the wrong way, to step out through the sandbags at the entrance of the BBC. The walk up to the hotel was along some very poorly lit back streets and the crews, normally supportive, would never go with you.

Once at the Europa, it always seemed to be party time. They had a kind of Bunny Club up on the top floor which tended to distract some of my colleagues. On one occasion, we came back from a difficult evening in a Catholic enclave called the Short Strand and found my BBC 'fixer' in his bath with two of the Bunny girls. He was very good at fixing things, for himself at any rate.

The Europa got bombed eventually and we moved further out to a smaller hotel called the Wellington Park which, in busy times, the BBC simply took over. We had a huge late-night gambling session there, twenty or so of us all flush with our advances from the BBC cashiers. I did not bet much, because I never win, but most people lost out to one of our senior editors, a shifty man with buck teeth. By 2 a.m. he had a great pile of £5 notes in front of him, £600 or so we thought and a big sum for those days. In a typical gesture that was both grandiloquent and mean he flung his arms wide and yelled across to the barman: 'Waiter! Let's celebrate! Ham sandwiches, all round!'

He was keen on military matters and was something big in the Territorial Army. He floated the idea that we should carry guns in Northern Ireland which would have put paid to quite a few of us if he had had his way.

Later that month the Wellington Park got bombed. The terrorist got through the outer door but not the inner one so left his device on the mat so to speak. The alarm was raised, but in the confusion quite a few people stepped over the bomb on their way out without realising it. Fortunately, everybody was clear before it went off, but it did a lot of damage and, for a time, we had to find other accommodation.

There were killings nearly every day and we reached new bloody landmarks all the time. In one 48-hour period I did a report on the 50th policeman to lose his life, shot as he manned a barricade outside Newton

Hamilton police station, and the 1000th person to die in the Troubles the next day. It was richly ironic that he blew himself up with his own bomb. I got there the following morning to find a gaping hole in a row of terraced houses in the Protestant Edgarston district of Portadown in County Armagh. Joseph Neil, a 25-year-old very amateur bomber, had been fiddling with 10 lbs of gelignite when it had gone off. They found his wife still alive but he had been spread very thinly over the back wall.

There was a crowd outside when we arrived, seething with anger, not at the murderous young idiot who might have killed quite a few of them, but at *us*. This was a problem because I needed to do a couple of pieces to camera to set the scene for a long background report I had prepared looking back on the Troubles so far. I was with one of our London cameramen, Chris Marlow, and we sensibly retreated to work out what to do. There was a large green in front of the wrecked house and we thought if we pulled up there we would just about have time to record the two pieces before the mob saw us and could get close enough to be a problem. It was fine in theory, but when we got out of the car Chris's camera jammed. I can see him now, red in the face and shaking his camera as if he was trying to kill it. The mob was halfway across the green before he got it working. My bosses in London remarked later on how moved I looked and how clever it was to have that demonstration of sympathy closing in behind me. I should have told them it was all down to cowardice and bad luck, but kept quiet. Reporters have their pride.

It was towards the end of just that sort of day when I got a call from Christine in the Belfast newsroom. This was the biggest and best story of all.

ELEVEN

I HAD BEEN KEEN to have children for a couple of years. I think it was a lot to do with my childhood, an urge to create the conventional family life that I felt I had never had. I liked the idea of babies, in an unfocussed, male sort of way. Besides, I was 26 and getting on a bit for fatherhood by the standard of the times. Christine, who was a year younger, was more reluctant. She had a much more realistic idea of how a child would turn our lives upside down. She also felt the ghosts in my family background had to be laid to rest before we began a family of our own. The mystery of my missing father nagged at her more than it seemed to worry me; I had fitted in with the general family denial and suppressed my emotions and my curiosity for a long time. She found this extraordinary and was determined to find him so she could put me into some sort of family context before we tied ourselves down with a baby. 'Eventually,' she would say, 'when we have found your father.'

So 'eventually' arrived for Christine not long after we came back from Canada, early in the New Year of 1973. She gave up the Pill. We were told it would probably take at least six months to get pregnant and we hoped for a baby in the summer of the following year. So much for planning. It happened almost straight away, as far as we can tell, on a rather tipsy journey home in our two-seater Volvo sports car from a wedding of two Radio Bristol friends. The breathalyser had yet to be invented.

I was delighted. I think Christine was rather taken aback and felt a bit cheated at being 'caught', as people used to say then, so soon. She was determined to stay at work until the last minute. The pregnancy was a worry almost from the start. Our GP was astonished at how fast she was swelling and suggested, very early on, that she might be having twins. He referred her to a very dour Scots obstetrician who pooh-poohed the idea. He put her through a series of investigations over the next few months, but told us firmly that, whatever was happening, it wasn't twins.

Christine was one of the first patients to have a scan at Southampton General Hospital. The consulting room was packed with medical staff, crowding in to see this astonishing new technology. The pictures looked like the TV used to look when you switched on the Hoover – madly oscillating snow. 'Twins,' said one of the crowd, 'Triplets,' another.

'Single baby with a very large head,' said a third. We became more and more concerned. As the months rolled on and Chris got bigger and bigger, we wondered just what she was going to produce.

We found out six weeks before the baby was due in December. By now, she was very large indeed and the doctors had felt it was safe enough to have an X-ray to find out what was going on. I had been working for weeks on end, mostly in Belfast, trying to store up time off for later. That day, I had been covering a shooting at the Divis Flats. I had been abused and spat on by some Catholic harridans and pushed around and punched by a gang of Protestant yobs. I suppose you could call it editorial balance, but I was feeling pretty low when I got back to the BBC in Ormeau Avenue and the phone rang.

'It's twins,' she said.

'We're having twins,' she repeated, thinking I hadn't heard. I was so shocked I couldn't stammer out a reply.

We were both so excited and so relieved. Twins. Something we'd heard of. It sounded normal, unlike some of the darker fears we had both had and sometimes shared. We were mercifully green at the time and knew nothing of the much greater risks of multiple births throughout early development, during delivery and later.

I went back to that bleak and pointless murder. What greater contrast could there have been between the casual rubbing out of life in the emotional wastelands of Northern Ireland and the other news I was much keener to share? We had a terrific party in the Europa Hotel and I slept right through two bombs that went off close enough to shatter the windows in the buildings just down the street.

The day after the X-ray, Christine went to work and straight away gave in her notice to the *Southern Evening Echo*. The perfect picture of the two little skeletons, squashed together inside her, had made her suddenly realise she was exhausted. There was no point in trying to hang on to the last vestiges of a professional life with motherhood rushing up so fast. She wasn't just tired but increasingly uncomfortable. She could not sleep and apparently had unbearably itchy feet, which she could no longer reach of course. Less than two weeks later she was admitted to hospital. Against 'reason for admission' on the slip she had to take with her, the GP had written 'tired and miserable'.

We knew what to expect. We had both been to the classes. Christine had learnt how to breathe and then rest between contractions. I had learnt how to be helpful, reassuring and calm. We'd watched the film where the pregnant woman wakes and says sweetly to her husband, 'I think it might be time to go to the hospital now, dear.' Our plan when we thought we were only having one baby was for it to be born in the homely local GP unit. It would be just the two of us, with the midwife Christine had got to know very well by now. Instead, she went into a ward of 'problem' pregnancies that was heavy with, largely unspoken, fears. The woman in the next bed was in the ward because the last time she was pregnant she had to give birth to a child she knew was already dead. On the other side was a 40-year-old woman who was expecting her first and longed-for baby. Even Christine, by then 26, was considered old to embark on motherhood and labelled 'elderly primigravida'. In those pre-amniocentesis days, a baby at 40 was a cause for special concern and her neighbour was being watched very closely. The child she called Joy was hastily renamed when they realised she had Down's Syndrome.

We were both going into a world with much potential pain as well as happiness. For me, the hospital smells, the sounds, the raw emotion washing up and down the corridors and wards, all brought back my mother's last days. I tried to tell myself this was different, that the same sort of place was just as much associated with the beginning of life as its end. But it just gave me a sense of foreboding every time I went there. This was where you lost people. These were the rituals of disease and death, not of birth and life. I found the visiting hard during the weeks of waiting. I tried to keep it to myself.

Despite the total rest Christine's blood pressure climbed steadily. Eventually, one of the doctors said: 'We'll have to induce you tomorrow, if it's up again.' I arranged time off. She washed her hair. We both felt a mixture of excitement and dread. It was no great surprise that her blood pressure was up again next day. Mine was too.

I arrived early, armed with magazines and a pack of cards. Chris was looking very beautiful, in full make-up, with the newly done hair. Her waters were broken and a drip had been put up. Nothing much happened for a while and I began to think it was a bit of an anti-climax. I went off to buy some sandwiches. I wasn't gone long but when I got back I found her in intense pain. Her hair was damp, the mascara smudged. She was panting hard. This was nothing like the classes. 'When's the "rest"? I need the rest,' she gasped. She had gone from feeling a mild back-ache to agonising, prolonged contractions in a matter of minutes. The whole thing felt out of our control and we were both frightened. It went on like that all day. The magazines never got read. The sandwiches were never eaten.

An eternity later she was wheeled into the delivery room. Looking back, I suppose it was more of an operating theatre. There were glaring overhead lights and everyone, including me, had to scrub up and get into green outfits. Christine was flat on her back on a table with her legs in stirrups, saying it was like major surgery with your eyes open. 'What about the epidural?' said someone. 'Too late,' was the reply. It was still not the usual thing for the father to be there at the birth and they were always asked to leave if it was anything other than straightforward. Christine had said she really wanted me there, so I could not leave her. I sat at the head-end, clinging on to her hand, more than half wishing someone would notice me and throw me out. But I was indistinguishable from all the staff in my green overalls. It wasn't the same, God knows, but in different ways there was no relief for either of us.

The room was hot and crowded. There was a team for each of the baby resuscitators that were waiting in the corner, a registrar who was in charge, the chief nursing officer, who was encouraging Christine, several assistants and any medical student or trainee midwife who hadn't yet seen a twin delivery for good measure. I did not catch anyone's eye. I spent most of the time staring fixedly at the wall, praying for it to be over. Simon was born first, delivered with forceps. There was only time for a quick glance at a little pink figure covered in what looked like bluish-grey mud before he was whisked away and everybody focused on 'twin two'. There were seven long minutes before Roland arrived, also by forceps and left foot first. We barely caught sight of him. He was rushed off to intensive care. We had no chance to hold either of the babies. There was no time for bonding.

The registrar looked down at her blood-soaked shoes and said: 'I must get some Wellingtons.' It had taken nine and a half hours and was all over, bar the clearing up which looked as though it would take some time. It was 5.30 on a gloomy Friday afternoon at the end of November. I was absolutely elated and very relieved. Not surprisingly, Christine was exhausted.

I went off to celebrate with friends, leaving her to sleep. When I came back several hours later I found her still on the delivery table. She had collapsed and had to have heart massage and a transfusion of two pints of blood. I sobered up very quickly. It wasn't over at all. In many ways it was just beginning.

The boys were quite a good weight – 5lbs 12ozs and 5lbs 10ozs. Christine had managed to carry them nearly to term, which is unusual for twins. In the end they had been induced only a week early. But there were obviously problems. They were both put in incubators to 'warm up'. By day two Simon had been transferred into an ordinary little Perspex cot but he was still dressed in a woolly hat and giant knitted boots even though the special care unit felt sweltering to us. His cot was pressed up against the incubator where Roland lay with eyes still tight shut and a feeding tube up his nose. On the morning of day three Christine went into the unit to feed Simon and express milk for Roland and was told by a rather insensitive sister that he had 'died' five times in the night, but would probably be all right now. We were terrified, rather than reassured. Their lives were so important to us and seemed so fragile.

Christine had always wanted to feed 'the baby' herself and she was even more determined when she found it was two, seeing the alternative as a life drowning in Milton. She practised on Simon and went on a machine called a humilactor to extract milk for Roland and build up the supply. She was soon producing enough for half the special care nursery. After five days they were allowed out of special care and she started to devise a method of feeding them both at once. It would be several more days before they were allowed home but things seemed stable so I went back to work to build up a bit more time off.

The BBC were pretty understanding. The Foreign Desk was overruled when they tried to send me off to the Middle East. Instead, I was ordered down to Sunningdale to help Martin Bell cover the first, ill-fated attempt to negotiate a power-sharing agreement in Northern Ireland. My mind was back at Southampton General and it was difficult to concentrate on the intricacies of the deal they hoped would bring the troubles to an end. But I could still smell the hatred on the Belfast streets and wondered how the agreement, being hammered out in the grand and leafy surroundings of the Civil Service Staff College, would ever stick. The shape of a new devolved government that was meant to share power so the minority Catholics were not tyrannised by the majority Protestants had already been agreed after months of anger, walk outs and personal abuse; the point of the Sunningdale talks was to set up an all-Ireland political dimension that reassured the Nationalists without selling out the Loyalists. The formula was to reappear in many guises. As would the opposition and its leader, the Reverend Ian Paisley, who boycotted the Sunningdale talks yet cast a large shadow over them. The negotiations lasted four days and nights. The Prime Minister of the day, Edward Heath, his Irish counterpart Liam Cosgrave, and Brian Faulkner the

Unionist leader, on whose survival the whole edifice depended, shuttled back and forth between their delegations.

The glimpses behind the scenes were fascinating. Faulkner's Unionists decided they should not use the drinks cabinet that had been thoughtfully provided for them, in case it affected their judgement. They sucked Polo mints as the sessions dragged on while their drinks allowance was shared out between the other delegations who seemed very thirsty and had no such inhibitions.

It was interesting to see the contrasts between public and private positions and how personal relationships developed between political antagonists in that hothouse atmosphere. I had not covered an important political conference before, but even I could see how it depended on both sides claiming they had got up from the table with more than their opponents. It only worked as long as your supporters did not listen to what the other side was saying. I did not see then that Faulkner had been pressed into too many concessions to give the deal a chance. To be honest, I could not wait to get back to my new family but I did not think I was rushing away from an historic peace settlement, and so it proved.

The agreement lasted five months before Paisley and the Ulster Workers' Council launched a general strike that brought the entire province to a halt, with no electricity and the bodies unburied. They blew Sunningdale away in a fortnight. Harold Wilson was Prime Minister by then and he upbraided the Unionists for 'sponging' on Britain and then undermining democracy. 'Who do these people think they are?' he said. Next time I was there, many Protestants were proudly wearing bits of sponge in their lapels. Northern Ireland had to wait a generation for a newer version of the same basic solution to have any more chance of success.

I had more important things to worry about. Doctors then had an absurdly paternalistic attitude to their patients; they didn't need to be told what they might not need to know. We were not specifically warned that they were concerned that Roland's brain might have been damaged by the loss of oxygen after Simon's birth. Presumably they thought that, as he might be all right, it was best for us not to know. We weren't stupid, though. It would have been difficult to miss the whispered conversations, the meaningful looks, the odd shake of the head, even if anxiety had not made us extra-sensitive. It was much more frightening to piece together bits of information gradually and find yourself staring at a nightmare.

Christine had the worst time while I was away, watching them regularly measuring Roland's head. She was distraught when one well-meaning nurse tried to reassure her: 'Never mind, dear, you've got one perfect baby.' She couldn't contact me in those days before mobile phones and just had to cope with the support of her sister until I turned up again. News can be cruel on families.

I went to bring them all home on a snowy morning just before Christmas. My sleek, ice blue sports car had been replaced by an acid yellow Renault 4 hatchback, with a twin pram in the back. Christine came out on to the steps of the hospital, breathed in the crisp, fresh air for the first time in five weeks and cried. It must have been a mixture of joy, relief and apprehension. We had both been through the best and the worst experiences of our lives.

Christine set up a regime of feeding the two of them simultaneously but it didn't work for a while because Simon and Roland couldn't glug back enough to cope with the amount of milk she produced and the supply got blocked up. I panicked a bit but a trip back to the hospital to pump off the excess sorted it out – baby care is really a matter of fluid mechanics – and we soon established a neat, if ruthless system of demand feeding. Simon's demand, as it happened He always cried first and my role as First Gentleman of the Bedchamber was to wake Roland and carry them both through to Christine. She eventually became so expert at sitting up in bed surrounded by pillows to prop both babies in position that she could knit or read at the same time. It was relaxing for everybody concerned apart from me. My responsibilities, and soon my expertise, involved the other end. I became something of a specialist with Terry nappies folded into kites, liners, pins, and plastic pants.

My job was not quite as family unfriendly as you might have thought. The work pattern on the reporters' 'taxi rank' in the London newsroom then was four-days-on-four-days-off. I was being sent all over the country and the world. If you got sent on some story for more than four days, you got the same number of days off. So I was either around all the time, or I wasn't there at all. When I was around I was completely indispensable, of course. I am still not sure how Christine coped when I wasn't.

We had the boys christened on a glorious summer Sunday in the church where we had been married nearly six years before. I wish I had been there.

Christine went ahead to Hereford to cook and prepare the buffet we planned for the 25 guests. Late on the Saturday afternoon I was in the newsroom in London at the end of my shift, filling in my expenses with some care and wondering how far they would go in Mothercare, when all the phones started ringing. A factory was on fire just outside Scunthorpe in Lincolnshire. The details started to come in more quickly than usual and each piece of information made it look worse and worse. 'You'll have to go, christening or no christening,' said the man on the home newsdesk. 'There's nobody else.'

'Bugger,' I said. 'I don't care how big it is, I've got to be back in Hereford tomorrow. Where is it anyway?'

'A little place called Flixborough.'

From the air you could see the thundering pillar of black smoke 40 miles away, drifting across the Lincolnshire plain under a strong south-westerly wind. We had been very quick off the mark and I was airborne with one of the BBC's best film crews, Peter Beggin and Roy Benford, in a chartered plane from Denham airfield within an hour of the first call. The pilot tuned in to different radio stations as we headed north and by the time we caught our first sight of it we knew it was a chemical factory, that it had been blown to smithereens and that anybody who had been in the main part of the plant was dead. The planning, for once on these occasions, went perfectly. Our little plane landed at a small strip at Kirmington, about 25 miles from the factory. The helicopter was waiting for us, its rotor blades already turning.

From above, it looked as though the gates of hell had opened. Great gouts of flame spurted from amongst the blackened remains of what had been one of the biggest plants of its kind in Europe. A dozen fire engines were already there but looked about as useful as piddling on a volcano. It was already seven o'clock and I was trying to do complicated calculations about how long we could afford to stay and still have a chance of getting the pictures on the main evening news. I reckoned about five minutes.

We landed inside the cordon, which was the first stroke of luck. The police sergeant who came across in a panda car was the second. Instead of throwing us out, he drove as close as we could get into the heat and noise.

Flixborough, at the height of the fire midway through Saturday evening, was an assault on all the senses. The fire was fuelled by tons of cyclohexane, a liquid much more flammable than petrol, pouring out of a ruptured valve. It was impossible to hear for the roaring of the flames. Our noses were full of the stench of burning chemicals. It looked for all the world like an atomic bomb had been dropped on the world's largest Meccano set. The big office block had been reduced to a 30-feet-high pile of rubble. There was nothing left of the key section of the plant closest to the source of the explosion. The men inside might have heard the first, small explosion, but were all incinerated in a massive fireball a second and a half later. Twenty-eight men had died, though I don't think we knew that figure for sure yet. We knew that it could have been 500 if the explosion had not happened at the weekend. As it was, we were already aware that we were looking at Britain's worst industrial accident in peacetime.

The flames glowed white for a moment and the blast of heat almost knocked us over. I had already done a couple of snatched interviews with the firemen and now did a hurried piece to camera against a fiery background. Peter muttered about contrast problems which seemed almost funny at the time.

It was as we turned to run back to the helicopter that I saw the man's leg sticking out of one of the steaming lagoons of water contaminated with chemicals escaping from the plant. It was bent at the knee and wearing a rubber boot. A single glimpse of what was probably the only recognisable human remains left after the blast.

There was no time for more. Less than ten minutes after we landed we were airborne again heading for the BBC in Leeds and the seconds were ticking away. We were met on the steps by the news editor, wringing his hands. 'You can't bring it here,' he said. 'We can only process black and white film. You'll have to take it to Manchester.'

That would have meant no chance of getting on the air at all that night. I told them to push the colour film through the black and white bath. It was a gamble with such priceless and historic footage but we had no choice. There was eighteen minutes to go to the main news. I asked the processing man how long it would take and he said: 'Twenty minutes, if you're lucky.'

In fact, I had the roll of unedited film in my hands about three minutes before the programme went on the air. We edited a couple of shots and managed to incorporate some even more extraordinary pictures shot by Paul Berriff, a freelance cameraman who lived nearby, but then we ran out of time. The telecine man loaded it into the machine and his hands were shaking, though not as much as mine. We ran the first frames as the headline for the programme and then re-racked it and waited for the end of the newsreader's introduction.

We ran most of the footage raw, as it was shot. I sat in the corner of the studio, trying to ad lib a commentary from scraps of notes I had made on odd bits of paper. For the first time, but not the last, it struck me how the adrenalin of a big story carries you through all sort of technical crises. In truth, the damage was so devastating, the pictures so dramatic, I could have sung the National Anthem over it all and people would still have been on the edge of their seats. I restricted myself to adding details that were not obvious from the film they were seeing. What we knew about the plant (it made caprolactam, the main component in the manufacture of nylon fibres); about the casualties and about the damage in the surrounding area. It had blown the roofs off houses in Scunthorpe, four miles away.

It was pretty ragged, I imagine, but it did not matter. The news editor returned after the dust had settled with fish suppers for us all and some much-needed alcohol.

I rang Christine at about 10 p.m. that Saturday night. 'Can we postpone the christening?' I asked weakly and got a slightly dusty but, under the circumstances, remarkably understanding answer: 'No. We'll manage without you. I suppose I will have to get used to it.'

The plant was still on fire, 3,000 people had been evacuated from the surrounding area and there was no chance Television News would let me leave the story. I did not really have any choice. I saved my regrets for later and drove back to Flixborough and a night in a hire car.

It was short and uncomfortable. But by dawn it looked as though the whole BBC had arrived. It was the full outside broadcast unit that had been covering rugby at Headingley for *Grandstand* the previous day, backed up by a convoy from the BBC in Manchester which included a 60-foot hydraulic mast, radio links vehicles and several mobile generators.

They had taken over the place, commandeered phone lines, sweet-talked the police and even served breakfast by the time BBC1 opened up at 8.30 a.m. that Sunday morning and I began a day of being almost continuously on the air. From time to time our broadcasts had to be interrupted when it looked as though we might be blown up in a second massive explosion. It was not a nice feeling to hear klaxons and whistles going and glance over your shoulder to see firemen racing towards you for all they were worth. It was even worse when they ran past you and kept going. The alarms, fortunately, were all false, but the plant blazed away uncontrollably for days. The firemen finally had to let it burn itself out.

Back in Hereford the christening went ahead on time at 4 p.m. We hadn't been to the church since our wedding but it was the same vicar who had married us. Christine told me later that, as she stood at the font, surrounded by a posse of godparents, she saw his eyes rake the crowd, desperately searching for a face he recognised who might be the father. She was still a sub-editor at heart and spent some of the ceremony composing headlines like MOTHER OF TWO JILTED AT FONT.

When the time came and went with me standing in a flattened cornfield under a blackened sky a hundred odd miles away, I felt rather sick. There would be many more times when I would miss some important family event but that was the worst and most difficult to forgive. I went through life without a father myself and did not want it to happen to my children. Yet I failed at the first hurdle and went on failing. It was certainly a talking point at the christening. After they had all eaten the buffet in the garden they trooped indoors and watched me do my bit on the early-evening News. I was half tempted to send them some sort of message but realised I was getting overwrought and wisely shut up.

Christine took the boys for regular follow-up appointments at the special care clinic but we both knew long before they were signed off that Roland wasn't brain-damaged. It was the best, the most wonderful of times. We took intense pride and pleasure in their every breath. They developed in tandem, with all the teeth coming through in the same order, sitting up at the same time, sliding around in the same leopard crawl, dragging themselves along on their tummies, with their elbows. They took great delight in each other, sleeping contentedly in the same cot at the beginning and later pushing each other around in a little trolley. Roland walked unaided first, probably because he did most of the pushing with the trolley, while Simon did the riding. Simon watched his brother's staggering efforts and two days later he got to his feet. They walked shakily towards each other. They both laughed and laughed. We were besotted with them.

From a rather wizened and wrinkled start they grew into the most beautiful blond babies and attracted a lot of attention wherever they went. I loved showing them off, trying hard to be offhand, but always failing. Everyone would ask us, 'Are they identical?' The truth was we didn't know. Their different births had meant they didn't look that similar when they were born. Simon's head was shaped by his longer delivery, while Roland's was an unmoulded dome. The doctors had said they seemed to have had only one placenta, a sure sign, but it could have been two that had developed so closely they had fused. The difference could be really important, not just for sentimental reasons. Identical twins are created when one egg splits shortly after fertilisation; the later they split, the more alike they are. They have an identical genetic package and they are a perfect blood or tissue match for each other; who knows, one day they might be able to save each other's lives. Fraternal twins, on the other hand, happen when the mother produces two eggs at once, an inheritable predisposition. Fraternal twins are no more alike than any other siblings and are no more likely to have matching tissues.

As they got older they soon began to look very alike but we wanted to know for sure. We went for a blood test when they were two. I was horrified to find I had to have blood taken too but had to be brave in front of them.

We went for the results. Monozygotic. Identical. 'How did it happen?' I asked the consultant. 'We don't really know. Maybe you simply have aggressive sperm,' he said. I had a great idea for a T-shirt with SUPERSPERM written in bold letters all over the front and back. I never quite had the nerve and rather regret it now, in a childish sort of way.

Captain Gordon Buerk, an officer but not quite a gentleman. My father, the ladies' man, in his prime.

My mother before her fateful meeting with my father.

Before the fall. I am pretending to be Winston Churchill, my father is pretending to be a legally married husband. My mother and grandmother are unaware of the storm about to break.

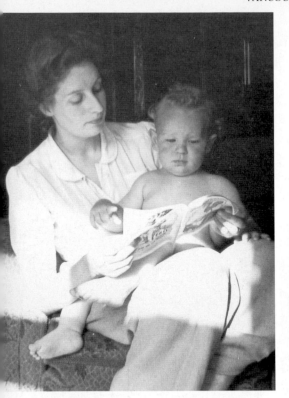

The newsreader. With my mother in the apartment near Stanley Park.

Fishing with a friend on the Vancouver quayside. Round the corner, my father's business was facing ruin, like his marriage.

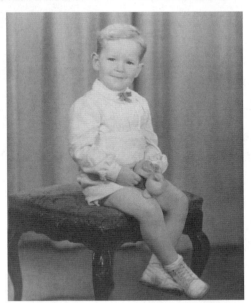

Aged 2, on best behaviour in full toddler dress uniform. I am hanging on to the boxing gloves, though, just in case.

My father and mother out shopping, snapped by a Vancouver street photographer in 1949.

First day at school.
Every inch the 1950's
prep schoolboy in my
Cedarhurst uniform.

My last day at school.
Under-officer Buerk marching
not, as he fondly hoped, into the
services, but onto a building site.

The young newspaper reporter
on the lookout for a story.

The *Bromsgrove Messenger*'s answer to James Bond.
The cigarette was a Woodbine, unfortunately, not
handmade for me by Morlands of Bond Street.

Athwart my beloved Austin Healey
outside my other beloved's family butcher's
shop. Sunday in the 1960s and Hereford's
High Town looks as if it has been evacuated.

I had got the gear, but I was still looking
for the 60s. Why I was searching for them
in a Bromsgrove graveyard is a mystery.

The banquet fit for a queen. Sue Lawley serves the royal reject sturgeon for me, Christine and her boyfriend at the time, Chris Potter. Full-on 60s chic, kaftan, Liebfraumilch and all.

Bristol fashion. Radio Bristol reunion, a quarter of a century after we launched the first of the BBC's big wave of local radio stations. With Kate Adie and Roger Bennett in Studio 1.

The perfect day. Christine and me on our wedding day in September 1968. The press newspaper put this picture on the front page, headlined 'Journalists' Romance'.

First day home with the twins. Proud father, tired mother. Simon (left) and Roland are too preoccupied to notice.

The Mulberry Bush after the Birmingham pub bombings in November 1975.
All that was left of the bar, which, like the other target, the Tavern in the Town,
had been packed with youngsters. The bombs were so powerful they blew holes in nine-
inch thick reinforced concrete. They killed 21 people and injured hundreds more.
It was the biggest murder case in British criminal history.

Flixborough, the day after the
Nypro chemical plant blew
itself to pieces, looking 'like an
atomic bomb had been dropped
on the world's biggest Meccano
set'. It blew roofs off in
Scunthorpe four miles away but,
because it was a weekend, 'only'
28 people lost their lives.

The natives were friendly but how could you tell? With the Zulus on Shaka day in Natal. So that is what it must have felt like at Rorke's Drift.

Resisting arrest. After talking yourself out of being 'necklaced' by the black 'comrades' you had to run the gauntlet of the white South African police. Standing up for cameraman Willie Qubeka during the township uprising.

" This is Michael Buerk reporting from South Africa."

Keeping my distance as the Zulu Inkatha party demonstrate with their so-called 'traditional weapons' in Johannesburg.

Reporting under censorship. How Mahood of the *Daily Mail* saw my attempts to get round South Africa's draconian emergency regulations.

TWELVE

THE TELEVISION CENTRE CLUB was a rowdy and democratic place. There were two bars and a rather grubby roof terrace where, in the summer, you could watch the airliners sliding down into Heathrow and a famous producer of classic comedies sliding under the table with the same air of graceful certainty. The club was rather like those churches in Bethlehem whose floor space is divided up to the last millimetre between rival sects. Though there was nothing to indicate as much to a stranger, each corner was the territory of a particular class of BBC person. The horny-handed riggers held robust court in the centre of the main bar by virtue of their physical presence and need for rapid replenishment. The actors favoured a corner by the window where they could catch reflections of themselves in the plate glass. The suits liked a raised area furthest away from the bar. They had an instinct for hierarchy and, anyway, there was a constant flow of sycophants to bring supplies over to them. The ice never had time to melt in their gin and tonics.

Most of it has gone now, replaced by a crèche and a gym, as neat a metaphor for social change as you could wish.

News had more or less taken over the small bar. We were resented and envied by rootless weaklings from accounts or engineering who were anxious to carve out *Lebensraum* for themselves. But there were a lot of thirsty people in news and many of them had time on their hands. Our territory was never left undefended.

I was down there one summer lunchtime, a couple of months after I had arrived. An ambitious local radio lad called Chris Cramer had come to look me up and have a sniff around the glamorous world of television news. I was in the middle of telling him it wasn't as exciting as it was cracked up to be when the deputy foreign editor came flying into the bar, flung out his arm in a dramatic gesture and said: 'Go. Go now. Go . . . to Istanbul!' I just had time to notice he was pointing in the general direction of New York, which seemed to confirm everything I had been told about the foreign desk's grip on geography.

Within ten minutes I was on the road to Heathrow with a handful of cuttings, a couple of thousand dollars in my pocket and a sinking feeling in my heart. I hadn't been given the least popular crew that worked for Television News but it had been a photo finish for the title and they had only just lost out. Mike was not a bad cameraman in the sense that most of his pictures came out. In fact, he had been trained at Pinewood Studios during the war to be a battle cameraman. Rumour had it he was dropped with the Paras into Arnhem and the wits in the reporters' room said it must be true because there only ever two useable shots of the episode subsequently immortalised as the 'bridge too far'. Mike's real problem was that he had been soured by life. He loathed most things and most people, but particularly the work he had to do and the reporter with whom he had to do it. He probably thought I was uppity and naïve. I certainly reckoned he was idle, surly and uncooperative. We were both right.

Stanley the soundman was a living legend. Mike might have been idle, but Stanley was famous. Some rated him as the laziest person they had ever met. He was commonly known as 'clean hands', a soubriquet that speaks for itself. He moved with the glide and shrug of a practised spiv and, when you nerved yourself to ask him to do anything, he would cock his head to one side and fix you with a beady eye, like a sparrow watching a cat. They weren't the ideal pair to go with on my first big foreign story.

We were going to Turkey because there had just been a coup on Cyprus and the Turks were mobilising their army, threatening war. Turkish Cypriots were in a minority on the island and a delicate constitutional deal had been done when it became independent of Britain to safeguard their interests. This had been overthrown, along with the President, Archbishop Makarios, when the Cypriot National Guard, officered by Greeks, attacked the Presidential Palace. Makarios himself skipped nimbly out of the back door as the National Guard machine gunned the front. The plotters wanted *Enosis*, union with Greece, and if the Turks didn't like it they knew which way to swim. There was heavy fighting going on in the bigger towns, Nicosia, Limassol, Larnaca and Famagusta, as well as freelance bloodletting between villages that had always hated each other. The coup leaders announced a new president, an Eoka terrorist called Nicos Sampson who the British had once sentenced to death but, in a moment of weakness, reprieved.

This was a full-blown international crisis; a coup, bloody battles and rumours of massacres on a strategically important Mediterranean island. Two mortal enemies (ostensibly Nato allies) snarling at each other across the Aegean and moving their armed forces on to a war footing. Britain, the former colonial power, wringing its hands, the UN powerless, the Soviet Union meddling from the sidelines. It had it all.

The Turks were never going to accept the coup and as soon as we landed in Istanbul it was obvious the country was in the middle of a classic war fever. We needed to get to Ankara, the capital Kemal Ataturk built as an alternative to Istanbul in the centre of the country, but the internal flights had been suspended because of the emergency. We spent an hour or so hunting for a taxi which wasn't a wreck and a driver who wasn't a madman. We had to compromise on both counts, but were finally able to set off as darkness stole over the Golden Horn.

The 350-mile trip from Istanbul to Ankara across the Anatolian steppe rates as the longest nightmare drive of my life. Our driver was merely reckless to an almost suicidal degree. Everybody else on the road that night was obviously insane. Round every bend we found a truck heading for us at full speed on the wrong side of the road with the driver either fast asleep or gibbering. We saw at least three accidents actually happen in ways that made it extremely unlikely anybody involved could survive. There were more wrecks than signposts and several of them were still glowing. Just round one blind bend in the mountains our headlights picked out a plume of white smoke rising from the ravine below. We stopped and looked over the edge. It was obvious a lorry had just driven straight over but it was too far down to climb and not much to be done, we felt, when we got there.

I was extremely grateful to get to Ankara. It may have been a grubby urban sprawl in the middle of semi-desert but it was only half a step short of paradise just to be alive. The Buyuk Ankara Hotel was suitably modern and expensive. The *Efes* beer was a great restorative when taken in large enough quantities. I perked up. The crew had had enough, but they had reached that stage before checking in their silver boxes at Heathrow and couldn't entirely blame Turkish road safety standards.

I was keen to press on down to the south coast where the Turkish Army was said to be massing but the foreign desk insisted I stay on in Ankara to cover the political developments. This consisted of dogging the Prime Minister, Bulent Ecevit, with the help of a sharp young Turkish journalist called Metin Munir. As ever, the trick was to find out where power really lay. The answer seemed to be with the army. The generals have a special role in Turkey. They regard themselves as the guardians, not just of democracy, but of the nation's secular soul and have a habit of stepping in when they think the politicians are getting it unacceptably wrong. Besides, this was an issue of national pride and even territorial

153

integrity. The army was driving things, not the earnest and even chatty Mr Ecevit.

I sent a couple of film reports back to London by a roundabout route but most of the time I reported live from what looked like a broom cupboard in the Turkish television headquarters. These were later described as 'pioneering' broadcasts and looked like it. I was in black and white, often apparently in a snow storm or, at the very least, suffering from terminal dandruff. But it was live, from the capital of one of the protagonists, and I occasionally had something interesting to say.

After a few days, it was obvious even to the foreign desk that this was no longer a political story, we were on the edge of war. We hired another taxi driver, even more reckless than the first but thankfully just as lucky, and we set off for the south. It was nearly 400 miles this time. I peeled myself an orange as we left Ankara and had revolting sticky fingers for the next 18 hours. Every time I covered my eyes in a reflex action caused by the many near catastrophes, I smothered my face in the stuff. It is little things like that you remember when the recollections of horror and joy fade away; curious isn't it?

The next day we stopped at Adana, an overgrown town heavy with humidity in the centre of the Cilician plain. I bought some Adana kebabs from a street stall. They are made with hot peppers and served with onions and a major dusting of paprika. It was lucky the windows were open. Our stomachs began to rumble almost as much as the tanks we began to see as we headed down to the coast.

Only a Turkish taxi driver could have threaded his way through the 29th Armoured Division that was heading south to join the main body of the Turkish 2nd Army then camped out on the coast. Mike cheered up a bit at the chance to do something devious and approached the task of sneaking pictures of the column with something that looked almost like enthusiasm. He hid the camera in a pile of coats on the back seat. 'Clean hands' looked the picture of injured innocence, his stock in trade. I smiled a lot.

We hit the coast road west of Mersin, the Turkish port that was only 50 miles from Cyprus. The horizon was blotted out by a great naval convoy which was obviously the invasion fleet, the transports for the army, with five warships as an escort further out to sea. They were heading to pick up the invasion force from Mersin and from Iskenderun further to the east. This was not just proof of Turkish intentions, it was the clearest possible indication the invasion was only hours away.

We took a few shots from the shore, but the convoy was three miles out and I wanted something closer. I got the taxi driver to go on to the next fishing village and pushed a big handful of dollars at a fisherman who was mending his nets on the stone quay. He was reluctant, but it is amazing what people will do for a lot of money in cash. Fifteen minutes later we were right in the middle of the Turkish invasion fleet, filming as if we were an official crew at a Portsmouth naval review. The gall of it was some protection. If I had a plan, it was to appear so confident they would assume we were filming with high-level government permission. I am not sure I thought about it much at all. I just wanted the pictures at any risk and at any cost.

We had a charmed life for a while, cruising up and down the lines of landing craft – I counted 20 – and circling the two big troop transporters. Just when I thought we had got enough and it was time to cut and run, a patrol boat packed with Turkish marines roared up and pointed lots of guns at us. The fisherman said: 'Over. It over. They arrest you.' He made his fingers into a pistol, pointed to his forehead and pulled an imaginary trigger. Oh, shit.

The jail in Mersin was dark and dirty and smelt of fear, mine probably. You could just see the sky through a small, barred window high on one wall. There was a lot of rustling in the dirt on the floor which I thought was a rat but it was only a cockroach. I stamped on it with a shudder, wondering if I would rot in a Turkish jail for long enough to get to know the cockroaches by name and call them friends.

Mike was in the next cell. Now he really did have something to complain about his bloody-mindedness took on a rather heroic tinge. I let him do the talking. All those years defending false overtime claims had made him impervious to questioning. His speciality was a kind of creative stupidity that none of our interrogators could penetrate. It made these local Turkish officials angry and threatening. They told us we were spies and hinted that the penalty for espionage in Turkey might be death or, at the very least, a long term of imprisonment. A little light torture was apparently traditional while they decided between those two options. One of them fingered something black and cylindrical that looked to me like a cosh. I could see myself being banged up with Mike in some Levantine oubliette for the rest of my days, a fate that made the death penalty look positively attractive.

The truth was that the threats were empty, we were not going to be tortured, they did not know what to do with us and were waiting for instructions from somebody important in Ankara. Anybody with any common sense would realise that the Turks needed all the friends they could get and doing away with a BBC crew would not be the best way of going about it. Mike knew it and I should have done, but it was a novel experience and I was in something of a panic.

We had one consolation. Stanley was safe. It wasn't his personal well-being that concerned me, in fact there were moments when it would have given me keen pleasure to have him hanging by his toenails from the wall in the next cell. But Stanley was carrying with him our film of the Turkish invasion fleet. It was a world exclusive and I fancied it would make my name.

It had been easy enough to change magazines on the fishing boat. The Turkish marines did not watch us very closely; they were too busy being officious. We were not only able to swap magazines but to unload the exposed film into a can and hide it in our bags. We knew there was nowhere within 500 miles where the new film could have been processed and our trick discovered.

I don't know why they let Stanley go. Perhaps they thought he was not really part of our enterprise – a conclusion I had reached long before. Perhaps they realised they would not get anything out of him. Stanley's blank obduracy was not a pose. Either way, he walked out of the jail a free man with a bulge in his pocket that the BBC would be pleased to see.

We had been released ourselves – with a great deal of surly reluctance from our jailers – by the time Stanley got to London. Our film did, indeed, make a big splash, but it lasted less than a day. By then, the invasion was under way and our effort was totally eclipsed by an astonishing stroke pulled off by ITN.

It was sheer luck, like most journalistic triumphs. The reporters on the island were all staying in the old Ledra Palace Hotel in Nicosia and they were tipped off the invasion was on its way a couple of hours before the troops actually landed. Within minutes a convoy of cars set off at high speed across the plain north of the capital heading north towards the mountain range and the port of Kyrenia beyond, that was bound to be the first objective of the Turkish forces.

The BBC won the race to Kyrenia but, in every sense, lost the war. Just south of the mountains, the ITN car broke down. Their reporter, Michael Nicholson, and his crew were beside themselves with frustration as the dust from the BBC cars settled and the last sound of their engines died away. Nobody with any sense was going in that direction. They were still ten miles from Kyrenia and there was nothing for it but to walk.

They were actually jogging when the sky suddenly went dark with Turkish paratroopers. Showing considerable presence of mind, Nicholson and his crew walked up to the first soldier who landed and started to interview him. Instead of shooting them out of hand, the paratrooper replied courteously and in reasonable English.

ITN had an extraordinary scoop. The BBC had nothing in comparison. The crew that had got to Kyrenia was bottled up in the Dome Hotel for four days until they could be rescued by the British Navy.

When I got back to London, the BBC was more traumatised by defeat than the Greek Cypriots. Naturally, I tried to console them all by recalling my own exploits but these were brushed aside in the general mourning and, wisely I think, I shut up and joined in.

The fighting was fierce while it lasted. The Turks had thrown in 7,000 troops and 40 tanks and their Skyhawk jets strafed the National Guard wherever they tried to make a stand. The military junta in Athens fell. Angry Greek Cypriot mobs attacked the British and American embassies, killing the American Ambassador and stoning the British High Commissioner's Rolls-Royce. The BBC did not do badly in covering all this, but the Nicholson scoop was all anybody remembered, another lesson in journalism.

Worse, much worse, was to come. There was a lull in the fighting after a ceasefire was negotiated in Geneva. It is perhaps paradoxical, but that is when it gets more dangerous for journalists when the fixed points formed by battle become more fluid and risk is less easily defined. A convoy of journalists accidentally drove into a minefield in the north of the island. A BBC soundman called Ted Stoddart, one of the very best and a good friend, got out of his car to warn the others and stepped on a mine. It blew his chest open. His last words were: 'I've had it. Look after my wife.' They had three small children.

The talks in Geneva did not go well and when the Turks set a 24-hour deadline for their demands to be met, I was sent back there because, they said, I was now the Turkish 'expert'. The difficulty was that the Turks had closed their airspace. The only realistic way in was to fly to Sofia and go into Turkey by train. This time the crew I was given were young and keen, both very good at their jobs but, unfortunately, as ignorant of geography as me. We were nearly at Heathrow and talking about getting some local currency when we realised that none of us knew which country Sofia was in. Swallowing our pride, we called up the foreign desk. 'Yugoslavia, old boy, surprised you didn't know that.' We got ourselves a pile of Yugoslavian dinars which proved of no use at all when we landed in Bulgaria.

I had fondly imagined we would sweep into Turkey in some luxury *wagon-lit* sipping Champagne by candlelight and fighting off the attentions of beautiful blonde Soviet agents, perhaps on the Orient Express itself. Instead, it was a local train packed to the parcel shelf with peasantry, and chickens running wild up and down the aisles. I spent the entire journey trying to hold on to my bag and my nose at the same time. Mike Viney, the most fastidious of soundmen, was worried about the creases in his safari suit. The cameraman, Nick Lera, was absolutely in his element but threatening to ruin our trip before we even got there.

Nick had two interests in life at the time, women and trains. It was not clear what order they came in. We used to speculate what would happen if he came across a damsel in distress tied to a railway line and about to go under the wheels of an interesting locomotive. Most of us thought he might be too busy taking the loco's number to free the girl, but we all agreed it would be a tough call for him.

That Balkan rail journey must have been better than sex for Nick. At the time, Bulgarian and Turkish railways depended on old German steam locomotives that, to the knowledgeable eye, had the voluptuous, period glamour of, say, Rita Hayworth. Nick spent most of the journey hanging out of the window, whining with pleasure as all this elderly metal chuffed by. The trouble was he was filming them all. We only had a limited amount of film stock and little opportunity to acquire any more. I made this point on the odd occasions when Nick's head was back inside the carriage but he kept telling me that there would never be another chance to film a Dusendorf Belcher and there were always plenty of wars. I prayed for nightfall.

With Nick and Mike I retraced my steps with more nightmare taxi rides across that vast country, down again to Mersin where I had been jailed the previous month. The BBC was keen to see events from the Turkish perspective, as nearly all the coverage so far had been from the Greek Cypriot side.

It took some negotiation, but the Turks eventually agreed to fly us into Cyprus with their reinforcements. We got to the airfield just as their troops were being drawn up. Something about one of the soldiers irritated his officer who simply punched him in the face as he stood there at attention. Discipline in the Turkish Army was fierce. I was pleased all over again that I wasn't still in one of their jails.

We crossed to Cyprus in an American-built Huey helicopter. Nick had just got a terrific shot of a huge Turkish flag on the top of the Kyrenia mountains when we saw a dozen or so puffs of smoke. Mike started to say 'They're shooting at us' but only got as far as 'shoo . . .' when the Huey lurched sideways and started to skid all over the sky. We thought we were going to crash but the pilot was just taking evasive action. There did not seem to be a lot of difference.

It was a great relief to be down safely, particularly when we saw that the strut that holds the tail rotor had five bullet holes in it. The pilot thought it was a great laugh. I smiled as best I could with my teeth chattering.

The fighting had broken out again while we had been on our long journey south. By the time we arrived they were trying to negotiate a new ceasefire in Geneva but, by now, a third of the island was in Turkish hands. We filmed in the mountains just south of Kyrenia, particularly the beautiful village of Bellapaix which had been immortalised by Lawrence Durrell's book *Bitter Lemons* and was now in Turkish hands. Everywhere we saw and filmed the Turkish build-up across the north of the island. Hundreds of marine commando reinforcements had landed at the new military airstrip behind us. It was obvious they were determined to hold on to what they had taken and I said so in a commentary I recorded to go with the pictures we had shot.

The problem, as always, was in getting the report out. It was solved for us when we ran into another BBC crew that had crossed the front line in a UN convoy under truce. They took it back with them, to be airfreighted out to Herzliya in Israel where it was processed, edited and sent by satellite back to London.

We did several other reports from the north and the eastern panhandle where no other journalists had been. We looked for evidence of Turkish atrocities but, in that area at least, found no evidence of them. The first villages we came to as we went east were empty except for the old people who could not run away; widows in black, toothless men with grey stubble, all wary of the invader and burdened by the sadness of being deserted by their families. But they did not seem especially fearful and they made few complaints. Perhaps old people whose world has suddenly been turned upside down retreat from it all to some place inside themselves where others cannot go. Perhaps the Turkish troops were watching too closely.

There had been no escape from Yialousa, the biggest town in the north-east of the island, near the end of the panhandle. The Turks had taken nine young men they suspected of being Greek Eoka B fighters and would not say what had become of them. They had confiscated all the guns and knives in the town. There was no water or electricity and nobody was allowed to leave but Yialousa seemed strangely normal. The small change of daily life carried on and everybody ignored the Turkish military patrols as if they did not exist.

We did stumble across terrible things that happened in the chaos that followed the coup. In one village north of Famagusta a Turkish major was supervising a couple of mechanical shovels. They had uncovered five bodies, two men and a woman apparently clutching two children in her arms. He thought there were 40 more bodies underneath. The village was Turkish and in the general outpouring of communal hatred two Eoka B men had toured the Greek villages nearby looking for recruits to attack their neighbours. One Greek village turned them away. But they got 30 men from one of the others armed with sten guns, shotguns and rifles. They surrounded this Turkish village and took away most of the men and boys who were never seen again. They came back the next day and took away the women who they raped repeatedly for four days before shooting them and burying them in a cornfield next to a clump of trees. This, at any rate, was the story from two old people, a woman and a shepherd, who managed to hide themselves and survive. All the evidence at the time seemed to support what they said. These were whole communities, living almost alongside each other, but hating the other so much as to collude in mass murder, for the Greeks had similar stories of atrocities. Their instinct was to kill and degrade but they and their enemies were ordinary people, living for the most part ordinary lives. Anybody who fondly believes in the essential goodness of human nature should take a trip to some of these places. Cyprus would be a useful start, but there are plenty to choose from.

After the second so-called ceasefire, the most dangerous area was to the west of the Kyrenia mountains, the citrus-growing area round Morphou. The Turks kept pushing forward to straighten their front line and the fighting could, and did, break out at any time and without any notice. Somehow, Nick, Mike and I managed to get trapped in no-man's-land between the two sides when the Turks opened up again and we were forced to take refuge in a UN post near the Turkish-Cypriot enclave of Lefka.

The post itself was idyllic. It was a big wooden building near the beach with a balcony that jutted out towards the sea. The building was a perfect vantage point from which to watch the two sides lobbing shells at each other. They passed almost directly overhead and occasionally fell quite close. It was a beautiful setting but not exactly restful.

The UN men had done their best to bring some of the comforts of home with them. They were Danes and nearly all seemed to have been seconded from the Copenhagen Vice Squad. At any rate, they had a truly extraordinary collection of pornographic books and magazines, piles of them in every corner of the post. There was a set routine when the firing started. Their officers would get on the radio to the two sides to appeal to them, in the name of the UN, to desist. When that did not work they all settled down with a can of Heineken and their own pile of porn to lose themselves in the sexual antics of Scandinavian love goddesses as the shells screamed overhead. They were extremely hospitable and, once we had taken what few pictures we could, we were soon getting through hostilities with a beer and a bonk, albeit a vicarious one. It was extremely effective. I can't say it calmed my nerves entirely, but it took my mind off the possibility of being blown to bits by a wayward Turkish gunner better than anything short of a general anaesthetic.

The UN got us out eventually and I was rather sad to leave the Danes and their seaside porn depot. We went off to film the Greeks retreating up into the glorious Troodos mountains. Fifty thousand of them were packed into the little red-roofed villages with their spectacular views down through the blue haze to the sea, waiting there as the National Guard dug in round Mount Olympus for a last stand.

Later, we got caught in a firefight at the airport in Nicosia. When I threw myself into a makeshift shelter I landed on one of my school-friends, now a captain in the Parachute Regiment seconded to the UN. It was strange having those 'do you remember the time old Swatty Ansell threw the board rubber and knocked out Spud Taylor by mistake' conversations as the bullets whistled overhead and the shells crumped around the airport perimeter.

I was not sad to leave Cyprus. It was a strange country then, part beautiful Mediterranean island with its pomegranates and its plum-coloured mountain roses, part British suburbia surviving in the stifling heat. There was hatred and anger everywhere and it made Aphrodite's island into an ugly place.

I was given two days R and R in Beirut and fell in love with it on the ride in from the airport. I stayed in the St George Hotel on the Corniche in a room panelled so beautifully it was like living in a cigar box, surrounded by luxury and deference. I ate wonderful *mezes* in a rooftop restaurant round the corner, watching the belly dancers performing for off-duty sheikhs or just staring out over the city and the sea cloaked by the velvet night. This, I thought, was where I wanted to live; a beautiful and cosmopolitan city in a peaceful corner of the Levant. My instincts were spot on as usual. Within two years Beirut was torn apart by the Middle East's most devastating civil war. The St George was reduced to a pile of scorched bricks and Lebanon became a byword for danger, death and destruction.

It had been my first risky foreign assignment and was also my first experience of the difficulties of settling back into the normal routines. The boys were nine months old by then and spending all day with them was a delight. But work seemed suddenly flat. The standard London assignments seemed pretty unexciting now, but there were always compensations. Television reporters have very privileged access to places and events. It was fascinating to see behind the scenes in Downing Street or Buckingham Palace or the Arsenal boardroom. It was always interesting to meet the leading figures of the day and see politicians under pressure, trade union leaders manoeuvring, the trappings of wealth in the City and the consequences of poverty in the back streets of Tower Hamlets.

Some of these encounters could prove embarrassing. On the night the French president Georges Pompidou died we brought in the Conservative politician, Edward Heath, to record a brief tribute. Mr Heath had forged a close relationship with M. Pompidou which had been instrumental in securing Britain's entry to the Common Market and he was the ideal person to give a dignified assessment of Pompidou's place in history on the day of his passing. After it had been recorded, we felt we ought to offer him a drink but did not think the BBC Club bar, by that time of night crowded with thirsty stage hands, was the right place to take a man who, after all, had been Prime Minister until a few months before. We decided to take him to the editor's office where there was a cocktail cabinet. It was never locked because Derek Amoore, the editor at the time, rarely stopped drinking.

There was no reply to our knocks and, after some hesitation, we opened the door, ushering Mr Heath in before us. The room appeared to be empty apart from the soles of a pair of Hush Puppies facing us on the big editor's desk. Mr Heath went round one side and we went round the other. Amoore had been drinking with his feet up on the desk and at the point at which even his capacity had been reached, he had slid off the chair and come to rest on the floor, still clutching a cut glass half-full of gin and snoring gently. We attempted to wake him but he did not seem to recognise his staff let alone the former Prime Minister and soon subsided back into a bibulous doze. Mr Heath had a drink and talked for a while across the body of the editor but the conversation was a little strained. He took his leave without any direct reference to what had occurred.

One wet Thursday night in November, 1974, I was getting ready to go home when the newsdesk phones started to ring in the way they always did when something terrible had happened. In any newsroom, tragedy has its own special kind of momentum. The first calls said only that there had been a bomb in the centre of Birmingham but they were coming in fast and getting more serious all the time. I was on the road north within about five minutes.

I don't know exactly how fast we drove the big crew car up the motorway, but as the news got worse the speedometer pushed up until it showed well over 100 miles an hour. We got there in the middle of the chaos that followed the worst terrorist atrocity Britain has ever seen.

The IRA had put bombs into two crowded pubs in the city centre. The Mulberry Bush was at the base of a circular, 20-storey building called the Rotunda, which dominated Birmingham's skyline. The Tavern in the Town was in a basement 150 yards around the corner. We went to the Mulberry Bush first. There was just a big black hole full of wreckage where the pub had been. The bomb was so powerful it blew holes in nine-inch-thick reinforced concrete and brought the roof down, leaving only the steel bars in position. Two bodies were still lying face down in broken masonry and girders. People were staggering around in the street, those that weren't lying in bags on the pavement that is. The explosion killed eight people in the bar and two more who were unlucky enough to be walking past when it went off. Everybody else inside was injured. There were ambulances around, but many of the wounded were being taken away by taxis and private cars. As we arrived a man clutching his arm jumped on to the roof of a passing Vauxhall and was driven away. Another man in a double-breasted blazer covered in blood stood looking at the rubble and crying. The blast had blown the Mulberry Bush sign off

163

the front of the building and the big red letters lay smashed, but still legible, out in the street. That peculiar bomb smell was still in the air; a mix of chemicals and burnt meat.

The Tavern in the Town was even worse. They say there were 200 people crammed in there when the bomb went off, most of them teenagers, sales assistants from the big stores in New Street. The explosion blew a crater in the floor. Eight youngsters were killed outright, two more were to die during the night. The barman lived with his horrific injuries for nearly three weeks before he finally died and took the total death toll to 21.

Three of Birmingham's biggest hospitals were swamped with the wounded. The bombs injured 167 people. That night, I talked to one of the senior consultants who told me the dead were 'unrecognisable'. He had tried to save one of the casualties who had lost both his legs but he had died of shock in Casualty. He told me every person he treated had severe flash burns. He described one of his patients whose face and arm had been 'burnt to a cinder' and, the way he said it, you knew it was not a cliché but the literal truth. He looked as though he had been crying. At another hospital the director of the Accident and Emergency unit told me about a pretty young girl aged, he thought, about 20 who had lost the sight of both eyes, blinded by a shower of molten metal fragments. 'They should never have abolished hanging,' he said.

Another consultant showed me a chair leg that he had taken out of a boy's hip. I asked him if it had been difficult. 'Not really,' he said. 'It's something you can get hold of, isn't it?' He had spent the night digging smaller bits of wood and metal out of young bodies and looked numb with it all.

They let me speak to the more lightly injured, though they were all covered in dried blood and some were heavily bandaged. They talked of the blinding flash and then a bang that 'went on and on'; of being buried under bodies and finding themselves covered with other people's blood. I was crass enough to ask them what had gone through their minds as they lay there. They all said the same: 'God help us all.'

We finally checked in to a hotel at around three in the morning. The bar was still open and my soundman asked for an Irish whiskey, a taste he had acquired during long stints in Belfast. The barmaid tugged the Jameson's bottle off the optic and smashed it on the floor then ran out in tears. It was not a good thing to be an Irishman in Birmingham that night.

The following morning I interviewed the Home Secretary, Roy Jenkins, who appealed to people not to take it out on the large Irish community in the city and said he was preparing emergency legislation. The Prevention of Terrorism Act was passed eight days later.

Trouble had been predicted that day in Birmingham. Feelings had been running high for a week since an IRA man called James McDade had killed himself, trying to plant a bomb at the telephone exchange in Coventry. There was so little left of him he had to be identified by a thumb print. That day there had been a Republican demonstration and some fighting as his body was taken from the morgue to Birmingham airport. It was meant to be flown to Belfast, but the airport workers there refused to handle it and the coffin eventually left on an Aer Lingus flight to Dublin.

As it was in the air, at 8.11 that evening, the *Birmingham Post* received a bomb warning. It was too vague and too late. Ten minutes later the Mulberry Bush exploded; another two minutes and the Tavern in the Town was destroyed.

The police got five of their suspects that night, though no announcement was made for another four days. They were all Irishmen who had been living in Birmingham for many years. They had been spotted by an alert booking clerk at New Street station who had sold them tickets for the train to Heysham. They were detained as they tried to board the Belfast ferry.

All of them claimed they were going to visit relatives, but they were actually on their way to McDade's funeral. When the police searched their luggage they found Mass cards that they had arranged to be signed by sympathisers at the Crossways, an Irish pub in Kingstanding where most were regulars. A Birmingham police team, who had seen the carnage in the pubs that night, were interrogating the five before dawn the next day. The evidence against them piled up and a sixth man, who had seen the others off at New Street, was arrested the following evening. The Birmingham Six were in the bag. They were charged on the Sunday night and all six eventually faced 21 separate counts of murder.

The biggest mass-murder trial in British criminal history opened the following June and I was the BBC reporter assigned to cover it. The defence successfully maintained that it would be impossible for there to be a fair trial in Birmingham, so it was moved 150 miles north to the medieval castle at Lancaster. The strongest security there had been provided by Norman and even Roman architects. The walls of the ancient Shire Hall where the hearings took place were ten feet thick. The castle was guarded round the clock by more than 100 armed police with dogs. I was issued with three different passes and had to go through six checkpoints to get from the street to the press bench. We were all body searched at least twice on our way in.

The six took their places every day in a specially constructed dock. I would like to say I had my doubts about their guilt but I can't remember any. There were certainly aspects to the case that made me uneasy, but it never seriously crossed my mind at the time that they were innocent.

The case against them rested on three legs. The first was their associations with the IRA. Several of them collected money for the dependants of Republican internees in Northern Ireland. They were friends of 'Lieutenant' James McDade who might have been described in court as a drunken layabout but by then had an honoured grave in the IRA martyrs' section of Milltown cemetery. They were even on their way to his funeral and had been hanging around New Street station at exactly the time the bombs were being planted.

The second leg was the forensic tests. These were confusing to the jury and contested by the defence. All of the defendants had been tested in several different ways for handling explosives. Three proved negative throughout. One showed positive traces, but so infinitesimal that no judicial weight could have been put on them. But the prosecution scientific expert said he was '99 per cent' certain the remaining two had been handling explosives.

The trial really hinged on the third element of the prosecution case, the confessions. The defence tried to have them ruled inadmissible on the grounds that they had been beaten out of the six suspects, but the judge allowed them to stand and the six were doomed from that moment.

There was no doubt that they had been severely ill treated. There were photographs of them covered in bruises which were still livid at one of the preliminary hearings I had covered. The question was whether they had been injured by the police as they forced them to confess, or whether it had happened at Winson Green prison after they were remanded. The six said the ill treatment began not long after they were first detained and that their admissions were extorted out of them under physical and psychological duress. The jury was evidently as sceptical about this as the press bench. We sat in the Lancaster pubs after we had filed our stories for the day talking about how much you would have to be tortured before you would admit to so terrible a crime. We probably had insufficient imagination to think what it must have been like to have gone through the treatment they said they received. According to them, they were not just beaten up and tortured with lighted cigarettes, they were deprived of sleep and food, threatened with a gun and a noose and repeatedly told their homes were surrounded by screaming mobs that wanted to kill their wives and children.

Nobody emerges with much credit from all this. No policeman or prison officer was ever convicted. The defence solicitors should have done more to protect them, the doctor who examined them was later accused by a judge of 'producing false evidence to protect his cronies in the prison service'. Even the judicial system itself seemed incapable of grappling with the idea that they might be innocent. Lord Denning, the Master of the Rolls, would later dismiss their appeal on the grounds that: 'if they won, it would mean the police were guilty of perjury; that they were guilty of violence and threats; that the confessions were involuntary and improperly admitted in evidence and that the convictions were erroneous . . . *that is such an appalling vista that every sensible person would say "it cannot be right"* . . .' (my emphasis).

We reporters were just as bad. I remember one afternoon sitting through the medical evidence of what happened to those poor young people in the pubs. Big splinters of wood, and the tubular metal that was fashionable in furniture at the time, were blasted through the soft flesh and brittle bones of all those packed bodies. Several people had to rush from the court with their faces in a handkerchief. The relatives who had stayed sobbed or looked sick. It did not put you in the mood to be finicky about fair treatment towards those who seemed to be responsible. Yet that, in the end, is what justice demands.

We ought to have been a bit more sceptical about the inconsistencies in the case. We did wonder why a group of IRA bombers would be stupid enough to plant their devices and then take a train to a known IRA man's funeral on a day of high tension when the police were bound to be on alert. They did not look very bright, but could they really have been that foolish?

If you looked closely at the confessions they contained little that the police did not already know, or could reasonably infer. They were also wildly contradictory right down to completely different versions of who placed each bomb and how. None of this bothered me much at the time. Besides, it was a much better story if they were guilty. I hope that wasn't the main reason I wanted them convicted, but it might well have been. I spent weeks on a background film to go out at the end of the trial. I was extremely pleased with it. To my mind, it showed, graphically and conclusively, how the worst crime in our legal history was committed and who did it. It included a dramatic reconstruction of the six gathering in the Taurus bar at New Street, transferring the explosives in white plastic bags in the way they described in their confessions (like the court, I ignored the forensic evidence that they had been in suitcases). I had interviewed some of the men's workmates. One of them said they had boasted of planting other bombs; several said the defendants had warned them to stay out of Birmingham that night. Detectives described how they had caught the six and how they were certainly the bombers, though several others who had been part of the conspiracy had escaped to the Irish Republic.

It would have been very inconvenient if they had been acquitted.

They weren't. On the day they were convicted my reports filled up more than half the *Nine O'Clock News*. I sat in an expensive hotel room in Manchester watching it go out over a very expensive room service dinner and a bottle of Champagne and was showered with the con-gratulatory messages that, in the trade, we call 'herograms'. The case had done my career and self-esteem a lot of good.

The Birmingham Six had a rather different evening, in a dark and, for them, deadly dangerous prison at the start of an apparently endless jail sentence. They served sixteen and a half years before the appeal court finally ruled that flawed forensic evidence and doctored police notes meant their convictions were 'unsafe'.

Justice may have, belatedly, been done to the Birmingham Six, but what about the parents of Lynn Bennett, who was only 19 when she was blown apart in the Tavern in the Town? Nobody now is held responsible for killing her, for the worst mass murder in our legal history. The only consolation Lynn's parents had was an offer of £43 from the Criminal Injuries Compensation Board.

THIRTEEN

I DREAMED OF PATROLLING the souks of Arabia for the BBC and I ended up on Shetland. I yearned for hot climates and passionate intrigue but found myself in parts of the Far North that were then being described by shivering Texan oilmen as 'outer space with bad weather'. How it happened was a story of pride and prejudice, of misplaced ambition and bad management. To be honest, it was a ghastly mistake but it turned out all right in the end. Looking back, it may even have been one of the happiest times of my life.

I had tried to get posted to the Middle East. The Cairo correspondent's job fell vacant and I applied for it, even though it came under the aegis of the World Service and it would mean returning to radio. I had always admired the BBC World Service, its high standards and extraordinary international reputation. Besides, I had come to the conclusion that how much you enjoyed working for the corporation was directly proportional to the amount of distance you could put between yourself and whoever was telling you what to do.

I only dimly realised that I was trying to cross one of those cultural chasms that litter the landscape of the BBC. My television colleagues thought the World Service dependable but dull. For a promising young TV reporter to go there was rather like Hamlet opting to play Rosencrantz. The World Service saw it differently, of course. In their view, they were not only the guardians of the BBC's integrity but the bannermen of liberty, freedom and truth around the globe. Television, to them, was an upstart medium, where the facts – if anybody over there bothered about facts – were fatally compromised by the way they were presented. Both sides adopted a *de haut en bas* attitude, on the rare occasions when they had anything to do with each other.

I had never been to Cairo but couldn't see why that should matter. I did not speak a word of Arabic which was slightly more of a problem. I bought a *Teach Yourself Arabic* book on the way to the appointment board at Bush House in the Strand. I was good at bluffing even then and thought I made quite a good fist of sounding falsely modest about my language studies. I talked in an offhand way about how tricky the transitive verbs were (a point I had picked up at the bottom of page two of the book – as far as I had got) and changed the subject as quickly as I could. But the World Service editors knew a chancer when they saw one. They politely peeled back the layers of bluff and pretence to reveal an internationally inexperienced wannabe quivering in all his nakedness. They appointed one of their own without, I imagine, the need for much discussion.

My pride was wounded. It was a long time since I had failed to get a job I wanted and it was especially hurtful that my colleagues thought it was beneath me anyway. While I was slightly off balance the job of television industrial correspondent came up and, in a moment of madness, I applied for it.

In another moment of madness they gave it to me. I found out later that I had unwittingly tapped into some high-level corporate angst and was seen as the only one of the candidates 'who realised what was at stake here'. The BBC had been under pressure over its industrial coverage for years. This mostly consisted of an endless round of strikes and closures, a fair picture at the time of the country's economic decline. But the corporation was under attack from all sides for being too 'negative'. Television News had tried to cover itself by launching a special programme called *Made in Britain* which was meant to laud our manufacturing heroes and went out in some obscure corner of the BBC2 schedule. I had done a couple myself and in both cases the companies concerned had gone bankrupt. One, about how Triumph and Norton were going to capture the world motorcycle market back from the Japanese with a new breed of 'super-bikes', actually went out the very week they went bust. But the pressure kept growing and finally the BBC agreed to appoint a second industrial correspondent to give its television coverage more 'breadth'.

As luck would have it, the appointment board was held not long after I had come back from Aberdeen where I had covered the royal ceremony that marked the arrival ashore of oil from the first major North Sea field. The Queen had thrown a switch inside a marquee at Cruden Bay and the oil flowed from BP's Forties Field far offshore on its way to the company's refinery at Grangemouth. The technology was almost as awe-inspiring as the money involved. There was a lot of smoked salmon and Champagne. We were given a large slice of the *Nine O'Clock News* and had a good time all round. Until, that is, our little charter plane got caught in a storm over the Grampians and we nearly got killed. At the board I made quite a point about the oil and gas developments in the North Sea, bluffing away in fine style. This was Britain's third Industrial Revolution, I said, full of technical marvels, visually stunning, bags of drama and, above all, *positive*. I saw the way they looked at each other but did not realise what a chord I had struck. I got the job and hated it from the start.

It had some advantages. I was the BBC's youngest correspondent, a couple of ranks above a mere reporter in the corporation's Civil Service-style grading system. The salary was a good bit higher and that was important now Christine had given up her job to look after the boys. I got a slightly better car, a Morris Marina rather than an Escort. I moved into my own little cubby-hole and did not have to fight, sometimes literally, for desk space in the reporters' cockpit upstairs. But, God, it was dreary and, worse, I was at polite war with the incumbent industrial correspondent who hated the whole idea and, by extension, me.

Ian Ross was a saturnine and prickly Scotsman who knew his job and did not suffer fools – a category which he felt embraced the entire BBC management – gladly or, indeed, at all. He patrolled the front lines of Britain's industrial battlefields night and day. He knew everybody who mattered on both sides and delivered his judgments with gravelly authority. He was indispensable and he knew it. He was indignant and we knew it. It would not have been so bad if my appointment had not come with a fanfare about a new commitment to positive coverage. He not only read it as a criticism of his efforts but he was also keenly aware that 'positive' stories were often the jollies that made his endless grind bearable. It had also been a mistake to appoint me on the same level as him, rather than as his deputy. He resented the fact that I had, in theory at least, equal status, even though I didn't know a boilermaker from a bandstand. He settled on a strategy of non-cooperation. He made it clear it was nothing personal against me and then proceeded to act as if I did not exist.

This began by being uncomfortable and then became unworkable. The BBC News management were generally pretty spineless and seemed particularly frightened of Ian. They just wrung their hands and sent me on a senior management course. It was held in a spectacular stately home out in Buckinghamshire. I proved brilliant at billiards but hopeless at the management games the corporation's future leaders have to play. A group of us were tasked with producing a strategy for recruiting secretaries. The corporation had no trouble in finding secretaries for the glamorous jobs, the television entertainment department, for example, but the deputy assistant transmitter maintenance administrator in Acton had been without a handmaiden for months. There were three of us, a correspondent, an editor, and a documentary producer (who went on to be a famous playwright) – all simpletons. It took us half an hour to reframe the question and solve the problem. The first thing to do, we decided, was work out who really needed a secretary. About one in ten of those who had them, we decided. The problem then was the salaries, which were well below the market rate, certainly in London. Simple, pay them more out of the money saved from getting rid of the 90 per cent we did not need. We went back to the billiards, thinking this management business was a doddle. None of us got a step further up the BBC ladder. We had missed the real secret, which is to waste a lot of time and make it look complicated.

That was certainly what they were doing when I got back. It was clear they were not going to tackle Ian and I started looking for another job. It was coincidence, or fate, but a few weeks later I was headhunted by Alastair Hetherington, the former Editor of the *Guardian* who had just been appointed Controller of BBC Scotland. The corporation had wanted to have a politically savvy heavyweight in charge up there at a time when there was a lot of talk of Nationalism and even Independence. Alastair must have seemed ideal. He was, after all, a brilliant broadsheet editor, a Scot who had made a mark in London and not stayed, mewed up and resentful, on his own tartan turf. It turned out to be a disaster. The problem was not that he knew little about broadcasting – lots of senior BBC people haven't a clue either – but that he had no instinct for survival in the treacherous cross-currents of the corporation's politics. He was clever, but fatally naïve as it turned out.

He told me that one of his conditions for taking the job was that there should be a specialist energy correspondent, based in Scotland, to cover the vast industry being built offshore. It was a hybrid job; the main responsibility would be to the network news in London, but I would also do longer programmes for the BBC in Scotland. I didn't like the idea of moving to Glasgow (too rough) or Aberdeen (too far away) but he said I could base myself in Edinburgh which sounded OK. I talked it over with Christine and we jumped at it.

I am not suggesting it was anything to do with me, but it is curious how that couple of years in the late seventies was the only time the great North Sea oil adventure really impinged on the public consciousness. It was the biggest industrial enterprise since the explosion of the railways, more than a century before. Whole towns were built on stilts in some of the most inhospitable waters in the world. Some of the platforms were higher than the Post Office tower. They were serviced by swarms of helicopters and fleets of supply vessels. They had generators each of which could light a whole city. It all cost maybe £100 billion and earned the country double that amount. It cost scores of lives, too, on platforms that buckled and burned, and hundreds of feet below the surface where dozens of heroic divers died lonely deaths.

Yet there are hardly any popular books about North Sea oil. Few of the politicians rescued by its revenues even mention it in their memoirs. There are no toy rigs, no social studies, no celebration of the roustabout as the infantryman of progress, as his predecessor, the navvy, was glorified in the 1840s.

The oilfields were miracles of human ingenuity. The concentration of financial and technical resources was unmatched outside a world war. It arguably saved the country from economic collapse. More arguably, it gave Margaret Thatcher the elbow room for her particular revolution. It changed our prospects, if not our lives, and most of the time we simply ignore it, out of sight and over the horizon.

I got to Scotland just as the main phase of development was getting under way. Oil had only been discovered six years before. The drilling-rig *Sea Quest* had been looking for gas, 150 miles east of Aberdeen, hoping to find something similar to the gas fields already being developed off East Anglia. The oil was such a surprise the geologists did not have a proper container to put a sample in. They used an old pickle jar. Then they poured some into an ashtray and set it alight. The ash tray shattered and the burning oil spilled all over the floor. It was a small beginning and an ambiguous metaphor for what was to come.

Successive governments leased 'blocks' of sea, each 100 square miles, to the oil companies who then played what amounted to a giant game of 'battleships' at £2 million a throw. What they were looking for would be 9,000 feet below the seabed, four times further down than the deepest coal mine.

I used to fly out to drilling rigs whenever they would have me. The red, white and blue Sikorski helicopters buzzed in and out of Dyce airport near Aberdeen and Sumburgh on Shetland like flies landing on a carcass. You lined up well before dawn with a group of scruffy, hard-looking men in quilted jackets, carrying duffel bags. You all had to get dressed up in an orange survival suit which was surprisingly stiff and heavy; most of us kept it unzipped as much as possible to avoid suffocation. They told you it was worth the discomfort; if the plane had to ditch it might keep you

173

alive for all of ten minutes in the freezing water. The noise inside the helicopter was shattering and the weather was normally bad so it often bucked and roared through a series of storms. Even the most experienced oilmen hated it but there was no other way.

It was always a wonderful moment to drop below the cloudbase and see the big semi-submersible tethered by half a dozen fifteen-ton anchors at some fixed point over the great grey waste of sea. There was a real sense of drama about the drilling process. You would stand in the shrieking wind looking down into the 'moon pool' below the latticework derrick, 50 feet or so above the boiling waters. You could see the whirling rotary table that controlled the drill bit cutting into the rock thousands of feet below; the gushing mud that lubricated it all; the hard physical labour of the men with their strange hierarchies, the toolpushers, roughnecks and roustabouts grappling with each 90-foot section of pipe and wrestling it into place. They, too, would be covered in the greasy, pungent mud and would look like prehistoric warriors. It seemed primitive and almost unimaginably technical at the same time. Behind it all there was the sense of fortunes being gambled on these floating steel islands. The prize was truly enormous wealth, but the wild card was the weather that might end the game at any time.

Onshore, a vast industry had to be invented almost from scratch to build the giant structures that were needed to exploit the new oilfields. There was a lot of controversy about whether Britain was getting a fair share of the work that was going. As I started the job a Church of Scotland minister in Aberdeen was complaining that 'the only things we are supplying oilmen with are whisky and whores'. The sudden demand for complex projects certainly shone a cruel light on Britain's declining manufacturing capacity. It exposed its failures of enterprise and management, its skills shortages and edgy industrial relations. The oil industry was dominated by American companies who liked dealing with other American companies and that did not help either. Even after government intervention the true British involvement in supplying our native oil industry barely rose above 50 per cent. Mind you, our stranglehold on whisky and whores was never seriously challenged.

The big platforms which formed the centrepiece of nearly every field *had* to be built close to where they were going to be used because they were so vast and unwieldy. The concrete platforms were amongst the world's most extraordinary sights. The one they constructed for the Ninian field at Loch Kishorn, an inlet of the Minch under Applecross, was said to be the biggest movable object on earth. We went to see it when it was hauled out of its dry dock into the Sound of Raasay, and again when they capped it with its great deck. In all, it weighed over 600,000 tons, almost ten times the weight of St Paul's Cathedral. It stood more than 700 feet high and was topped off by a deck larger than a football pitch. To travel north in a helicopter and find it in the fjordland of West Scotland, looking for all the world like a giant mushroom sticking out of mounds of spinach, was a magical moment. I hung out of the aircraft just over my cameraman as we swooped around it, trying to grasp just how enormous it was and what a feat of organisation and engineering it had been to build it in a place where there had only been a shooting lodge and a handful of crofts.

We followed the platform as far as we could on its 850-mile journey around the North of Scotland and the tip of the Shetlands. It took seven tugs and 80,000 horsepower to move it. The biggest problem was right at the start, in the Minch. It drew 252 feet and had only 18 feet clearance over the sandbanks. It was finally dropped, pinpoint perfect, on its spot east of the Shetlands, kept in place by its own vast weight and five miles of chains and anchors. I thought there was drama, even romance, in the story of Ninian Central and I think, for a short while, we managed to capture the public's imagination with it. Kishorn never built another platform. The place where half a million tons of concrete had arrived by train and barge to be fashioned by 800 men into one of the engineering feats of the age was soon as derelict an industrial monument as was ever seen on Clydeside.

I spent a lot of time with the politics of North Sea oil, the arm-wrestling between government and the oil companies over who was going to get what from the spoils. The companies had the upper hand from the start. Their strategy was to minimise the potential and maximise the difficulties, suggesting all the while that if taxation and regulation were too onerous they wouldn't bother. By the mid-seventies, though, it was clear there was a lot of oil there and the quadrupling of prices by the Arab countries after the 1973 Middle East War had made Britain's reserves economically and strategically very valuable. As Armand Hammer, the boss of Occidental Petroleum, put it: 'The British government treated the potential bonanza as carelessly and complacently as any untutored sheikh and, in those early days, practically threw it into the hands of the Seven Sisters (the oil majors).'

The Labour government wanted more, and the negotiations between the Energy Department and the companies seemed to have had something of the flavour of a Western saloon about them. The Energy Secretary at the time was Tony Benn whose chief spin doctor was Bernard Ingham, who went on to be equally effective and belligerent in the service of Margaret Thatcher. I used to fly down from Scotland and haunt the corridors of the Department of Energy and the headquarters of the oil companies. The backstairs lobbying was intense. It was all fascinating for a while. I could see how politicians and, for that matter, political correspondents get their kicks. There are few things more seductive than having the inside track on some high-level manoeuvrings, or thinking you have anyway. It was all a matter of quiet briefings in out-of-the-way restaurants, a whisper here, a phone call there. The government won the public relations battle hands down. The oil companies were endlessly keen to buy you an expensive lunch and talk off the record but would rarely put anybody in front of a camera to argue their case and so, on television at least, they were at a considerable disadvantage. Whether they lost the real tussle is more open to question. The government's initial objective was for the state to own 51 per cent of the oil, but that ended up as the right to buy 51 per cent of the oil at the prevailing market price which, to say the least, was not quite the same thing. A British National Oil Corporation was set up to buy and sell this crude and to take a major part in North Sea developments, but that was abolished by Margaret Thatcher within a decade.

Plans to put all the oil money into a separate account and treat it as a windfall to be spent on special projects, like improving the country's transport system, were dropped. It was subsumed into general state expenditure, cushioning Britain's relative economic decline. History might say we blew it but that is for historians, not reporters.

North Sea oil was often a simpler story of life and death and I was forever racing off to Dyce airport because a helicopter had come down, a supply boat was lost, or one of the platforms was under some sort of threat. The danger of getting killed on one of Britain's offshore rigs at the time was 11 times higher than on a building site, and nine times greater than down a coal mine.

The divers had the riskiest job; at times they were dying at the rate of one a week. Divers were always needed to install pipeline junctions, maintain the control networks and look out for corrosion. In little more than a decade they had gone from working for an hour at a time, at no more than 50 feet, to spending four weeks in 'saturation' working long shifts at depths of around 450 feet. They spent all that time under compression and breathing a mixture of helium and oxygen. They commuted from a pressurised chamber on the surface to the diving bell that took them to their workplace in the black depths under the platforms. Anything could, and did, go wrong and it was usually fatal. Propellors could slash lifelines, they could get trapped in metal tangles on the seabed, the compression system could be faulty. They were vulnerable all the time, even when the job had been done. It took four days for them to decompress properly; anything more rapid and they developed nitrogen necrosis or 'the bends'. A human error on the diving support ship *Byford Dolphin* led to five divers dying in agony in front of a crew who could see and hear what was going on, but do nothing to save them.

I made a television documentary about North Sea divers and, at the end of a moving interview with the widow of one of the first to be killed, noticed she still kept his ashes in a casket above the fireplace. I thought it might make an excellent opening sequence for the programme if she scattered the ashes out on the North Sea. She considered it for a while and then agreed. A fortnight or so later we set off in a small charter boat with my television crew and the diver's wife and two daughters, all dressed in black and looking strikingly like those advertisements for the Scottish Widows insurance company. The budget would not cover more than a couple of hours' boat hire but it was sufficient for our purposes to be just far enough out for the land not to be in shot. The family were already looking pale, though it wasn't clear if it was the motion of the boat, or the emotion of the occasion. Either way, I felt it best to get it over with quickly. Unfortunately, neither I nor the widow had taken much account of which way the wind was blowing. When she flung the ashes over the side, with the most dramatic of gestures, they slapped back across my face and, worse, the camera. By great good fortune, the family were all weeping. Their eyes were either firmly closed or filled with tears and they did not see me picking their beloved husband and father out of my teeth, nor my cameraman blowing him off the lens. They thanked me at the end of the day, which made me feel worse. They said it had helped them come to terms with his death and move on. It was some time before I got over him myself. I kept finding ashes in my ears and hair and clothes and it was the devil's own job editing around his impromptu last appearance.

I did quite a bit of exotic travelling with the energy job. I went to the heat of the Middle East and the humidity of Lake Maracaibo in Venezuela where a thousand 'nodding donkeys' peck for oil in the shallow waters. I spent a lot of time in cold Norwegian winters and had two long trips to the 30-below-zero Arctic wastes of Prudhoe Bay in Northern Alaska where the oil companies had built small cities under bubbles, like space stations on the moon. We could only film for a few minutes at a time before the oil froze in the camera and the umbilical cord to the sound recordist snapped like a stick.

During one of these American tours I went down to Houston in Texas to interview the legendary oilfield firefighter 'Red' Adair. He was more than hospitable. As soon as I checked into the Hyatt Hotel, I got a phone call from a sultry southern belle called Francine down in the lobby. 'Red said you might need a little comfort and company tonight, honey,' she said. Say what you like, it was a friendly gesture but it frightened me to death. I locked my door and did not come out until breakfast next day.

When I met him, Red turned out to be a portly little old guy with his hair cemented into the John Wayne style of a fifties cowboy. John Wayne had actually played him in a Hollywood film called *The Hellfighters*. He gave me a Zippo lighter with his name on it as a keepsake, and a warning about the North Sea. 'There'll be a disaster, sooner or later,' he told me. He said by the time trained personnel got there it would be out of control. 'Hardware to deal with a disaster?' he said. 'At the moment, for a real blowout, you don't have anything.' I took it as a shrewd piece of corporate advertising and wondered if he was a bit past it. Three weeks after the interview was broadcast it happened, and he wasn't.

I was in London when drillers on the Ekofisk Bravo platform, just inside the Norwegian sector of the North Sea, managed to put the blowout preventer on upside down. It's a bit like the cap on a pressure cooker. Without it, the riser pipe blew out and spilled a torrent of oil and mud into the sea. By a miracle, it did not ignite, and the crew got away safely. But the industry's response was shambolic. None of the safety craft based in the North Sea was able to stop the oil gushing out at a rate of 3,000 tons a day. The operators, Phillips Petroleum, made a total mess of handling it, and handling the media, too. With all the other reporters, I was trying to cover what was happening from Stavanger airport in Norway. The company told us nothing, but sent a series of timid press officers to face an increasingly angry and unruly crowd of the world's press with nothing to say.

The BBC had an outside broadcast unit there and I did a series of live reports in which I tried to explain the purpose of a blow-out preventer by inventive use of my hands. I was pleased with myself for the simple and graphic way I was explaining a complex technical issue. The foreign desk, when they managed to stop laughing, said it was the first time they had seen a reporter wanking on air. It was all very unsatisfactory.

Phillips had said they could cope without Red Adair but eventually had to call him in. It took him a week to cap the well. By then 22,500 tons of oil were covering over 900 square miles of sea. The oil industry's reputation for technical omnipotence, and even competence, had been blown out along with the Ekofisk riser.

It was an interesting job, but the best thing about it was being able to spend time with my family. Top television reporters have little control over their lives. Their work pattern is unpredictable by definition. A select few never seem to stop travelling and never seem to stop working. You can do it for a while, but you eventually get burnt out, generally a few years after your second marriage has collapsed. I was on the fringes of that group when that chapter of accidents shunted me on to the sidelines. Because I knew more about my speciality than anybody else at the BBC, and because I worked for several different parts of the corporation, I was generally left to organise my own life. I got home most evenings and most weekends. We could do things as a family in a way we would never have been able to do if we had been in London. I saw my children growing up and enjoyed them more than I would have enjoyed skating around the top international stories and not seeing them. It took a little while for this to dawn on me, but I began to realise it was a golden time. You can recover a career, but you can't recapture your sons' childhood.

Besides, we loved Scotland. Everything looked similar, but was really so different. The pubs sold 'heavy' and '50 shilling' instead of mild and bitter. You could get deep-fried haggis and even, it was said, fried Mars Bars in the local fish and chip shop. Scots were serious about only two things – footba' and bringing on early heart failure. Pushing my tray along the counter of the BBC Glasgow canteen, I said, 'No French fries, thank you', probably a touch primly, to the purple-faced wifey who was serving. 'Chups is compulsory,' she said, and buried my plate in them.

When we looked for a house we found there were no estate agents. Instead, we went along to a shop set up by Edinburgh's lawyers, known, exotically, as 'writers to the signet'. All the properties available were listed by district and price, with the bare details and none of the ungrammatical and misleading hyperbole you get down South. The price listed was the minimum the seller would accept, rather than the most they thought they might get away with. The process was simple and swift. You went round the house at a set time. If you wanted it, you arranged your finances and put in a sealed offer by midday on the closing date. Generally, the highest bid was accepted and it was then binding on both parties. The knack was judging just how much you had to offer to beat everybody else. We managed it at the sixth attempt and moved into a big Victorian stone cottage on the links at Musselburgh, backing towards the Firth of Forth. The links were the original home of the Honourable Edinburgh Company of Golfers, now more comfortably installed at Muirfield down the coast. These days it's all a municipal open space, with a few greens for keen but impoverished golfers and a rudimentary racecourse. Most of the time it was really a giant playground for my kids and their friends. The occasional race meetings, and particularly the trotting races, just made it more exciting. Twice a year the circus would come along and the boys would follow the elephants up our little road willing them to crap outside somebody else's house.

We had a wonderful family time. Winter and summer we were always down on the golden East Lothian beaches, which began only a couple of miles from our house. When it snowed we would take our toboggan out on the Braid Hills. We explored down in the borders and up into the Highlands, staying in cabins by the side of lochs and once, memorably, shoving the boys in their pushchair up the Knock of Crief.

The public services were better in Scotland. Simon and Roland went to a playgroup at three and a local primary school at four that had not been influenced by then fashionable educational theories. Pinkie St Peters had no frills. It served a working-class town and most of its pupils came from the 'scheme' rather than private houses. But the teachers were respected and they knew how to get children to read and write and do their sums. Our boys walked to school and slipped effortlessly from Received Pronunciation to broadest Musselburgh as the lollipop lady helped them across the busy A1.

Edinburgh was a magnificent place, large enough to have all the theatres, restaurants and museums you could wish for, but small enough for you to have friends on the other side of the city and still be able to see them regularly. We had lots of friends, some really close that we have kept to this day. My office was in Queen Street, in the New Town. I remember thinking what a privilege it was to work in the middle of the most complete example of Georgian town planning in the world; to be able to walk around the corner and see the castle standing on its great volcanic plug, and the medieval town stretching down to Holyrood Palace.

We liked the Scots. There was a sense of social cohesion about the place and a generally sturdy attitude to life, its duties and its pleasures. That's what made their endless chippiness about the English even more odd. There is a strange disjunction between the attitudes of the English and the Scots to each other. The English, in the main, feel affection and not a little admiration for the Scots. Most Scots' accents are accorded automatic respect, particularly when uttered by teachers or doctors. To a generation brought up on *Dr Finlay's Casebook* it is the voice of wisdom, of authority and a special kind of stern rectitude. When a Scot hears an English accent he thinks only of a spineless, inbred toff who is out to swindle him. There may be deep historical reasons for this but it is a long time since we English handed our throne to a Scots king who came south with most of his belongings and all of his money in a box. Since then Scots have taken over most of our institutions, including, from time to time, the government and the BBC. The average Scottish family has a quarter of its members living south of the border and yet there is an institutional racism, that was evident in the seventies and, in my experience, is worse now. It rarely seems to be personal. It always seems possible for you, the individual, to be exempt from the generalised anti-English critique. But it is pervasive and rather childish all the same.

BBC Scotland was the same, only worse. There the chip dwarfed the shoulder and BBC Glasgow looked south to London with a kind of thunderous sulk. It was not helped by the extraordinary success of those Scots who had made it in London and seemed to be running most of the programme departments, and occupying most of the key posts up to and including the Director-General. This appeared to make those who chose to stay behind feel like failures, in many cases an accurate analysis. This resulted in what amounted to a conspiracy to sabotage anything to do with London. The Scottish news department would do its best not to tell network news in London about anything that was happening. If, by chance, London did get to hear of some story north of the border, every effort was made to ensure that the coverage did not reach them, certainly before it had been seen on the Scottish programme, often not at all.

Shortly before I had joined Television News there had been a disaster at the Rangers football stadium, Ibrox Park. More than 60 of the club's fans had been crushed to death on stairway 13. Worried that they would get very little from BBC Scotland on what by any standards was an international tragedy, network news sent my predecessor, Michael Clayton, up to Glasgow. As soon as he set foot in the BBC Scotland newsroom, apparently, he was ordered out and, when he hesitated, was frogmarched to the front door by the commissionaires. The network news had to cobble together whatever pictures they could find and Michael had to do his commentary from a telephone kiosk in Queen Margaret Drive. In true BBC style, no action was taken about this. The incident was regarded as 'unfortunate' and the relationship 'sensitive'.

It took a new Scots Editor of Television News, Andrew Todd, to do something about it. He called me down to London and bought me a large and expensive lunch in Odin's restaurant, round the corner from Broadcasting House. We talked for some time about the fate of Alastair Hetherington which was the talk of the BBC at the time. He had been squeezed out in a messy and ruthless way which would have made him into a Scots martyr if it hadn't been done by a Scots Director General, Alasdair Milne, who wore a kilt on all reasonable occasions and played the bagpipes on many unreasonable ones.

Andrew was old-style BBC. He was not a particularly talented editor, but he was regarded as a safe pair of hands and was surefooted as a cat around the corporation's treacherous corridors. His take on Alastair Hetherington's short and bewildered BBC career was a master class in BBC politics. I did not have time to dwell on the irony of one rather average editor passing cruel, if shrewd, judgment on another who was very much his intellectual and journalistic superior. Andrew Todd was worried about BBC Scotland. He was concerned about the growth of Nationalism and the increasing demands for devolution and self-rule. The network news had to take Scotland seriously and if BBC Scotland could not, or would not, cover what was going on for the network, the only answer was to appoint what would effectively be a foreign correspondent for Scotland. I was already there. I got on reasonably well with them. I was at least half accepted by the Glasgow newsroom. Would I do it? Och, aye, I said. Andrew didn't laugh. He was the stern type. Besides, he had the kind of sculpted white moustache that made laughing difficult.

I had my own crew and spent a very enjoyable couple of years going all over Scotland doing stories for the *Nine O'Clock News*. A lot of it was the usual news-bulletin fare: train crashes in Dundee, strikes at Ravenscraig steel works, prison riots at Peterhead (a jail that made hanging look like a soft option), the inevitable violence at 'old firm' matches between Celtic and Rangers. I charted the slow decline of the once mighty Scottish fishing fleets, the lobstermen up against cheap Canadian imports, the mackerel men of Ullapool who were refusing to fish on a Sunday, the great Scottish scampi glut – I brought three boxes home from that one and have never been able to look one in the eye since.

Best of all was the chance to go to the further corners of that beautiful country. I loved working in the Highlands, out of Aberdeen where the BBC was run by a spry veteran newsman called Arthur Binnie, who had become a good friend. I trekked for miles carrying a camera tripod across the Isle of Harris to Britain's most remote community, Rhenigidale. The crofters were about to have a road that would link them up to the outside world and were touchingly excited and yet worried about it all. The older ones thought they would be losing more than they gained, an argument I can appreciate more now than I did then. I went to schools in the Highlands where there was only one teacher and one pupil. I got to Gruinard, the island that was used for Anthrax experiments in the war and was only visited once every twenty years. I landed in small planes on white Hebridean beaches. I drank the manager's special whisky in the loft of the Laphroaig distillery on Islay. It looked and tasted to me like a solution of chain-smoker's lung, incidentally, but the setting was out of this world.

I learned to hate seals.

It was a story that gripped the nation for a week or two. Seals breed on the remoter Orkney Islands before setting out into the North Sea to hoover up the fish and get up the noses of Scottish fishermen. According to them, the number of seals was spiralling out of control and they must be culled. They won the argument but, inevitably, lost the battle for public opinion.

The emotional context for the seal fanciers was the dramatic pictures of baby seals being clubbed to death in Canada that had only recently been shown on the front pages of most British newspapers. To be fair, the Orkney seal cull was not going to be done by battering the pups into pulp with the nearest blunt instrument. They had hired a team of Norwegian marksmen to pick them off from a safe distance.

They had reckoned without the soft hearts of the British public, the networks who could see how the mass murder of cuddly animals would make wonderful television, and Greenpeace whose stock in trade is their ability to manipulate public concern without being overly worried about the subtleties of the argument. They sent their converted trawler, the

Rainbow Warrior, to the islands to track the seal cullers' boat and get in the way of the executioners.

I was fairly neutral on the issue. I hate cats, but am mildly fond of dogs and, if I thought about seals at all, would have put them somewhere halfway between the two in the scale of my affections. The argument for controlling seal numbers was a powerful one, but hinged on how fast the population was growing and how much impact they were having on fragile fish stocks. Though most scientists seemed to say that was a lot, in both cases, there was a rump of expert opinion, as there often is, that took the opposite view. I was more worried about ITN. Their reporter, Sue Lloyd Roberts, now a BBC colleague, had charmed her way on to the *Rainbow Warrior* and was busy wrapping Greenpeace round her little finger. I had to hire a lobster boat and the three ships spent the next fortnight playing tag around the Orkney Islands in winds that got up to gale force.

Sue had a grandstand view of any confrontations between the main protagonists, but I was not at as much of a disadvantage as I had feared. For a start my boat went where I wanted it to go, whereas Sue was stuck with going where Greenpeace wanted. My lobster fisherman knew the Orkneys, and where the seals actually were, much better than either of the other two skippers so we got lots of winning pictures of the snow-white babies all unaware the hunters' guns were closing in. It was while supervising the filming of a particularly touching little fellow on a clump of offshore rocks in a howling wind that I turned against them.

Baby seals look particularly attractive and, more to the point, vulnerable if you can get them to tilt their heads back and look directly up at you. When the cameraman was ready I stepped up to it, just out of shot, and tried to attract its attention by talking to it as you would a pet Labrador. Without a moment's hesitation, it sank its filthy teeth deep into my shin. It was agony. Swearing at the top of my voice I aimed a ferocious kick at its head, missed entirely, lost my balance and toppled backwards into the freezing sea. I nearly died waiting for the crew to stop laughing and pull me out.

The seal hunters were heroes as far as I was concerned from then on. Whenever they got near to a colony, I was willing them to get the machine gun out and not mess about with mere rifles. But the world has become a spineless place. Public opinion, ignorant of the vicious nature of baby seals, could not bear to see them killed and the Norwegians were eventually called off.

A couple of months later I did what amounted to an ironic postscript to the seal cull story. The Americans, who I'd always thought had a sensible attitude to animals (i.e. they eat them in vast numbers), had an attack of sentimental insanity about seals and banned the import of products made out of sealskin. This had a particular impact on Scotland, whose major industries might have been crumbling away, but who were still world leaders in manufacturing one product – the sporran. Unfortunately, sporrans are made from the skins of seals and America was the biggest market; the Scottish sporran industry was facing the greatest crisis in its history.

I interviewed anxious sporran makers all over the country, and just when I thought this would be yet another report on the demise of another proud bastion of British manufacturing, a big wheel in sporrans came up with a solution: artificial fibre. It was very neat. The sporran was saved because it would now be made, ultimately, out of North Sea oil. The industry would survive because it had found a moral sporran.

The important story was the rise of Scottish Nationalism in the seventies, fuelled by the Scottish National Party's skilful use of the slogan 'It's Scotland's oil'. In the 1974 election the SNP got 30 per cent of the vote and seemed to be threatening Labour's hegemony in Scotland with far-reaching constitutional and economic consequences for Britain as a whole. By 1977 polls showed the SNP with 36 per cent support, but it proved to be a peak from which it went into a nose-dive. The government was pushing forward its ideas for a devolved assembly for Scotland, a half-way house to independence that split the nationalists. When it was put to a referendum in March, 1979, everything had come unravelled. The weather was cruel, Scotland had been smashed in the World Cup, the unions had had their winter of discontent. There was a bare majority for devolution, 33 per cent of eligible voters said 'yes' against 31 per cent 'no', but the Scotland Act required 40 per cent of the total electorate to vote for it so it all collapsed.

The SNP brought the Callaghan government down and, in the ensuing general election, were almost wiped out. They lost 9 of their 11 seats and their share of the vote fell from 30 per cent to 18. Callaghan himself said the SNP were like 'turkeys voting for Christmas'. Scotland had ushered in Mrs Thatcher.

FOURTEEN

FROM THE FAMILY point of view, Christine and I would have cheerfully stayed in Scotland for ever. It was a good place to live, we had great friends and I had more control over how, when and where I worked than most television reporters. The boys were happy and we thought we could just about afford to send them to one of the fine Merchant Company schools in Edinburgh when they were a bit older. They might have ended up part of the Scotocracy and I might have learned to play golf, the short-cut to acceptance in those parts. It would not have been a bad life.

I was only dimly aware of the seismic shifts at BBC News in London that cut across our plans. There were changes at the top and a couple of the senior executives with whom I was only on guarded terms were replaced by people who thought I was pretty good. The BBC can be rather like the Chinese Communist Party at times. Outsiders, and most of the insiders for that matter, can only really work out what's going on by seeing who is in favour and who has slipped down the pecking order. My star was, apparently, in the ascendant.

Part of the reason for this was that a lot of the old dinosaur reporters had gone bellowing off to some different swamp, or in one case, into prison. Martin Bell had been posted to Washington, Keith Graves was off to the Middle East. There was a shortage of experienced television reporters and I had a stream of phone calls saying I was needed back in London. I might have been reluctant if it just meant going back to a reporter's job, but they offered me what amounted to the top international fireman's slot and the title of 'special correspondent' which, of course, impressed me no end. I did think of renewing my passport so that I could put that as my occupation, but left it as 'representative' in the end, which proved a wise decision. In the places I would be going it was often best to be ambiguous about who I was and what I was up to.

The special correspondent's post had a short and troubled history. It was created for Martin Bell. Although he was, by some distance, the most brilliant BBC television journalist of the day he was still, by his own choice, a general reporter and so hierarchically inferior to the most junior specialist correspondent. Making him, effectively, a correspondent with-out portfolio corrected this absurdity and when he left for Washington they kept the post open and eventually used it to lure me down from

186

Edinburgh. I had just enough of the James Bond fantasist left in me to see this as being promoted to 'double O' status, though it was actually not a licence to kill, more a licence to be killed, as it turned out.

The job had already created a lot of envy and jealousy. After Martin left one of the other senior reporters contrived to get himself appointed special correspondent by threats that rumour at the time said included suicide and mass murder.

Michael Sullivan was kind and funny but, at the time, cracked. He was tall and prematurely white-haired and probably the most naturally talented journalist I have ever come across. He was entirely capable of delivering an impromptu comic monologue, writing an elegant television script and finishing off a bitingly funny cartoon, all at the same time. It was all done without effort or even, it seemed, a great deal of conscious thought, which was just as well. He needed all his concentration for his feuds. His domestic life was going through considerable turmoil which had left him slightly unhinged. He was pretty well homeless at the time and lived in a storeroom next to the basement garage of Television Centre, where he was constructing aeroplanes. He would emerge from time to time to inveigh against the injustices of life in general, or the iniquities of his enemies in particular. It was easy to fall into the latter category. Though the most decent and considerate of men normally, when Mike got what he called the 'red mist' one wrong word put you on the receiving end of the wildest, wittiest and most belligerent man in London.

Poor Nicholas Witchell came in for it for no better reason than that he was short and had red hair. Nick was an exceptionally able young reporter at the time, whose only fault was that he, perhaps, took himself a bit too seriously. Too seriously, in Sullivan's view, for someone of his age, stature and hair colour anyway. He constructed what, in the end, became one of the longest epic poems in the English language, entitled 'Ode to a Carrot', each verse of which took poor Nick to task for some presumed ambition or pretension, each one exploded by the inevitable refrain: 'But his feet don't touch the ground'. Nick took it all with his characteristic dignity though, as he told me once, there was really no choice. Even being ridiculed as a prick was better than looking as if you couldn't take a joke.

From his cubby hole, down in the basement, Mike ran a one-man dissident campaign against the BBC establishment and its favourites. His main weapon was the cartoon. They were beautifully drawn and our bosses and their henchmen were caricatured to within an inch of their lives. Every physical peculiarity and character trait was mercilessly ridiculed in cartoons that appeared on every Television Centre notice-board in the middle of the night. They tried to buy him off by offering money for the cartoons 'as a souvenir'. They sent security men round in secret to tear them down, but Sully had a photocopier down in his lair and all night to pin them back up again. The management was at a loss, a characteristic position. They did nothing, an equally characteristic response.

When the special correspondent's job came up they had their revenge. Mike was the most senior, and most able, reporter there even if he was temporarily half bananas. He certainly felt he was the right, inevitable, indeed only, choice and when the appointment board looked like turning him down the red mist fell with a vengeance.

The story was that he made it known to the editor of the time that he was a qualified pilot with access to a 'plane, and nothing to lose. He knew exactly where the editor's office was – he had been carpeted there, often enough – and he was capable of piloting the 'plane through the window with pinpoint accuracy.

Sully said the story was made up by the more malignant of his enemies. He agreed – indeed, it was widely acknowledged – that he had got the job by threatening dire consequences for those who withheld it from him. He said that, by being less specific, he made it all more menacing. His threats certainly threw the management into a panic. The editor then was a skinny little man with, despite his preoccupation with guns and the military, no great reputation for personal courage. Perhaps he felt an injustice really had been done. Either way, the appointment board was instructed to appoint Sully special correspondent the following day, on the editor's personal authority, and he retired to his underground work-shop mollified, at least for the time being.

Sully was not often to be seen when I arrived back at Television Centre; his aircraft were reaching a critical stage in their construction. The editor had moved on, too – a promotion and an office whose windows faced safely into the central courtyard, though that might, of course, have been a complete coincidence.

First stop as a special correspondent was Paris to cover the presidential and parliamentary elections that brought the Socialists into power. The French make a meal of their elections, like they make a meal of their meals. The whole thing went on for three months and was a total delight. My schoolboy French did not improve quite as much as my ability to bluff my way through without it. I became a leading authority on at least three different kinds of asparagus and can tell the difference between a *belon* and a *fine claire* with my eyes shut and, if need be, a peg on my nose. It's all texture with oysters, you see.

The BBC Paris correspondent's job was, by tradition, a radio appointment. The incumbent then was, thankfully, not interested in doing television and, in any case, a lifetime at lunch had left him with the sort of bomb-damaged face and livid complexion that would have required the BBC to put out one of those warnings that 'what you are about see might upset you'. He spent much of the day in the Restaurant du Beaujolais round the corner from the office with a giant napkin spreading down from his scarlet jowls, in lumbering pursuit of some gastronomic nirvana. Mind you, so did I, when I could.

The BBC had sent out John Sergeant, who was then a radio reporter, to ensure that the strain on the Paris correspondent should not be too intolerable. He carried a copy of *Le Monde* with him wherever he went and generally made a better fist of pretending to speak French than I did. I had bumped into him on other assignments but had never realised how funny he was. He was a droll dinner companion, frequently making me laugh so much I very nearly threw up. It could be a real problem, especially with oysters.

The BBC office in Paris is splendidly situated in the fashionable Faubourg St Honoré, just up the road from the British Embassy which was originally commandeered by the Duke of Wellington, along with several of the Emperor's mistresses, at the end of the Napoleonic Wars. The BBC had a floor in a block mostly occupied by the kind of exclusive tarts the French call *poules de luxe*. The lift stank of Chanel and one's fellow passengers were never less than eye-catching.

Despite its Gallic flavour, it was a typical BBC office, in as much as only two of its permanent staff seemed to have anything to do with broadcasting, and then only reluctantly. The rest had ill-defined administrative roles which we were given to understand dealt with much higher purposes than making programmes.

Passions ran high between the two broadcasters; hate, as it happened, not love. The wattled Paris correspondent could not stand his French woman assistant and his feelings were reciprocated to an unusually keen degree. They did not speak and went to elaborate efforts not to run into each other. The correspondent spent much of the day at lunch. His assistant brought in great cast iron saucepans full of the marinated wedding tackle of small rodents, which she rummaged through gloomily at intervals during the day. There was an elderly freelance reporter who acted as a go-between, a charming and emollient old boy called Jack Starr, who had once been the *Daily Mail's* man in Paris. He tiptoed up and down the corridors, carrying a glass of *kir* like a flag of truce. It was unnerving, he said, operating in a no-man's-land between warring factions, but he made a good living from BBC programmes relieved to find someone in Paris who was willing, available and uncomplicated.

The most intriguing feature of the BBC Paris office was an impromptu mural that had been drawn in the reception area by the famous French artist, poet and director, Jean Cocteau. He had been invited in to take part in some radio programme, probably in the hope he would be bitchy about his old rival Picasso, and been kept kicking his heels in the outer office for an hour or so. He used the time to draw all over the walls. According to legend, the great modern master was told off by the rather bluff BBC mandarin in charge for despoiling corporation property. By the time I arrived, the Cocteau mural was reckoned to be worth as much as the building. To the French staff it had become a symbol of their nation's higher artistic sensibilities; they could see a masterpiece, the benighted English could only see graffiti. We Brits shared a secret joy when the Paris correspondent was called in over a weekend and found the (French) cleaner scrubbing it off and moaning about vandals.

The election itself was a contest between the two most arrogant men on earth. Valery Giscard d'Estaing, the incumbent President, was tall and haughty. Francois Mitterand, his Socialist opponent, was a small man with a truly colossal sense of self-importance. Neither was a natural campaigner. They seemed to be at their best over the banquets that, happily, punctuated every few hours on the campaign trail. Uncritical reverence for the local cuisine was the tactic they both employed. The sight of two such fastidious men glorying in *la terre* and its more robust products could be amusing. It struck me if either of them was presented with a baby they might be more inclined to eat it than kiss it.

Like all elections it was a story of issues as well as personalities. The right had held power for twenty years, but the economy was in trouble, unemployment was rising and Giscard himself seemed to many cold, distant and incompetent. We criss-crossed the country looking at France's troubled industries. We profiled the *bourgeois* and their fear of the left. I drove round Paris in the back of a Rolls-Royce interviewing its owner, a millionairess called Mme Toussaint du Wast who seemed to see the Socialists as akin to the barbarians who sacked Imperial Rome. Later, taking tea in her opulent drawing room, she spoke as if her magnificent surroundings would soon be turned into a hostel for Arab anarchists; she and her maid shivered together in anticipation of *le déluge*. Later the same day I went to the so-called 'Red Belt', the swathe of working-class Paris the tourists never see, that was the heartland of the Communists and their saturnine leader, Georges Marchais. We followed Michelle Bernard, a single mum, as she walked down a filthy street to pick up her children from some flea-pit of a school. Over tea in her tiny flat, she spoke of the election, and a victory for the left, in almost redemptive terms. It was a simplistic, but instructive, way to personalise conflicting social attitudes. It was also interesting to see how social divisions could be as deep, if not deeper, in a republic as in a monarchy.

I caught up with Giscard in his heartland, the Auvergne, and found him lofty in every sense, but he could be witty, in a condescending kind of way. I got less change out of Mitterand whose immobile features seemed rather sinister when I interviewed him, though he might simply have been tired. It might also have been the difference between the incumbent who knew he was going to lose and the challenger who knew victory was inevitable, as long as he did not trip up. I tried to make a film about Mitterand's distinctly dubious wartime career and his links with the collaborationist Vichy government, but found most of the doors closed and bolted and did not have the time to come up with anything conclusive.

Paris went mad when the first exit polls predicted a sizeable Mitterand victory and Giscard conceded defeat. The Champs Elysées was flooded with hysterical young French people, screaming and hooting and waving flags. Everybody in the cars, often including the driver, was hanging out of the windows bellowing slogans or singing patriotic songs. They talked of a new dawn for France in the kind of vaporous, overblown language that makes their magazine advertisements so incomprehensible. It was all very enjoyable, particularly when I was kissed by a passing blonde, whose passion, sadly, was entirely political. It was like VE Day without the war. It all made wonderful television, of course, but I could not help thinking that if they could work up such enthusiasm for a pompous little collaborator, what would the celebrations have been like if they had had someone like the great Iron Duke on *their* side?

By the time I got back from the National Assembly elections, which ended with the same result, a victory for the Socialists, and the same high-octane celebrations, we were faced with the big move back down South. Selling in Scotland was a dream, a couple of weeks on the market, then into Messrs Archibald, Campbell and Harley, Writers to the Signet, to open the sealed (and binding) bids that were lined up in a row of expensive-looking envelopes. Buying in the South-East was the usual nightmare. We had taken a long time to find where we wanted to live. The big decision had been whether to be inside or outside London. Housing was so much more expensive, the idea of paying for the boys' education would have to be shelved. We did not so much look for a house, as a school. Most of my colleagues who lived in London were worried sick about state schools for their children. Those outside were happier, so I would be a commuter.

We drew a semi-circle round the west of London, from St Albans in the north, to Reigate in the south, and started hunting. We were looking for good schools and a place that was a community in itself, not just a rootless suburb with nothing but a couple of estate agents and an off-licence. We found a place we liked, Guildford, about as different from Musselburgh as it was possible to get and still stay on the same planet. We found a house we liked, too. The surveyor we employed said it needed some work, but he would organise it all for us. It would be no problem. He was rather vague about how much it might cost, but he was sure that would not be a problem either.

We bought the house and the surveyor presented his plans for making it habitable. We felt rather like Louis XIV must have felt when he first saw the plans for Versailles, except that Louis wasn't already heavily in debt to the Abbey National and could, presumably, go out and buy a pizza if he wanted without a lot of careful calculations. The surveyor was disappointed with our lack of ambition and we parted company. We sat in our ruin, too tired to sob.

We were rescued by Pete and Dave, the builders from heaven. They were saints who worked like demons. Every morning before I went to work myself I would look at them bent over the concrete mixer and wonder if those two lumps on their backs were really shoulder blades or, perhaps, folded wings. The house was an uncomfortable building site and would be for months, but Christine, Pete and Dave were in complete accord on everything, including my overall uselessness with anything remotely practical. I was OK for unskilled lifting and carrying but after I had tried to make a hole in the wall with the blunt end of a drill bit and the guffaws had lasted all morning, I realised my only real function was to provide light relief. Special correspondents weren't at home very much and it was just as well.

Most of the time I got the tougher stories near the top of the bulletin, but I did do some softer trips, too. Sometimes they were almost as dangerous. I was sent off to the United States to make a film about the 200th anniversary of the Battle of Yorktown, the crucial test of strength that led to America's independence. Lord Cornwallis surrendered to General Washington and his army of colonists, stiffened by French regulars. The whole thing was being re-enacted with considerable enthusiasm and attention to detail by almost as many people as took part in the original battle. In the middle of a scrum around President Reagan I tried to suggest to him that if the replay came up with a different result he ought to abide by the consequences. He looked worried, I thought, and went into a close huddle with his advisers. They said he was making last-minute changes to a big speech he was making that night on East-West relations, but we thought he was checking that Strategic Air Command would not be off at a weekend barbecue if the Brits started to make a better fist of it.

I reported on Yorktown II dressed as a redcoat officer, which was a first for a BBC correspondent, and got reprimanded for compromising the corporation's reputation for impartiality. It might have been a joke; with the BBC it is often difficult to tell. I replied, with a straight face, that though we were always required to be fair and truthful, we could not be expected to be absolutely even-handed between our own country and an enemy in time of war. This was to prove a richly ironic foretaste of what was to happen a couple of months later when we argued about these issues in deadly seriousness, with Mrs Thatcher and her government barracking from the sidelines.

Unfortunately, on this occasion, it had little effect on the outcome. The wrong side won again. An American patriot seemed to take offence at my description of him as a 'treacherous rebel' and clipped me behind the ear with the butt of his 'Brown Bess' while my back was turned. He swore it was an accident but I knew better. They weren't to be trusted then and they certainly aren't now.

I was sent off to Munich in a tearing hurry when a German women's magazine, *Die Aktuelle*, published what it claimed were bugged phone calls between Prince Charles and the then Lady Diana Spencer. The Prince's lawyers said the transcript was a fake but went to great lengths to get an injunction preventing publication. The magazine went to equally elaborate efforts to circumvent the legal restrictions, rushing the issue into print before the injunction could be served. A million copies, almost twice the usual run, hit the streets with a front page showing the royal couple and a headline *Kein 'skandal'. Sondern liebe, sehnsucht und ein bischen kummer.* (No scandal. Just love, longing and a little sadness.) It was fairly mild stuff, in comparison with later indiscretions, but it created quite a commotion at the time. The best thing about the story, from my point of view, was an opportunity to stay in the Vier Jahreszeiten, one of the finest and most expensive hotels in Europe. I was pampered as if I was the Prince himself at at time when any bed that wasn't full of dust and grit was a luxury. My phone calls home were tinged with guilt.

I went to northern Italy to cover the world chess championship between Anatoly Karpov and Victor Korchnoi and learnt a lot about the fevered intensity of top-level chess, and the equally fevered political subtext of a Soviet champion head to head with a Soviet exile. I spent a bizarre week chasing the Springbok rugby team as it tried to go on a secret tour of the United States. Only Ian Wooldridge of the *Daily Mail* and I found out where the match was being played. They had managed to avoid the anti-apartheid demonstrators, but they had given their supporters the slip, too. Ian and I were the only people in the small and bewildered crowd not wondering why these footballers were so underdressed.

Most of the time was spent, as ever, in Northern Ireland, where the hunger strikes in the H-blocks were reaching a grim and inevitable conclusion. The IRA men wanted to be treated as political prisoners, to wear their own clothes and be able to move freely within the prison to associate with their comrades. They had been given these privileges in the desperate days of 1972, but they had been withdrawn in 1976. They had tried everything to get them back. They went 'on the blanket' – refusing to wear clothes at all – and they smeared their cells with excrement. The hunger strikes were the ultimate form of blackmail. It was a war to the death over apparently trivial things that really went to the moral heart of what was happening in Northern Ireland. Were these men freedom fighters or callous murderers? The relatives of those in the security forces and in the wider community who had been killed by the IRA were in no doubt. They pointed out that their fathers, husbands, brothers had no choice about dying, and there had been no opportunity to plead for concessions to save their lives.

Their voices were drowned out by the maelstrom of emotion whipped up by the long, slow, self-imposed agony of the hunger strikers. When Bobby Sands died, with a golden crucifix given him by the Pope round his neck, 100,000 people – one in five of the Catholic population in the province – turned out for his funeral. I was there shortly afterwards as Raymond McCreesh was on his deathbed. He was 26 years old and was serving 14 years for attempted murder. He had gone blind and couldn't even hold down the water which was the only thing he would let past his lips. It was said that he had wanted to give up, but he was hopelessly confused by then. There were reports his family, especially his brother, Brian, a Catholic priest, had persuaded him to go through with it. Father McCreesh denied the allegations, even though they were apparently backed up by transcripts of conversations said to have been taped in the hospital. Either way, he did not allow any medical intervention after his brother lost consciousness.

It was a rough night in Belfast. Kids in the Catholic areas siphoned petrol out of parked cars to attack the army and police, and we spent hours dodging in and out of the barricades. It was worse when Thomas McIlwee died on my next trip there. He was the ninth to go, but his death coincided with the tenth anniversary of internment and it happened over a weekend. McIlwee was an unlikely martyr. The bomb he planted in Ballymena killed a young mother. But feelings by then were running very high. The timing of his death ensured that Catholic areas all over the country erupted. I spent two nights commuting from riot to riot, mostly in Belfast and Portadown, but parts of Lurgan, Newry, Armagh and Dungannon were also in flames. The army fired 1,000 plastic bullets in one night. One of them whacked the cameraman I was working with on the shoulder. Another killed a middle-aged man who was walking home from the pub.

On the face of it, attitudes on both sides were hardening. But we were already hearing whispers that the government was secretly negotiating with the IRA behind the scenes, whatever Mrs Thatcher might be saying in public.

One Friday afternoon I was sent to Belfast for the fourth time in a month. There was no time to pick up any clothes, I just had the little overnight case with a spare shirt and spare set of underwear that went with me everywhere. Don't worry, they said, you'll be back on Sunday. I did not get home again for three months.

I did not stay long in Northern Ireland. The hunger striker who had been at death's door seemed to recover. Talk in the Catholic pubs was that he had given in to the temptation of toasted cheese; there was a lot of head shaking at the deviousness of the English. (In fact his family had said enough was enough, and the government had secretly backed down. After 217 days and ten deaths the strike was called off. Three days later the government effectively granted nearly all the strikers' demands.) At any rate, he was in a rather better condition than Martin Bell, who had gone down with dysentery while covering a particularly vicious little war in El Salvador. Forget Belfast. Central America, please, you'll just catch the overnight flight. Do not pass go and your underwear will just have to last.

Spare underpants weren't a luxury, they were a necessity for a nervous reporter in El Salvador, at the time probably the most dangerous place on earth. It was the original banana republic, a fertile little place, full of nice peasants being murdered by nasty people who wanted them to be Communists, frontier guards for American capitalism, or simply slaves. Only 4.5 million frightened and bewildered people lived there, in a country not much bigger than Yorkshire. Yet it was the cockpit of the cold war then, a battle ground for competing ideologies operating through the most ruthless and rapacious gangsters in Latin America. In the middle of the war, they were trying to hold an election, a crucial test of almost anything you might care to mention according to the editorial writers. The eyes of the world were on the steamy, deadly little dump.

I thoroughly frightened myself by reading up on the background on the flight over, and any gaps in the undiluted horror story were helpfully filled in by the ever-knowledgeable Peter Beggin, battle cameraman and walking encyclopaedia. I did not mind him being a know-all. It was his uncomplicated bravery I could not stand. He could not wait to get stuck in, to get close to the fighting and win another award. I could not wait to get out again without a bullet in the back of the head (a speciality of the right-wing death squads) or my *cojones* stuffed in my mouth (the trademark of the left-wing guerrillas). The soundman, Roy Benford, was calm and laconic. I was reading him yet another account of an atrocity in some place called San Francisco Gotera when I realised he had dropped off to sleep. I envied him his nerves.

If I was scared when we landed, I was terrified by the time we got to the hotel. Martin had thoughtfully sent his driver, Carlos, to make sure we got in safely. Carlos was an extraordinary fixer and guide, but his running commentary on the road in from the airport made it increasingly difficult to keep my bowel movements under control.

'Thees place here is where they killed and raped the four nuns,' he said, pointing to a sinister-looking patch of waste land. His description of the barbarous deaths of these blameless ladies left nothing to the imagination. A few hundred yards further on was where an army patrol had been massacred. Just past that was the spot where an American 'observer' had been decapitated. Everywhere you looked in San Salvador itself there had been some terrible killing; every rubbish dump, and there was a lot of rubbish in San Salvador, would have its quota of new corpses in the morning.

The most chilling moment was when Carlos described the deaths of a four-man Dutch television team, who had been lured out of the hotel by someone who said he could take them to the rebels. It was a ruse and they were taken straight to one of the death squads who shot them all neatly behind the right ear and left them in a ditch.

'How did it happen?' I asked naively.

'They were naïve,' said Carlos.

'When was this?' I was having difficulty getting the words out. It was probably the heat.

'Couple of days ago.'

Even Peter Beggin was looking preoccupied as we turned into the hotel car park. I just wanted a stiff drink and a door I could lock. If the drink was stiff enough and the lock strong enough, I wasn't ever going to come out.

The Camino Real Hotel was packed with the world's media. The car park was full of network trucks and the windows sprouted satellite dishes the way a rotting tree trunk is covered in fungi. Most of the journos were too sensible to go out of the capital; a fair number never left the hotel, and you could see their point.

I felt this was a story best reported from the cocktail bar but Martin Bell had other ideas when we gathered for a council of war in his room. In his view, it was all happening out in the war-torn countryside, an extraordinary story of life and death, of oppression, rebellion and democracy. History was being made down the Pan-American highway, out in the flat valleys pimpled with volcanoes where silver rivers slithered down to the crashing Pacific. It was the biggest, most exciting story in the world and we were very, very lucky to have a chance to cover it.

'Righto, Martin,' I said. 'On you go. I'll hold the fort here.' I tried to look keen, as if I was struggling hard to hide my disappointment. 'You're the senior man. My time will come.' Not if I can help it, I thought.

Martin was obviously torn and, for the first time, I noticed how ill and drawn he looked. He could barely stand up, in fact, but I was so windy at the time, so busy dreaming up excuses, it had not registered at all.

'I wish I could,' he said – he did, too, mad devil – 'but it just won't work. It will have to be you.' He looked at me with envy in his eyes. I looked away to disguise the terror in mine.

It seemed only the British television crews were going out into the badlands. Jon Snow and his ITN team seemed to be providing most of the 'bang bang' for the American networks with whom they were allied, just as Martin had been for the BBC's coalition. The crew doing all the nasty stuff for the CBS American network, which operated on its own, turned out to be British, too.

We set out early the following morning, as the garbage workers were pulling the night's harvest of corpses off the tops of the rubbish tips. The death squads had been even more productive than usual, hoping to wipe out every leftist sympathiser they could reach by voting day. Political campaigning amongst the peasants was not very subtle. It appeared to consist of telling them: Do what you're told or we'll kill you. Thirty thousand had already been murdered, out of a total population, remember, of only 4.5 million.

President Jose Napoleon Duarte, the leader of the American-backed junta that ran the place, was, in every sense, sanguine about this. When we put it to him that a lot of peasants had been killed under his rule, he did not demur. 'Naturally they have,' he said. 'Most people in El Salvador are peasants.'

Although President Duarte had tried to introduce some reforms in the two years he had been in power, El Salvador was still a very feudal banana republic. Power and wealth was still firmly in the hands of an oligarchy that treated the peasants like slaves. Two per cent of the population owned half the country's land and received nearly half the nation's income, and most of the people lived in extreme poverty as dependent workers on plantations. Eight out of ten of them didn't get enough to eat, nine out of ten were illiterate. The leftist guerrillas, the Farabundo Marti National Movement, were strong in the mountains of the north and east and came down from them from time to time to cut the highways and attack the towns. The United States' nightmare was that the guerrillas would topple the dominos of central America and even Mexico, bringing Communism to the very banks of the River Grande. They poured money and advisers in to El Salvador to stiffen the army and the government.

The guerrillas saw no point in contesting the election and said they would stop it taking place. The country was tiny, the people downtrodden, the rulers squalid and the politics a matter of competitive bloodletting, but the global power and reputation of the United States had somehow come to be at stake. That's what made it important.

The vote itself boiled down to a choice between the extreme right and the not-so-extreme right. President Duarte's main opponent was a strikingly handsome torturer called Major Roberto D'Aubuisson, who had played a leading role in 'interrogating' captured guerrillas. Even the American Ambassador described him publicly as a 'pathological killer' which D'Aubuisson regarded as an endorsement and his supporters seemed to feel was the ideal quality they needed in a leader. I filmed him at a rally of his ARENA (National Republican Alliance) party. He was smooth and dapper, wearing a black SS-style windcheater that had the cross of medieval crusading knights emblazoned on the front.

He told me that if he won, he would wipe out the guerrillas 'in three months'.

'How?' I asked him.

He did not reply directly, he just drew his finger across his throat. When I looked sceptical, he fired off an imaginary machine gun in the general direction of the crowd. His supporters called him the *maximi lider* – the great leader – and kept screaming, '*Patria si! Communismo no!*'

The capital was frightening enough. It wasn't so much the cough of mortars as the guerrillas tried to fight their way into the working-class suburb of San Antonio Abad, at the foot of the volcano overlooking the city. That seemed almost comfortingly far away. It was the sinister-looking men driving round, four to a car, clearly armed to the teeth. The death squads seemed to be everywhere, and they might kill anyone.

It got worse as we travelled east. We hit the first rebel roadblock about 12 miles from the city. They seemed to be drunk or, at the very least, extremely overwrought. They pushed their guns through the windows of the car demanding money and cigarettes. We had supplied ourselves with cartons of Marlboros for this kind of eventuality, but they persisted with their demands for about half an hour before they let us go.

Less than a mile further on we ran into a government roadblock. They wore slightly more recognisable uniforms but they acted in precisely the same way, even dragging us from the car to search us for weapons. My nightmare was that the rebels would come round the corner as we were trying to buy the government troops off with cigarettes and we would get caught in the middle of a firefight. After we were finally released, our guide said that was the least of our problems; he had overheard two of the soldiers discussing whether it would be best to kill us so they could take the camera and our personal belongings. I was so glad I could not speak Spanish.

We hit three more roadblocks on our way to the provincial capital of Usulutan, some 80 miles south east of San Salvador. There had been garbled reports of heavy fighting there and the rebel radio Venceremos had claimed it was in the hands of the guerrillas. The suburbs seemed deserted as we drove slowly into town. The windows were all shuttered tight and most of the walls were chipped by bullets, but in that early afternoon the only sign of war was the muffled crack of a single shot on the other side of town.

It turned out we had arrived in the middle of an unofficial siesta. Just as we approached the centre of Usulutan, it started up again, all around us. We tumbled out of the car and sheltered behind a half-ruined wall while we tried to work out what was happening and what to do.

It did not require a great deal of strategic insight to see that the focus of the fighting was the battle for control of the main street . We found ourselves amongst the government troops, most of whom were firing wildly down the road in the general direction of the rebel positions which were round the main church they were using as a strong point. There were about 200 of them, apparently, and for three days now the fighting had been a bloody stalemate.

It all had something of the Wild West about it. Across the street, a shuttered cinema still had a poster, in Spanish, advertising *Gunfight at the OK Corral* and the real life in front of our eyes seemed to be aping the celluloid fiction. The soldier lying in front of us in the gutter would roll out into the centre of the street to fire off a burst, before rolling back again as the rebel bullets puckered the dirt around him. More soldiers were firing snap shots from windows and behind pillars. From time to time, a sergeant with a heavier machine gun would dash out into the street and fire a longer burst. But the fifth or sixth time he did it he got hit in the shoulder, which spun him round and knocked him over. He managed to crawl back behind cover where his mates seemed to have trouble stopping the bleeding.

Beggin was in his element with all this. He was filming it off the shoulder, steady as the proverbial rock and with about as much imagination about the danger he, and we, were in, to my mind. But then, he was conspicuously brave, and the chattering of my teeth was louder in my head than the machine guns. After about half an hour, Beggin decided the view would be better from the other side of the street. It was madness, of course, but I could not talk him out of it. Worse, much worse, he wanted me to go with him to bring his spare tapes and batteries. Nothing I said did any good.

Beggin was a bulky man and I made sure he was between me and the rebels firing at us down the street. Left to myself, I reckon I could have set some sort of record for a short-distance sprint, but Beggin took it at a stroll. Then he stopped, right in the middle, and started to film.

'For fuck's sake,' I shouted, as I edged up behind him, making sure no bit of me was showing.

'Won't be long,' he said. 'It's a marvellous shot, you can actually see them shooting at us.'

'Great,' I said. 'That's the main thing.'

I don't know how long we stayed there. Long enough for me to consider, in some detail, how unlikely it was that even a body as well nourished and obtuse as Beggin's would stop a high-velocity bullet. Long enough for three or four rounds to buzz past our heads, a couple to slap into the roadway and several more to whang off the kerbstones. Long enough to film an extraordinary 'point of view' shot, as it is known in the trade. Peter was tickled pink.

The fighting slackened off after that and it wasn't long before the rebels pulled out of the town and back to the hills. They took their dead and wounded with them, but left the corpse of one of the local oligarchs lying naked in the gutter with a notice, listing his sins, stapled to his chest.

The street was littered with cartridge cases. The church was a wreck, pockmarked with bullet and shell holes. In the silence, the church clock started chiming and people began emerging from their homes, carrying white flags. Their faith in the ethics of neutrality was touching. As far as I could see, they weren't bystanders; they were the targets.

It was a relatively short but perilous journey up to the Pan-American highway to the provincial capital of San Vicente, huddled in the shadow of Chichontepec volcano. San Vicente was an important crossroads and a key objective for the rebels in their campaign to stop the election happening. We managed to slip into the town in a military convoy and found the strong government garrison at full stretch trying to hold the guerrillas at the perimeter. The fighting seemed pretty continuous. The crump of mortars and chatter of small-arms fire went on all afternoon and through the short twilight, only slowly dying down when it got pitch dark.

We got some of the fighting, but Peter wasn't satisfied. Soldiers just firing into the distance wasn't enough for him any more. It wasn't real, it wasn't dramatic, without *incoming* fire. I was not sorry when it got dark. There was no point in filming any more and it wasn't so easy to see my hands shaking.

We managed to find a hotel in San Vicente. The tourist trade was understandably going through a quiet period. It had been built as a quadrangle and all the rooms faced into the courtyard, which gave it a spurious feeling of safety and made the sporadic gunfire sound comfortingly remote, though the front line was only a couple of hundred yards down the street. My room was on the first floor. It had an iron bedstead, some filthy bedclothes and that was it, except for things that scuttled across the concrete floor, barely visible under the dim and flickering light.

I dropped off into a feverish sleep and dreamt of flesh wounds and, oddly, cricket. It was three in the morning when I woke up, slowly aware of a tramping noise that first inserted itself into my dream and then became so loud and insistent it snapped me awake. The world seemed on the move, beyond the rusty metal door of my room. The shuffling of hundreds of feet was mixed with muttering and coughing and a rhythmic thudding and grunting that sounded strangely familiar. I could not make out what was going on, which turned me, in an instant, from highly nervous to dead scared. I pulled the patched sheet over my head and pretended I was at home in Surrey. It didn't work.

After a long internal debate I summoned up enough courage to open the door and look outside. The government army, practically all of it as far as I could see, was drawn up in the hotel quadrangle. Soldiers queued, three abreast, up the concrete staircases to the landing where they broke into single files leading to almost all the rooms. As I watched, two of the doors opened and soldiers came out, buttoning up their uniforms, and those at the head of the queue disappeared, eagerly, inside to take their place.

It was obvious, even to me, famously innocent about these things, that we were staying in a brothel. It was doing, in every sense, a roaring trade. I stepped quickly back into my room and did my best to lock and barricade the door. I was sure I wasn't quite what the licentious soldiery had in mind, but they did seem to be getting impatient and the light *was* very poor. I had already imagined a hundred horrible fates, but to end up as the sexual plaything of the notorious Atlcatl battalion, thanks to a mix up over room numbers, would have been worse than any of them.

There was no point in trying to get back to sleep. I got dressed and spent the rest of the night staring out of the cracked and grubby window. I wondered how long it would take the rebels to realise the defences were deserted and they only had to stroll up the street to catch the entire army with its trousers down. I was glad when dawn broke, almost as pleased as San Vicente's prostitutes, I imagine.

This was the election day. The rebels had threatened to kill anybody who cast a vote and they still had the town under siege. In the early morning we made our way cautiously through the broken buildings back to the perimeter lines, where soldiers and civilian guards were blasting away at rebel positions less than a hundred yards away. The guerrillas were obviously going to mount a serious attack and, for about half an hour, we were pinned down under pretty well constant machine-gun and mortar fire. Peter got his 'incoming', nearly a belly-full, in fact, as he crossed a patch of open ground in search of a better angle. Eventually, even he was satisfied and, in a brief lull in the fighting, we pulled back into town.

The streets were packed. People streamed out of the houses where they had mostly barricaded themselves in since the siege began, to cast their votes. They stood for hours in the courtyard of the polling station, which was only a hundred yards from some of the fiercest fighting, and bullets were fizzing overhead. I could not work out if this was an extraordinary example of the power of democracy – it was, after all, the first so-called free election in El Salvador for 50 years – or whether they were more frightened of the soldiers in the town than the guerrillas on the outskirts. I talked to a dozen or more of the voters. They all said they were determined to vote, but they all looked anxiously over their shoulders at the same time.

It was the same everywhere we went that day. We slipped away to San Miguel in the east and then back through the scary roadblocks of both sides to the capital.

I thought we would be safe as we reached the suburbs, but gunfire broke out only a block away from us and it turned out a rebel offensive had penetrated to within a mile of the city centre. They had attacked nine different parts of San Salvador. Helicopter gunships and an old Dakota were machine-gunning the slums yet, even there, people were voting.

*

It took several days for the votes to be counted. Even when we knew the result, we did not know who had won. President Duarte and his American-backed junta had only 40 per cent of the vote. The remaining 60 per cent was split among parties of the far right who talked of a government of national unity under the sinister Major D'Aubuisson and letting the army loose with a vengeance.

He was still manoeuvring for control when we left. I felt sorry for the people of El Salvador who were hospitable and brave and did not deserve their fate. I would have felt sorrier still if I had known that their war would go on for another decade, eventually killing 75,000 people and, incidentally, costing the American taxpayer $6 billion. I hope they think it was worth it.

I have never been so happy to get out of a place in my life. Even the BBC realised it had not been the easiest or most straightforward of assignments and told us to stop off in Miami for a couple of days 'R&R'. Peter, Roy and I were by no means averse to this idea and checked into the most expensive hotel we could find. We did not even have time to unpack. I was thumbing through a list of seafood restaurants when the call came through from London. Argentina had invaded the Falkland Islands. The only chance of getting there was through Chile. 'R&R' was off. Next stop, Cape Horn.

Punta Arenas, at the entrance to the Straits of Magellan, is the end of the earth. The shoreline is littered with wrecks that did not make it round the Cape. The wind shrieks across a grey and gritty landscape and through the streets of the town itself, a frontier kind of place made mostly of corrugated iron, with time on its hands. The people were friendly. A surprising number had red hair and were called Williams or McGregor. They were sympathetic to the British, generally, and even more so now that we were on the brink of war with their neighbours, Argentina. There was little love lost between the two countries, especially down there where there was constant arguing over how the boundary should be drawn through the Beagle Channel.

We had our seafood dinner. The prawns at the Cabo de Hornos Hotel were probably better than anything we might have had in Miami. But the menu was rather limited. If you did not like prawns or mutton, you were in for a thin time. In any case, we were not planning to stay long. The idea was to find some means of getting to the Falklands, 500 miles away in the South Atlantic. Jon Snow of ITN was also in town on the same errand. Every morning we exchanged guarded greetings and then set out to ransack the place for some ship or aircraft that would make the perilous journey, desperate to buy it up first. For several days Jon and I were in a bidding competition for some flat-bottomed car transporter that would have killed either of us if the owner had been stupid enough to make the journey. Peter spent most of his time on the trail of a flying boat that was supposed to be locked up in some shed in a remote valley stretching north to the distant Andes. Slowly, it dawned on all of us that this was not going to work. There was no vessel or aircraft there capable of getting to the islands. Even if we had found something, the Chileans wouldn't let us go, and the Argentines would kill us or lock us up if we ever did make it. I began to get sick of prawns.

I was rescued by another phone call from London ordering me to Buenos Aires. It may have been the capital of a potential enemy, but after the nightmare of El Salvador and the boredom of Punta Arenas, I could not wait. I left Peter and Roy to carry on the fruitless search with a series of other BBC correspondents who were sent to kick their heels at the edge of the world over the next couple of months.

Peter came to see me off on the flight back to Santiago. I was sorry to be leaving them both. He was a strange man, but good-hearted as well as brave, and there is an indefinable bond between people who have risked their lives together.

I never saw him again. The day he returned from South America he took his wife for a drink at their favourite pub outside Henley-on-Thames. The pub car park was full so he dropped her off and left his car a hundred yards further on. As he crossed the road, he was knocked down by a Mini and killed instantly. It was a stupid, bathetic death for a man who had been in the thick of a dozen wars, who had courted so much danger. I went to his memorial service. We had a lot to say, but it was all paradox and no meaning.

FIFTEEN

Si siente, si siente, Galtieri presidente!
    We can feel it, we can feel it, Galtieri is president!
    Si siente, si siente, la Rienna esta calente!
    We can feel it, we can feel it, it's getting hotter for the Queen!
    The crowd was enormous. They say more than 200,000 Argentines tried to pack into the Plaza de Mayo that day. Big though it was, the square could not hold them all. The streets around were jammed; the city was at a standstill.
    It was like a football crowd, though no stadium in the world would have been big enough for them. They were gathered for a partisan purpose, defined not just by who they were, but who the enemy was. Us, in fact. The mob bellowed: 'Death to the English'. Not for the first time, I wished the camera did not have BBC stamped on it.
    All afternoon that great mass of sweltering people stood in the square, fanned only by the thousands of blue and white Argentine flags sweeping back and forth, back and forth, over their heads. All the bellicose pride of an insecure nation welled up out of them and spat defiance at the empty blue sky. It was as if all the complexities, all the difficulties, of living in a military dictatorship on the verge of ruin had been swept aside by this much bigger thing. This looming fight over territory had set free feelings as old as man himself. A hard-pressed and emotional people swapped their troubles for simple rage.
    That was the idea, of course. And, as the heat started to go out of the day, the man who dreamt it all up to save his neck came out on the balcony of the Casa Rosada. It had been the platform for many a dictator. Evita Peron used that balcony to harangue her *descamisados* (literally 'shirtless ones'). You could chart Argentina's political, moral and economic decline in snapshots of the guilty lording it over the gullible from the second floor of the Pink Palace.
    General Leopoldo Fortunata Galtieri stubbed out his cigarette, drained his Scotch and went out to meet his people. He was a limited man, ruthless rather than clever, who had come to prominence in the dirty war against the left after the military took over in 1976. Galtieri had seized power the year before in a bloodless coup. He was the senior member of a three-man junta, with the head of the navy and the air force.

From that balcony, feeling the adulation of all those emotional people, he must have thought he was looking at destiny, when he was really seeing disaster.

The cameraman struggled with the contrast between the crowd in the square, still sweating in the sun, and the General who was shaded by the bulk of the palace behind him. 'If the British come,' he said, 'let them come. We will do battle.' Neither he nor I believed it would happen. We were both wrong.

Britain was still a long way from war with Argentina when I touched down in Buenos Aires a day or so after leaving Punta Arenas. But there had been a lot of hostility and much belligerence since the Argentine Army had invaded the Falkland Islands and there was already a strong sense of arriving in the enemy camp. I was worried that I would be arrested and interned. Instead I got a long and patronising lecture on British iniquity from the immigration official, who seemed to hold me personally responsible for our bloodstained imperial history in general and our criminal occupation of the Islas Malvinas in particular. I was relieved to get in to the Sheraton Hotel where the BBC had set up its operation under Elwyn Evans, a senior producer from the television newsroom and an old friend from my days back in South Wales. Elwyn told me he had been so scared that he had replied to all the questions at the airport in pigeon French. There had been nobody to meet him either there or at the Sheraton and he assumed all the British had been thrown in jail, or worse. He barricaded himself in his room, with the wardrobe wedged against the door, and prepared to sell his life dearly. In fact, they had all been out at a boozy lunch and he felt rather foolish when he had to be coaxed out of his room, several hours later.

Feelings were certainly running high in Buenos Aires, but at first I found it difficult to see how the two countries could go to war over a few scraps of land one stop from the end of the earth. The Falklands were of little strategic or economic importance. They gave Britain some legal say in the Antarctic but that was hardly worth fighting over. There was talk of oil under the famously hostile waters around the islands, but that is all it was, talk. The Falklands ran at a loss. They were a relic of Empire, from the days when the Royal Navy ruled the waves and needed coaling stations in the far corners of the world. The Navy had evicted the original inhabitants in 1833 and replaced them with British settlers with a taste for solitude. There were 1,800 on the islands when the Argentines invaded. They called themselves 'kelpers' after the ubiquitous seaweed there.

I spent hours in the Sheraton talking to Harold Briley, the BBC's veteran Latin America correspondent and the only journalist to be a more or less regular visitor. Harold had a copy of the Falklands' 'newspaper', *Penguin News*. Issue number 19 was the last to be published before the invasion and painted a picture of a society where practically nothing happened. It consisted of 15 stencilled and stapled pages. The main story, indeed the only thing of any consequence that appeared to have happened in the previous month, was a report of a road accident in the capital, Port Stanley. A Land Rover had collided with a Hillman Imp 'inflicting possibly irreparable damage on the latter vehicle', as *Penguin News* put it. There were only 12 miles of made-up road in the islands at the time, according to Harold who found the story surprising, if not newsworthy. 'It's difficult to find anything to have an accident with.' It was odd to think that a dead-and-alive place in the middle of nowhere was now the centre of human attention, that great issues of peace and war hung on who would control it, that all the forums of mankind and half the world's statesmen were trying to find a solution. Harold worried about his friends on the islands. He fretted about how they were coping with the occupation and what would happen if their little homeland became a battleground.

You only needed a couple of days in Buenos Aires to realise what a deeply cynical move the invasion had been. The country was riddled with internal divisions and stumbling over an economic cliff. At the turn of the previous century, Argentina had been one of the four wealthiest countries in the world and should have been still. Everything grows on the vast pampas that stretches from the coast to the Andes. There were three times as many cows as people, a skilled and energetic workforce, and the makings of a first-world infrastructure. It should have been a land of limitless opportunity. Instead, it had been ransacked by a series of blundering dictators, its middle class was on its knees, its working class, betrayed by cardboard heroes, increasingly sought excitement and even salvation on the streets.

Just after dawn, one morning soon after I got there, I went down to the headquarters of Buenos Aires' largest finance house. It was besieged by thousands of hysterical investors. It opened its doors, but not for long. It paid out the equivalent of $250 million in the first hour and then shut down, for good. There were queues at all the banks. Everybody wanted cash, fearful that the banks would go bust, too, even though they knew that, with inflation running at 150 per cent a year, the value of their money would just dribble away through their fingers. I talked to some of the people standing in the queues about their lives. All the white-collar workers told me they had to have two full-time jobs just to get by and they tried to negotiate pay rises for each of them four times a year to keep up with inflation. The working men said they were worried about losing their jobs. One in five was now unemployed, in a country which thought there would be a job for everyone, even in the bad times. We saw, and filmed, Argentines searching through skips for something to sell so that they could feed their families. Industrial production had fallen 8 per cent in a year, the peso was sliding on the currency markets, the foreign exchange reserves were exhausted and the stock exchange, as I found when I went there one day, barely functioned any more. The country was in a mess and, until the invasion, blamed Galtieri for it. It was widely believed in Buenos Aires that the other two members of the junta were already preparing to dump him when he ordered the invasion. Overnight, he became a national hero, but he was only postponing his downfall at the cost of many lives.

Interestingly, the opponent he chose was also deeply unpopular. A Gallup poll at the end of 1981 suggested the British thought Mrs Thatcher was the worst Prime Minister in the country's history. Galtieri went to war to save his own career and only succeeded in rescuing his enemy's.

The men and women in the queues outside the banks, indeed every Argentine I met, were convinced that right was on Argentina's side. Port Stanley was, after all, 6,939 miles from London. Rio Gallegos, the closest point on the Argentine mainland, was just 426 miles away. They saw it in colonial terms and from the point of view of a nation that had thrown off its own Spanish masters nearly two centuries before. British ownership of the Falklands was an insult to national pride, and to a nation largely made up of excitable southern Europeans, insults were not to be borne. They did not understand why the Falklanders did not want to become Argentine and didn't much care. The wishes of 1,800 people, in their view, should not stand in the way of historical and geographical justice.

It never seemed particularly personal. We covered massive demonstrations where the British were accused of being murderers and oppressors and where the chant was 'Death to Mrs Thatcher', but it always seemed to be the American crews that got beaten up. In part, this was because of their lack of experience in filming potentially hostile crowds. We had learned the hard way in Northern Ireland that you got in close enough to touch and be touched and part of what was going on, or else you stayed a long way away and out of trouble, filming on a long lens. The worst thing to do was to hang around on the fringes, within reach of troublemakers, but having no real contact with the crowd. You soon became a target, whoever you were.

It was more than technique that kept us safe, most of the time. The Argentines genuinely liked the British, which made it all so strange. The British built the country or, at any rate, the railways, the phone system, the finance houses and the meat-packing plants. There were still 17,000 British passport holders in Buenos Aires alone and as many as 100,000 Argentines who claimed British descent. The main store in the capital was called Harrods, the most attractive landmark in the city centre was called La Torre de Los Inglesias (the English Tower), a loose replica of Big Ben that had been donated by the British community in 1910. There was an Hospital Britannico, a British orphanage, a British Sunset House for the Elderly, the St John's Anglican Cathedral and a dozen British churches and schools. Every year, the British community council raised £200,000 at their fêtes and raffles for the city's poor and sick.

The Argentines seemed as fond of the British who were their enemies as they disliked the Americans who were, for a time at least, in the role of peacemakers. One of the government's first acts, after the invasion, was to issue a decree that British lives and property were to be protected. A guard was placed outside the English Club in Buenos Aires, where elderly gentlemen in sports jackets dozed in big leather armchairs in front of a giant photograph of central London. There was little for him to do, and only the odd pink gin slipped out to him by sympathetic members to relieve the monotony. The Argentines managed somehow to distinguish between Britain, the oppressor they hated, and the British, the people they looked up to and liked. It was an odd position to be in.

The British community itself was deeply upset by it all and made a number of, probably ill-advised, attempts to smooth things over. We followed the Anglican bishop's plans to fly to the Falklands with a delegation of Anglo-Argentine farmers to tell the islanders how pleasant it was living in Argentina. No doubt the Right Reverend Richard Cutts was well intentioned but I remember thinking it would be difficult to dream up a more naïve and misguided idea. The bishop was slapped down very swiftly by his boss, the Archbishop of Canterbury, who removed the Falklands from his jurisdiction and forbade him to leave Argentina.

Argentines of all ages and classes seemed actually to aspire to different kinds of, often idealised, Britishness. The young were obsessed by the Beatles and the Rolling Stones. In the middle of one of the biggest demonstrations in the Plaza de Mayo I got surrounded by a gang of lads who followed up their spittingly angry denunciation of Mrs Thatcher with a word-perfect rendering of 'She Loves You'.

The most popular cinema film in Buenos Aires throughout the Falklands crisis was the British movie about the 1924 Olympics, *Chariots of Fire*. The night we went down to see what was going on, we found queues out round the block, hours before it was due to start. The cinema was packed, as it had been, apparently, ever since it opened. The Argentines booed the American athletes and hissed at the manoeuvrings of the French Olympic officials. But when the Englishman, Harold Abrahams, won his gold medal and the Scotsman Eric Liddell got his chance to run, they went mad and practically took the cinema roof off with their cheering.

It was the rich of Argentina who most wanted to look and sound English. The holy of holies for them was the Hurlingham Club, some ten miles outside the city. When we went there the Argentine cricket team, who were due to play in the World Cup that June, were practising on one of the pitches. A young man in whites, standing on the boundary, said it was the 'softest, slowest grass in the country. It's so important to adapt to English conditions, old boy.'

There were vintage MGs in the car park and young men in cavalry twills and brogues. There was only one polo match going on, but most of the 18 tennis courts were in use, and the 18-hole (par 71) golf course was dotted with Pringle sweaters. Inside the magnificent, ivy-clad clubhouse nobody was talking about war even though Air Force Mirage jets came screaming overhead to land at their base nearby. My questions about it were regarded as a lapse of taste. The only excitement came from a backgammon game in the corner of the bar. P. G. Wodehouse would have been at home at the Hurlingham, but I could not think of anywhere in Britain that was that English.

I was covering Buenos Aires with a very experienced colleague and old friend, Chris Morris. I had known Chris since he ran his own news agency in Spain. He was a grown-up, hard-working and competent. From the start we came to an agreement between us to prevent the kind of silly rivalries that had undermined the BBC coverage of this kind of story in the past, which both Chris and I had seen at close hand. We took it in turns to be in charge. One day I would do all the leg work for him, the next he would do the same for me. It worked brilliantly.

We spent most of the time trying to track the diplomatic efforts to head off war. The American Secretary of State, General Alexander Haig, must have done the equivalent of flying to the moon and back, shuttling between London and Buenos Aires three times as the British Task Force headed south. At first, some sort of compromise seemed to be possible. The Argentine Foreign Minister, Nicanor Costa Mendez, seemed much more flexible than his military masters and was continually hinting to us that their position was softening and agreement was very close. We also got wind of divisions between the members of the junta. The Admiral, Jorge Anaya, was taking a tough line (while keeping most of his fleet well out of the firing line). The Air Force commander, Brigadier General Basilio Lami Dozo, was apparently pushing for a settlement. The more we found out what was really happening behind the scenes, though, the more it became clear that it was all about Galtieri's survival. Anything less than a British agreement to negotiate handing over sovereignty of the islands would be the end for him. Put simply, if the Argentine flag was pulled down there, he would be toppled too.

The British government had acted in the past as if the Falklands were an inconvenient embarrassment, an attitude that played its part in Galtieri's massive miscalculation. But if there was any chance of a compromise it pretty well evaporated in the wave of patriotism that surrounded the sailing of the Task Force. Even so, British public opinion might have wobbled in the weeks it took the fleet to reach the South Atlantic but for the will of Mrs Thatcher, the bellicosity of the London newspapers, and a BBC scoop in Argentina. It was an exclusive for which we could claim no credit, though we milked it for all it was worth.

Almost every newspaper and television organisation in the world had been begging the Argentine government to let them go to the Falklands. We certainly did, on a daily basis, to be met with a shrug if we were lucky, a lecture or a frog march to the door if we were not. Finally, the Argentine military took an American crew from our colleagues, NBC. They probably did it to ingratiate themselves with the Americans, but it backfired in the most spectacular way. Instead of showing the NBC crew only what

212

they wanted them to see, the Argentines allowed them to talk to the Falklanders. The island people were obviously intimidated, but still managed to use the opportunity to appeal for help to the outside world. The Anglican minister, the Reverend Harold Bagnall, pointed to an Argentine conscript and asked the camera crew: 'How can you talk to someone who is pointing a gun at you? The only communication we have with them is when a soldier makes a gesture with his gun.'

But the woman who may have made war inevitable was the wonderfully named Madge Buckett who made a direct and emotional appeal. 'For Christ's sake,' she said, 'somebody out there do something.

'We are trying to keep smiling, only because we dare not annoy the Argies. Somebody do something, please. Many of the islanders are afraid to set foot outside their homes, especially the older ones. Some of them stand at their doors and beg for food, too frightened to go to the shops.'

Because of our reciprocal deal with NBC we had access to all their pictures and interviews. We used more of them than they did, painting a picture of a very British-looking and -sounding community under enemy occupation. The reports gave the whole issue a human focus; it was no longer just a question of high politics or abstract principle. The British weren't fighting for a bunch of rocks any more, but for real people. Madge Buckett had given them a voice and a face.

For the rest of the time we tried to show, as accurately as we could, what was going on in this country with whom we would shortly be at war. In my view, the responsibility for it lay not with the Argentine people, passionate and misguided though they might often be, but with their cruel, bungling leaders. They looked like pantomime figures in their Ruritanian uniforms and their mock-heroic posturing. But they were veterans of a secret war against their own people which wiped out not only the leftist activists in the country, but anybody who was sympathetic to their cause and even those who had been in relatively innocent contact with them. As many as 15,000 people were taken away, tortured and killed. Nearly all of them disappeared leaving no trace at all. Their relatives never found out exactly what happened to them. They were left with nothing, not even a body to bury.

I used to go down to the demonstration that was staged every week in the main square by the 'Mothers of the Disappeared', the Madres de Plaza de Mayo. It was a silent protest, by meek women in the main, who walked round and round the Piramide de Mayo in the centre of the square, under the towering palm trees. They carried placards with photographs of their lost loved ones, a description, perhaps, and a note of where they had last been seen.

The police had harassed them, but they kept coming back and now the authorities mainly left them alone. They were a weekly reproach to the General who sat in his Pink Palace at one end of the square. They were the people he had climbed over to grab power. He had been a little-known combat engineer when the so-called 'dirty war' started in 1976. He was good at organising secret killing and impatient with any moral ambiguities that might have deterred better men. 'I am a simple soldier,' he told us once when we were allowed an interview. 'I like simple words and clear ideas.' He never came to the window when the mothers were parading down in the square but sat chain smoking and drinking his favourite Scotch, ignoring them and the shame they brought him.

Our position as the BBC in Buenos Aires was, to say the least, ambiguous. We had the freedom of the city. I would spend hours talking to the Mothers of the Disappeared, for instance, practically under the dictator's window, without undue interference from the police. Yet at other times we would be targeted almost as enemy aliens and there would be veiled threats of expulsion or internment. For a long time we were able to satellite our reports directly from the Argentine television headquarters. It was all handled by a colourful Australian called John Arden who worked for our sister agency, Visnews. He managed to create great confusion there about the reports he was feeding and ours got mixed in with those for Ireland, Canada, America and Australia. John was a strikingly handsome and persuasive man who was as successful at confusing the moral defences of Argentine ladies as he was at finding a way through the censorship of the country's officials. He was tired all the time, which was scarcely surprising, and bore his nickname – Juan Hard-on – with weary resignation. Eventually the Argentine technicians rumbled him and we had to charter a plane every day to take our report across the muddy estuary of the River Plate to the Uruguyan capital Montevideo, where John was soon being received, in every sense, with open arms.

Life in the enemy capital was extremely comfortable. The Sheraton was a splendid hotel in a fashionable part of San Martin. It was a high-rise building with magnificent views over Buenos Aires at the front and, if the port and the railway station at the back were less glamorous, they were at least busy and gave us a sense of the pulse of a great city. There was a swimming pool, tennis courts and a gym so we could keep fit, and room service was courteous and efficient.

The hotel was full of British reporters. We had a cricket tournament that was played along the corridors of the fourth floor. It began as a knock-out, but turned into a league when we all realised we were going to be there for the long haul. We played schoolboy jokes on each other all the time. The ITN correspondent, Norman Rees, was unwise enough to tell us he was going downstairs to get his hair cut one morning so we got one of our translators to tell the barber Mr Rees wanted all his hair off. Norman, who did not speak Spanish and was nursing a ferocious hangover, only noticed when half of his hair had been reduced to a film of fuzz. Relations with ITN were strained until they got their own back, fortunately not on me.

Our favourite restaurant was a marvellous little place by the railway station called the Mosca Blanca (White Fly). All the glories of Argentine cooking were on show there, mainly the wonderful meat that came in truly heroic quantities. 'Baby beef' was the smallest portion, and that flapped over the edges of a plate the size of a small table. The menu had an eccentric English translation that required a great deal of lateral thinking to work out. 'Roast Reproductive Gland' was an accurate enough description, though not one calculated to appeal to fastidious British tastes. 'Alligator' and prawns turned out to be rather less exotic avocado; the translator had obviously had a glass or two of *vino tinto* too many when he looked it up.

We grew very fond of the Mosca Blanca and they did of us. The manager confided to me one night over a table covered in the juices of dead animals and pressed grapes that no man had ever made so much money out of an enemy. He came up with a wonderful Spanish expression, a mixture of ill winds and silver linings, that I promised myself I would remember, but lost hold of as I lurched back to the Sheraton. That night I managed to get a rare phone call through to Christine in Guildford. She did not seem overly concerned herself, but she told me they were praying for me in our local church. I told her the biggest danger was overeating and she thought I was trying not to worry her. I felt something of a fraud.

All the time the days to war were ticking by. The British declared an exclusion zone around the islands, deadlines came and went; still it felt unreal. Then, one Sunday, the phoney war came to an end. It had been a particularly boisterous day for the flower of the British press corps in the Sheraton. Most of the newspaper reporters had spent their time in the bar adapting the *Dad's Army* theme tune, the Bud Flanagan song with the opening line 'Who do you think you are kidding, Mr Hitler?' for this new conflict. There were nine verses in all and copies had been circulated to every British journalist in the hotel. Halfway through dinner, the Sheraton dining room rang to the very first performance of 'Who do you think you are kidding, Galtieri?' (it sounds best with two glottal stops). As we were singing, a news report was being passed from table to table, but it wasn't generally announced until after the ninth verse had been sung with appropriate gusto. The biggest of the Argentine warships had apparently been sunk, many of the sailors on board had been lost. Some of the waiters were crying. One smashed a plate against the end of a serving table. I would have smashed it over the nearest British reporter's head if I had been him.

That night the hotel was surrounded by an angry mob. Cars circled the square honking their horns and loudspeakers shouted: 'Death to the British'. The banners showed the Union Flag spattered with blood and the words: 'Now to the death' and: 'We gave our blood for the Malvinas and will kill anyone who tries to take them away'. It felt threatening for a while but seemed to have been officially orchestrated. It had never happened before and it never happened again.

The torpedo that sank the antique American cruiser the Argentines called the *General Belgrano* killed more than 300 conscripts and made the war suddenly real and bloody. I don't think we ever had any doubt about the outcome. We had some sense of the weaknesses of the Task Force and how exposed it might be, so far from home, against determined air attack. But we had seen British troops in action, the marines and paratroopers especially. More to the point, we had seen the Argentine Army. For a hundred years their soldiers had fought nobody but themselves. The conscripts did 12 months in the army and the 9,000 who were sent to the Falklands certainly drew the short straw. Argentine television showed pictures of them most nights and, however carefully they were edited, they always looked miserable. The South Atlantic winter was drawing in and they were sleeping two to a tent in the bleak countryside. The state radio and television appealed to patriotic Argentines to knit them sweaters and bake cakes for them. With 600,000 sheep on the island they were not likely to starve, but Galtieri's boasts about 'fighting to the last drop of our blood' looked absurd when you saw the miserable, gloomy boys he wanted to be heroes.

War creates difficult moral dilemmas for reporters in the enemy camp. You have to report what's going on there, without just repeating enemy propaganda. I interpreted this as a duty to give British viewers a flavour of what ordinary Argentines were being told, while pointing out the inconsistencies that showed up exaggeration or outright lies. Sometimes it was very difficult to strike that balance. Fortunately, the Argentine government was deceitful and incompetent in this, as in everything else. The Saturday the British attacked the Falklands themselves the state radio and television issued a flurry of communiqués, most of them contradictory. The main message was that the Task Force had been compelled to withdraw with heavy losses, but there were so many inconsistencies to point out, within them and between them, that justified the scepticism of our reports.

We filmed Argentines going to Mass the next day, most of them under the impression their forces had won a great victory. We filmed an ordinary Argentine family as they waited in front of their television for more news. Why had the captured Harrier pilots not been put on display? Where were the pictures of the British soldiers who had been killed and captured? The television just showed an interminable John Wayne film. They continually promised a nationwide broadcast from General Galtieri, but kept postponing it. Eventually, two hours after it had been scheduled, the last gunfight in the film was interrupted by the emblem of a flaming torch and crossed swords. They played the National Anthem and then the special Malvinas song.

The picture dissolved into aerial shots of the airfield at Port Stanley. The commentator, who sounded as if he was describing the second half of a cup tie football match, claimed it had been taken late the previous afternoon, after the British attack, and it showed how the runway was untouched. It was unfortunate for them that the airfield was bathed in brilliant sunshine in the picture, and we knew that there had been heavy, low cloud there at the time.

At last, General Galtieri himself came on. He looked tired and sounded confused. He contradicted himself several times. He talked of brilliant victories, yet seemed also to acknowledge heavy Argentine losses. Our family went very quiet.

The Argentine authorities tried to recover their position in the propaganda war after that; they filled the Sheraton with banks of televisions and gave endless briefings, but their credibility was zero and nobody believed them.

At home, some of Mrs Thatcher's ministers criticised the very idea that the BBC should report from the enemy capital at a time of war. The BBC chairman at the time, George Howard, seemed sympathetic to this; at any rate he said that it was 'a curious state of affairs when we can interview an admiral on the active list who commands the marine forces of a country with which we are at war'. Indeed.

I think we served a constructive purpose. We showed that the enemy was human, or at least that the ordinary citizens of that country were not monsters and were subject to passions and pressures it was useful to know about. It was right to show the real nature of the Argentine junta and particularly the dictator, General Galtieri. I think it was important for British viewers to know what sort of man he was so that they could judge whether he was best dealt with by compromise or confrontation. I would argue it was right to report what ordinary Argentines were being told and what they believed, particularly when their official communiqués could be tested against provable facts. In any case there is always a value to knowing your enemy.

I have another, more personal, reason. I liked most of the Argentines I met and thought the war between the two countries was absurd and obscene. Once the invasion had happened and the Argentines would not withdraw on acceptable terms, I think Mrs Thatcher's government was right, and brave, to press ahead with recapturing the islands. But it was tragic that British paratroopers and guardsmen, and young Argentine conscripts, should be sacrificed to a dictator's ambition.

The BBC Director General at the time, Sir Ian Trethowan, summed it up rather well. 'The BBC,' he said, 'could not be and was not neutral as between our own country and an aggressor. But one of the things that distinguish a democracy from a dictatorship is that our people wish to be told the truth and can be told it, however unpleasant it may be.'

The fighting on the islands was still going on when I returned, by a necessarily roundabout route, to London. Part of me wanted very much to stay in Argentina until the conflict, and the fate of the Falklands, had been decided. But I had been away for more than three months by then. I was missing Christine and the boys a very great deal and was extremely tired. I also needed to lose weight after all those meals at the Mosca Blanca – not something I raised when I was met at Heathrow by a welcoming party of BBC bosses who seemed to think I was something of a hero.

I did make an effort to explain that life in the enemy camp was neither a hardship nor dangerous, but nobody seemed to listen. I tried several times to point out that El Salvador, on the other hand, had been a blood-curdling nightmare that we were lucky to have survived, but everybody had forgotten I had even been there. Television news is such an ephemeral business; your triumphs (and disasters) don't even last long enough to wrap tomorrow's chips.

By the time I got home, Christine had accomplished most of the renovation of our new home but our angelic builders were still putting the finishing touches to it. The boys did not seem fazed by their father returning from the war and seemed to have taken the prayers for my safety at the church where they were choristers in their stride. I settled down to what I hoped would be a few weeks' leave and made some pathetic stabs at home improvement before being relegated to my old job of unskilled assistant labourer.

I had only been home four days when I got a phone call from the Editor, just before lunchtime. 'Would you like to present the *Nine O'Clock News*?' he said. His voice seemed a bit strained.

I was surprised. I had never wanted to be a newscaster. Like most reporters, I resented how they got all the glory just for reading out loud, while we did all the work and took all the risks. Michael Cole and I used to describe ourselves as 'Angela Rippon's little helpers' when we were particularly put out by what we regarded as this triumph of celebrity over worth. Irritatingly, most ordinary people took this at face value. I was pretty sneery about 'announcers', but the thought of doing it myself made me extremely nervous.

'When?' I said.

'Oh, tonight. Just for tonight.'

I had lots of questions, but the editor was evasive. I only pieced together what had happened over the next few days.

At the start of that year, the BBC had at last decided that its main news programmes should be presented by proper journalists. They had come to this conclusion a couple of decades after ITN and the American networks. In the early days, the BBC did not want television news presented by any kind of human being at all. It was all maps and slides; the only animation was an occasional hand that pointed a stick to emphasise something of special interest. It was only with the greatest reluctance that the BBC allowed a human face to be seen reading the news. Even then, only the most reliable of its radio announcers were given the job, with terrible warnings about the neutrality of their manner, lest by some movement of the eyebrow, or pursing of the lips, they should hint at 'views'. For a generation, this suited the BBC fine. The ex-actor newsreaders were distinguished-looking men, with mellifluous voices, and, most importantly in such a producer-led organisation as the BBC, were no trouble. They never argued about what the lead should be or how it should be put together.

As they approached retirement, the mood had changed, even inside the BBC. They saw how much extra credibility news programmes carried when the audience knew the person presenting it had been out at the sharp end himself. The research showed they thought he was much more likely to know what he was talking about. Besides, technology had moved on, enabling programmes to respond to news that broke while they were on the air. It would be reassuring to have somebody fronting the news who might know about the story and the editorial pitfalls of extempore news broadcasting.

They chose two of the BBC's greatest journalists to present a new-look *Nine O'Clock News*. John Humphrys and John Simpson came from radically different backgrounds and had contrasting personal styles. John Humphrys was the son of a French polisher, born in Splott, one of the poorer districts of Cardiff, and had come up through local newspapers and regional television. He was, and is, quick and combative, an under-dog with attitude. John Simpson's background, while unconventional, was more patrician and he came to the BBC via Oxbridge. His manner was cultured and self-deprecating, an essayist more than a hack. In fact, they had a great deal in common. They were both brilliant reporters and driven men, head and shoulders above most of their colleagues. Their head and shoulders were promoted on to the screen.

One worked, the other did not. John Humphrys, an ambitious show-off like most of us, loved it and it showed. John Simpson was not happy with the job. He had given up being political editor to become a newsreader and been heavily criticised by those who thought he was squandering his talent – which was true – and I think it must have got to him. He had several programmes where there were technical problems, not of his making, which inevitably reflected badly on the presenter. He began to lose confidence and fluency. He stumbled a lot and it got steadily worse. To anybody who had known what a superbly natural broadcaster he had been before this episode, even more to those who know him as the magisterial commentator of his later career, it seems inexplicable. It can happen to the very best. In the early summer of 1982 it happened to John.

The day I was called in, the Editor of Television News had been ordered by the Director General to take John off the air, not the next month, or even the next day, but there and then. I had to do that night's *Nine O'Clock News* with no experience, no training, not even a rehearsal. Actually, there is not much to it. In any case, I was lucky. It was a straightforward programme with no surprises and no cock-ups. They were also kind enough to frame the cameras so you could not see my hands shaking.

'Just for tonight' became 'just until the end of the week'. By the end of the month it seemed to be permanent. To start with, I did not mind. I had been away such a long time, it was good to have mornings and weekends with the family. The Falklands War was reaching its climax so the programmes were full of important news and watched by huge audiences. John Humphrys and I alternated between presenting the programme and being its senior editor, spending half the night having noisy, and hugely enjoyable, rows with each other.

When the war ended, they let me out to cover the fleet's return, but then it all turned into routine. I had always wanted to be a foreign correspondent, based abroad, and when I came back from Buenos Aires got all the peculiar BBC signals that this was on the cards. Now, though, I came under increasing pressure to become a permanent newscaster. My salary was comparatively low at the time and they said they would double it if I carried on reading the news. Curiously, this was not as difficult to resist as the appeals from editors I liked, who had been good to me and whose company I enjoyed.

In the end, I did a deal with them. I agreed to present the programme for a year, on condition that I would be the next Africa correspondent, based in Johannesburg.

It gave them breathing space to consolidate the idea of the journalist/ presenter. It enabled us to plan the move to Africa. But I was desperate to go and, in some ways, it was the longest year of my life.

SIXTEEN

AT 36,000 FEET SOMEWHERE over Juba, the African sky outside the 747 was velvet black, shading to blue on what must have been the night's horizon like the ink on an old love letter. The jet stream sighed under the big plane's wings. From time to time it would rock in the clear-air turbulence but mostly it slid smoothly through the sky on its long journey from London to Johannesburg. Inside the Club cabin there was a kind of sprawled and restless silence, broken only by the whispers and occasional clatter of cutlery from the stewardesses beyond the galley curtain, or a mutter in someone's broken dream. The boys, now nine years old, had been excited for the first few hours but were now deeply asleep, looking like they'd been flung on to their seats from a great height. Christine had finally slipped off into a fitful doze. I couldn't sleep at all. This was what I had been waiting for most of my life; a real foreign correspondent at last, not a fireman dashing out from London every time the alarm bells rang. I would have a whole continent to myself, to live in as well as report on; to sink roots into, rather than rush across; to try to understand, rather than glibly summarise. That British Airways flight to the golden city at the other end of the dark continent felt like a journey to some personal destiny.

My colleagues called it the gravy train. They were all envious. It was the ambition then of every BBC reporter to be a foreign correspondent for television. BBC salaries at the time were relatively low, the expense account at home was as nitpicking and bureaucratic as only the corporation's genius for administrative complexity could make it. The foreign correspondents, though, led autonomous and relatively luxurious lives on allowances that were based loosely on those of senior diplomats. They did not pay tax. Their living expenses were all covered: nice house, car, utility bills, schools for the kids, entertainment. The BBC wouldn't pay for servants even in those postings where servants were customary, which its featherbedded foreign contingent then considered to be the height of meanness. But if anybody looked closely at the accounts the correspondents submitted, the servants' wages were in there somewhere, under 'garden maintenance' perhaps, or 'replacement of BBC crockery'.

Thanks to the almost legendary reputation for independence and accuracy long since established by the BBC Radio World Service, the corporation's foreign correspondents were treated like alternative British Ambassadors. In those African countries whose own newspapers never got off their knees in front of whatever corrupt and murderous dictator happened to be in power, and in those where the British diplomatic mission was sunk in the water-treading torpor that afflicts so many of our High Commissions in the tropics, the BBC correspondent mattered even more. His arrival (always *his* then; the job was far too important, and fraught with too many potential hardships and embarrassments, for a woman to be even considered) was a matter of great suspicion to the local authorities, and sometimes some hope to those under the current Big Man's heel.

Television correspondents were even better off. They were given a magic porridge pot of money, a so-called 'imprest account'. They could spend what they needed out of the account and every month the bookkeepers in London would dutifully fill it up again. Television is a costly business and considerable sums flowed through these accounts. The more financially creative and less scrupulous correspondents made small fortunes, particularly in those troubled parts of the world where unstable currencies offered even more profitable opportunities on the black market. One of the more famous BBC men was seen quite regularly on the streets of an African capital hawking currencies from a leather bag. Another made one of his many fortunes trading carpets across the troubled frontiers of the Middle East.

Part of the reason for the indulgent way television correspondents were treated was because there were so few of them. Each was regarded as an individual case, with special requirements that did not fall under the almanacs of rules and regulations that constrained the corporation's reporters based in Britain. BBC TV had only five full-time foreign correspondents who divided the world between them. Johannesburg was the pick of the postings. You were not stuck in the miserable climate and Soviet lifestyle of Moscow. You were not out on a limb with one story a year like the man in Hong Kong. The Middle East correspondent was trapped between Jew and Arab in a cauldron that always simmered, sometimes exploded, but where there was never much relief from short-range nastiness. Washington was pleasant to live and work in, but too busy. That, and the ready availability of American network television pictures, meant it was always difficult to get out of the bureau to go and see things for yourself; a treadmill; fast food and fast television.

Johannesburg, they said, had it all. The climate was wonderful. The life was luxurious. The living was cheap, especially as someone else, the viewer and his licence fee in fact, was paying for it. It was not so busy then that you could not regularly head off into the bush with your crew to discover and film something new. And yet it had a very serious, long-running story on the doorstep, perhaps the most striking moral issue of the late twentieth century. Unlike most other vexed ethical questions of our times, it was absolutely clear who was right and who was wrong. The detail might have been complex. Heroes and villains tended to get rather mixed up in disconcerting ways. But apartheid was simply and obviously evil.

Johannesburg, then, had everything a reporter could wish for. It gave you a chance to stake out a showy position on the moral high ground. There were lots of opportunities to align yourself with, and report movingly on, the poor, the disenfranchised and the downtrodden. Then, come the evening, you could sip white wine by the side of your own swimming pool and think how unjust the world was – for others. It wasn't complacency, or hypocrisy – well, maybe it was. But, heading south at ten miles a minute, it seemed I was going to the most wonderful job in the world. There would be a worrying ambiguity about enjoying the fruits of unfairness while decrying it from the highest of media rooftops. But I would find out they were right; it *was* the most wonderful job of all.

I only half understood these things as we crossed the continent that was to be our home, and my workplace. The flight seemed endless. Africa is huge – four times the size of the United States, 7,000 kilometres from Cairo to the Cape. It is old, formed out of the most ancient rocks three billion years ago, which left a rich legacy of minerals but poor and relatively infertile topsoils. This was where man was born, and where his life is still often short and painful. Somewhere underneath the port wing was Laetoli in Tanzania where they found the earliest known evidence of man's ancestors walking on their hind legs. You can see the fossilised footprints of three people, upright but not yet very bright, frozen by some geological accident at that moment in time, nearly 4 million years ago, when they left the woodland to go down to the plain in search of animal carcasses.

It was down there that modern humans evolved and began to spread across the earth; first East Africa, then the length and breadth of the continent, finally the world. Genetic research, that was actually being stitched into a persuasive theory as BA 56 carried us over humanity's cradle, suggests we are all descended from one woman, the 'African Eve', more than ten thousand generations ago. The genetic variations of today's Africans show how most of human history was played out on the continent that is now so impoverished and marginalised. It seems the rest of us are descended from a small band of Africans, perhaps as few as 50 people, who crossed the land bridge to the Middle East a hundred thousand years ago and went on to populate the globe. For us that night, for all of us any time, flying to Africa is a homecoming.

These were things I sensed, but did not really know, as the dawn came up somewhere beyond Zanzibar and the plane, caught in a weather front, shook itself like a dog coming out of a pond. What I did know, from the satchelful of newspaper cuttings I had brought with me, was something of Africa's recent history. The way the colonial powers had met in Berlin a hundred years before to carve up their imperial conquests. They drew straight lines on the map, arbitrarily chopping Africa's 2,000 tribes and 200 languages into bite-sized colonies. My little library of books and cuttings told how those colonies had been off-loaded with unseemly haste over the previous two decades, half-developed and unprepared for the independence that came so much sooner than anybody, European imperialist or African activist, could ever have imagined. How a cohort of tyrants, incompetents and naïve idealists had taken this half-baked inheritance and, in their greed and lust for unchallenged power, made it all much, much worse. Two-thirds of the countries over which we flew that night were worse off than they had been at Independence. The average income of the people who might have seen our jet's trail from their shacks or their huts was around 50 pence a day. More than half of them were malnourished; one in eight babies was dying before their second birthday. In half the countries we crossed, those children who did survive could not expect to reach 40, and many are not alive today. Eventually I would discover a positive side to Africa, but it was not to be found in those newspaper reports that I read and re-read under a single overhead light in that darkened cabin.

They served breakfast to a bleary, frowzy set of passengers as we crossed the River Limpopo and left 'black' Africa behind. We were now flying over the richest, most powerful country on the continent, where the white man kept not so much a toehold as a stranglehold on power and wealth. We had reached the pariah state.

The boys were glued to the windows as we came down through the cloud that covered the Highveld like thin semolina, and took a wide sweep above the khaki-coloured, late-winter countryside around the towers of Johannesburg. I hugged them as we landed at Jan Smuts and told them it was going to be the start of a great adventure.

And, in many ways, it was.

'Hullo,' I said, to one of a line of unsmiling white immigration officers as I handed over my passport and work permit. He did not bother to reply. He said something to one of his colleagues in Afrikaans, which seemed more like a throat infection than a language. As soon as he saw the letters 'BBC' on the document he wrote something laboriously across it and stamped it four times. He had cut my work permit, and my family's permission to stay, from six months to three months.

'Welcome to South Africa, Mr Buerk,' he said. He was pleased, but still had trouble smiling.

Egoli, city of gold. How it shimmered in the dry and copper-coloured air that morning as we got our first real sight of Johannesburg. Coming in on the network of motorways from the airport and the East Rand, there's a moment where the high rises and the mirrored office blocks and the telecom towers of central Johannesburg are silhouetted in a dip on the skyline. There's only one reason for its existence; the 'banket' reef of gold-bearing rock that spreads, like the Afrikaners' toffee after which it is named, through broken strata up to a mile or more underground. The city centre sits surrounded by its own waste on the low range of hills called, in Afrikaans, the Witwatersrand – the ridge of white waters. A century before there was nothing but a few sheep. Then the cry of 'Gold!' brought hundreds of thousands flooding here. Johannesburg was built on greed, almost overnight. Its gold made the Rand Lords the richest men on earth, precipitated a cruel war between Briton and Boer, for a time underpinned the whole world's economy, and for all time destroyed the agrarian society and customs of both whites and blacks. The old paternalistic accommodation between the two was swept away by an urgent need for millions of units of labour, with consequences that South Africa lives with to this day.

The M2 motorway swung south round the city centre, past the great dumps of spoil, the mountains of rock that had been crushed into hills of dirty, sulphur-coloured sand in the search for gold. Then north and on to the M1 through the skyscrapers, almost within touching distance of the dreaded security police headquarters at John Vorster Square. Blacks taken there for 'questioning' did not always come out intact, or even alive. That day, and every time we passed, we craned our necks to see if we could see someone being tortured. It was happening but, with unusual sensitivity for the South African security police of those days, not normally in front of passers-by. The interrogation rooms were on the tenth floor, far above the passing cars. It was high enough for the threat to be thrown out of the windows to be particularly effective.

The M1 crests a low rise before swooping down into the northern districts of the city, the reservation for rich whites which was to be our home. The first impression was how green it was, even at a time of drought at the end of the bone-hard Transvaal winter. There were trees everywhere in those gracious garden suburbs, built across what had been bare veld; so many trees that some say white Johannesburg is the biggest man-made forest on earth.

We spent the first few weeks in a hotel in Rosebank. The boys were instantly seduced by expense-account living. They developed a habit, which they have not yet managed to shake off, of picking the most expensive choices on the menu. They were aided and abetted by the black waiters, men of overflowing good humour who badgered them into bigger and bigger blow-outs, until we feared they would burst. The waiters were personable and charming but not long on memory which was a shame because it seemed a point of pride for them never to write anything down. For the first few nights we were impressed as they took a mental note of our complicated orders and strode confidently off to the kitchens. It was only when they came back with trays full of food we didn't want that we realised their method was rather flawed. It annoyed us for a while and we took to writing out the order ourselves. This was always loftily disregarded. In the end, it became a long-running joke and we just accepted that every evening was pot luck. Except for the boys, of course, who automatically got the most expensive dishes available, even on the very rare occasions when they had not actually asked for them.

It was early spring by the time we moved into our new home, a sprawling single-storey house in a district called Saxonwold. Developers there were keen on Merrie England and Home Counties names. Their clients were mostly lower-middle-class English-speaking whites who, because of the system, were living lives of considerable privilege and liked to ape what they imagined were the manners of Edwardian Wimbledon. Ashwold Avenue was beautiful. It was heavily shaded by jacaranda trees that branched at head height and rose up into a dense canopy, dusted with lovely lilac-coloured flowers. Black garden boys (as they were universally called, even if they were old enough to be my grandfather) lackadaisically raked away at wide verges or perfect lawns. The houses were mostly open at the front then, not the fortresses for frightened people they would soon become. An ibis in the tree opposite our house sneered and cawed at us over his long curved bill as we turned up the brick drive, past the big swimming pool in the front garden, and parked under the porch. A lion roared quite close. Our heads knew it was in the Johannesburg zoo, two streets away. Our hearts knew we were in Africa.

We barely had time to unpack our bags before a lorry turned into the drive, loaded up with the BBC furniture. On top of a precarious stack of tables, armchairs and sofas that had furnished the previous correspondent's home sat Caroline, the BBC servant, with her trademark red woolly hat. She was a cheerful woman, by now long since accustomed to the unusual sensibilities of liberal British journalists. She had already worked for John Humphrys, John Simpson and Philip Hayton.

We had all tried to stop her calling us 'master'. The conversation was always the same.

'Don't call me master,' I'd say.

'No, master,' she would always reply.

It was always said with a straight face, but I think she saw some advantage in our discomfort. She was cleverer than any of us. She knew how to work the ambiguities of this relationship to her best advantage, and was much envied by the maids down the street. We used to get lectures from neighbours about what a bad example our treatment of Caroline was setting for the entire servant class.

We very definitely had not wanted a servant. Not, to be frank, because we were keen to do our own housework, or that we had profound moral objections to the whole idea of servanthood, but because of the restrictions having a stranger in the house would put on our lives. I, in particular, have an alarming habit of striding round the house stark naked, which I had to curb for fear of bumping into Caroline. I think I was worried she would laugh.

We tried hard to stop her coming; to pay her off. But she became increasingly desperate to be with us and provided us with our first personal lesson in the realities of apartheid. A job with us, that we might regard as demeaning, was a lifeline for a family fractured by official racism. Because she worked for us, she could live at our house. Not *in* our house exactly. Like most homes in the northern suburbs, the maid had a room in the yard opposite the dog kennel. Apart from the iron bedstead jammed into it and raised up on bricks to stop the *thokoloshe* (evil spirits) climbing the legs, it was little different. But it was regular money for undemanding work in secure and pleasant surroundings – privileges enjoyed by very few blacks at the time.

This was the only way an ordinary black person could qualify to live in a white 'prescribed' area. Her husband Victor was a mechanic at the Volkswagen garage down the road. His job qualified him to travel to a white area every day, providing his *dompas* (pass) was up to date, but he was not allowed to spend the night there. He could not officially sleep with his wife. He did have permission to stay in Soweto, the giant black township on the outskirts of Johannesburg, and millions of marginalised blacks envied him the privilege. In fact, he used to shin over our garden wall when it got dark. It would have been prison for him, and a hefty fine for me, if he got caught.

Caroline and Victor had two little girls. They did not seem to be authorised to live with their father or their mother, but had to stay in the so-called 'homeland' that had been designated for their Tswana tribe – a mini, make-believe country called Bophutatswana, 80-odd miles away, where they lived with their granny and only saw their parents once or maybe twice a year.

Now that I was, effectively, harbouring a criminal, I tried to find out how a black person could qualify to be in a prescribed area and was referred to the Black (Urban Areas) Consolidation Act.

> A 'qualified person' means a black referred to in section 10(1)(a) or (b) who is not a black referred to in section 12 (1) and any descendant of such a black who is a black referred to in section 10 (1) (a) or (b) and . . . also any black who is not a qualified person but falls within a category of blacks recognised by the Minister by notice in the Gazette as qualified persons for the purposes of section 6A and 6B and the regulations relating thereto, or who has in any particular case been expressly recognised by the Minister as a qualified person for such purposes, as well as any person who has in general or in any particular case been expressly recognised by the Minister, subject to such conditions as may be determined by the Minister, as a qualified person for said purposes: provided that the said conditions may also provide that a person shall be recognised for a particular purpose or for a particular period or until the occurrence of a particular event only.

The truth was that most of South Africa was 'prescribed' and most blacks were 'disqualified'. The huge body of law, and the miasma of legalisms that surrounded it, gave blacks no rights at all. A favoured few had a temporary immunity to arbitrary arrest, but white functionaries could change that on a whim. The bigger point was that this was what made South Africa morally repugnant. Not cruelty – many, if not most, African regimes could be more cruel. Not oppression and unfairness; other African countries proved even worse. What was uniquely evil was that a modern state, claiming to be acting in the name of civilisation, institutionalised racism. It defined and legislated blacks into inferiority at every level of society and, in terms of citizenship, out of existence entirely. Four out of five South Africans, the ones whose skins were dark, were foreigners in their own country.

It was great to be white. Johannesburg was really a metropolis of more than 4 million people, but only 900,000 of us with pale skins were allowed to live there. The blacks lucky enough to have permission to be in the area at all had to live in satellite townships. Nobody knew how many lived in the largest of them, Soweto (a contraction from SOuth WEstern TOwnship); 2 million, maybe more. That was only one of the black dormitories that circled the city, along with other townships specially designated for Indians and (mixed-race) coloureds. The result was that we lived close to the centre of one of the world's great cities but had the elbow-room you could only find far out in the suburbs of a normal society. In English terms, it was like having a Surrey country house in Islington. Occasionally in the winter we would catch a whiff of the countless coal fires in the townships on the evening breeze. As far as our neighbours were concerned, that was the only evidence of their existence.

Everybody told us when we arrived that apartheid (literally, 'apartness' or 'separatehood') was being phased out, everybody official and white, that is. The South African Ambassador in London had told us before we left, the Information Minister repeated it like a mantra in my first interview, the thin-lipped and disapproving Miss Van de Merwe at the Home Affairs Department in Pretoria said so as she rather reluctantly handed me my first work permit renewal. Government jobs, at all levels, were reserved for Afrikaner whites. Postman Joubert told me apartheid was dead when I met him at the bottom of our drive. He looked sad about it.

He needn't have been. The truth was that the government of Prime Minister Pieter Willem Botha was making a few cosmetic adjustments;

some of the more absurd rules on segregation were being quietly dropped in the more liberal areas. He was wooing Indians and coloureds with offers of second-class citizenship. But the master plan of Grand Apartheid, a plan that acknowledged blacks (73.8 per cent of the population) as an economic necessity but pretended they did not exist politically, was being cemented into place, apparently for all time.

Even the changes in so-called 'petty' apartheid were slow and painfully uneven. There were fewer 'Whites Only' signs around than there had been, but segregation, in almost everything, was still all around us. When Caroline fell ill she was taken in a blacks-only ambulance to a blacks-only hospital where pregnant women slept on the floor even though there were dozens of beds free in the maternity unit of the white hospital down the road.

Some of the cinemas near us were still segregated, and the films they showed were not only restricted by age group but sometimes also by race. Blacks were not allowed to see blacks in America living on equal terms with whites, for instance.

The nearest post office to us had pulled down the partition between the blacks' counter and that for whites, but the next one was strict about not allowing both races to queue together.

The Zoo Lake park near our home where I took the boys on their bikes was open to blacks but, up the road in Pretoria, the administrative capital of the government supposedly abandoning apartheid, it was different. Soon after we arrived, the council voted to close 17 of its parks to all blacks (except white children's nursemaids) and fence off the other three into white and black areas at a cost of £100,000.

Blacks could get served in the Rosebank Hotel, where we had been staying, if they waited long enough. But only five per cent of South Africa's hotels were allowed the 'international status' to accept all races and, even there, mixed dancing and mixed swimming were forbidden; in fact, both were officially a crime.

There was a big fanfare as we arrived about desegregation on the railways. Some pro-government newspapers declared it as the symbolic end of apartheid. What actually happened was that trains started to have a few mixed carriages where whites, if they chose, could sit amongst blacks. But there were still whites-only carriages for those who could not bring themselves to rub shoulders with people of colour.

The truth was that everything that mattered was still segregated, from where you were born, through school, what job you could do, who you could have sex with and marry, where you could live, and finally where you could be buried.

It all seemed to me both obscene and absurd. The assumptions of superiority and inferiority were bad enough, but the detailed way it was all regulated and enforced often verged on the surreal. It didn't so much hit you in the face as creep up on you as you encountered layer after layer of accumulated, institutionalised prejudice. It became the way things were, slowly darkening your snow-white soul.

I talked it over endlessly with the BBC's cameraman in South Africa, François Marais, a jolly little barrel of a man with a lush moustache. François was a descendant of French Huguenots who'd arrived in the Cape fleeing religious persecution, an Afrikaans speaker who loved his food, loved his wine and took beautiful pictures. He used one of two soundmen, both of whom had had more than their fair share of misfortune. Mac Mclean was a Rhodesian who had somehow managed to get a burst of machine-gun fire in his bottom from his own troops during the bush war. Five bullets in the backside had nearly killed him and he was left with a slight limp and a tendency to brood. A perforated behind, he would say, does tend to make you moody.

Peter Henderson was a sturdy Capetonian who had contrived to get half his hand chewed off by a lion, which bothered him not at all. Indeed, it was something of a talking point, particularly with visitors from England. He generally managed to gloss over the fact that it had all happened in a zoo when he had been leaning against the bars of the cage and paying less attention than the lion.

It was with this crew that I set off to find out about apartheid.

SEVENTEEN

I STARTED ON THE beaches of Durban, the Blackpool of South Africa. They even called the stretch in front of the 'international' hotels the Golden Mile. This was where the surfers ('waxies' from the wax they put on their boards) rode the big Indian Ocean breakers. This was where families paddled and sunbathed, or took shelter from the humid heat under blue beach umbrellas. Only white surfers and only white families. Section 37 of the Durban beach laws reserved the entire stretch for 'the white race group'. The only blacks allowed there were selling ice creams, or nursemaiding white toddlers. While I watched, a couple of young black women, fully dressed and very tentative, crossed the sacred sand to dip their black toes in the pristine sea. They were headed off before they got to the water's edge. A beach patrolman, a stringy old white man in khaki shorts and a military-style shirt, barked into his two-way radio before giving them an ultimatum: leave immediately, or be carted off to jail.

The African beach was a bus ride out of town, beyond one reserved specifically for Indians. We were there at a weekend. It was standing room only, out up to chest-high in the big, breaking waves. Durban's city council was, by the standard of the times, liberally minded and wanted to drop the beach segregation altogether, saying it gave the city the 'wrong image'. But thousands of whites protested against the idea, and a campaign, led by Peter Wilmer, an English immigrant and former member of the National Front, stopped desegregation in its tracks. It was, he told me, a question of 'levels of sophistication and behavioural norms of the non-white populations'. I asked him when he thought non-whites would have progressed to the stage where they could be allowed to bathe alongside him. He shrugged a safari-suited shoulder: 'Who knows?'

The city council was embarrassed. It even discussed draining all the municipal swimming pools so nobody of any race could use them. But in the end they compromised. They kept segregation but put up notices saying it wasn't their fault. 'Liberal' white South Africans sometimes turned ineffectiveness into an art form.

The beaches were a side show really, except perhaps in the way they touched on the most visceral of white fears about blacks' physicality and sexuality. I had laughed at the rasping Mancunian editor of the BBC early-evening news who'd taken me aside at my leaving party in London

233

and told me what he thought really lay behind apartheid. 'Remember, Mike,' he growled. 'It's all about black hands on white thighs.' In a way, in the furthest Freudian recesses of white minds, he was right.

Real apartheid, though, was about social engineering on the grandest of scales. All the while the government was protesting that apartheid was over, they were pushing ahead with the twisted vision of Dr Hendrik Verwoerd. He solved the problem of black South Africans by arranging things so there weren't any. His idea, and there was an amoral logic to it, was to set up a series of tribal mini-states on marginal scraps of land within South Africa's borders. Every black could then be assigned to one or other so-called 'homeland' which would eventually be given independence. In this way, three-quarters of South Africa's population was allocated 13 per cent of the land and effectively made foreigners in their own country. Millions of blacks were shovelled away from countryside now designated white into these reserves, kept there at a distance and under control, and only allowed into white South Africa if they were of economic use to the master race.

Mogopa was one of the so-called 'black spots' that we watched being ruthlessly rubbed out. The Bakwena tribe had owned land in the valley, south-west of Johannesburg, since before the First World War. Their title deeds were signed by a government minister before 'natives' were forbidden to buy land from whites by a British administration. It was a successful community with boreholes, settled houses and a church; prosperous, contented and a threat to no one. But they were on the list. They were told they would have to move to a bare hillside at Pachsdraai, in the 'homeland' of Bophutatswana. It was ready for them, the white officials said, though when we went there we found row after regimented row of tin toilets and nothing else.

For a time, Mogopa caught at the world's imagination. Something about the dignity of the Bakwena and the unfairness of it all struck a chord outside the country, and churchmen like Bishop Desmond Tutu and the Reverend Alan Boesak joined them in emotional night-time vigils. We filmed them singing hymns together as the cold of the evening settled on the slopes of their valley. The old men with their rheumy eyes and white beards stood painfully erect, singing out strongly and staring into an uncertain future.

Force won in the end. Under constant pressure and harassment, many Bakwena tore their own homes down to salvage the window frames and doors. They cried over the family graves, and left. Those that remained were overwhelmed by a big police operation a few weeks later that sealed their valley off. They were reportedly handcuffed and arrested, but we don't know for sure because we weren't allowed near. We did film an abandoned dog, looking mournfully after the last lorry as it left their home for ever.

Few communities escaped this fate. It took the Queen to save the Ngema tribe who lived on a farm in the Eastern Transvaal. They had been given the land by the British Lieutenant-Governor in 1904, as a reward for their help in the Boer War. The officials arrived one morning and told them they would have to pack up and leave. They painted numbers on the brown doors of their mud-brick houses and thought it no more important and troublesome than the hundreds of other black communities they had razed from land now designated white.

They had reckoned without the patriarch, Alfred Ngema, a baby when the Boer War was being fought, now an old man, shrivelled and bent but undaunted. He said he would die rather than leave and got his son to write to the Queen, pointing out the land had been given them in the name of her great-grandfather. 'We love this land,' the letter said. 'Since England gave us this land, how can South Africa take it away?' Alfred's son confidently told me: 'When the Queen reads my letter, she will get the government of South Africa to leave the people in peace.'

Fat chance, I thought. But it worked. Prime Minister Botha was making a European tour at the time, trying to shake off the country's polecat status. Mrs Thatcher invited him to Chequers and read out the Ngema's letter which the Queen had passed on to her. The Ngema were given a temporary, and grudging, reprieve.

Most, though, were hustled off into bleak and remote bushveld or sometimes terrible resettlement camps, like one we found south of Bloemfontein at a place then called Onverwacht ('unexpected' in Afrikaans). There, nearly a quarter of a million blacks had been dumped in a place that wasn't even half-built. They were being shipped in on lorries at the rate of 1,000 a week. There was a grid of poles and tin toilets, but few houses. Corrugated-iron shelters stretched almost as far as the eye could see. Babies crawled through mountains of garbage. Kids rolled old tyres down the rutted tracks. Women queued for hours to fill buckets out of the few communal taps.

The busiest place was the graveyard. We filmed the seventeenth funeral there in four days. A little girl called Alice Jantjies who'd never been well since she was taken to Onverwacht and died just before her ninth birthday. She was brought to the graveyard in a small white coffin and lowered into one of a row of empty graves. An old priest threw dirt on to the coffin lid as he said a prayer, while the undertaker stood impatiently by with his shovel. The women, wrapped in their plaid blankets, sang a soaring hymn that made the hairs on the back of my neck stand up. It was difficult to speak.

I asked the undertaker about his job. He said the graveyard had been opened a couple of months before and was already half full of children. I asked him why they were dying. He said: 'Through this water. They say the water's no good.' I asked him how many children he had buried. He swung round and made a gesture that embraced dozens and dozens of graves behind him. 'Whoooa,' he said. 'It was opened and in a week we had all those graves.' Then, with an even bigger gesture that covered a whole landscape of mounds: 'In two months we buried all these children here.'

After he and the rest had gone, we stayed in the graveyard while I tried to find the words to sum up what we had seen. There was a lump in my throat and a faraway look in François' eyes, François, the eternal optimist about South Africa. Later I checked the death statistics. Five hundred children had died there in the last year and, at that time, they were dying at the rate of three or four a day. For all the talk of change, this was apartheid, and it wasn't really changing at all.

Onverwacht would soon be renamed Botshabelo, which means 'beautiful place' in the Sotho language – Pretoria had a taste for laughably inappropriate names – and incorporated in the' homeland' of Qwa Qwa, a territory as ramshackle as it sounds. At least it was in more or less one piece, unlike KwaZulu, the Zulus' notional homeland, which was scattered like bird droppings across the map of Natal, an archipelago of scraps of countryside whites felt they could do without.

And it was not as sinister a tyranny as Ciskei, a Xhosa tribal 'homeland' in the Eastern Cape, which Pretoria had already declared 'independent' though they were the only people in the world that recognised it as such. On Independence Day in 1981, the flagpole fell over when they tried to raise the new national banner for the first time. Under 'President for Life' Lennox Sebe and his secret police it went downhill from then on. Farce turned to tragedy in the packed Ciskei township of Mdantsane, the nearest place most blacks could get to jobs in the white city of East London. When people there staged a bus boycott over an 11 per cent increase in fares, Sebe sent in his army and police, together with his party vigilantes. They mowed the demonstrators down, eventually killing up to 90 people. A thousand more were rounded up and detained without trial, including a leading churchman called Father Smangaliso Mkhatshwa, Secretary-General of the Catholic Bishops' Conference, who had gone there to address a students' meeting and simply disappeared. He had been missing for six weeks and there was growing international concern.

Journalists were not welcome in Ciskei, and several had been arrested and beaten up by the time François and I arrived. Sure enough, within a few minutes of crossing the 'international' border, a van-load of heavily armed secret police forced us off the road. They all had natty suits and open-necked shirts, with bulges on their hips and under their arms. They frisked us, searched every inch of our hire car, leafed through notebooks and picked over the camera equipment. All the while they spoke of the 'accidents' that could happen to strangers there.

I did not need convincing. I was pretty frightened and talked rather fast; the letters BBC came out every other word. Instead of being beaten to a pulp and dropped back over the border – or worse – they decided to take us to see the dictator himself, the man who was already being called the Papa Doc of southern Africa.

However impoverished and desperate these homelands were, they all had a smart little toytown capital where the puppet leader and his white advisers were sealed off from the people they ruled. Sebe had Bisho, a clutch of new administrative buildings, 18 very grand official residences and a palatial mansion for the President for Life. He arrived there in a brand-new £50,000 Daimler with darkened windows, followed by a BMW with heavily armed guards. Soldiers with machine guns stood outside his office. Inside, he oozed menace. He was big, thick-set man, straight out of the villains' file in Central Casting. He had scratchings of grey hair over a moon-shaped face and tiny eyes half hidden by big, glinting silver spectacles. He was dressed like prosperous funeral director, which, I suppose, in a way he was. A medal hung from his left lapel, from whom, for what, we never found out. He spoke like a cartoon villain, too. 'Those people that were, umm, keeeeled,' he said, seeming to savour that word and roll it round his thick tongue, 'had only themselves to blame.' Hollywood could not have done it better.

I had recovered my nerve enough to ask him about Father Mkhatshwa and he flew into a rage about interfering priests, muck-raking journalists and the difficulties of maintaining order amongst his ungrateful people.

Then, to everyone's surprise, not least his own security guards', he said we could see the priest.

We were taken off by a gang of secret police, miles into the Ciskei, to a remote detention centre and told to wait in the office. After half an hour, the bewildered priest was brought in, looking very much the worse for wear, dressed in a filthy red track-suit top and ragged jeans.

It was one of the more bizarre interviews I have done. Father Mkhatshwa was obviously terrified. He was surrounded by thugs who looked as though they would fall on him if he uttered a false word. One picked his teeth and hissed all the time. Another took his gun out and pushed it meaningfully around the table in front of him. Father Mkhatshwa was being diplomatic, as if his life depended on it, which it might very well have done.

How was he being treated?

'As you might expect in the Ciskei.'

How long will you be here?

'Only the Ciskei knows, just as only the Ciskei knows why I was detained.'

The priest was hustled off after 15 minutes or so of this careful conversation, shooting me a rather desperate look as he was pushed, none too gently, through the door. He was released a few days later, unlike many Ciskei detainees, who simply disappeared. That bizarre interview might have saved his life, or at least saved him from more brutal treatment that was the norm in Ciskei's cells, but it is difficult to be sure. The homelands of apartheid were beyond reason, let alone law.

This was quite a scoop to take back to the BBC base in Johannesburg. This was a shed in François' back yard, tacked on to another, similar-sized box where Jack the gardener lived.

Jack was rather alarming until you got used to him. His eyes rolled slowly round as he talked to you. He rubbed the side of his head incessantly. One shoulder hung down. The opposite leg didn't seem to work very well and he had to drag it behind him using a rake as a crutch. It was worse when he was drunk, which seemed to me to be most of the time. He didn't appear to do much gardening and preferred to come and watch me editing our pieces on the video machines. François would mildly reprove him from time to time in Afrikaans, but it made little difference.

Our other spectator was Cholmondley, François' Springer Spaniel. Cholmondley was a dedicated news hound who liked nothing better than to watch us editing, to the point of making what he evidently thought were helpful suggestions. He would bark when I was trying to record the commentary. François reckoned he was correcting my grammar.

Cholmondley would not react at all to his aristocratic name. The only words he ever responded to were 'bugger off'. This had been shouted at him so often he was convinced it was what he was called, and would come rushing up, wagging his tail, whenever the words were uttered.

The deadline was 4.30 in the afternoon, which just gave the shipping company messenger time to get the package on the overnight flight to London. Satellites cost nearly £2,000 for ten minutes and were only for the most urgent and important news. At the time, the BBC did not seem to regard apartheid as either. The reports were run on the main bulletins because they were touching stories, well shot, well written and well put together, but there was not much sense at Television Centre that this was one of the great issues of our times. There was more a feeling that this was an old story; that every new correspondent sent to South Africa 'discovered' apartheid, got obsessed with it for a while, but eventually got over it. Pretoria and its embassy in London monitored the BBC coverage very closely and kept up a barrage of complaints if they felt apartheid was being given undue prominence, or that 'progress' was not being properly acknowledged. There were threats, of varying degrees of subtlety, that the BBC bureau would be closed and I would be thrown out, if my reporting concentrated too much on issues of discrimination. Miss van de Merwe's lips were even thinner at the Home Affairs Department in Pretoria. My work permit was again reduced from six months to three. She could not say why. 'Perhaps you have not been behaving yourself, Mr Buerk,' she said

To my bosses' credit, I was never told to stop reporting on apartheid – just to tread more carefully and to find stories in South Africa that had nothing to do with race. The problem was that apartheid permeated every aspect of human life in the republic. You were only really safe with animals.

I went back to the Durban beaches to make a film about sharks, racing out in speedboats through the surf with the excited Zulus of the Natal Sharks Board to check the nets that were supposed to protect bathers of all races. They were not that effective. The sharks could swim above them, below them and around them. The morning we were there the Zulus found several big sharks that had got caught up in the nets and had died because their gills only work when they are swimming freely. All of them were on the inside. The director of the Sharks Board was a tiny but feisty woman called Dr Beulah Davis who loved her work and absolutely adored sharks. We put her next to a giant white, about three times her size and looking dangerous even though it had been dead twelve hours and was hanging upside down from a hook.

'They're the lions of the sea,' she told me, patting it like a dog and positively glowing with affection for the ghastly thing.

I said they were ruthless killers, a nightmare with fins. That seemed to be what she liked about them. I reminded her that the last shark they had opened up had two human feet in its gut.

Yes, she said but they were Indian.

She seemed a decent woman and I don't think she meant it to sound as if she thought an Indian's life was of less account than a white man's. It was just that your race was the most important thing about you, in death as in life. Even though most of you was now unidentifiable shark excreta, your feet were still Indian, and that's what counted.

It counted so much that people were endlessly trying to get themselves 're-classified', normally to a lighter category of skin colour and therefore more privileged racial caste. There was an entire government department devoted to this, holding bizarre hearings to decide these matters. The laws were, to say the least, imprecise. A white, for instance, was 'any person who in appearance obviously is, or who is generally accepted as, a white person, other than a person who, although in appearance obviously a white person, is generally accepted as a coloured person'.

The tests the classification boards applied were even more farcical. They used light meters to judge shades of colour. They were particularly interested in your hair. Applicants would be instructed to push pencils into their hair and shake their heads. If the pencil stayed put it was a bad sign, an indication your hair was curly, like a native, and a cross was more likely to be put against your name.

That first year I was there the board published a list of changes made over the previous twelve months.

Cape Coloured promoted to white	722
Cape Coloured to Chinese	4
White demoted to Cape Coloured	3
White demoted to Chinese	15
White demoted to Indian	1
Indian promoted to White	1

Indian to Cape Coloured	34
Cape Coloured to Indian	39
African to Cape Coloured	109

It was not absolutely rigid. Exceptions were made in some cases. Coloured singing or sporting stars might be given the status of whites for the brief period of their engagement in South Africa. Japanese were treated as honorary whites, in recognition of their economic importance in the world, as long as they were not taken to be Chinese, a lowish sub-group in the racial caste system and generally referred to as 'coolies'.

It was rigid enough to leave hundreds of people, particularly children, in a racial limbo. I went to a centre, just outside Soweto, where they put children the state was having trouble classifying. Because nobody could decide what race they were, they could not go to school. Most just ran wild, except 80 or so, aged between 4 and 12, who had been rounded up by a charity and were being given at least some lessons in a makeshift hall. We filmed them as they lined up outside in their threadbare shorts, each with his or her hands on the shoulders of the child in front.

Norman Johnstone was 11. His mother was a mixed-race coloured, his father was black. The authorities couldn't, or wouldn't, decide which he was, which meant he could not go to either a black or a coloured school. He seemed a bright and lively youngster. He told me he wanted to be a doctor. He had a long way to go. When I met him he had not had a day's formal schooling in his life.

Thabo Buchanan, who was 11, and his sister, Tinky, who was 10, were beautiful children, both with heart-shaped, coffee-coloured faces and long lashes over their brown eyes. They had been going to a black school in Soweto, but as they got older they came to look more racially mixed. They had been taunted and attacked by the other children, until the headteacher expelled them for being a disruptive influence.

All the children had similar stories. Young lives shipwrecked by the system before they had barely begun. They just had to wait until officials got round to measuring their skin tones or the curliness of their hair to decide what breed of human they were and which racial pigeon hole they should be put in. The obscene thing about South Africa was that the only thing worse than being racially categorised as inferior was not being classified at all.

Being declared white was the ultimate prize. It was still pretty important how far down the scale you slipped. It was better to be coloured than black, for instance. Generally speaking, you could live in a slightly better area, go to slightly better schools, and, if you lived round Capetown, have apartheid half on your side.

Capetown was where the first white Dutch settlers, led by Jan van Riebeeck, had come ashore in 1652 and begun to mix with the Hottentots and the Bushmen. Coloured people are the result of the miscegenation that van Riebeeck and his successors tried so hard, and so unsuccessfully, to prevent. Van Riebeeck planted a hedge of bitter almonds to keep his randy Dutchmen from the Hottentot women. Some of the hedge remains to this day. Part of it runs through Bishopscourt, the official residence of the Archbishop of Capetown. When Desmond Tutu lived there he showed me the hedge, laughing uproariously at the folly of trying to curb human nature with vegetation. Today's 2.5 million people who were officially classified coloured have come through the physical and metaphorical gaps in that hedge and are now, as then, to be found in their greatest numbers in and around Capetown.

The truth is that the 'whites' who were doing so much to protect their racial superiority and separate identity were themselves 'coloured'. The science of genetics was already showing those Afrikaners who regarded themselves as pure white were, on average, 6.9 per cent black.

Under apartheid, the Western Cape had been declared a 'coloured preference area'. A black could not legally be given a job unless it could be shown there was no coloured person who could do it. This was not because of any residual affection for these stepchildren of white domination. They were, after all, kept separate from whites in their own townships in unattractive areas round the city. It was partly the policy of sub-divide and rule, partly also the laager mentality at work. The Cape, where the white man first landed, might one day need to be his last stronghold. It was never official policy but it was in the back of the policymakers' minds.

So blacks were doubly disadvantaged in the Western Cape. The law tried to restrict the permanent black population to 20,000 families. The rest were declared to be 'illegals' and subject to an endless campaign of harassment and expulsion with guns and dogs and armoured vehicles. The whole paraphernalia of 'influx control' was particularly strict where it tried to keep the millions of poor and marginalised blacks in the Eastern Cape from flooding westwards. It was ruthless and often brutal. But it was no more successful than Jan van Riebeeck's hedge.

I met Vera Pindi very early one morning out on the Cape flats, the dusty scrubland east of Capetown that was, and remains, a dumping ground for the poor and black. The Cape is one of the most beautiful places on earth but the flats are a bleak armpit of marginal land, between the airport and False Bay, that is too poor for animals and where no human who had a choice would want to live.

It was the pearly-grey half-light well before dawn, and Table Mountain was just a dark presence behind her, rather than the sharply defined backdrop to a daily tragedy that it would become over the next few hours. She had already been up for some time, busy in her blue and white headscarf and green housecoat, coping with another relentless day. I don't know why she stands out so sharply in my memory that, even now, I can remember every detail of how she looked, what she did, what she said. It may be because of the extraordinary difference in our circumstances and prospects that owed nothing to worth, or reason, or justice. It was just a chance meeting between two people who might as well have been creatures from separate universes. The trajectory of our lives, intersecting for just a few minutes in the pre-dawn on that blasted heath, tells you all you need to know about white privilege and black repression; about apartheid.

I had come the easy way. Christine and I had eaten lunch on the verandah at home with the sun bouncing off the swimming pool, now back to a glassy and blameless blue. They were tricky things, swimming pools. Just when you thought you were getting the hang of the chemicals and the rather sinister pool-cleaning gadget known locally as a Kreepy Krawly, it would suddenly sicken and turn into a giant bowl of Vichysoisse. The pool doctor had been a regular visitor and Christine and I talked about whether there was any way his exorbitant fees could become the responsibility of the British television licence payer over our salmon salad and sweet, golden *Spanspec* melon. A light wind rustled the trees and purple jacaranda blossom settled like snowflakes on the lawn as François and Mac arrived in the crew Mercedes for our assignment down to the Cape.

We always travelled first class on the South African Airways Airbus that took just under two hours to get to Capetown from Johannesburg. I can't remember how we justified it to the BBC accountants in London, or if we ever felt the need. We probably told them first class was a better excess baggage deal for all our camera gear. It might have been true, for all I know. In any case, we felt we deserved it.

This was first-world South Africa, efficient, luxurious, self-indulgent.

We did not want to spoil our dinner so we only had two glasses of Champagne and just a nibble of the canapés being served by slightly effeminate stewards. The cabin crew were all-white, and SAA seemed to have cornered the market in camp Afrikaners.

François, the gentlest and kindest of men, was politically incorrect like cameramen everywhere. On the flight he told jokes about van de Merwe, the archtypically thick Afrikaner, and his black servants. About how van de Merwe would never buy a washing machine because he had two 'Kaffirmatics' in the back yard. I laughed along with everybody else.

We hired a big BMW at Capetown's D.F. Malan airport, now Capetown International, which had been named after the Prime Minister who had promised to make South Africa 'a white man's land'. There were 200,000 blacks and browns in tents and shacks and regular houses on the plains around the airport that bore his name. The fact that many were 'illegals' did not mean they didn't exist, however hard the country's rulers tried to pretend they were invisible, however hard their officials tried to get rid of them. Vera's squatter camp was only just across the motorway from the airport. The plane had flown right over it on its final approach. But work was for tomorrow. We swung the hire car right, on to the motorway into white Capetown.

Once you left the belt of squatters and shanties behind and got past the sewage works that throws an invisible curtain of nastiness across the N2, Capetown and the great grey wall of Table Mountain unfold gloriously in front of you. On the side of the mountain is the monument to Cecil John Rhodes, the immeasurably rich Cape Prime Minister who added a million square miles of Africa to the British Empire and, arguably, laid the foundations of apartheid. (Sixty years before the Afrikaner Nationalists came to power he told the House of Assembly in the city: 'The native is to be treated as a child and denied the franchise. We must adopt a system of despotism, such as works so well in India, in our relations with the barbarians of South Africa.')

The N2 rushes past the bare mountainside studded with stone pines whose tops are bent over by the south-easter that can blow hard for days. Past Groote Schuur Hospital where the first heart transplant was performed, then over a ridge and down into the city bowl. We branched left on the high road called de Waal Drive. Down to the right you could see that a large stretch of the city's centre was a strangely bare wasteland, save for half a dozen dilapidated churches and mosques. This was District Six, once the liveliest and most raffish area in the city, part London's Soho, part New Orleans' Vieux Carré, where the races mixed in clubs and bars and seamen's brothels. It was bulldozed out of existence by the engineers of apartheid in the seventies with a blast of racist moralising. But a cloud of ill-feeling and guilt settled on District Six. No developer would take it on. It was an open wound in the heart of Capetown, and remains so to this day.

Our destination, though, was the Mount Nelson, a Capetown institution and one of the finest hotels in the world. It is a magnificent pink-washed building, or series of buildings, set among palm trees and beautiful tropical gardens right under Table Mountain. In its heyday, the English aristocracy would come out on Union Castle liners and stay there to escape grey British winters. It felt like the Dorchester had been shipped from Park Lane to Paradise and been kissed by the setting sun. We loved it.

There was time for a swim and a pre-dinner drink in the extremely English Nelson Bar. Mac and François amused themselves about the upmarket and very elderly people out under the long-case clocks in the lounge. They reckoned the only way you could tell whether they were alive or dead was to look at the dates on the newspapers behind which they were apparently dozing. I used the hotel telex to tell the foreign duty editor in London, a nice man bowed down by a monster mortgage, three difficult children and a nightmare commute, how hard we were working. Then we went to dinner in an open-air restaurant facing the sea. *Kingklip*, a native South African white fish, and a couple of bottles of smoky Simonsig Vin Fumé, I remember. We weren't late. We had an early start.

Vera Pindi's journey to Crossroads was rather different. She had grown up on a white-owned farm, somewhere in the Orange Free State. She and her family were 'surplus' blacks, who were swept off the land where they had lived for several generations and 'resettled' in some God-forsaken corner of a Xhosa tribal homeland called the Transkei. She and her husband and three children had lived in a two-roomed corrugated-iron shack, 20 miles from the territory's capital, Umtata. There were no jobs there. There was no work anywhere they could find in the Eastern Cape. They hated the squalor in which they lived. They were hungry. The children were always sick. They were desperate. Vera and her husband decided to defy the system and join the flow of 'illegals' heading west-wards towards Capetown. They left two of the children in the Transkei with relatives but took the youngest, then aged two, with them on the bus for the 750-mile journey to the Western Cape. They didn't make it. Somewhere near Beaufort West they had run into one of the many police roadblocks set up in the name of 'influx control' to try to hold back the black tide.

It was unclear what had happened. Vera did not know herself. There was a mêlée as the blacks on the bus tried to escape, to get away before they were rounded up and shipped back to the Transkei. In the confusion, Vera became separated from her husband and from her daughter, who had been picked up by another woman as they ran off into the bush.

Vera had made her way in stages to Crossroads. She had found out that her husband had been caught and taken to Pollsmoor Prison, outside Capetown, but she did not know whether he was being held for trial under any one of the dozens of laws he might have broken in his failed effort to find a better life for his family. She still did not know where her daughter was. She looked every day round the squatter camp and tried to send messages back to the Transkei to find out if the woman had taken her back there. She was beside herself with worry. All she could do was carry on with the new routines of her life as an 'illegal' squatter, and hope her husband and child would somehow turn up. Survival was difficult enough. She had found occasional work, cleaning up in some factory in one of the poorer parts of the city. She had staked out a patch of sand in Crossroads where, every evening, she built a tent out of sticks and plastic. She would push the sticks into the ground and bend them at the top so they could be tied together to make a frame. Then she would gather up the strips of black plastic sheeting she had had to buy for £1.50 a piece and tie them together, on top of the frame, with bits of wire. It made a primitive kind of yurt, enough to keep out the chill of the night. It was still early spring and out there on the flats it could be bitter. After she had cooked herself some *mielies* over a small wood fire, she would wrap herself in an old blue blanket and sleep on the hard-packed sand.

When we met, at half-past five that morning, she was in a hurry to dismantle her home. She knew the white officials would be coming to bulldoze these pathetic hovels and arrest those blacks they found without the state's permission to be there. All around, blacks in sweaters and balaclavas were scurrying through the dust and woodsmoke with bits of scrap metal. A young boy on a rusty iron bedstead blinked awake as his mother ripped the cardboard roof from over his head.

Vera paused a moment to look at a cut on her hand from the wire fastenings she was tearing out of the plastic and explained to me what she was doing, patiently, as if I was very young, or very slow.

'Every morning I do this, and later come back from work, I can build again. If I don't do this the white men will burn everything I have, and if they don't take me in the vans I will have to sleep outside.'

The more I found out about her, the more admirable she seemed to be. She was a strong woman, coping with the kind of misfortune, discrimination and desperate poverty that would have crushed most people I knew. Despite her problems, she was warm and funny. She deployed her quick wit at my expense, once she knew I meant her no harm and showed no sign of moving away. She had a sustained running joke about the sanctity of my shoes and the unmentionable things I might step in if I was not careful. She spoke at least four languages as she chivvied the others around her to hurry up before the white men came.

I went with her as she looked for hiding places for the bits of her home. She buried the plastic in the sand dunes and salted the sticks away amongst the shacks in the part called New Crossroads which was, for the time being at least, not the target of the authorities. Then, with a wave, she was gone.

At eight o'clock precisely – apartheid was a punctual tyranny – the men from the Administration Board arrived. They came in a convoy of white vans, the Europeans in the front, the black labourers who would actually do the work of destruction in the back. The white men carried automatics very obviously on their left hips. Behind them rolled three armoured personnel carriers, the ones the South African Army called Casspirs. A mailed fist on wheels, in case the resentment exploded into violence.

There was no resistance. This was routine, for both sides. What was left standing in the camp was gathered up and burnt on a huge pyre. The white officials spoke only to bark orders at their labourers. They completely ignored everybody in the camp. When the job had been completed to their satisfaction, they got back in their vehicles and drove off. The blacks of Crossroads gathered round the bonfire as the flames leapt twenty or thirty feet in the air and sang hymns. An old man with a woollen hat and a beard that was almost pure white dabbed his eyes.

I stood in front of the fire and tried to sum up what we had seen for the camera. I tried hard, as I was trained, to find some balance in all this, even though in my head as well as my heart I knew what was happening in Crossroads was cruel and inhuman with no qualifications. 'It's a symbol to many,' I said, 'of the heartlessness of apartheid. It's a symbol to some of the increasing need to control the movement of blacks who they think might otherwise swamp South Africa's cities.' It was lame and I knew it.

Then we went back to the Mount Nelson for breakfast.

It only took us twenty minutes to get back there. Forty minutes and we had showered off the smells of the squatter camp and were sipping freshly pressed orange juice on the terrace under the palms, waiting for our Eggs Benedict. The fierce south-easter – Capetonians call it the 'Doctor's Wind' – had scoured away every trace of pollution and the air was like Champagne. The great mountain was grey and pachydermatous under a sky of eggshell blue. The gardens were still damp from the overnight watering. Gaudy flowers dripped diamonds in the rising sun.

We had most of that golden Capetown day to ourselves. I had a couple of appointments in the gracious Parliament buildings, but they were only a short walk away, through the gardens that Jan van Riebeeck originally planted in the 1650s to supply the scurvied Dutch sailors who touched there on their way to the East, and they did not take long. We took the BMW south, out of the white beachfront suburbs of Green Point and Sea Point and along Chapman's Peak Drive, the world's loveliest road. It soars up out of the city to cling to the side of the sandstone buttresses they call the Twelve Apostles and then down to the towns and villages of the Capetown Riviera – Bantry Bay, Clifton, Camps Bay and Llandudno. The water up the west side of the Cape comes straight from Antarctica. It is cold and a dark greenish-blue before it thunders into foam on the Riviera beaches. We drove through the nature reserve at the Cape of Good Hope, the symbolic southern tip of Africa (though the southern-most point is actually Cape Agulhas). They tell you there that the Cape has the richest and most varied vegetation on earth, 8,600 plant species, more than half of which occur nowhere else. (Britain has 1,500, many of which are not native.) It is that blessed. We returned along False Bay, up the east coast of the Cape, through Simon's Town, where the British once had their naval base, and Fish Hoek. We walked on the long beach at Muizenberg, where the Indian Ocean water is 10°F warmer than on the Cape's western shore, before returning through the mountains and Constantia, where the mansions of the rich sit amongst the pines, to the Mount Nelson for tea. Sir Francis Drake had called it 'the fairest cape of all' and he was a good judge. I wondered how Vera had spent her day.

We went back to Crossroads in the late afternoon, looking for her. But she did not come back. Her belongings, her sticks and plastic, were still where she had hidden them. Nobody seemed to know what had happened to her. Most likely she had been swept up in one of the regular police raids and shipped back off to the Transkei. Perhaps she had got word of her daughter and gone to find her. I hoped so. I discovered later her husband had been given a three-month jail sentence and always meant to try and find her through him, but I was away a lot and somehow never got round to it. I used to ask about her whenever I went back to Crossroads but never found any trace. Vera was just a small and insignificant part of the great human flotsam of apartheid, and her story would have vanished as surely as she did.

Television gave this brief snapshot of Vera's life and the daily rituals of oppression at Crossroads a particular poignancy and an audience of millions. It made a considerable impact, not least with the South African Embassy, who complained, more in sorrow than in anger, they said, about negative reporting.

Two weeks later, my bosses flew out from London to say they were thinking of closing the bureau down, and we should plan for returning to London.

EIGHTEEN

I SHOULD HAVE KNOWN something was up. BBC executives are as seasonal as migrating wildfowl. They normally arrive in February, when the weather is at its worst in London and at its best in South Africa. The State Opening of Parliament in Capetown is in February. They like an excuse to go down there; the scenery and the restaurants are better than Johannesburg, and then, as now, there was less chance of being mugged or murdered. But this was November in Johannesburg, and two colleagues I liked and admired were telling me the job I had wanted all my life, and had only held for four months, might well be over.

I had known Chris Cramer since he was a scruffy young reporter on Radio Solent, unsavoury-looking even by the standards of the day, not that he had exactly turned into Hugh Grant in the meantime. He was sharp and funny. (Much later he would open contract negotiations with Martin Bashir, after his world-famous Princess Diana interview, with the words: 'Well, Martin, you've peaked now, haven't you?') He runs CNN these days, but then he was probably the best news editor the BBC had ever had. Peter Woon, his boss and mine, had revolutionised both Television and Radio News. He had started out as a pretty hopeless TV reporter but sensibly changed tack to become a talented editor and a generous, inspirational chief.

At first I thought the BBC had been got at by Pretoria, which would have been bad enough. But the problem was not in South Africa at all. The problem was Robert Mugabe.

The Zimbabwean leader had been threatening for some time to stop us reporting on his country and now the situation seemed to be coming to a head. Chris had worked there as a BBC field producer. He had formed an emotional attachment to the place and at least one of its war widows. Over the first of a series of large and expensive meals, he said 'the feeling was' (a trademark BBC phrase) there was no point in having an African bureau if Zimbabwe was to be off-limits. Over dinner at our house, I argued for hours. I said that these restrictions were always porous and would not last.

But my main point was that Zimbabwe wasn't the only story; it wasn't even the most important story in that part of the world any more. Christine was working for a charity in Soweto at the time and described

250

the daily routines of discrimination as seen from both sides of the racial divide, and how we both sensed the issue of apartheid was coming to some sort of crisis. We threw a party for Chris and Peter at our house and invited Afrikaner politicians (who rang to ask if they needed dinner jackets), diplomats and other correspondents and their wives. They all waded in on my behalf, as they tucked into the giant barbecued fish called a Cob and the legs of pickled pork out in the garden. Somebody very dignified fell into the pool. The party was deemed a big success but we weren't sure about our campaign for survival. Chris and Peter did not seem entirely convinced but when we went to bed that night we felt we had won some sort of reprieve, albeit a qualified and temporary one.

BBC Television's Johannesburg bureau had originally been set up in the mid-seventies to cover the war in Rhodesia. It was a secure base a couple of hours' flying time away from Salisbury and had all the facilities Rhodesia lacked. Even after Rhodesia's whites finally gave up their unilateral declaration of independence, Zimbabwe was still the BBC's main preoccupation in Africa. There were some good reasons for this. Rhodesia had been near the top of the news agenda for so long it was obviously important to see how majority rule would settle down. Mugabe was already showing signs of the despotism that has since ruined that beautiful country more effectively than the bush war. He had started interfering with judges and overruling the courts. And he had sent the notorious Fifth Brigade of his army into Matabeleland to crush the minority Ndebele tribe who supported his old rival, Joshua Nkomo.

Even so, I would sit having breakfast in the old Meikles Hotel listening out for his convoy of limousines and army trucks as they screamed into town with all their sirens going – we called this daily event 'Bob Mugabe and the Wailers' – wondering if I should be spending so much time there. After all, it was four years since Zimbabwe had become independent. There was a case for saying that it was now just another post-colonial African country being screwed up by another apprentice tyrant. There was the kith and kin connection, of course, but half of them had already left. Its birth as an independent country had been more long drawn out and bloody, but I wondered if it should get so much more attention, say, than Uganda, whose President, Idi Amin, kept his opponents cut up in the fridge; than Angola and Mozambique, both racked by civil wars ten times worse than what had happened in Rhodesia; and particularly more attention than South Africa, which was immeasurably richer, more powerful, more strategically important, and, crucially, the place where institutionalised white superiority was making its last stand.

That said, I liked going to Zimbabwe. If the BBC still wanted to cover every twist and turn in the story, I didn't object too much. Despite the war, both races were more open and relaxed than they were further south. Zimbabwe was beautiful and more like my idea of Africa than the *Platteland* of the Transvaal and the Free State, or the *Boland*, the Mediterranean-style hinterland of Capetown. The hotels were comfortable, especially Meikles, where the BBC Radio correspondent, Ian Mills, Rhodesia-Zimbabwe's once and for all time ice-dancing champion (they had closed the country's only ice rink), would play the white grand piano into the small hours. The only thing wrong with Meikles was Zimbabwean wine, which locals reckoned was made from the urine of elderly township donkeys. We used to bring up lots of South African bottles in the silver camera boxes and were very popular as a result. It must have been a bit like being a GI (or a Canadian Army captain, indeed) in 1940s Britain.

Now, though, all that was at risk. Mugabe had got so annoyed at the foreign media telling the world what he was up to that he was trying to keep them out of the country altogether. He had imposed a ban on foreign journalists who were based in South Africa. Nearly all of us did live in Johannesburg because it was the economic epicentre of the region and the hub for all its communications. Mugabe argued that we had been 'tainted' by apartheid. He wanted a 'new journalistic order', attuned to the needs of developing countries, who did not see everything through the prism of their white, western preconceptions. There was an interesting argument to be had about this, but not with Mugabe. He wanted a foreign press like his own: fawning, uncritical and blind to his growing tyranny.

His attempts to corral foreign correspondents had been a dismal failure. He had banned us from Matabeleland but we had slipped in anyway and come out with evidence that the North Korean-trained Fifth Brigade had been systematically torturing and killing his political opponents there. Stung by the international protests that resulted, the government organised a facility trip with the army that was meant to show that the allegations were untrue; that what was going on was just a routine policing operation. It was set up with a great fanfare and we were summoned from Johannesburg for what was billed as 'conclusive proof of foreign media lies'.

We had all got to the Holiday Inn in Bulawayo the previous evening and prepared ourselves for the morning in the way you might expect from 60 or so thirsty reporters and cameramen in the vicinity of a well-stocked bar.

At any rate, we were all up and ready by 0730, the scheduled departure time for the trip to clear Zimbabwe's reputation. There were some government officials there, a bus and a few soldiers. But not General Rex Nhongo, the army commander who we were told would take us wherever we wanted to go. While we waited, we finalised the list they had specifically asked us for, of places we wanted to go and people we wanted to talk to. It was a long list. You can't kill and torture hundreds of men and women and leave no trace for determined journalists to find. We pared it down to places and people close to Bulawayo and conveniently near tarred roads. We did not want to leave General Rex any excuses.

He arrived precisely three hours late, in a big convoy of armoured vehicles. He said he had been 'at a trade fair'; he had clearly been drinking. He stood swaying in his new fatigues, with his staff red lapel badges and red-banded British general's hat, and repeated the govern-ment's promise: 'We are at your disposal,' he said. 'Anywhere you want to go, we will take you.'

We gave him the list and he disappeared into a scout car near the front of a column that by now seemed to contain most of the Fifth Brigade. We were loaded into an old bus which was immediately surrounded by armoured cars. It was necessary for our protection, we were told by the officials who were with us. It was scarcely likely to encourage witnesses to come forward but, in the event, it made no difference. The general led us in precisely the opposite direction to that in which we wanted to go.

After a few miles, the whole convoy swung off the road and into uninhabited bush. For seven hours we ploughed through the sand and thorn trees until we got bogged down in a dried-up river bed. The general had disappeared; back to 'the trade fair' perhaps. It took several hours to dig the bus out and then only by chaining three armoured cars together to get enough towing power. By now the reporters were feeling more rebellious than the Ndebele. I stood in front of the camera, with the whole mess behind me, and tried to drip as much acid into my voice as possible: 'This much-heralded operation to clear Zimbabwe's name,' I said, 'began in frustration and is ending in farce. We've been to none of the places we wanted to visit, we've seen nobody, we've spoken to nobody. Soon it will be dark.'

Worse was to come. We got bogged down again, and the soldiers confessed we were hopelessly lost. After ten hours of this fiasco what was left of our patience snapped and we demanded to be taken to the nearest road. The trouble was that the soldiers said they did not know where it was. We spent the night out there and did not get back to the Holiday Inn until ten o'clock the following morning.

What the Zimbabwean authorities thought they would achieve, apart from demonstrate their total contempt for their media tormentors, God knows. We all wrote and broadcast long pieces that majored on the Zimbabwean Army's incompetence and the atmosphere of high farce in which the whole operation had been conducted. The Zimbabwean authorities came out looking clownish, capricious and cruel. A pretty accurate impression, as it happens. What was happening to the Ndebele was not funny. The dead were already being counted in hundreds and the killing did not stop. That was when it looked like the curtain would come down on us for good .

But the ban on South African-based reporters proved to be as porous as I had thought. Mugabe could not seal himself off from the outside world. He needed aid. He wanted to be taken seriously as a great international statesman, the 'teacher' lecturing the rest of the world on morality. Besides he loved his own trips abroad. All the scheduled passengers on Air Zimbabwe's only intercontinental aircraft were often bumped off at the last moment so he and his hangers-on could commandeer the plane to go shopping in London.

So the blanket ban on us was watered down. We had to apply in writing every time we wanted to go to Zimbabwe, specifying where we wished to go, what we were reporting on, who we were trying to meet. This was actually no different from many other African countries. I was allowed back to do a report on the three-year-long drought in the country, probably because Mugabe wanted to get more money from international donors. We went to the east, where starving refugees had fled across the border from the civil war in Mozambique and had only grass to eat. We filmed normally fertile farms that had been turned into dustbowls. They insisted we went to a rally at the Independence Stadium where thousands of children and supporters of the ruling party waited for hours under a broiling sun with their Mugabe T-shirts and Mugabe flags for the man himself to bother to turn up. It was four in the afternoon before he came. Colonial-style policemen in solar topees and khaki shorts pushed the crowds back as he walked in, loose-wristed and straight-backed, looking for all the world as if he was cross-country skiing, without the skis. The chant went up: 'Long live Comrade Robert Gabriel Mugabe, long live!'

He barely acknowledged them; just a perfunctory wave before he jumped up on the podium and, as heavily armed soldiers took up position behind and underneath him, laid into the sins of the imperialists. He took a high moral tone, standing there in his Mao suit, his eyes flashing behind his thick-rimmed glasses. Britain was trying to maintain its old colonial control over Zimbabwe by undermining his people's revolution, he told them. Britain's agents were the 100,000 or so whites who had remained after Independence, but the day was soon coming when that problem 'would be dealt with'.

I had spent the morning at the tobacco sales in Harare and watched as the auctioneer went up and down the sample leaves with a gabbling chant that never seemed to require drawing breath. Zimbabwe's white commercial farmers had earned the country £1.5 million in three hours that morning. They were paying for the rapid personal enrichment of Mugabe and his henchmen. They were paying for the army and police that were crushing all organised opposition to him in the country. They were paying for the £50 million international conference centre being built outside the capital to fulfil Mugabe's dream of hosting major conferences of African leaders.

We manoeuvred ourselves round the back of the podium into a narrow passageway where he would have to come close to us to get to his waiting convoy. I ducked between two of the soldiers and threw him an anodyne question to see if he would respond. He did, of course. His appetite for windy moralising was endless. I have been lectured a lot down the years. Margaret Thatcher used to do it like Moses the Housewife, parcelling out eternal truths as if they were stone tablets for me to distribute to the great unwashed. Ronald Reagan and Bill Clinton both did it with their hands on my shoulder and a vapid kind of sincerity shining as brightly as their make-up. Mikhail Gorbachev did it for what seemed like hours with a tweed hat and a fiercely wagging finger. But you would have to go back to a fourteenth-century Chinese emperor to find someone so secure in his moral superiority as Comrade Robert Gabriel Mugabe. Those Jesuit missionaries at Zvimba who raised him have a lot to answer for.

It was a mercifully short lecture, strong on the 'malevolence' of the British generally; the BBC were 'lackeys' and 'troublemakers', and white

Zimbabweans were a problem that history, presumably in the shape of the comrade leader, would soon have to resolve once and for all. He looked steadily at a point a foot above my head as he talked. He was not interested in answering questions. A flap of the hand to dismiss us and he was gone.

The report that I filed that night was about Mugabe's anti-white rhetoric, the economic importance of the whites, particularly at a time of severe drought, and the difficulties of reaching a just accommodation between the races after the long and bitter bush war. They did not like it much, but the Information Minister Dr Nathan Shamuyarira grumbled rather than yelled when I called him later that week from Johannesburg. They might let me back in from time to time if I behaved myself. Meantime, he said, my family and I could always go there on holiday.

So we did.

Dawn on the Zambezi comes suddenly. Blink, and it feels like somebody just switched the light on. The hunter had woken us up half an hour before, while it was still pitch dark on the sand strip beside the river where we had camped. There were no tents to pack. We had laid out our sleeping bags on canvas stretchers to keep them off the ground, and slept under the stars. There was nothing to muffle the roars of big game, startlingly close it seemed to us, and the thousand sounds of killers and killed out in the darkness. It was amazing how easy it was to sleep in those circumstances. How resentful you were when the hunter shook your shoulder in the pre-dawn.

It only took a few moments to pack the two-man canoes. They were 15 feet long, made of fibreglass but shaped like the ones the Red Indians used, rising in a sharp and graceful curve at both ends. The food and drink was packed into a big box in the centre of the boat, and the sleeping bags and spare clothes were used as cushions for the paddlers or tied on at either end. We said very little as we slipped the canoes into the water, hopping in quickly in case the crocodiles had made an early start, too. We were heading east, so the sun broke over the escarpment directly in front of us. A red glow, an orange flash, a semi-circle of rose-gold, and then the sun was free, seeming to suck the mist up off the river as it lit the world with morning.

Just as the sun broke we were paddling close to a high bank of the river. Christine and I were in the second canoe, a few yards behind Roland and the hunter, who were leading. Without warning, a huge shape loomed at the edge of the overhanging bank and, gathering itself in a moment, soared over Roland's canoe, blotting out nearly all the light. It landed with an almighty crash in the water just beyond them. For minutes afterwards, the image of the great bull hippo was still imprinted on our minds. Two and a half tons or more of solid animal, stretched in mid-flight over my son, for all the world like the cow jumping over the moon in a child's nursery rhyme book. Roland was very nonchalant about it when we stopped for breakfast. He gave the hippo two points for style, three for difficulty and only one for artistic merit.

Hippo were a big part of the briefing when we first met the hunter at a field by the river, just downstream from the Kariba dam. There were the four of us, Martin and Mary Ann, friends we had made in Scotland, a laconic Australian to make up the numbers and the hunter himself. He was a blond, well-built man of about thirty with a double-barrelled surname and the brand of clipped English reticence you only get in pre-war movies – as if Tarzan had gone to Sandhurst. He radiated competence and some deep-seated unhappiness. It turned out he had been in the 'Recce' battalion – the Rhodesian SAS – during the bush war. He was courteous and patient but he did not smile a lot. You got the impression the canoeing gave him time to wrestle with his inner demons.

He obviously knew his job. He briefed us on the animals that could kill us without breaking into sweat; it was a long list. The river was teeming with homicidal wildlife. There was a crocodile for every 50 yards of the Zambezi riverbank, but it was the hippos we really had to watch. He told us there were thousands in the river between us and our destination, 150 miles and seven days' paddling away, where the Zambezi crosses the Mozambique border. He said they bathed in the heat of the day but came out at night to graze on the river banks. The one that had jumped over Roland had stayed longer than the rest of the herd and had been frightened by the splashing of our paddles. He told us not to be misled by their benign expressions. They could be dangerous. Male hippopotami in particular were easy to anger. They weighed up to three tons but could move with surprising speed, in the water and on land, and could bite the boat in half, not to mention its occupants, with no trouble at all. The boys were staring at their trainers at this point. Christine and Mary Ann were looking thoughtful. Martin and I tried, not very success-fully, to appear manly and protective.

As if reading our thoughts, the hunter said there was one sure-fire way of avoiding trouble. 'Don't worry,' he said, 'hippos only ever attack the last canoe.' You could also bash the side of your canoe with the paddle, which apparently gives the hippo a headache, but this was a more risky tactic. Speed through the water was the thing. The hunter made it sound more than that. He made it sound like life and death.

Self-preservation made the boys disloyal. Before the subject of who would go with whom was even raised, Roland opted to partner the hunter. Simon bagged the Australian, who looked a sturdy, outdoor type; survival of the fittest, obviously. Martin was an English public school alpha male but still pasty from the London winter. The boys were well aware of the physical limitations of their father. They were already able to run further and faster, and I was becoming grateful I had opted for a consensual style of fatherhood. I was none too sure I could take them on in a fair fight even though they were still only ten, and used to give up quite early in the affectionate rough and tumbles at home, claiming concern for the furniture.

Canoeing proved a great deal more difficult than I had anticipated. We covered the first half-mile going backwards. An hour after we set off on the great journey we encountered our first family of hippos, who surfaced like new islands right in front of us. They blew water out of their nostrils in what I thought was a rather friendly way, and waggled their little pink ears. It might have been the beers at lunchtime but I found it difficult to see these amiable-looking creatures, each one of which looked like the laughing policeman emerging from a mudbath, as killers. But everybody else paddled like crazy and I was caught up in the general hysteria. Canoes never went so fast.

Direction, though, was a different matter. We careered straight at one animal the size of a small mountain, which looked surprised at such an unorthodox tactic and crash-dived like a U-boat. No sooner had I congratulated myself on this unintentional triumph of will than the canoe veered 90 degrees and rammed straight into the bank, narrowly missing the most surprised crocodile in southern Africa. The other canoes had vanished. All that was left was their wake, like the trail of several torpedoes.

Years later, introducing yet another news item about the British quadruple Olympic gold medallist, Steve Redgrave, I wondered how much better a rower even he would have been if only his trainer had had the foresight to stock that training stretch of the Thames with a few hippo.

*

The next few days were amongst the happiest I can remember. We were out of reach of bleepers and phones, in tune with nature in one of the most dramatic wildlife areas on earth. Paddling down the great river, starting in a wide plain between low mountain ranges that then narrows as you get further east, was an unforgettable experience. The river banks were riddled with the nests of carmine bee-eaters. Crocodiles slithered into the water at the first noise of your approach. Buck and elephant come down to the river to drink as we passed by. We saw a leopard – rare sight – in a branch on the edge of the Mopane woodland, and the footprints of the sacred ibis on the sandbanks. There were villages of thatched huts on the Zambian shore and, from time to time, their dugouts would pass us, going far faster upstream than we could manage going down with the flow of the river. It was dangerous, but most of the time we were not in the least afraid. We had a fright when a big bull elephant came between us and the canoes one lunchtime. It kept getting annoyed as we tried to work our way round it to get back out on to the river, trumpeting at full volume and hosing us down with mud. After half an hour, whacking its great ears back and forth and screeching, it became bored with its own outrage and shuffled away.

I had an even worse moment when I woke up at four in the morning and saw a rhino padding and snuffling round Simon's sleeping bag. I held my breath longer than I have ever managed in my life and prayed quite hard. Eventually, somebody coughed in their sleep and it sauntered, jauntily, into the bush.

The hunter did all the cooking. The fresh stuff lasted a couple of days, some other perishables lasted longer packed under ice, and for the last few days we were on tins. He was a good cook, though and we were always astonishingly hungry. The wine ran out, slightly to our surprise, midway through the trip, but it was so awful it was not a major blow. Martin kept talking about pouring it into the Zambezi to kill the crocodiles, which might explain why it did not last. He trailed beer bottles behind his canoe to keep them cool, but sometimes there would be a jerk and the rope would come up, bitten through and the bottles gone. If the Zambezi is now stocked with the world's first alcoholic crocodiles, Martin is to blame.

The river flows through the Mana Pools National Park, with its forests of giant acacia and mahogany, where it splits into channels half covered in hyacinths. We saw lions patrolling near the riverbank on the lookout for warthogs, their favourite food. We saw a chase once, the warthogs fleeing with their ridiculous tails like radio aerials sticking up from their backsides, the lions kicking up a lot of dust but not quite getting into the position where warthog was dish of the day.

The boys were very cool about close encounters with wild beasts. They were only really worried by our toilet arrangements. These consisted of a shovel and a toilet roll and instructions to head a sufficient distance downwind into the bush. It was something about their particular vulnerability in these circumstances, vis-à-vis a passing predator with ill intentions, that seemed to make them nervous. Actually, it was the thought that the encounter might be the opposite of vis-à-vis, that they risked being bitten in the tail by anything from a scorpion to a full-grown lion, that concerned them most. Like most boys, they were also intensely private about matters of this kind and rejected all offers to stand guard. At Mana Pools they were in every sense relieved to find a real latrine. It was a long drop, up on a rise, enclosed on three sides but wide open where it looked up the river. I went up there at sunset and saw a zebra, a large antelope and two buffalo while attending to my domestic needs. It is our all-time favourite lavatory. Truly a loo with a view.

We paddled on through the Nyachidzilo mountains and under the towering cliffs of Mupata Gorge before we reached Kanyemba on the Mozambique border and our journey's end. We finally asked the hunter the question that had intrigued us all through the trip. Where had he kept his gun? We just assumed he had got one. All hunters carried guns and, besides, how otherwise could he keep us safe? 'What gun?' he said. Ever since the war, he had gone off them. Thank God he had not told us at the beginning of the trip, that's all I can say. Mind you, he was the kind of chap who would probably be able to kill a crocodile with his bare hands. Crocodiles, it turned out, were his only real worry. He had never taken children our boys' age on the river before and was worried every time they played in the water. When they splashed about the crocodiles were likely to think they were an animal in distress, apparently, and come up licking their lips.

As it happens, the very next canoeists who did the trip were attacked by crocodiles. A lad, quite a lot older than our boys, had his arm bitten off while he was trailing his hand in the water. His father won a tug-of-war with the crocodile for him, otherwise he would have met that most awful of fates, to be chewed up and drowned, then left to rot in some reptile's underwater larder until considered sufficiently toothsome for a crocodile buffet.

*

The canoe trip was only one of many marvellous holidays we had while we were in Africa. We watched a million wildebeest, tracked by prides of lions, on their annual migration out of the Serengeti into the Maasai Mara in Kenya.

I tried to drive our minibus round the 1,000-foot-high sand dunes in Namibia and got us stuck and lost in the desert, miles from anywhere. Christine's forebearance on this occasion was heroic.

We lived for a few days in a tree house in the Hwange National Park, pulling up the ladder at dusk and holding the furniture tight as a herd of elephants took turns to scratch their backsides on the trunk.

And, most magical of all, we flew up to Maun in Botswana and then on into the extraordinary Okavango swamps. In winter, when the Okavango river floods out of the Angolan Highlands and into this depression in the Kalahari Desert, the swamps cover 15,000 square kilometres. We hired two local men, Justice and Albie, to pole us around what was no more than a corner of the swamps in two dug-out canoes.

It is a land of crystal-clear rivers and a thousand wooded islands. The waterways are covered with waterlilies and hyacinths, the banks lined with papyrus. The whole area teems with wildlife, great and small. It all adds up to the greatest single wilderness in southern Africa, and it was Justice and Albie's element. Two hours into the trip they spotted a new lion kill, an impala that had been left by its killer. Before the vultures could get there, Justice and Albie had butchered it. Strips of meat were spread out to dry along the canoe (and in the trees where we camped) and the horns were mounted on the front of Simon and Roland's canoe.

At night, Justice and Albie would make a tent for themselves out of old *mielie* sacks and build up the fire. Water buffalo were the problem, more ill-tempered, active and dangerous than lions. They would gather round our tents at night. We could hear them, rumbling and stamping, just out of the ring of light cast by the flames. Occasionally we caught sight of their wicked eyes reflecting the firelight. We would huddle down in our sleeping bags while Justice and Albie stood guard with their spears, feeding the fire and defying the circling animals until dawn.

The land north of the swamps was no place for a holiday. Angola was in the throes of Africa's longest-running civil war. It was fuelled by super-power rivalry, funded out of the country's fabulous mineral wealth, and driven by one man's lust for power. Jonas Savimbi was the son of the first

261

black man to become a station master on the Benguela railway. Savimbi Senior eventually won the status of an *assimilado*, with, in theory at least, most of the rights of a white Portuguese colonist. To become almost white in this way was quite an achievement in a country which had only abandoned slavery some 40 years before and did not bother to give Africans even primary education. Savimbi Junior was not impressed. He was taught by missionaries and, according to his biographer, Fred Bridgeland, early on showed the personality trait that would eventually kill half a million people. The missionaries organised a football match between their black pupils and the white children in the local town. The whites produced the referee, Savimbi provided the ball. When the referee disallowed a goal Savimbi thought he had scored, he picked up the ball and walked off with it. The game had to be cancelled.

That's exactly what he did when he lost out to the Marxist MPLA in the struggle for power after the Portuguese fled in the mid-seventies. It had all been very sudden. In historical terms the Portuguese vanished almost overnight after a left-wing military coup toppled the government in Lisbon. A quarter of a million colonists, who had said they would fight to the death to keep Angola, just legged it, stripping their homes, destroying everything they could not take. They even threw away the keys to the cars they were forced to leave behind.

By the time I first met Savimbi, he had been in the bush for nearly 20 years. He had started with a borrowed pistol and a small group of followers from his Ovimbundu tribe, and a set of initials, UNITA (the National Union for the Total Independence of Angola). By the mid-eighties, he had a well-drilled and impressively armed force of 40,000 men that controlled a third of the country and turned much of the rest of it into a nightmare.

It was difficult to get to him. You had to be invited. But Savimbi knew the value of publicity and how to play to different audiences. Inasmuch as he had any political philosophy beyond an obsession with gaining untrammelled personal power, he was an African peasant socialist and admirer of Chairman Mao. Yet in the West he talked the language of liberalism, fluently, in four languages. On his tours of western capitals he was stylish and sophisticated; his handlers called him the 'Gucci Guerrilla'. The South Africans supported him openly, but they had their own agenda for destabilising black-ruled countries on their borders. Western help, mostly from America but also from the intelligence services of Britain, France and Germany, was covert. Savimbi wanted more. He wanted public recognition, and when his soldiers captured a group of British engineers in central Angola he saw a way to get it.

It was a tough journey. We gathered in the pre-dawn at Lanseria airport, outside Johannesburg, to be loaded into a World War II vintage Dakota. The first part of the flight was bad enough, as it bumped and banged across Botswana. But as we approached the Angolan border, the South African pilot took the ancient plane down to 50 feet to avoid the government MIGs and, within a couple of minutes, the flower of the foreign media were hurling their breakfasts into any receptacle they could find.

We landed at a dusty airstrip and packed ourselves into the back of a UNITA lorry that set off along a barely discernible track through the bush. It took an excruciating ten hours to reach Savimbi's headquarters at a place called Jamba, a town of thatched huts arranged with military precision, half hidden in groves of trees. By then it was near midnight, but we were greeted by a very smart guard of honour and taken off to one of the larger huts to be given a silver-service dinner. The waiters were soldiers who served us risotto and broccoli in white gloves and stood to attention between courses. The food was excellent. The wines were the very best South Africa had to offer. The sheets in the sleeping huts we were eventually allowed to stagger off to were shining white and freshly ironed. It wasn't Claridges, but it was not what you might expect from a rebel hideout in one of the most ravaged countries on earth.

The next day Savimbi put on an elaborate military display to honour a distinguished visitor from Britain. To secure the hostages' release, Mrs Thatcher's government had agreed to send out one of the most senior officials in the Foreign Office. He had had to fly, illegally, to the lair of a rebel fighting a government Britain officially recognised. Now the two of them were seated side by side up on a dais, a study in contrasts. Savimbi: in his immaculately pressed fatigues, a green beret with three gold stars over his dark, bearded face, a pearl-handled revolver on his hip, toying with an ivory-tipped cane. The man from the FO: pink and perspiring, in what looked like his gardening shirt and a pair of khaki slacks that had obviously been made for a less imposing figure many years before. He was unfazed and affable. As far as I could hear responding to Savimbi's lengthy lectures with a diplomatic 'really?', 'most interesting', or 'jolly good'.

The military display that unfolded in front of us had clearly been rehearsed for months. The latest armour rolled past, regiments of immaculate soldiers performed complicated drill manoeuvres in the dust, while a big crowd of supporters went wild against a frieze of triumphalist posters showing Savimbi and his victories that stretched across three sides of the parade ground.

Savimbi was a rich rebel and it showed. South Africa was giving him money and arms. America was paying him as much as $60 million a year, though we did not find out about that until later. Most of all, he had Angola's diamonds. You could pick diamonds out of the river banks of north-east Angola, which his forces controlled. It is estimated he was making £250 million a year from them.

His enemies, the Marxist government in Luanda, were bankrolled by the Soviet Union who gave them around $800 million a year in military aid and paid for the 30,000 Cuban troops, the backbone of the army that kept them in power. Savimbi might have the diamonds but the government had the oil. They controlled the rich fields in the Cabinda enclave. Angola's mineral wealth was not so much a blessing as a curse. It paid for an endless war of destruction.

Savimbi was a mass of contradictions and they were all on show that day. He was carrying on a polite conversation about international politics with a distinguished British diplomat up on the stage, while the praise singers who gathered in front of him treated him like the most traditional of African chiefs. They talked up his sexual potency in terms which might have disturbed even the Foreign Office mandarin's equanimity, had he understood what they were saying. They spoke of his lust for blood, which was certainly true, and not only for that of his enemies. He would frequently purge the ranks of his followers and publicly burn whole families alive in front of large crowds on that very square. Mind you, if anything, the MPLA were worse.

It was a long day, but by mid-afternoon even Jonas Savimbi was satisfied. Getting the Foreign Office man to Jamba, he told me, was like winning a battle. 'He came here on humanitarian grounds, we know. But for us, it is recognition, and that is a victory.'

We were all taken off to meet the hostages, who were being very British and, from the standpoint of an interviewer, deplorably understated about their imminent freedom. Graham Popplewell, sporting a beard grown over 80 days in captivity, said they had been treated well. But they had been told they would never be released if Margaret Thatcher didn't back down and send a high-ranking emissary to beg for their freedom. 'Our Prime Minister is known for her' – he searched for the right words –

'umm, staying qualities, so we didn't sleep very well that night.' Mrs Thatcher's MI6 was busy helping prop up UNITA, so maybe it was not that great a sacrifice of principle.

The last time I saw Jonas Savimbi was in that camp at Jamba. I forget precisely why we were there. All I can remember now was a bizarre celebration that evening for 'the wounded'. They lit the bonfires when it got dark and several bands broke into infectious African rhythms. Soon the square was filled with thousands of cripples, men, women and children, who had all lost at least one leg. Some hung on to each other for support. A few just hopped around, dancing on their crutches. One side of the square was reserved for the wheelchairs, which rocked back and forth in time with the music.

For years, landmines had been the biggest crop sown in Angola's soil. Nobody knew how many had been planted by both sides, but there were certainly more landmines than people in Angola.

I have seen some sad sights in Africa, but that last dance for the legion of the legless was one of the saddest. It said everything you needed to know about ambition, and proxy wars, and the tragedy of Angola.

Dr Hastings Kamuzu Banda of Malawi was a different kind of African leader, in style, anyway. Like most of the others, he was an autocrat who had appointed himself President for Life. He ruled by fear. His opponents disappeared on a regular basis; some were dropped with their feet encased in concrete to the bottom of the giant lake that takes up much of the country. He encouraged a relentless cult of personality. It was his personality that was different. He was not a warrior like Savimbi or a Marxist ideologue like Mugabe. He had been a GP in Harlesden, North London, and he was still an elder of the Church of Scotland. Banda was a very conservative kind of African Nationalist who did not think much of the ability of black people, other than himself, to run things. He was well into his sixties, and had even been suspended from practising medicine for running an illegal abortion clinic, when the headlong rush to decolonise left him, seemingly, as the only person to lead six million people from colonial Nyasaland to independent Malawi.

We were very rarely allowed into Malawi, and I was only able to talk to the *Ngwazi* (chief of chiefs) once. He, too, was keen on great parades in his stadium at the administrative capital, Lilongwe. He had a private army of women, the *Mbumba*, who were fanatically committed to the old man and permeated through to every corner of Malawian society.

Thousands of them, dressed in identical long blue dresses, dragged his open Land Rover into the stadium that Independence Day. A younger Hastings Banda was printed across every ample bosom and seemed to wink in time with every step. They chanted out the endless praise of the *Ngwazi* that was, apparently, public policy. Adulation was required by law, but the *Mbumba* were not doing their thing under duress. They were enthusiastic to the point of ecstasy.

Banda himself was an anachronism. He was well into his eighties then, dressed in an immaculate three-piece suit, dark glasses and a big black Homburg. He swished his trademark flywhisk delicately over the backs of his faithful followers, his lips pursed with a very elderly and very superior kind of delight.

The whole column wound out of the stadium to be replaced by armed Malawian police in their British-style tropical kit, who rushed up and down stabbing the turf as if it had suddenly rebelled against the President for Life. The witch doctors had their turn, one with 16 pots stacked up on his head (I counted) and a pair of motor cycle goggles, another driving just the steering wheel of an old Morris, two more with great animal heads who writhed and subsided in perfect unison.

Then he was back. The Homburg had been swapped for a shield and spear. Bare-headed, but still dressed appropriately for morning service in a Scottish church, he joined in a stately dance with warriors whose formal dress consisted of ready-to-wear skins. He might have been arthritic, even slightly camp, but there was no doubting the force of his personality in the cauldron of that stadium.

He was less impressive close to, sitting next to his 'official hostess', Miss Cecilia Kadzimira, who was said to wield the real power in Malawi. Her role during our interview was to adjust the presidential hearing aid, not that the *Ngwazi* bothered to listen much, even to my questions. He defended his dictatorial rule, and his unfashionable friendship with South Africa, on the grounds of Malawi's self-sufficiency. 'Only Malawi feeds herself,' he said, scrabbling with one hand for the flywhisk. 'The rest of Africa has to beg the British, the Americans for food. We do not. Thanks to me.' I asked him why he tolerated no criticism but he ignored me and gave me a lecture on why Africa, in his view, was falling apart: 'The ignorant have now got hold of power,' he said. He was more racist than any white South African. In his view, only one black man was capable of being a ruler and there were no prizes for guessing who that was.

I wondered aloud why he had banned bell-bottomed trousers and mini-skirts from Malawi, and he got very worked up about the childish vulnerability of his people and the loose morals of the West. So worked up that the 'official hostess' got fidgety and shot us threatening looks. The *Ngwazi* found his flywhisk and at the end of a rather incoherent sentence about England losing her Empire through moral collapse, he flicked it abruptly upwards and the interview was over.

Not all the African leaders I met were cruel and corrupt megalomaniacs, but many were, and in those days of breast-beating guilt over our colonial legacy it was not always easy to point it out quite as forcibly as I might have liked. But for every President Bongo of Gabon, a tiny man under five feet tall, who wore built-up heels and banned the word 'pygmy', and who raced round his destitute capital in a gold-plated Cadillac followed by a silver-plated ambulance, there was a President Samora Machel who was the complete opposite.

Machel was a tall, upright man, absolutely incorruptible, driven by his vision of Mozambique as the first real Marxist African state. It was a crazy idea and he was always doomed to fail. Marxism could never work in Africa, where there was no long tradition of centralised power, and where there has never been a mindset sympathetic to the general common interest as opposed to the interest of the family, the clan or the tribe. Machel would have had no chance, even if the country he had inherited had not been ruined by the mass exodus of the Portuguese, who left only a dozen doctors for 10 million people. He had to fight a dreadful civil war against the Renamo rebel army, sponsored first by the Rhodesians, then by South Africa, whose only purpose was destruction.

It was an hour and a half's flight in a small charter plane from the skyscrapers and shopping malls of Johannesburg to the ruins of Maputo, where, on one visit, the main department store only had a packet of rubber bands to sell. On another, I was told no woman in the country had been able to buy new knickers for eighteen months, and even in the capital women would queue all day for milk or a loaf of bread. In the country it was worse. We found people in the north who had returned to the Stone Age, clothed only in bark and living on weeds. Yet Machel, all flashing eyes and endless energy, worked 20 hours a day trying to create his Marxist utopia, even compromising all his principles to negotiate a showy 'accord' with the whites in Pretoria who had done so much to destroy him and his people. He was still trying when he died in a mysterious plane crash in 1986.

*

For every Mobutu Sese Seko, the kleptomaniac who ransacked billions from the rich mineral wealth of Zaire, there was a genial Kenneth Kaunda, who might have led Zambia into economic disintegration but would cry in public about it. For every Jean-Bédel Bokassa, who crowned himself as a Napoleonic-style 'Emperor' of the Central African Republic at a ceremony that cost a quarter of his country's annual revenue, and was known to be a cannibal, there was a Julius Nyere, who translated Shakespeare into Swahili and was personally charming, the most scholarly and simple of men. But he was equally destructive; his particular brand of socialism comprehensively ruined Tanzania. Its slogan was self-sufficiency, but it made the country utterly dependent on handouts and managed to waste hundreds of millions of pounds of aid.

They only had one thing in common. They all, or very nearly all, made a mess of their countries and a mockery of the idea of independence.

Two African leaders dominated most of my time in Africa: the white conservative P. W. Botha whose strategy of modernising apartheid destroyed it, and the black Marxist military dictator of Ethiopia, Colonel Haile-Mariam Mengistu, who was only prevented from letting 3 million people die by a television camera.

NINETEEN

A SUCCESSION OF ACCIDENTS had first brought me to Ethiopia in the summer of 1985. It was not strictly in my patch. I had enough on my hands in southern Africa with the beginnings of an uprising in the Transvaal's black townships and wars in the surrounding states. The same drought that was gripping the Sahel and the Horn of Africa had dried up most of the south of the continent, too. The same mix of drought, war and incompetent governments was also starving southern Africans to death.

One Friday morning in July, 1984, I had a call from the Foreign Desk in London. The voice was apologetic. It was a difficult request; in fact the caller, a pleasant and experienced Foreign News executive, knew it was next to impossible, but they were keen on the idea in London *at the very highest level* . . . BBC speak for 'our boss is being leant on by his boss'. They wanted me to get to an African famine area and out again with both a dramatic story for the news, and footage for a charity appeal that was to take place the following Thursday, in just six days' time. The idea was less noble than it seemed. The appeal, by the Disasters Emergency Committee of UK charities, was going out on all the channels to coincide with an hour-long ITV documentary that had been months, if not years, in the making, called *Seeds of Despair*. The BBC had just woken up to the fact that the appeal would promote its competitor as well as raise money for the starving, and had, very late in the day, decided to beat them to it.

Mozambique was the obvious place to go. There were plenty of people starving there, but the war with Renamo, the almost complete lack of transport and, most importantly, the mind-numbing bureaucracy and delay ruled it out. The last time I had been there it had taken a month of badgering to be allowed into the country with a film crew at all, and then another week camped out in government offices to get a permit to leave Maputo and head upcountry. Mozambique was impossible, given the time available.

I sent off a telex that night to Paddy Coulter, the Head of Communications at Oxfam and an old friend. He's a wickedly amusing Irishman with a conscience, the most worldly and effective of do-gooders. 'Help,' I wrote. 'Have had request from the BBC in London, relating to an appeal to be televised next Thursday, entitled *Famine in Africa*. You will probably know far more about this than me (you could hardly know less). The Beeb had this nice idea of me satelliting in a piece with a "and today here in . . ." to be incorporated in the appeal, presumably at a cost that would keep Upper Volta in asparagus for years. Need urgent advice on where I can leap in and out quickly with pictures of harrowing drought victims, etc. to be edited and satellited from either Joburg or Nairobi. Apparently money no object, nor distance, only time.' The telex ended up on the Oxfam notice board for years afterwards, a slightly embarrassing testament to the symbiotic relationship between the media and the aid agencies.

Paddy replied that they were most worried about food security in Ethiopia. There was no hope of getting permission to go north, where the government was locked into wars with Eritrean and Tigrayan rebel movements. But the situation in the south, where there was no fighting, was bad, too, and if we all pulled every string we could find, it might just be possible.

Next I had to find a camera crew. South Africans were persona non grata in East African countries then so I could not work with François or any of the cameramen I filmed with in the south. I called Mo Amin. We had already done several assignments in East Africa together, including a couple of dangerous trips into the Luwero triangle of Uganda where the army was butchering and burning the Baganda. I admired him as the most forceful and wily of operators, a brave cameraman with a sense of mischief that made working with him fun, even in the worst of situations. But Mo had fixed himself up with a more attractive assignment, filming two episodes of the American television series *Lifestyles of the Rich and Famous* with the Hollywood actress Brooke Shields in which famine victims were unlikely to figure. Mo said he would chase up his contacts for me, and he put me on to his alter ego in Nairobi, Mohinder Dhillon. The two Mos had a lifelong love-hate relationship which was then, though not for long, going through a friendly phase.

Mohinder was a tall and distinguished Sikh with silver hair and a trim beard, impressively dignified, yet with a droll sense of humour that survived, was even improved by, an heroic stutter. Mohinder was another legendary African cameraman. He had once been Emperor Haile Selassie's personal photographer and had been in and out of the continent's war zones with a film camera for decades

I picked up Mohinder and his brand new electronic camera in Nairobi.

It was the first he had ever used and he spent most of the flight to Addis reading the instruction manual. This was not reassuring, but there was so much else to worry about I tried to push it to the back of my mind. I asked him if everything was OK as we stepped off the plane. He didn't reply. I put it down to the stutter.

Ethiopia is a place out of time, quite literally. The day begins at 6 a.m. Their Julian calendar, which has 13 months, is seven years behind ours so they are still, as I write, in the twentieth century. But, when you travel outside the capital, you feel as if you have stepped back a millennium and more; into a pre-industrial society of subsistence farmers living in exactly the same way as their ancestors did in the time of Christ, using Iron Age agricultural technology that has not changed for 3,000 years. Seven out of eight Ethiopians still live this way.

It is a country twice the size of France. Most people live on less than 70 pence ($1) a day and cannot expect to live much beyond 40 even if their lives are not snuffed out by war or famine. They are Coptic Christians, followers of a church that was cut off from the rest of Christendom by the sudden sweep of Moslem conquest. They believe the right arm of the true cross is buried at Gishen, the Ark of the Covenant is at Axum, and the solid gold cross you have to bribe a greasy priest to see at Lalibela miraculously appeared in the stone under a mason's chisel. Their religion is that of the fourth-century Holy Land. Their God is from the Old Testament, fierce and unforgiving. They are fatalistic and have much to be fatalistic about.

Within fifteen minutes of arriving at Addis airport we were on the road south to the province of Wollaita. It began to rain as we approached the town of Soddu late in the day. The countryside was lush and green. The villages we passed through looked prosperous by Ethiopian standards, but deserted; it did not seem possible for this to be a famine area, with so much water dripping off apparently healthy vegetation. But that is what it was. The rain had come too late for their crops and they were not used to perennial shortages like those who lived in the northern Highlands; they had no culture of coping with sustained suffering. The rains did no more than cover the land with false fertility. The final irony for many in Wollaita that summer was to die of drought in a sea of mud.

A million people were going hungry in the region and there were only a dozen or so feeding stations across the whole province. We watched people queuing in the rain for relief food doled out on plastic plates by a homely Catholic nun from Rotherham called Sister Colette, who had dedicated a lifetime to these people and never seen them go hungry in this way. A short walk further on we found a village where people had just given up. One woman was dying in her hut after burying her two sons outside its door. Her husband tried to comfort her, though he was weak and almost helpless himself. Nearby, two mothers sat listlessly side by side, their gaunt and hungry babies sucking on their empty breasts. Children lay around, swollen or pathetically thin and covered with flies. A funeral passed us, a small coffin covered with a mat balanced on two poles. Seven thousand people a month were said to be dying. And still it rained.

Most of this we managed to film in the end, though for long periods Mohinder could not get his new camera to record. He would tut and suck his teeth over his instruction manual and poke a fastidious finger into its workings. I fretted in silence. The dying were patient; they didn't care either way.

A series of miracles got us back to Nairobi with enough usable material for a lead report on the *Nine O'Clock News* that went out before the ITV documentary (no doubt to the intense satisfaction of my masters) and an insert into the disasters appeal. The impact was immediate, though how much was due to our hasty efforts, and how much to the intelligent and polemical documentary on the other side, it is impossible to say. It was so overshadowed by what was to come almost everybody has forgotten it ever happened. Yet the money poured in; millions of pounds over August and September, and with it a succession of demands from the foreign desk to go back to Ethiopia to see how the money was being spent and how British viewers were saving African lives.

The truth was rather different. The famine in the south eased as late-planted crops ripened and relief food that had been locked into store by paralysing bureaucracy eventually found its way to the hungry. But in the north the failure of the main *Meher* rains, for the third year running, tipped a crisis into a catastrophe. It happened out of sight of the rest of the world and an evil government which had other things on its mind.

Even by African standards, the *Derg* ('committee' in Amharic) that ruled Ethiopia were monsters. They were a group of young Marxist army officers who had slowly stripped the 80-year-old Emperor Haile Selassie of his supporters and his powers and waited for the chance to overthrow him. It came with a British television report of another famine in the autumn of 1973. Jonathan Dimbleby smuggled out a film of mass suffering, largely ignored by the feudal lords and ramshackle imperial bureaucracy. The *Derg* arranged for pictures of the *This Week* film to be shown in Ethiopia, intercut with the Emperor's banquets. The Throne of Judah tottered and the following day the officers struck. The Emperor, descended, or so he claimed, from King Solomon and the Queen of Sheba, was driven away from his palace, squashed between two sergeants in the back of a green Volkswagen. He was never seen alive again. He was apparently strangled and then buried under the palace lavatory. The revolution was followed by mass murder of university students and senior officials. Later, there was a more widespread bloodletting, inevitably called the 'Red Terror'. A hundred thousand Ethiopians are said to have died. Their bodies were left to litter the streets of the capital, on the orders of the new Emperor, Colonel Mengistu, who ruled in the name of Marx but swiftly acquired the tastes and trappings of absolute monarchy.

To lie unburied is the most terrible of fates for people in such a traditionally religious society; a final twist of cruelty, meant as an awful warning. After dark, some of the sons and daughters of the dead tried to recover their fathers' bodies but the soldiers were waiting and hanged the children from the lampposts. In August and September of 1984, as the worst famine of modern times spread across the north, Mengistu and his government could only think of celebrating. He was determined to mark the tenth anniversary of their murder of the old Emperor with the biggest military parades in the country's history. His nation of starving peasants, the poorest on the planet, had the biggest and best equipped army in Black Africa with which to fight its own citizens. Ethiopia was already billions of dollars in debt to the Soviet Union for all their tanks and Migs. Now he was spending as much as $200 million on glorifying his rule. For two months, all official business was put on hold. Nearly all applications to travel out of the capital, from aid officials and diplomats as well as journalists, were refused. A curtain fell across the north and death came in behind it.

The roads of the capital were resurfaced. Government departments, including those charged with drought relief, were instructed to use part of their budget to beautify their offices.

The rehearsals went on for six weeks. North Koreans were flow in to orchestrate the great day. They trained thousands of schoolchildren to create heroic Soviet backdrops with coloured cards in the stands that fronted on to Revolution Square. Columns of mud-brown tanks forever lurched past the saluting base with their gun barrels dipped in respect. Soldiers goosestepped and peasants stepped bravely into the future shaped by scientific socialism. Everywhere there were triumphal arches, huge pictures of the great leader wearing an uncharacteristic smile, and snappy slogans like 'Long Live Proletarian Internationalism'. On the big day the parade stretched for more than three miles. There were banquets for distinguished visitors and endless speeches. Mengistu himself spoke for more than five hours without mentioning the hungry. They were nowhere to be seen. The beggars and street children of Addis had long since been trucked away, and the starving peasantry were kept from approaching within 50 miles of the capital by a ring of army roadblocks.

Ethiopia has a long tradition of uncaring rulers and an even longer tradition of famine. The earliest references are in the Ethiopian synaxarium, a work of religious instruction, which talks of mass starvation in the middle of the ninth century AD. 'Great tribulation hath come upon our land and all our men are dying . . . our beasts and cattle have perished and God hath restrained the heavens so that they cannot rain upon our land.' Like all the others recorded down the centuries, including a famine so bad in 1890 that mothers reportedly cooked and ate their children, it was blamed on the people's sins and their God's righteous anger.

It was happening more often. Despite the deaths, the population trying to scrape a living from the thin soils of the Ethiopian Highlands had grown and made the land on which they depended less and less fertile. The plots got smaller, the earth more exhausted. The mountains which were once heavily forested were now almost bare. The rains, when they came, washed the topsoil down into Sudan and Egypt – millions of tons of it a year. When the rains failed, the winds blew it away. In 1984 you could see it from space, a red smear on the satellite photographs spreading out for hundreds of miles across the Indian Ocean.

By the late-twentieth century, famine was meant to be impossible. The Third World was full of earnest and well-intentioned aid agencies. The vast bureaucracies of the United Nations, with their bewildering acronyms, were there to protect and uplift the poorest of the poor. Many of them were actually headquartered in Addis. The First World's governments had programmes for dispensing the surpluses built up by their subsidised farmers. And the First World was stuffed with food. In the rich north, where most people's problem was eating too much, the 1984 harvests were the biggest ever recorded. There were bumper crops in the United States and Europe. Britain produced

4 million tons more grain that September than she had ever done before.

The harvests in Ethiopia, though, kept failing. The highland farmers nearly all depend on the rains and, for three consecutive crop seasons, they did not come. By March, 1984, it was clear what would happen. That month the government's own aid department, the Relief and Rehabilitation Commission, called a meeting of all the big agencies and donor countries to appeal for help. The RRC was remarkably accurate in its estimates. It said one in five of the population would need assistance to prevent a 'major tragedy'. The agencies didn't believe them; they thought Ethiopia was crying wolf.

The RRC said it needed 900,000 tonnes of grain to avert mass starvation in 1984 but acknowledged, perhaps fatally, that it could not transport and distribute that much and formally requested half that amount, 450,000 tonnes. The lead UN agency, the Food and Agriculture Organisation, looked at the figures, thought about them for months, and slashed them by more than two thirds. The UN called for 125,000 tonnes, and that is the figure that went to the big international donors.

They were not falling over themselves to help. President Reagan's United States had no time for a cruel Marxist military regime across the strategically important trade routes to the Suez Canal. Though full of slogans – 'a hungry child knows no politics', 'we don't care who's sitting in the palace when there's starvation on the street' – the one country which could have prevented the famine sat on its hands. The Thatcher government in Britain and the countries of the European Economic Community took a similar view. The right hated the *Derg* for being Soviet stooges; the left were in love with the Eritrean and Tigrayan rebel movements and what they saw as their David and Goliath struggle against oppression. Ethiopia, the poorest country on earth, was getting less aid per capita than any other Third World nation. That summer the world did practically nothing. The March estimate that 900,000 tonnes of grain would be needed to avert mass starvation was actually an underestimate. By August, less than 100,000 tonnes had been promised and hardly any had actually been delivered. Ethiopia's emergency food stocks simply ran out.

The terrible consequences of this miscalculation and indifference were only rumours as August slipped into September, and the efforts of journalists and aid experts to get up to the north were blocked by officials.

My friend Mike Wooldridge, then the BBC's East Africa radio correspondent, had tried everything to get out of the capital when he had been there covering the anniversary celebrations, but met a wall of denial and fear. Back in Nairobi, he continued to badger his contacts on an almost daily basis.

On Friday, 12 October, Mo Amin returned to Nairobi after filming the lifestyles of the famous rich and started to call in twenty years of favours to film the lifestyles of the starving poor. I chimed in, as best I could, from Johannesburg. BBC Television insisted I should go, more to follow up the July story than because any of us really knew what was going on.

The permissions finally came through at the beginning of the following week. On the Tuesday night I flew up from Johannesburg and joined Mo and Mike on the Wednesday morning Ethiopian Airways flight to Addis. The customs officials at Bole airport tried to impound the camera gear but were no match for Mo. To see him whirling around his pile of silver boxes, one minute spitting with artificial anger, the next beaming with bonhomie, was to watch a great performer at the very top of his form. We checked in at the Hilton – Mo characteristically insisting he should have one of the top-floor luxury suites rather than the senior UN official who had reserved it – and set off to pay homage to bureaucracy.

The first stop was the headquarters of the Relief and Rehabilitation Commission where we found our travel permits for the north had been abruptly withdrawn. The head of the press department looked nervous. There was a lot of nonsense about 'you people' only wanting to film 'negative things'. The truth was someone higher had decided the famine should stay hidden. We argued that the lives of countless fellow Ethiopians might be at stake, but he laughed. In a fear-ridden tyranny that is the weakest of arguments.

We went to the Ministry of Information who seemed relieved at not having to endorse the travel plans of dangerous foreigners and were completely unmoved by the humanitarian arguments we put forward.

When we returned to the RRC the next day, the press department man had disappeared. We tried to see the Commissioner, head of the whole organisation, but he was out at a meeting. Eventually the three of us managed to corner the Deputy Commissioner in his office. He was surprised we had ever managed to get permission to go north in the first place, let alone had it withdrawn. At first, he seemed as indifferent as all the others. Mo oozed charm; Mike was courteous, persuasive and transparently decent. I would have beaten the bastard to a pulp out of fury and frustration given half a chance, so settled for looking earnest. He made a couple of phone calls and slowly we seemed to win him round. Whether he made his own decision that it was time the truth of what was happening got out, whether the regime itself had come to that conclusion and he had been authorised to clear us, none of us know to this day. There was a third possibility. The places we wanted to go to, Korem and Makele, were hundreds of miles away in a war zone. No charter planes would fly there and they were several days' journey on terrible roads. Even if we were given a travel permit it did not mean we would ever be able to get there.

It was Mo who solved that problem. He got a call from the Christian evangelical charity Worldvision. They put a higher priority on publicity than most charities. They were rich enough to lease a Twin-Otter plane to operate in Ethiopia and keen enough on media exposure to be looking for a cameraman to film television appeals for money in the famine area. Mo stitched up a Faustian deal with its two representatives, a silver-haired Australian doctor called Tony Atkins and a cheerily cynical Englishman, Peter Searle. Mo would film them with the starving babies, if they took us where we wanted to go. We did the rounds of the offices again. We got our permissions stamped, reluctantly, by the Information Ministry then spent an uncomfortable hour at the sinister security police headquarters outside the city. Early Friday morning the Twin Otter took off from Addis, cleared for the north.

We flew over a tortured landscape of jagged khaki-coloured mountains that soon became grit-grey, tinged with red. It was a world scorched by drought, racked by war and now visited by famine. From the air you could see little collections of the conical huts called *tukuls* clinging to the mountainsides like button mushrooms. There were few other signs of life. The only splashes of green were the trees that surrounded the circular churches, which the peasants were not allowed to cut down for fuel. Everwhere else was bare. A century before, the mountains had been covered in forests. By 1984, only four per cent of the land had any trees.

According to the flight plan, we were meant to stop at Lalibela, the village whose twelfth-century churches, hewn from the living rock, are considered by many to be the eighth wonder of the ancient world. While we were in the air, we decided to push on to Makele and it was as well we

did. That very day the TPLF stormed Lalibela. Had we landed, we would
have been captured and marched off, to be released, if we were still alive,
three months later in Sudan. By late morning we were circling Makele,
the capital of the province of Tigray. The Canadian pilots wondered
whether the airstrip was safe for us to land. We were more concerned
about the massive crowds of people who seemed to be swarming over a
barren stretch of land on the southern outskirts of the town. We didn't
know it, but that was our first sight of the famine.

We commandeered a truck. The road into town was full of shuffling
people who shook their upturned palms at us as we passed. The men
hung their arms over sticks carried cross-wise across their shoulders, in
the Ethiopian way. They do it for balance but it looked that day like a
parade of the crucified.

Several times we had to stop because mothers had put their babies in
front of our vehicle and run away. The driver said it was a trick to get the
feringhees to take the child and save its life. He seemed to regard it as
cheating and drove carefully around each of the bundles without a
backward glance. The mothers had not really run away, he kept assuring
us, they would be watching from somewhere in the crowd.

In a wide swathe around Makele, 85,000 people lay about without food,
without water and without hope. They'd walked there from all over the
province and just sank down where they had come to a stop. All were
hungry, all were exhausted, some were literally dying on their feet. We
watched an old woman who had just arrived as she died, face downward
in the dirt. An old man, probably her husband, stood over her body
fingering a cross and staring out towards a horizon bare of any kind of
hope or consolation. Food could only get there by armed convoy. The
last had come nearly a month ago. There was hardly any food. There were
a few sacks, stamped with a picture of a handshake and the words
'furnished by the people of the United States'. But they were old and
empty and only useful as shelters from the scorching sun. We found a
group of women picking over a donkey's dung, looking for some
undigested grain they could eat themselves.

Officials had taken over a compound surrounded by a low wall. They
selected – God knows how – a handful of people every day and brought
them inside to be given a few cans of butter oil and a small scoop of grain.
They had the gift of life. The wall was what struck me most; so few
fortunate people inside, so many thousands outside. They stood, three or

four deep, at the wall, staring in at those being given a chance to live, in a resigned kind of despair. When we went outside they held up their children, stripping them of the few rags they wore so the *feringhee* could see how much they suffered, how deserving they were of a chance to live, too.

The compound had been a barracks for the soldiers, but they had moved out and the tin sheds had become charnel houses. Forty people died inside them the day we were there. Some struggled as they died. A middle-aged man with a greying beard lay on his side with his eyes closed, his mouth open and his Adam's apple jerking up and down his neck like a piston. It stopped. He seemed to give a shrug and was gone. His daughter, the only survivor of the family of seven that had set out from their village, rocked back and forward on her heels, too much in shock even to cover his face.

Next to him was a four-year-old boy who had died half an hour before. His eyes were open and he stared, in a puzzled way, at the ceiling. There was nobody to mourn him; his mother had died the previous night. A nun bustled by with tears in her eyes. I wondered how she survived the sorrows of that place, but had no chance to ask her.

When darkness fell we went to the Ghion Hotel, a three-storey, castellated building on top of a small hill in the centre of the town, surrounded by flowering shrubs. Somehow I had thought there would not be any food, that there *should* not be any food. But life seemed almost normal for the townspeople. It was as if the army of the starving encamped on their doorsteps didn't exist. We were served with *injera*, the rolled-up pancake made from *tef* that looks like grey vegetarian tripe. It tastes as bad as it looks – like rancid tea towel – and is used as both plate and knife and fork. We had *tibbs*, gristly bits of fried lamb, to go with it, and warm beer. I would like to say I was sensitive enough not to be able to eat in the near presence of so much hunger, but I finished it quickly and almost asked for more. We did not talk much. The experiences of the day were too profound to be lightly tossed around. I went to bed but lay awake for most of the night listening to the hyenas that now preyed on the living as well as the dead. When I got up I found Mike still fully dressed but sound asleep with his forehead resting on his Uher tape recorder where he had been editing the interviews from the day before. He was always doing it.

That morning I was woken by the sound of the horns the Tigrayans blow to announce a death in the family. The town was covered with a blue haze. The day smelt of wood smoke and eucalyptus, of shit and mortal corruption. The hotel gave us a boiled egg each and coffee that was sickly but strong.

At the edge of the town I found an improvised shelter for babies being run by an Anglo-Swiss International Red Cross nurse from Hertfordshire called Claire Bertschinger. She had about 550 mothers and their babies, about 1,000 people in all, but there were crowds more outside desperate to get in. They were all suffering from diarrhoea, vomiting fevers, scabies and chest infections. Many had tuberculosis. There were some with measles, though that was a sure death sentence. Their eyes were full of pus and their faces covered in flies. She and her local helpers fed those they took in three times a day with a high-energy milk drink made from dried skimmed milk mixed with oil and sugar along with some rice. Supplies were always about to run out. Every few days she would have room for a few more, because those she cared for had either died or become just well enough to take their chance elsewhere. The choice she had to make, and go on making, was obviously agonising. She had to select those amongst the hundreds and hundreds camped around her who should be let in – which babies should be saved, and which left to die.

She used the weight-for-height test, but no longer needed to weigh and measure. A quick grip of the baby's wasted upper arm was enough; enough to decide between life and death.

She had to lean forward to catch my questions in the hubbub. 'I feel terrible,' she said, 'because it is sending them to a certain death. Many will die within the night.'

I asked her how that made her feel, what did having to make that decision do to her, and got the answer I deserved. 'What do you expect? It breaks my heart.'

I thought she was a saint, she thought I was a prat. Long afterwards, she told me how she could not believe I could ask that kind of question. She told me lots of other things too. Of mothers who ate their babies' food and how it was difficult to tell if this was because of *akehaida*, the hierarchy of survival burned into their culture, where the man ate first and the youngest last, if at all, or because they did not want the baby discharged into a camp where there was nothing else to eat. It was meant to be supplementary feeding, but there was nothing else to be had.

She told me of the time she had some baby food left over one day and tried to give it to those outside the centre. Some got spilt and people threw themselves on to the ground to lick it up from the dust. She saw one of her little boys, a four-year-old called Kiros, asking his mother why she was beating him. He had diarrhoea and had messed his clothes because he was too weak to get up. She was so upset she wrote a poem about it that night, called 'Why?' It was the only question to ask in Makele, but there was no sensible answer. She described how she felt like a Nazi, condemning babies to death, and how she had hated herself ever since. Being told she was a saint did not make it better, it made it worse.

In her shelter, a mother held up her tiny, scrawny baby for Mo to film. He had the most amazing eyes, like a bushbaby, that looked in wonder around that dreadful place. His life, I thought, hung on a thread, on the thin chance the world would galvanise itself and stop a massacre of innocents caused, at least in part, by its neglect. It did not seem likely.

That afternoon we got back in the Twin Otter to fly to Alamata, the nearest airstrip to Korem. I thought nothing would compare with Makele, but Alamata was almost as bad. Tens of thousands of desperate people were clustered around a Worldvision feeding station. Mo kept his side of the bargain, filming the Worldvision doctor's stomach-turningly crass 'pieces to camera' appealing for money with dying children as props. I sneered behind my hand at what they were doing but, deep down, wondered if what I was doing was that different. I was also concerned that Mo's camera was chewing up its batteries and there was no possibility of recharging them. We weren't going to be able to film much more and we were already hearing that Korem was even worse than anything we had seen so far.

Darkness was starting to fall as we climbed through the hairpin bends in the road that led up a 2,000-foot escarpment from Alamata to the top of the plateau and Korem. There was just enough light to see the brightly coloured houses fronting on to the wide dirt street, with their roofs of rusty corrugated iron and unfaced side walls showing the mud and sticks from which they were constructed. We pulled up at the grandly named National Hotel, a shack with mud floors and a filthy bed on an iron bedstead Mo and I were going to have to share. When I pulled back the soiled sheet, there was a big insect that looked very like a scorpion to both of us. We were too tired, and too depressed, even for the black humour and mutual disparagement that normally kept us going. We set the clock for an hour before dawn and tried to sleep.

The night was peopled by mortal ghosts. The road was full of them. Wispy figures in grey flitting through the beams of the Land Cruiser's headlights with dark arms, thin as wands, that stretched for the car windows. We could hear their upturned hands rattling against the bodywork as we lurched through the potholes. Only those who pressed closest seemed human and they were hardly flesh and blood, just skeletons in cloaks, the skin of their faces dragged back against the bone in a rictus of suffering and supplication. Above the noise of the engine the pleading beat like surf on the car doors. As we turned off the rutted road on to the track that led to hell, the headlights swept across those who were beyond begging. An old man squirming in the ditch over uncontrollable diarrhoea. A woman on her knees, rocking back and forward over a small bundle in front of her, throwing an arc of tears that glittered for an instant in the passing lights. Two mounds of rags with legs sticking out, cramped up against a mud wall. A woman's face with braided hair fluffed out behind her ears caught in a scream we could not hear. This was the centre of Korem, northern Ethiopia, in the early hours of 19 October 1984. The camp outside the town was much worse.

We had arrived in the dark and it was dark still as we reached the outskirts of the town and swung left on to the plain that stretched to the harder shadows of far-off mountains. From a distance, in the sparse starlight, it looked like the ground was covered in old snow, dirty and grey in every direction. You could just see the near edge of it move as you got closer. Beyond, hidden in the night's shadow, thousands of shrivelled and starving people lay in their rags in a temperature that was close to zero. The living were restless. They groaned and wheezed; some cried out in their sleep though no nightmare could ever come close to this kind of reality. Only the dead were still and quiet. We unloaded the gear and waited for dawn.

Daylight pulled the curtain back on the biggest human tragedy of the late-twentieth century. The darkness evaporated and, in the pearly half-light, we began to see what a vengeful God, cruel rulers and an indifferent world could do to the toughest and most stoical flesh and blood. Directly in front of us a little boy got shakily to his feet. His head looked much too big for his shrunken body. His knees seemed to bulge between matchstick thighs and toothpick shins. It was his eyes, though, that I will never forget. They began tight shut but opened, wider and wider, as he took in the dying world around him. You could see it all in those eyes. Confusion. Loss. Fear. There was nobody left to comfort him. His lower lip trembled as he slowly turned his head. He began to wail, the high, quavering sound of the truly terrified. He had the dark tuft of hair that

Tigrayans leave on their children's foreheads so God can grab hold of them when they are in trouble and pluck them up to paradise. But God wasn't around that morning. Or maybe He was and we have got Him badly wrong.

I looked round for Mo to point the little boy out to him. I needn't have bothered. He already had him locked into close-up. He was a superb stills photographer and his work that morning would make him the most famous television news cameraman on earth.

It is difficult for a decent person to be a journalist in the middle of a human disaster. It requires the detachment of a doctor, without any of a doctor's justification. You are not there to help. Often you hinder. You may try to convince yourself that, by bringing this suffering to the attention of a wider world, you may eventually play a small part in relieving it, but you don't believe that at the time. Not when you are aiming the camera into the face of a dying old man or, in my case, hunting through the legions of the lost looking for pain and grief at its most graphic for your cameraman's next sequence. You don't like what you are doing. You don't like yourself. And you don't like the audience of overfed first-world couch potatoes whose taste for sensation you are trying so hard to gratify. It is not reasonable, and you will talk yourself out of it soon enough. But you feel hopelessly soiled at the time; the man who can exploit ultimate distress.

For that was what it was. Forty thousand people were on the very edge of death, out in the open and packed into an area the size of a couple of football pitches. They had flooded there from villages a hundred and more miles away. They only left their homes when they had nothing, when all their livestock had gone, when they had sold their implements, their utensils, every single thing they had owned. When they were eating their sandals, and their children had already started to die. Only then did they abandon everything they knew and stumble away looking for help. They headed for Korem because it was the furthest place north, on the great spinal road that stretches from Addis Ababa to Asmara, that was safe for the government food lorries. Thousands died trying to get there. The weakest children were abandoned to try to save those with more of a chance of survival. The old mostly sank into a trance when they could go no further. They would spend hours on their knees by the side of the paths before rolling over to die in some rutted ditch. Gangs of hungry *shiftas* – bandits – preyed on the starving, taking anything they could find and adding to the human carrion that littered the tracks across the parched mountainsides of Wollo and southern Tigray. Nobody will ever know how many died in that great exodus; certainly tens of thousands of those who set out for Korem never got there.

Those who did found there was nothing like enough food for them. When we arrived that morning we were told there was sufficient to give the barest ration to about a third of those who had turned up, and that only for a few more days. The numbers were growing all the time, for the newcomers far outnumbered the daily dead. Most seemed beyond hope, beyond even despair, sunk in some collective torpor, wasting away.

Starvation is a terrible thing to watch. They had already gone through the initial stages back in their villages. Generally, the racking pangs of hunger only last a few days. After that, the body goes about eating itself. It burns up the fuel reserves in the liver and systematically strips itself of its fat. Then it has no choice but to metabolise its protein, eating into the muscles, including the heart, sapping all strength. The mind starts to go then, long periods of being irrational, interspersed by bouts of unfocussed rage. That doesn't last either. It uses too much energy and the body is closing itself down. Men become impotent, women cease to menstruate, nursing mothers' breasts dry up. Mentally, irritation is replaced by indifference. Physically, the body is now, perhaps, half its normal weight, the buttocks and thighs and ribs just bones covered in a paper-thin skin that's become dry and piebald with a patchy pigmentation that looks like camouflage. Hair goes dull and falls out in lumps. The walls of the intestines start to come away and excrete themselves in severe and incessant diarrhoea. Pulse rate and blood pressure drop and the body loses the ability to shiver. Now hypothermia will kill as swiftly as the other diseases that are queuing up to finish them off: pneumonia, tuberculosis, bronchitis and 'flu. And that is just the adults.

It's worse for children. Kwashiokor (an African word that means 'the sickness of the first child when the second is born') is bad enough, with its mockery of good health. The swollen stomach apes jolly plumpness. The shining skin once led to them being called 'sugar babies', though it soon becomes flaky and covered in lesions. The hair goes red and anaemia sets in. Marasmus is worse, turning children into grisly little monkeys, looking like the windblown dead; a kind of living mummification. With it all comes blindness. Vitamin A deficiency causes Xerophthalmia. The whites of the child's eyes go muddy, the brown iris turns milky blue. The cornea softens and then the lens simply falls out and the whole eye begins to rot.

It was all there, out on the Korem plain, in the soft light and chill wind of that October morning. Overhead, the vultures and the carrion storks they call 'undertaker birds' circled patiently, riding the thermals, waiting like everybody else for death.

We worked our way slowly through the camp in the half-light. Here and there, a group gathered round the body of somebody who had died in the night, their high-pitched wails soaring above the groaning hubbub of the crowd. A child or an adult was dying every twenty minutes somewhere in the camp.

We found one of the few European aid workers. Dr Brigitte Vasset was a brave and dedicated doctor from Médécins Sans Frontières who seemed near breaking point. She was full of rhetorical questions which had no answer. Why was she there? What could she do, in the face of all that mass suffering? What was the point of being a doctor, of dispensing medicine and drugs, when there was no food? I asked her what she thought of the rich countries – our world – and how little had been done to help. 'I don't know anything about politics,' she said. 'I only know I am a witness of Korem and if something isn't done thousands of people will die' – she looked, almost wildly, at the reality around her and corrected herself – 'no, *already* thousands of people are dying, *hundreds* of thousands of people will die.' An old man in the crowd pressing round us folded up and fell to his knees, wedging himself in a thicket of bony knees. Brigitte turned away to help him with a look of such distracted despair I can see it still.

In a corner of the camp was the Save the Children supplementary feeding centre for destitute children that had been set up in December, 1982. It had taken courage to keep it open. The rebels ransacked it in April, 1983, and abducted Libby Grimshaw, the SCF country director (she was released in Sudan months later). Anybody who wants to plot a graph of the twentieth century's worst famine can see it all in the records of that feeding centre. In the first year, up to December, 1983, 2,000 children had been registered there for special care. In January, 1984, they registered another 1,000; in February, 2,500; in the first three weeks of March, 6,000, but by then it was out of control.

The process of selecting the worst babies was crude but the resources were pitifully thin and there was no point or time for sophistication. New arrivals – there were 114 in the hour we spent there – were weighed in a yellow sling under a tripod of poles and then laid in what looked like a big wooden pencil box to be measured. The results were compared with a table which gave the ideal weight for the child's height. None were anywhere near. Eighty per cent weight-for-height was the critical figure that defined severe and life-threatening malnutrition. By now, half the children being tested were below that level. Many were under 70 per cent, the level at which, the workers told us, they 'die like flies' and shouldn't have been able to survive the journey to get there. Only a few were getting help. Not the very worst, those under 60 per cent weight-for-height. The food would be wasted on them. Though their hearts still trembled and they could sometimes open their blank little eyes, they were living corpses and would very soon be dead ones. We turned away from the despair of the mothers whose emaciated children were judged too well to be fed. This, too, was meant to be a *supplementary* feeding station but for most of the starving Korem refugees it was the only source of any kind of food. The SCF workers had to live with it all; God knows how.

It was the same for the adults. Those that could drag themselves along to the waiting area stayed all morning, squatting in the dirt in long, long rows. They wanted food, but all that was being given out was a few bags of clothes, hand-me-downs from the wealthy West, for the poorest people on earth, almost naked and starving in the freezing nights. An official walked down the rows looking for those with least to cover them. He slashed at their foreheads with a felt-tipped pen to mark them out before the distribution began. Those who got something looked, briefly, grateful but you could see they wished they could eat it.

Without warning, there was a commotion in the far corner of the camp and people started to get to their feet and run towards it. First in twos and threes, then in dozens, then the whole camp was on the move. Thousands of people were hysterical with hope, dragging themselves through the khaki dust towards the rumour of food. We ran, too, alongside a boy, perhaps eight or ten years old, staggering on his stick-like limbs carrying his younger brother. His face was full of yearning; his little brother's showed only pain. The rumour was false. There was no food again that day.

The worst places were the sheds. The government had put them up to shelter the hungry and now they were places to go to die. Seven thousand people were packed into them that morning. We saw a naked three-year-old girl under a drip who had been taken in far too late. As we filmed, a worker came up and shook his head. He removed the drip, quite roughly, and took it away to someone else. Before he had put it up again the little girl shivered, coughed as if she was just clearing her throat, and died. Her mother was leaning on her haunches over her body, her dark face made hawkish by hunger and filled with an inexpressible sadness. Tears rolled down through the dust of her cheeks. This was the last of her four children. Her husband had died the previous day. She had nobody left in the world. Everything she had ever had, everyone she had ever loved, had gone.

We watched people dying, and filmed them, until we could take no more. Outside, Ethiopian officials on the back of a truck were choosing people to take their place. Hundreds crowded around pleading to go to the shelters. The officials pointed and bickered, then snatched a handful of people out of the mob and lifted them bodily into the back of the lorry. It seemed entirely random. Those left behind were at least as bad as those that had been chosen. After the truck left, they clustered around us, plucking at our sleeves, nudging us with their upturned hands. Most of the pleading was directed at me. The handful of Europeans they had ever met were all doctors, nurses and aid workers. *Feringhees* (foreigners) could save you, could feed you and make you well. At the very least they could pick you out for the shelter. They could not imagine that this *feringhee* was entirely useless. They thought I was just being cruel.

By now it was probably around 9 a.m. and the wailing, which had been a background noise in the camp ever since the sun had come up, grew into a crescendo. In the lee of a small ridge they were bringing all the bodies of those who had died during the night, and grief was gathering around them. All the corpses were bound in sackcloth, in the local fashion, tied tightly round the neck and waist and legs so that you could see the shape of the body inside. There was something impossibly moving about seeing the outlines of a child, trussed in its grubby winding sheet. A mother and her two-month-old baby were wrapped together in a grey blanket, still on the poles used to carry them from where they had died together in the night. Two pairs of dusty bare feet, adult and baby, stuck out of the end of the bundle. I don't think anybody could see those feet and not cry. Even the old men, the most dignified and stoical of people, were crying. The younger men beat their foreheads on each other's chests or on the floor. The women were uncontrollable, hurling themselves from side to side, resentful of any restraint.

The bodies kept coming for nearly two hours. An official made a list on a filthy scrap of paper. He had reached 37 by the time we moved on, and was still counting. It had been an exceptionally good night, apparently. The next week the nightly figure averaged 100. The bureaucracy of death was still underway when those who had already been logged were loaded on to poles again and taken out by long lines of people to be buried outside the camp. They headed for the low hills to the north-west, away from the town, and buried the adults in rows just where the land began to rise. They took the children further to a church that stood in a small grove of trees. There was no room in the graveyard but they dug the little mounds as close as they could so God might notice the babies who had died such agonising deaths and His heart might be touched enough to forgive their sins.

That was Korem, epicentre of the great Ethiopian famine. It was a small town, little more than a straggling village that few people had ever heard of. It was two days before the world woke up to what was happening and Korem became a metaphor for human misery and global responsibility.

After that terrible day in Korem we got back to the Hilton in Addis. I was grateful for its luxuries but resented them. I could not see how it could exist in the same world, let alone the same country. The shacks of the poor, the *Wuha Anfari* (literally, those who cook water), lapped up to the back wall (the hotel rooms that side were cheaper), but in front it had everything the spoiled expatriate might need. There was a huge swimming pool in the shape of a cross, fed by a warm spring. In the immaculate gardens there were tennis courts and a pitch and putt area for keeping up your golf. Inside, there were saunas and massage parlours and squash courts. There was a pastry shop as well as the bars and restaurants, and they were all full of people eating and drinking; people who took public money to stop Ethiopians starving. I was overwrought and full of disgust. I had my own sense of guilt to cope with, too.

The Hilton was really a UN hostel, a club for the fat cats of the aid industry. Many probably did good and even selfless jobs, but the UN agencies had a reputation for high living and a low work rate. They often seemed to be the first out when it got rough and the last to react when it became desperate. The people I saw wining and dining the night I came back from Korem were partly responsible for the famine. Their much-vaunted 'early warning system' was, in reality, a shambles. In 1984 it was routinely taking three months to process the malnutrition figures from the countryside. In August and September they went on their holidays so it took very much longer.

The UN's analysis of the nation's hunger was based on wildly out-of-date statistics and a hopelessly over-optimistic assessment of food coming into the country. They had muddled up the figures and double-counted promised imports. They confused the donor nations by painting an entirely false picture of the situation that contradicted the Ethiopian RRC's dire warnings. Worse, they told the donors that Ethiopia's ports could not handle increased shipments. In the event, the ports were able to process *three* times what the UN's World Food Programme said would be their absolute limit.

The minutes of the agencies' meetings held that summer show they virtually ignored the famine. Right up until October they were pre-occupied with trivial development issues and collections of agency 'round-ups', as if nothing out of the ordinary was happening. The RRC was so frustrated about the famine being ignored, they stopped sending their representatives to the meetings.

That night, as I lay in all the soft comforts the Hilton had to offer, I thought of the woman who had jumped out in front of our Land Cruiser up in Makele. I thought she must be trying to kill herself, but the Tigrayan driver had a different explanation. 'Because her family have all died,' he said, 'she thinks she has the devil on her back. She doesn't want us to run her over but to kill the devil.'

There were many devils on Ethiopia's back. And you could not kill any of them with a Land Cruiser.

TWENTY

JUST AFTER SIX O'CLOCK on the evening of 24 October 1984, Karen Eley, who was then 11, and her younger brother Russell, who was 9, went into the living room of their house on the Orrell Park Estate in Liverpool and found their mother crying in front of the television. They were an ordinary family, living ordinary lives in an ordinary street, but how they responded to what they saw over the next ten minutes would be multiplied by millions across the wealthier nations of the world and add up to one of the most extraordinary events of the late twentieth century.

Bob Hawke was only half listening when the ABC ran the news report they had just received on their daily satellite link with London. It was long, too long really for an Australian news programme, but it had so affected the journalists and technicians who had recorded it in Sydney that they tossed out several other stories to make room for it. By the end of it Bob Hawke was crying. He was an emotional man, but prime ministers don't normally cry at what they see on television.

At his home in London, an Irish singer was worrying that his pop career was over. He switched the television on to take his mind off his problems. What he saw didn't make him cry. He was ashamed. And angry; very angry.

The two Ethiopian famine reports that went out on BBC News – about Korem on 24 October and Makele the following day – are by far the most influential pieces of television ever broadcast. They prompted a surge of generosity across the world for Ethiopia. They started campaigns that raised more than $130 million from private individuals. They unlocked $1 billion in aid from governments that had largely shunned the place and its problems. It is impossible to say how many lives they saved, but they were counted in millions.

Television launched the biggest emergency rescue operation in history. More than a million tonnes of food would pour into the medieval highlands over the next few months, some of it airlifted by half a dozen of the world's air forces. Fleets of cargo ships bulging with grain sailed to Ethiopia's ports. Great convoys of trucks would stream across the eastern desert and up the winding dirt roads into the mountains. The force of world opinion pushed Mengistu and his henchmen to one side and saved his people from the full disaster he had done so much to create.

The two reports fused the sympathy of the First World to the urgent needs of the Third World in a way that has never happened before and has never happened since. They raised the curtain of cynicism and selfishness that divides the rich of the earth from the poor. People were moved enough to believe they could do something for others in distress; tens of millions all over the planet went out and did it. The same emotional and practical response embraced presidents and pop stars, old folk's homes and kindergartens. It was no overnight phenomenon. It snowballed for two years, through Band Aid and Live Aid and Sport Aid. The telethons, Comic Relief, Children in Need, and countless other events to help those less fortunate than ourselves, are its legacy.

We had got back to Nairobi at midday on 23 October on a Kenyan Airways flight out of Addis. I was upset and disturbed by everything I had seen and worried that I would never be able to convey what it was really like to be there. It is one thing to see it with your own eyes, to touch and be touched, to smell the shit, the staleness of despair and the sickly sweetness of the corpses, to have people trying to give you their dying child, to feel, so strongly, the sense of personal inadequacy at being a useless spectator at a mass tragedy. It was another to try to put all that over to people who would be watching it at several removes, seeing two-dimensional images on a screen, in the comfort of their living rooms, with all the distractions of their secure, so-different lives.

The BBC was worried about the competition. We knew we were the first news journalists to get to the north since the real crisis developed, but we also knew an ITV documentary crew had been allowed in too, possibly because their thesis, a comparison of the massive food surpluses of the rich countries with the hunger of the poor, had appealed to the Ethiopian authorities. We had met the *TV Eye* reporter, Peter Gill, in Addis and he had been generous in sharing information with us. My foreign desk was worried that his programme would go out first or, worse, they might give what they had shot to ITN. They had arranged for my Johannesburg tape editor, Mac Mclean, to come up to Nairobi on his Zimbabwean passport so that we could quickly edit the first report and satellite it in that night. But while we were in Ethiopia, ITV was paralysed by a technicians' strike. The documentary could not be broadcast. We had the field to ourselves.

In fact, after the BBC reports were broadcast, the ITV unions relented and Peter Gill's thoughtful and hardhitting *Bitter Harvest* was transmitted on 25 October. Later he wrote the definitive book about the famine, *A Year in the Death of Africa*.

Mac and I started to edit the pictures from Korem on Mo's primitive equipment in between a stream of phone calls from the BBC foreign desk in London. Mike Wooldridge's radio reports were already being run on Today and were creating a lot of concern. One of the newsdesk executives rang me to say there was a considerable 'appetite' for the television version. The insensitivity was unintentional and normally I would have laughed or let it past. Stupidly, it upset me. I was raw, and it sliced through to a lot of confused feelings about what I was doing, about the thin dividing line between reporting and exploiting, about using desperate people as raw material.

I was also worried about how difficult I was finding it to describe to them down the phone what I had seen. I suppose I was still in some kind of shock but I just could not discuss the detail of what we had been through as if it were a list of ingredients for a show. I needed some time and space to sort out my own thoughts and emotions. Television News hardly ever gives you that luxury, but on that day it did.

The satellite link from Nairobi has always been difficult. More often than not it does not work at all. Even when it does, the pictures or the sound often get distorted. By five o'clock that evening the BBC had decided to cancel the Nairobi feed and had booked me on the overnight British Airways flight to Heathrow.

Mac and I ran and reran the Korem tapes, putting the story together entirely in pictures; I would find the words later. It was obvious where to start, on the tracking shot I had told Mo I would never use. It set the scene like no other sequence could, circling around the sprawled and hooded figures in the grey half-light of early morning, a donkey in the foreground and a low moaning on the soundtrack. It looked exactly like one of the colour plates in the Bible I had at school. That is why it had such strange resonances for me and so many others from my generation and my background.

We worked through the sequences, trying to show the scale of it all and then paint a picture of horror with all those faces etched deep by loss and despair. We left the bringing out of the dead to near the end. I wanted people to think it could not get any worse and then hit them with that terrible sequence that showed so clearly the daily cost was in human lives and uncontrollable grief.

We had finished the picture cut by eight o'clock. The BBC had said they would probably take a three-minute piece, even four if it was 'really graphic'. I had cut eight and a half. With a detailed list in my hand that described and timed every shot, I climbed on board the 747 and was writing the commentary as it trundled down the long Jomo Kenyatta runway just after midnight.

It took half a continent to get the opening right, working and reworking the sentences with the shotlist in front of me but the mind's eye back in Wollo and Tigray. I tried to recapture what it was like to be there.

'Dawn, and as the sun breaks through the piercing chill of night on the plain outside Korem it lights up a biblical famine, now, in the twentieth century. This place, say workers here, is the closest thing to hell on earth.'

Cocooned and isolated in the half-empty Club class cabin, seven miles above the famine lands, I had time not just to think but to examine my own responses. I wanted to give the report an emotional dimension, in an unemotional way. I hate the lachrymose kind of reporting that tells people how they should feel, but no human being could be dispassionate in the face of such individual and collective suffering. I finished somewhere over France but, for a time, was too upset to sleep. I finally dropped off as the plane touched down in London.

I did not show the editors any of the pictures until I had put the commentary on them and the report was completed. One of the technicians in the dubbing theatre was crying by the time I had finished. The programme editors crowded in to see it and the normal cynical backchat died away as the black-and-white leader counted down to the opening frame. After it had ended, there was silence. People stayed looking at the empty screen. They coughed, cleared their throats, blew their noses. A voice at the back said 'fucking hell', just as a man next to me was saying 'God almighty'. I was not the only one struggling to find the words to do justice to what I had seen, I'd just had more time. Besides, I still had the smell of the famine camps on me and did not need the video to see the pictures.

The Korem report ran first on *News Afternoon*, the lunchtime pro- gramme on BBC1. But it was the *Six O'Clock News* that created the biggest impact. It had recently been relaunched under Ron Neil, a burly Scotsman who was the most brilliant and effective producer of his generation. He devoted well over half the programme to Ethiopia. It began with a long studio set-up by Sue Lawley to give viewers some context to the story along with a warning that it 'might upset' them. Afterwards there were reports on the European food mountain, the political reaction at home and abroad, and the response from the aid agencies. The Save the Children Fund's phones were already besieged by people wanting to give money, but their director, Hugh Mackay, wasn't pleased. He was angry with a rich and uncaring world that had let this happen, and said so. He was a mild-looking man with the air of an archdeacon but he looked out of the screen ablaze with frustration and disgust. 'What does it take,' he asked, 'before something is done?' He did not know it, but his question had already been answered.

Television News is a fickle business. The *Nine O'Clock News* did not think the famine was at all important. It was a dull news day but they managed to run it fourth, after an insignificant development in the long-running miners' strike, a state visit by the President of France, and trouble in the Vaal triangle in South Africa that I would have been covering if I had not been in Ethiopia. As far as I know, the *Nine O'Clock News* editor was never taken to task for almost burying the most impactful BBC exclusive ever broadcast. In fact, when it won the Golden Nymph at the Monte Carlo festival, the most important prize in Europe for television news and documentaries, he was the one they sent to receive it on my behalf.

By the end of the day that first report was being shown around the world. Joe Angotti, the European boss of NBC, the American network that was then tied in with the BBC, saw it at lunchtime. He and his staff spent the afternoon arguing with their colleagues in New York who had turned it down, unseen. Paul Greenberg, the Executive Producer of the NBC *Nightly News*, did not want to know. It's a busy news day, Africans are always hungry, did you know there's an election on? Angotti kept telling them how devastating the BBC report was and, on his own initiative and even against orders, put it on the regular satellite feed to New York that evening.

The feed is shown on monitors around the big network newsroom as it comes in, at around five in the evening New York Time. Normally, few people take much notice. That day, according to the veteran NBC anchorman, Tom Brokaw: 'The entire newsroom came to a stop. Not a breath was taken. I think people were washed in their own thoughts, deeply moved by what they had seen.'

'The closest thing to hell on earth.' Mo and me on the plain outside Korem, October 1984.

Makele, Ethiopia, at the height of the famine. We did not have much to say to each other as we worked among the desperate and dying. Words were not enough, but words had to be found to tell the world about an unspeakable tragedy.

Honoured by the Royal Television Society. One of many banquets where we picked up prizes for reporting on the starving. The irony was not lost on me, but I still went.

Live Aid, July 1985.
Not just the greatest concert ever held, but the biggest shared experience in human history.

With the rebels in the Tigrayan highlands at the height of the Ethiopian civil war. I did not normally work with a producer, but Mark Thompson was editor of the *Nine O'Clock News* at the time and my boss. Now he is the BBC's Director-General and everybody's boss.

MINISTRY OF INDUSTRY

The explosion in Addis that killed John Mathai and mutilated Mo Amin. This was shot from the Hilton, two miles away. We were right underneath it.

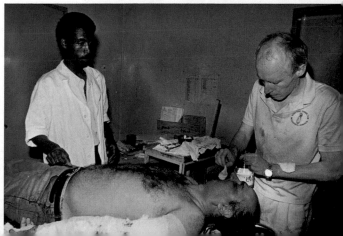

Mo, later that day, in a makeshift hospital in the middle of a city at war. Colin Blane is trying to keep him alive.

You cannot be serious; with my *Spitting Image* alter ego in the BBC newsroom.

So that's what they wear when they are off duty. The Rocky Horror quintet, Jeremy Vine, Jeremy Bowen, Sophie Raworth, Carol Kirkwood and me at *Children in Need*, 2002.

And that's what they wear under the newsdesk. With Vix, my future daughter-in-law, and some qualified admirers at the *Children in Need* party.

Making a prat of myself for *Comic Relief*. The surly look went with the wig.

On the road with 999.
For most of the 90s it was
the BBC's most popular
factual television programme.

The whiskers that never
were. I still regret shaving
the beard off, seconds before
the *Nine O'Clock News*
went on the air.

EVENING STANDARD 15 JULY 1997

"Torquil will be distraught if Radio Four drop 'The Moral Maze' "

The Moral Maze is meant to
be an intelligent programme
for intelligent people. If you
can't keep up, try Radio 2.
This is the *Evening Standard*'s
take on the remodelling of
Radio 4 in the late 90s.
The programme's existence
was never threatened, but it
was moved to the evenings
because a focus group told
the BBC they did not like
argument in the mornings.

Rites of passage. With Christine,
family and friends at the end of *This Is
Your Life*. The relief shows.

Brothers who took different roads.
I met Sergeant Gary Buerk RCMP for
the first time in 2003. As Christine said:
'He looks just like you really – only,
you know, *handsome*.'

Greenberg remembers: 'All the side talk, the gossip, the scuttlebutt about the presidential election, just stopped. Tears came to your eyes and you felt you had just been hit in the stomach.'

Brokaw says he turned to the *Nightly News* team and said: 'If we don't put that on, we shouldn't be in this business.'

'Even then,' he said later, 'what we did not anticipate was the impact it would have on the US. It moved the nation as no other single report has ever done.'

They ran my BBC report that night, half acknowledging their initial reluctance. 'Stories of mass hunger and death are not that uncommon,' Brokaw said, 'but with everything else that's going on these days, often these stories don't have much impact. They're just words from far-off places. Not any more . . .'

The response in America was as immediate and powerful as in Britain. Aid agencies were overwhelmed and money started streaming in. Ronald Reagan saw it and, visibly moved, promised an immediate $45 million. NBC took out full-page advertisements in the major newspapers to boast about breaking the story of such suffering. 'The Ordeal of Ethiopia. The Compassion of America' it said over a photograph of a haggard peasant with his starving son on his shoulders. A small box in the corner of the page said: 'NBC salutes Michael Buerk of the British Broadcasting Corporation and Mohamed Amin of Visnews', which was gracious of them.

The same thing was happening all over the world. The Australian Prime Minister, Bob Hawke, wept again, publicly this time, and launched a nationwide appeal. From Stockholm to Sydney, from California to Kobe, people started giving money and asking questions. What is our government going to do? What's the UN doing? What can I do? Altogether, 425 television stations around the world broadcast the Korem report and half a billion people saw it. The same happened the next day with the report from Makele. This time it led all the BBC programmes, in fact nearly all the world's news bulletins where journalists were free to make their own decisions. In both reports I pointed out that drought might come from nature but famine was created by man. War and misgovernment had turned a crisis into a catastrophe, I said, and the West's dislike of a Soviet-backed Marxist military regime was preventing any adequate international response. But, for the most part, I wanted to show people what was happening in the most powerful way I could. It was not the time for smart analysis of the ruthless inefficiencies of

Marxism, of the bunglings of the aid trade, of the cruelties done to poor people ground between Cold War rivalries. That was all for another day, another time. I just wanted to make sure people could not say they did not know.

The day after the second report was broadcast I had to fly back to South Africa where the township uprising had turned bloody. By then the most extraordinary response in broadcasting history was well under way.

It was the ordinary people who reacted first, who dug deepest into often not particularly deep pockets, who sacrificed the most.

Karen Eley and her brother, Russell, at home in Liverpool, were upset at the news report about Ethiopia, particularly when they saw children of their own age, little more than skeletons, wasting away. After the cosiness of children's television a few moments before she remembers what a terrible shock it was for an 11-year-old to see somebody die. Their mother had left the television on, despite the warning. Once it had started she could not switch it off, but sat crying, and that upset the children even more. Karen and Russell wanted to send some money but thought their pocket money would not be enough. It was just before Bonfire Night so the two of them decided to collect 'Pennies for the Guy'. They thought they would get more money if they took it in turns to be the guy themselves, dressed up to look like a dummy. They went down to the Oxfam shop for some old clothes and used the straw bedding for their hamster to stuff down the trousers. The 'guy' was strapped to an old shopping trolley and the other held out a bucket with a sign on it saying they were collecting for Ethiopia.

It was not a prosperous area but people were very generous. She remembers some who were short of money telling her to 'be there on Thursday when I do the big shop because I'll have more money then'. It was half term and they went out five days running, collecting more money than they had ever seen before. After a couple of days, Karen wrote a sweet little letter to the BBC children's programme *Blue Peter* describing what they had done. It is touching, and it was typical of what was happening with young people everywhere.

'I just thought you would like to know,' she wrote, 'how my brother and I have decided to help the children in Ethiopia. We went out collecting "Penny for the Guy". We took it in turns to dress up as the guy. We collected £87.81p on Saturday and have decided to go out again during the week which is our half-term. We'd like to raise £300 if we can.

When I was the guy I had a piece of chicken thrown at me, I got run over by a lot of prams, I was kicked, prodded and stepped on. A dog nearly went to the toilet on my brother. People could not tell whether we were real or not.'

Karen and Russell were real and so was the response they represented. *Blue Peter* had 2,000 similar letters that first week and the editor, Biddy Baxter, decided they would launch their own appeal, even though they already had one under way for the British lifeboat organisation, the RNLI. They collected bottle tops and scrap rather than money, in the programme's tradition, and by Christmas had raised £1 million. All over the country people were not just collecting money but making sacrifices for a faraway place few had ever thought of before, let alone cared about.

People like the West family in Scotland. Mrs Alick West had burst into tears when she saw the BBC that night. She, her husband and her 16-year-old son drew up a list of all the things they no longer needed and sold it all. The china, glass, furniture, a much-loved 36-year-old tractor and a caravan raised £2,500.

Janet Joss, who was six, put all her toys in a pram and went through her village selling them door-to-door. She collected £40.

An unemployed man sent his benefit cheque – £54, 'all I have', for Ethiopia's starving. A farmer's wife, in tears, rang relief offices, saying: 'I have looked in my larder and I feel guilty.' She sent a ton of wheat.

Oliver Walston was a farmer who watched that night's *Six O'Clock News* and could not bear the contrast between what he saw in Ethiopia and the grain mountains he was helping to build. He set up a famine relief scheme for wheat farmers like himself to send in the value of one ton of their grain, £100. Soon, he had to turn over his farm to his foreman while he and his wife became full-time charity organisers. Sackfuls of mail came in response to *Send a Ton to Africa*, from beef and dairy operators and market gardeners as well as arable farmers. Over the next few months he raised nearly £2 million and sent 12,000 tons of wheat to Ethiopia and Sudan.

Nigel Humphries, the Managing Director and chief pilot of Air South West, simply dropped everything to help. He and his colleague, Liz Amos, decided he should go to Ethiopia with their one 'plane, a twin-engined Beechcraft Queen Air. They appealed for money on local radio and got more than £10,000. They loaded up the 'plane with a ton and a half of plastic sheeting, tarpaulins and rope that was badly needed by one of the feeding stations run by Save the Children. For three weeks Nigel ran a taxi service for aid workers into the remoter camps in the Ethiopian mountains. When he returned he found Liz had raised another £70,000 so he went straight back and worked there right through to the spring of 1985. Liz so impressed Save the Children they recruited her and she spent the next 18 months working for them in Sudan and Kenya.

Everywhere people were giving concerts or staging Lovely Legs and Beautiful Eyes competitions. Julius Harper, a ten-year-old in London, raised £96 busking with his recorder in Camden Market. A hairdresser in Gillingham in Kent, Jerry Harley, set up his shaving stand in the High Street and took £150 by shaving ten people in four minutes – blindfold.

The Reverend Richard Kingsbury preached a nine-hour sponsored sermon at his church, St Peter's in Caversham, Berkshire, and raised £2,000. A hotelier in Devon called Leslie Oakland roared around Barnstaple in his old Land Rover calling on people to throw money in for a new Land Rover to go to Ethiopia. He collected £10,000 in three weeks. The telethons that grew out of the response to the Ethiopian famine have made this kind of fundraising seem normal. But, at the time, it was extraordinary. People queued to pay out for the most crackpot of schemes, grateful to give and to share in a communal act of caring.

The newspapers jumped on the bandwagon. The Brighton *Evening Argus* raised £46,000 from readers and flew a Cargo Boeing 707 out from Gatwick airport loaded with blankets. The *Sun* raised £100,000 for children in Ethiopia. The *Daily Mirror* went one better and set up a special fund that collected £400,000 in ten days. They hired a 'plane from British Airways and flew to Addis with 30 tons of food, medical supplies, tents and blankets. The *Mirror*'s proprietor went too and, as I was back there by then reporting on the avalanche of help that was starting to flow into the country, I went, under protest, to report on the grandstanding old crook's arrival. At the best of times I found Robert Maxwell difficult to take. But this turned my stomach, perhaps because it struck a chord with my own insecurities. I did a particularly sneery piece for the *News* that night, and that was before I found out he had threatened to take his food away again if he was not given a red carpet and a ministerial reception.

Shortly after it was broadcast in London, Maxwell called me up to the Presidential Suite of the Hilton. He sat there, overflowing a rather spindly dining chair in front of a table smothered with rich food: smoked salmon, canapés and cake. He seemed curious, rather than hostile. He was interested in the coverage of his visit but not at all in the famine. Our conversation petered out and I left before I was dismissed.

I found out later that the *Mirror* had not bothered too much about what to bring the famine victims. The consignment included cornflakes, tinned tomatoes, toilet paper and babies' nappies. The nurses were outraged that Maxwell's gift to the wasting babies included milk powder that required clean water that was not available, had instructions the people could not read and, if left for more than a few minutes, would be contaminated. A Red Cross nurse told me giving them milk power was like holding a gun to their heads. She was even more incensed when she sorted through a great pile of out-of-date drugs and found the man who claimed on his own front page to have come to the rescue of Ethiopia had brought the starving slimming tablets.

I had not been dragged away from the smoking South African townships to watch a rich megalomaniac dancing on the dying. I could not wait to get out of Addis which was packed with reporters and television crews, battling with officialdom and the impossibilities of Ethiopian transport. The Hilton, normally half empty, was heaving with anxious people in new khaki bush clothes trying to follow up our stories. They were interviewing each other as usual and the bar nearly ran out of drink. An assistant manager told me the squatters in the shacks behind the Hilton were complaining that the noise from drunken journalists in the thermally heated swimming pool late at night was keeping them awake. I had nodded sympathetically to the ITN reporter who had been ordered to do a piece to camera on the flight from London: 'Thousands of feet below me the greatest tragedy of the late twentieth century is unfolding.' I knew how he felt.

Mo and I chartered a ramshackle aircraft to take us north again. The pilot was a brisk and confident Ethiopian, but even he was alarmed when his seat rolled backwards as we took off. The 'plane lurched sideways as he tried to hang on to the joystick at arm's length. I was sitting behind him and just managed to push him into his proper position to stop us crashing alongside the ruins of a Soviet Antonov that was a permanent awful warning at the end of the runway.

We landed at the dirt strip at Makele, which had suddenly become an international airport. The pilots of the Twin Otter that took us on our first visit had been nervous about their little plane landing there. When we went back, ten days later, giant Hercules transports from the RAF, the German and the Italian air forces were clustered around the dusty edges of the strip. The grain they had brought was being trucked the short distance to the famine camp.

299

Claire Bertschinger, the ICRC nurse in Makele I had filmed on my first visit, told me how she had gone up to the little hut on the airstrip very early in the morning to wait for the first plane to arrive. It was only just light and she heard a low buzzing noise before she spotted a dot over the mountains to the south of the town. As she watched the dot become a thundering RAF cargo plane, loaded with food and manned by her hardworking, professional and caring countrymen, she had only one thought in her mind: 'We're saved.'

It was too little yet to make a big difference, there or at any of the other camps we went on that follow-up trip. But there was hope now where there had been none, a promise of more to come, a chance of survival. I wanted to stay, but events in South Africa had become even more serious and Pretoria had refused to allow another BBC reporter in to cover for me. I went back to the townships and the one country in the world that did not seem to care about starving Africans. The night I got back I saw bits of my first reports on the South African Broadcasting Corporation for the first time. An aptly named reporter called Freek Robinson was using them to construct a clumsy thesis about famine being the inevitable consequence of black self-rule. I sometimes used to wonder if there was ever anybody else with me in the middle ground between the racists and the idealists who would not tolerate any criticism of Africa and its leaders, who found it difficult to accept that black people exploit each other and thought white colonialists were responsible for all the continent's ills.

It was a scruffy, foul-mouthed Irish rock musician in the middle of a career crisis who seized hold of the situation and mobilised half the world to help. Bob Geldof was at home in Chelsea with his wife, Paula Yates, when the *Six O'Clock News* came on. He was distracted. He was having trouble selling his band's latest single, the album they were about to launch was obviously going to flop. Some sense of particular seriousness in the newscaster's voice caught his ear and then his eye.

'From the first seconds,' he said later, 'it was clear that this was a horror on a monumental scale. The pictures were of people so shrunken they seemed to be from another planet. The camera wandered among them like a mesmerised observer, occasionally dwelling on one person so that he looked at me sitting in my comfortable living room . . . it was clear that this was a tragedy which the world had somehow contrived not to notice until it reached a scale which constituted an international scandal. You could hear it in the tones of the reporter. It was not the usual dispassionate objectivity of the BBC. It was the voice of a man who was

300

registering despair, grief and absolute disgust at what he was seeing.'

For Geldof and millions of other people around the world that night, the pictures and the words would not go away. He felt he had to do something, as he put it to 'expiate myself from complicity in this evil'.

Band Aid started with a hesitant phone call to his friend, Midge Ure of Ultravox, and the beginnings of a song fleshed out in the back of a taxi. A month later practically the entire front rank of late-twentieth-century British pop music gathered at the ZTT studios in Basing Street, Ladbroke Grove, to record 'Do They Know It's Christmas'.

Phil Collins, George Michael, Sting, Duran Duran, Spandau Ballet, U2, Status Quo, Bananarama, Wham, Paul Young, Culture Club, Style Council, were all there. Boy George was in New York as the recording was about to start but got there by Concorde to take part. Paul McCartney and David Bowie, who were abroad on tour, sent tapes. Geldof wanted every penny to go to Ethiopia and bullied everybody in the pop music food chain to forgo their cut. ICI donated the vinyl. The record company, Phonogram, waived their profit, and their workers made it for free. The women who packed the sleeves worked all night for nothing to get them in the shops. The big retailers, Boots, Our Price, W.H. Smith, Woolworths and HMV, took no profit. The Musicians' Union waived the fees for playing it on radio stations. The Controller of BBC1, Michael Grade, shuffled his schedule to give it a special five-minute slot before *Top of the Pops*.

It was not the best song ever made, but that was not the point. It was a phenomenon. People bought boxes of them and used them as Christmas cards. They were going into stores, buying 50 and giving 49 back for resale. A butcher in Plymouth rang Geldof to ask if he needed special permission to sell records. When he was reassured, he cleared the meat out of his shop window and filled it with the single. The Queen's grocer, Fortnum & Mason, phoned to ask for two boxes to sell in their restaurant and eventually sold thousands there. Every record factory in Europe was pressing it – 320,000 copies a day – and it was never anything like enough. 'Do They Know It's Christmas' sold 50 million copies, the best-selling record of all time.

I took a holiday in the middle of December. I don't think I had had a day off for three months and I really needed it. I wanted to spend time with Simon and Roland, and my mother-in-law was visiting us for the first time since Christine's father had died, a few months before. We all piled in to our mini-bus and drove a thousand miles down to the Eastern

Cape and then west along the beautiful Garden Route towards Capetown. Long before we got there, the BBC had caught up with me, wanting me back in Ethiopia. It was the usual tussle between the family I did not want to leave and the story I did not want to miss. Twenty-four hours after leaving the sunshine and sweet luxuries of whites-only Capetown, I was back in the famine fields again.

By mid-December, the British charities were reporting that the public had already given them £25 million since the reports were broadcast and the money was still pouring in. American charities were saying the same; they would eventually raise over $70 million. Much more importantly, the extraordinary and sustained outburst of public sympathy forced Western governments to reverse their aid policies on Ethiopia. The American administration had begun shipping what would end up as a total of 500,000 tonnes of grain. Britain sent food and committed another £50 million (though Mrs Thatcher's opponents accused her of ransacking other aid programmes to do so). In Brussels, the famously featherbedded officials of the EEC gave up their Christmas to strip the community's industrial and social budgets to pay for emergency relief.

Not much of it, as yet, was getting through to Bati. That Christmas it was the worst of the famine camps and the daily death toll there had climbed to well over 100. Bati stands at the entrance to a pass up from the desert and on to the central Ethiopian plateau. It was a market town where the fierce Afars from the arid plains traded with the mountain people. Now the town was dead. In a valley outside, 22,000 peasants from the surrounding countryside were dying too. When I got there they had tents – rows and rows of them, like a Crimean War encampment – that stretched to the dun-coloured hills a mile or so away. There was some food. They had sunk a well for clean water, but it was too slow for all those people, often maddened with thirst. They drank from the foetid local river and went down with amoebic dysentery, typhoid and hepatitis.

Myles Harris, a British doctor working for the Red Cross, was trying to save as many as he could in this shifting city of the sick and the dead. I spent the day with him as he worked his way round dozens of scrawny children with sunken cheeks. He looked into eyes that were blank or blind, listened for fading heartbeats and the fluttering of flooded lungs, flexed stiffened necks and felt swollen bellies. 'What are their chances?' I kept asking. Most times his reply was: 'Fifty-fifty, fifty-fifty.'

He was a restless and complicated man who had seen the heartlessness of that totalitarian regime at its most cruel. 'Unremitting villainy', he called it. In the afternoon, he went looking for children who were being hidden away by their families, through superstition, or because of the deeply ingrained habit of these people, to let the weakest die to increases the chances of the strong surviving. Myles could not stand the idea of kids dying whom he might just be able to save. He prowled through the camp in his jeans and Beatles cap, stethoscope flying, poking and prying. He rooted under blankets in the back of the tents, here and there uncovering dehydrated babies covered in faeces – on the edge of death, or beyond.

'*Woolly hakun bit*,' he shouted at the mother. Bring him. '*Ahun.*' Now. Sometimes he would argue for hours with a mother for permission to try to save her child.

I went with Myles to the 'House of the Dead', a circular building with a conical thatched roof that stuck up in the middle of the regiments of tents. The light filtered in through half-open palisades on to the day's corpses, mostly wrapped tight in filthy grey blankets. Myles pulled one open to reveal the body of a boy, perhaps about 12, whose skin was so stretched across the bones of his face as to be almost transparent. 'I don't come here often,' he said. 'It's not good for the morale.' At night he read Sherlock Holmes which he reckoned was the only thing keeping him sane.

Thirty-two gravediggers worked, quarrying out the low hills to the north of the camp, to build an underground city of the dead in the iron-hard ground. They dug a hole, then cut a shelf round its wall where they would lay the bodies. They could not keep up. When I was there parents queued quietly for hours with their sons' and daughters' bodies in their arms, waiting for the graves to be ready. There was no ceremony; the burial was even stripped of emotion. Death had become routine. They had buried 3,000 children in six weeks at Bati.

In the charnel house I thought for a moment about one irony of the Band Aid song. They did not know it was Christmas because, for them, it wasn't. According to their calendar, Christmas is in the middle of January. By then the gravediggers would have filled the mountainside with 1,000 more bodies. You wondered how even these intensely fatalistic people could keep faith with such a cruel God.

I only managed to get back to Ethiopia a handful of times the following year. South Africa was such an important and intense story with white supremacy being maintained by oppression and brute force. The October reports won nearly every major award going, two from the Royal

Television Society, one from Bafta, two of the three most important awards in America, the top European prize and a quiverful of accolades from the United Nations and the Catholic Church. We even got a plaque from the Ethiopian government, handed over by the official who had done most to try to ensure we never got to the story. I didn't go to half of them but Mo and I were still fêted at one drunken occasion after another. Mo usually ended up with the trophy because, as a strict Moslem, he did not drink and was normally the only sober one left at the end of the evening. The irony of these endless banquets to celebrate our success at covering a famine was not lost on me but I am ashamed to say I loved it. Reporters are insecure people, by and large; I am, anyway, and recognition from my peers felt very good at the time. It was only afterwards that a queasy sense of self-disgust crept in with the hangover.

That was the main reason that, deep down, I was grateful not to be part of the great aid movement let loose by our reports over the next two years. I wanted the distance to retain my self-respect and not to seem like I was trying to capitalise on a journalistic stroke of luck that ended up doing some good for a change. I also wanted to stay the right side of the dividing line that separates the reporter from the campaigner. I wanted people to believe I was telling the truth, not worry that I might be trying to influence them, even for the most humanitarian of purposes.

On 13 July 1985, I was in one of the grimmer black townships on the East Rand, watching the kids throwing rocks and the white policemen smothering them, and me, with tear gas. It was a cold, clear Highveld morning with the sun shining from a cloudless sky, just as it was at Wembley stadium, where the world's biggest spectacle was being held for the starving of Africa. Bob Geldof told me once how he had left his home on that sweltering morning and heard the televisions through the open windows of the houses he passed, saying 'four hours to go to Live Aid and the greatest musical event of all time' and thinking 'oh, shit'. He needn't have worried. The world was on a high. Wembley was packed. The Guards' trumpeters sounded a fanfare. Status Quo launched into 'Rocking All Over the World'. Prince Charles and Princess Diana took their seats, rather incongruously amongst all those rock fans, and 17 hours of live television from Wembley and Philadelphia were under way.

The Live Aid concert was the biggest shared event in human history. Two billion people saw it. It's estimated now that 85 per cent of the world's television sets were tuned in to it. They were not just watching the greatest assembly of rock musicians ever gathered together, with very nearly every big name taking part. They were sharing in a worldwide act of human solidarity.

A lot of it worked perfectly. Many of the songs took on a new meaning in the context of all that suffering. The serious purpose of the day brought giant egos under control. There was a sense of everybody being involved, of rules being waived, willing it all to be a success. When things went wrong, when Paul McCartney's sound system died in the middle of 'Let It Be', the crowd just took over. The huge audiences at the venues, and the billions watching, never seemed to lose sight of the concert's purpose. It was pop's greatest moment, when its stars really did seem caring, rather than crass. Only Bob Dylan struck a jarring note. At the end of a disastrously bad set in Philadelphia with Keith Richards and Ronnie Wood, he said, 'It would be nice if some of this money went to the American farmers.' But by that time the concert had wrapped half the globe in a euphoric sense of goodwill. Old women in Ireland were trying to pawn their wedding rings for money to give to Ethiopia. One young couple sold their first home to give money to Africa. It was a truly extraordinary day.

It is easy to write it off as a short-lived phenomenon, but it went on for years. The following summer it was Sport Aid, which itself turned into the biggest sporting event ever held. Nearly 30 million people set off at exactly the same time (4 p.m. GMT) on 25 May 1986, to run six miles for Africa. There were 250,000 runners in London's Hyde Park. It happened in at least 250 other cities in 75 countries. Even an armed robber at Dartmoor did the distance round and round the exercise yard, paced by two warders. Sport Aid alone raised $100 million for the hungry.

For twenty years now people have argued why the Ethiopian famine – of all the great human tragedies of modern times – should have provoked such a unique and profound response across the world. Certainly the plight of those poor people was particularly moving. You could take in the scale of it all in an instant, because so many starving people had gathered together in only a handful of camps. You could see, in a series of snapshots, what they were going through. The camera caught so many emotions: the pleading of a mother with a dying child, the racking anguish of grief, the emptiness of loss. Yet there was also a visible stoicism in the face of what, to us, would be unbearable; dignity as well as despair.

These were people whose Nilotic features conformed to our ideas of handsomeness and grace. A trivial and rather unworthy thing, but it did make it easier for us to identify with them as individuals, even if their society and customs seemed a millennium and more away in time. That in itself served to underline how our world had advanced so much and *had* so much, leaving fellow human beings so far behind.

There was something going on with us as well. Britain was five years into the Margaret Thatcher era; Ronald Reagan had been in the White House for nearly four years. Everywhere, the notions of a corporate state and welfare socialism, the consensus politics of the post-war world, were in retreat. But even those who believe this was long overdue, by definition the majority of those who voted in the elections, seemed to be uneasy about it. Market-driven individualism might work better with the grain of human nature, it might make most of us more prosperous, but it sometimes made us feel selfish. There *was* something obscene about us piling up mountains of food we could not eat while millions of others starved to death, a few hours' flying time away.

There were other factors, of course. There was not much else happening in the world at that time. Television was a much more shared experience then than it is now. Audiences for those news programmes were twice as high as they are these days; even pop stars were watching. Nobody could have predicted that the first report would catch the eye of such an unconventional hero as Bob Geldof. For all his foul-mouthed scruffiness, he was and is a man of extraordinary sensitivity, intelligence and drive. He did more than rope in the big pop stars of the day, raise tens of millions of pounds and keep the issue at the top of everybody's agenda for a couple of years. He short-circuited governments, official-dom, tyranny. He cut through – or seemed to – all the bureaucracy, the process, the flannel, the heartless politics of it all. You can argue about how effective it really was in an historical sense. But he made whole nations of ordinary people feel they could make a difference. Articulate and coarse, he was shocking yet wonderful, and spoke for everyman. I was not there but I treasure the moment he walked up to Colonel Mengistu, one of the most evil rulers of modern times, and called him a cunt to his face.

All these things are part of the explanation but not all of it. Something very special happened that year, and some traces of it can still be seen. It might not have solved much in the long term but it made a difference then. We felt, we cared, we tried, and we saved millions of lives. Maybe the memory of what we did then will one day lead us to a fairer and better organised world where famine is described by historians, not reporters.

At the time, I was too busy to think about what it all meant. The South African townships were in flames and apartheid was making its last stand.

TWENTY-ONE

THE SMELL IS WHAT locks it all into place. You can remember what it looked like: the massed crowds, the running battles, the beating and the killing, and the bent figures huddled round their primitive acts of vengeance. That's easy; the problem is not remembering what you saw, it is forgetting. The noise, too. The shuffling rhythm of the *toye-toye*, ten thousand moving and grunting as one. The single versicle *Amandla!* ('power') and its collective response *Awetu!* ('to the people'), shouted with a forest of fists in the air. The guerrilla's lilting anthem *Umkhonto we Sizwe* ('Spear of the Nation'). And, most of all, the Methodist hymn that became a freedom song, *Nkosi sikelel i'Afrika* ('God bless Africa'), sung, hauntingly, on every occasion when it was abundantly clear He hadn't. But what makes it real, what jack-knifes you awake at three in the morning, is when you suddenly remember the smell. The sharp odour of thousands of live bodies packed around you in the heat of an African afternoon. The sweet, nauseous stench of the dead, putrefying in their cheap coffins. The bite of tear gas hanging in the air, a whiff of cordite, and everywhere the choking stink of burning tyres. I hate funerals. But in two years I must have buried more people than an undertaker manages in a working lifetime. The dead were all, in their different ways, victims of apartheid which was itself in its death throes, had we but known it.

The process had begun shortly after we arrived. The government had come up with a new constitution that offered mixed-race coloureds and Indians a share of power. They were each to have their own separate chamber in Parliament, which would give them some control over the affairs of their own, segregated communities and a small say in the running of the country as a whole. The whites, then around 15 per cent of the population, would still have the final decision over everything that mattered. The coloureds, about eight per cent, and the Indians, around three per cent of South Africans, would barely even be junior partners in government. The blacks, then 74 per cent of the population, were completely ignored. In a referendum, the whites agreed to go along with what had been sold to them as a decisive change that would not really alter anything. My reports tried to strike a balance. It was significant that, for the first time in living memory, brown people would have some say in

308

how they were governed. But it underlined, in the clearest possible way, that blacks were being treated as if they did not exist. In retrospect, the whole idea was preposterous. It was the spark that would burn the whole edifice of apartheid to the ground.

There was trouble in both communities in the run-up to their first elections in August, 1984. There were many coloureds and Indians who felt they were being co-opted to help run apartheid rather than change it; that they were voting for their own oppression as well as that of the blacks. Down in the Eastern Cape, I watched a coloured campaign meeting become a mass brawl with fist fights surging back and forth across the stage. In Lenasia, the segregated Indian township next to Soweto, voting day turned into a riot. Hundreds of young Indians gathered in groups round the civic hall, which was being used as a voting station. They yelled 'sell out' at the thin trickle of voters passing through the cordon of white police. There were more police backed up round the corner in reserve and it was not long before they were called in. They charged the demonstrators with whips and dogs. The crowd responded with stones. The police started beating up reporters and photographers, so we withdrew to a rooftop nearby. From there, we watched running battles break out across the wide car park in the centre of the township. The police used tear gas. Snatch squads pulled out those they had decided were the ringleaders. But the young Indians would not disperse. They caught a policeman and began stoning him, but he managed to crawl out of the way. As the evening drew on, the demonstrators turned to petrol bombs and the police fired volley after volley of rubber bullets at them. It didn't look like a new political dispensation. It looked like the stirrings of revolution.

The elections went ahead, though fewer than one in three coloureds, and one in five Indians, used their new vote. The day their semi-elected leaders were sworn in was the day everything really changed, but not in the way the government had planned.

The change didn't happen down in the Parliament at Capetown. There, the coloured and Indian leaders signed up for their salaries and their cars, but found their new status had old limits. They moved into the old Parliamentary Chambers but found the whites had moved into new accommodation, taking all the power with them. The coloureds were given the former Senate, which had voted to deprive them of the vote in the fifties, and tried hard not to look like assistant oppressors. I should have been there but had stayed on in Johannesburg for a prosaic and painful reason. I had toothache.

I was actually in the dentist's chair one morning in early September, 1984, when the message came through. The dentist was a weary young fascist who would wedge my mouth open before favouring me with his bloodcurdling ideas for solving what he called the 'black problem'. He had just given me an injection and was waiting for it to take effect. He was reaching for his instruments when my bleeper went off. It was an abbreviated message. Just one word, in fact. Sharpeville.

Sharpeville already had a special place in the history of South Africa. It had not long been built, as a black dormitory for the white steel town of Vereeniging, when passive resistance died a violent death there. On 21 March 1960, a big but, by all accounts, peaceful crowd gathered at the wire fence that surrounded the police station at the top end of the township to protest against the pass laws. The police inside had guns. They even had two British-made Saracen armoured cars. But they panicked and opened fire. The Saracens' machine guns raked backwards and forwards across the crowd, stopped, then did it again. It was a massacre. Sixty-nine blacks were killed, 180 were injured.

A quarter of a century later, resistance was no longer passive. It was murderous. By the time I got there, with half my face numb and wisdom tooth still painfully in situ, the road down into the township was half blocked by boulders and burning cars. Kids were trying to make barricades out of smouldering tyres. Vans loaded with armed police careered around, blazing away at figures crouching on the roadside or dodging into alleyways between the matchbox houses. Dark smoke was rising from a dozen major fires where the homes of blacks seen as co-operating with the system had been torched. The Deputy Mayor of Sharpeville had been the first to die, hacked to pieces on his front doorstep. Two others had been caught in their car. The mob set fire to it and would not let them out. They sang, we were told, as they watched their victims burn to death.

The flashpoint for what was to become a township uprising was economic, not political. The council, set up in Sharpeville as elsewhere as a limited form of local self-government for blacks, had put up rents. The anger focussed on the councillors who were seen as stooges for the white government, but it quickly became a wider campaign against the new political dispensation that so pointedly excluded them. It was no coincidence violent black protest broke out on the very day browns got their apartheid promotion. No coincidence either that the other main targets that day in Sharpeville were the Indian-owned businesses which were plundered and then burned to the ground. I caught up with two Indian businessmen who were standing outside the ruins of their store, fingering the pistols on their belts and looking bewildered. 'Everything we had we lost,' one of them said. 'Every Indian has lost everything he owned, everything he worked for. They're burning it all, one way.'

'Why have they done this to us?' said the other. 'We didn't even vote.'

By the time we packed up our gear and headed back to Johannesburg on that first day we thought ten people had been killed, but it was more. We had been unable to get right into the township and had filmed most of it on a long lens from the outskirts. On the second day they found four people strangled behind a ransacked garage and another burnt to death in a bottle store. All over the scrubland round the township crowds of people, looking from a distance like an army of ants, were carrying off everything they could steal.

By the second evening, the death toll had risen to 26. The police brought up more armoured personnel carriers and helicopters, the army took up position on the outskirts, but still they could not get Sharpeville under control. On the third day there was nothing left to loot, but the violence continued. For a few minutes history looked like repeating itself. In the middle of a huge crowd, hundreds of young blacks started taunting a double line of police, who responded by loading their guns with live ammunition. A local priest managed to get between them and somehow persuaded the crowd to sit down.

Afterwards, when I spoke to him, he said the people's anger had over-taken the rule of law. 'The police embitter everybody,' he said. 'They're here to uphold law and order. But it's an unjust rule and an unjust order.'

The trouble moved from Sharpeville to Sebokeng and Evaton, the two, larger, townships just to the north. Then it spread to the East Rand, the industrial belt outside Johannesburg. Soon it gripped the politicised townships in the Eastern Cape. We were down there for weeks after police opened fire on unarmed black demonstrators outside the white town of Uitenhague, killing 20 of them. That happened, with the symmetry that seems South Africa's trademark, on the anniversary of the 1960 Sharpeville massacre, and with even less justification. Eventually it was everywhere, an urban black uprising barely suppressed by armed force. As fast as the authorities slammed the lid down in one place, it broke out somewhere else.

By the time the dead of that first spasm of violent resistance in Sharpeville came to be buried a fortnight later there were 56 of them. In the clampdown, all demonstrations and most other forms of protest had been banned. But the dead had to be buried. It was next to impossible to stop the funeral turning into a political protest and so a rhythm began that was to be the pattern of my life – and was to end the lives of many others – over the next two years.

That day dawned clear over Sharpeville. A transparent blue sky was dotted with a few clouds no larger than a man's hand. The police were out in force in their armoured Casspirs. They tried at first to seal off the township but the crowds were too large. By the middle of the morning, waves of mourners were washing up to the doors of the Sharpeville church, passing coffin after coffin inside. They laid them out in three long rows in front of us and the singing began, hundreds of people swaying and waving in time to the freedom songs. The dead were blessed by priests, but it was much more of a political than a religious occasion. They were treated like martyrs even if they had been killed in some squalid settling of scores behind the shebeen, or shot as they looted a wrecked store. South African mythology is instant.

After a couple of hours inside the church, in response to some signal I did not see, the coffins were passed out to the crowds waiting outside. The authorities had said even walking with the coffins would be an illegal demonstration. But thousands picked them up and ran through the dusty streets of the township, calling white people 'dogs' and yelling: 'Death to the Boers!' It did not seem to be personal. We were the only white people there who were not in uniform, carrying weapons and hiding in an armoured car. But they washed round us, as we stood in the street, in the same way they swept past the police vehicles, leaving us all untouched.

Thousands more were in the graveyard, waiting in the swirling dust for the dead to arrive. There was no room to get to the graves so the coffins were passed from hand to hand over the heads of the crowd. There was not much room for solemnity or even respect in that swelling, angry mob. Some coffins went into the grave with a modicum of ceremony. A couple I saw simply toppled in with a crash that was barely heard above the slogans and the general hubbub.

Trouble broke out as the crowd began to leave. Cars and lorries were torched. The waiting police moved in and started tear-gassing the mourners. We ran back into the graveyard and coughed our lungs up into our handkerchiefs. It was only when I looked around that I realised I was in the section where they had buried the dead of 1960. The cycle of violence had taken more than two decades. Now it was to be every week.

Saturdays and Sundays were set aside for the dead and we had to be there. The dangerous time for us was getting into the township. Most had only a couple of roads in and out, so they could be easily sealed off. The police and, as the situation deteriorated, the army were usually out in force. They were normally jumpy and did not like us much. They would turn us back; sometimes they would arrest us and rough us up a bit. Occasionally, they would fire a tear gas canister in our direction and even the odd shot, close enough to scare us. We would start earlier and earlier to get in before the armed cordon closed. Sometimes we would leave the hire car (they were trashed too often for us to take our own) on the highway and walk in across the veld, but we did not like it. We all had nightmares about being caught by an angry mob, with no means of escape.

The first moments inside the township were crucial. You had to find a local priest, or the leader of the local 'comrades', to explain who you were. They were suspicious of whites and wary of cameras. The police had three times as many television crews as the foreign networks. Our very vulnerability, though, was our strength. No policeman in his right mind would place himself in the power of the township. We would point this out in the middle of what was often a hostile crowd. On at least two occasions they wanted to burn us to death. The letters BBC normally had a calming affect. 'Lord Reith's saved us again,' I would say in that first flush of relief when the crisis had passed. François would reply in Afrikaans if he was really rattled, with suggestions as to what I could do with Lord Reith that, mercifully, I did not understand.

The dead from a week ago would have been discharged from the mortuaries and would be lying in open coffins on the kitchen tables of their homes. Often they included tiny children who had either been caught by a stray bullet or had been suffocated by tear gas. The clouds stuck close to the ground and babies and toddlers who could not run away were particularly vulnerable. The family would be sitting around, the women wrapped in blankets. You could hear their keening a street away.

There would be hundreds inside the church, but thousands would join the march to the graveyard and turn it into a political demonstration, flaunting everything that was banned, flags, songs, slogans, guerrilla uniforms and wooden guns, at the police in their armoured cars. The security forces would normally wait, but close in on the burial ground once the crowds were inside.

313

The trouble would mostly begin before the bodies were interred. You would often hear the crack of the first shots over the rattle of dirt on the coffin lid. We would be by the graves and would see the streaks of the tear gas canisters arching into the sky. The crowd would run in all directions. Most would try to run away and find somewhere safe, but the teenagers would start stoning the policemen and, every week, some would pay for it with their lives. All this we would try to film from a vantage point where the police could not see us and then try to sneak out to get the tapes back to edit them for the evening satellite to London.

It made compelling television, and told a story of black resentment and defiance that was at odds with the official version of events. It was a story that had profound consequences for South Africa. The rand went into free fall on the foreign exchanges, the Johannesburg stock market was on the slide day after day. The country's international reputation was in shreds, now the world could see in its living room the gap between the rhetoric of reform and the reality of oppression.

I had some qualms, but not the usual ones about the part the cameras might have played in the violence. For a start, neither blacks nor whites in South Africa ever saw these pictures. Local television was firmly under the government's control and ignored all black opposition to it. And there was something purposeful about these crowds. You asked yourself: Would this be happening if we weren't here? The answer was always yes.

My main concern was getting killed, of course. It was a dangerous business; reporters, even more so the camera crews, were risking their lives three or four times a week, and I was more nervous than most. I was also worried about television's ambiguous attitude to violence. It liked to be excited but it did not like to be shocked. Visceral stories of mass confrontation and death, particularly set in the context of one of the overarching moral issues of the day, made a huge impact and led bulletins, night after night. But it must not get too real; the audience can only take so much reality. Now, perhaps, I have a better idea of how difficult these judgements can be. Then, under the strain of it all, and the paranoia foreign correspondents tend to have about the commuter deskmen back in London who deal with their reports, I thought they were sanitising what we were running the gravest of risks to film. It came to a head one terrible Saturday in the Transvaal township of Leandra.

*

That day's funeral was more emotionally charged than most. They were burying Chief Mayisa, the leader of the local 'comrades' in the township, who had been murdered by a gang of black vigilantes. The gang had the protection of the police who, it was said, had provided them with their weapons and ensured they were not brought to justice. When we got there that day, everybody seemed to know who the murderers were and pointed them out to us. They had not been arrested, or even questioned. Before the crowd began to gather they swaggered up and down the dirt road, making long-distance threats in our direction.

It was different when the township filled up with Chief Mayisa's supporters and 'comrades' from other townships. They hid away up an alley. The police put on an extraordinary show of force in the morning, sending a great armoured column slowly through the township. The killers thought they were safe.

It was after the church ceremony that the crowd formed into a long and angry procession and went looking for them. They were doing the *toye-toye*, working up their anger. The sun briefly broke through the clouds and glinted off the knives and axes that had suddenly appeared in their hands. François and I followed them, along with Willie Qubeka, a gentle and dignified black cameraman who worked for our allies, Visnews. We were all there when they found one of the young men they were looking for.

It was a short chase the lad was never going to win. He had one chance. If he could get to his own home and barricade the door long enough for the police to rescue him, he might just survive. He did not know the mob had been there before him. François and Willie had filmed them smashing the windows with their big knives, hacking at the front door with their axes. We heard his mother and sister screaming inside, and the mob saying they would kill them, too.

We were all there, ten yards or so from the house, when the terrified young man burst into the front yard. He hopped in huge jumps in front of us as the crowd behind him tried to bludgeon and stab him. He yelled to his mother to open the door, but she was too frightened. She didn't say or do anything. He hesitated for a fraction of a second – he must have known he was finished – and then ran round to the back yard. They were already closing in on him from two sides and, just by the back door of his house, they caught him. In front of both our cameras, they stabbed and hacked at him as he stood there. I caught glimpses of his face through the flailing arms. His lips were drawn back in a never-ending

315

scream. His eyes were bulging but already seemed sightless. He fell to his knees, then someone hit him in the back with a shovel and the force of the blow flung him full-length on the ground. A boy with a jaunty cap and a look of depthless evil on his young face leaned over him from behind and stabbed him in the stomach over and over again – a flurry of movement that brought blood pumping all over the front of his shirt. I have no real religion nor, indeed, any precise idea of what, if any, spiritual side there is to our lives. But I swear I knew the moment he died. There was a fraction of a second in which that live human being became a dead carcass, and it gave me the clear impression of a spirit leaving his body.

They did not stop when he was dead. They seemed to need to abuse his body, to hack at it with shovels, and kick his face and his groin. It was more than inhuman. It seemed to me a glimpse of the dark soul of man.

I don't know why we thought we were safe and that the mob would not turn on us. We had, after all, been a few yards away from them committing the most dreadful of murders, filming it like a television play on two cameras. I don't know why I knew that if we tried to interfere we would be killed. Maybe it is just an excuse, but we all felt that, and the others were both braver than me.

Willie was in a state of shock. Sometimes the camera distances a man from what he is filming, but not that day. He put his camera down and said simply: 'I can't do this any more.' I drove him back to Johannesburg, while François, very pale, took our car. I tried to talk to Willie on the way back, but he would not say another word.

It was difficult to know how to edit that night's report. Willie had filmed the murder, close-up and in full detail. François was a cleverer cameraman and more aware of the BBC's sensitivities. He had shot it in an impressionistic way. At the moment of the killing, you saw the knives rising and falling but you did not see the blows strike home. I used a couple of those shots, set in the context of the day and against a storyline that told of black divisions and police partiality. The viewer could tell something dreadful was happening but could not see exactly what it was. At the time, I desperately wanted to share with people at home what we had been through. I thought they needed to see it to know what was happening in the black townships of South Africa. More than that, I wanted people to feel what violence was really like; how sad and empty it was, compared with the exciting fictional violence we are fed all the time by television. I wanted to yell: 'Look at this! This is reality! This is what it really means!' I practically wanted to put it on the school curriculum.

The news editor I badgered half the night obviously thought I was cracked. He cut out all references to a murder. He left that glimpse of raw evil on the cutting-room floor to save the BBC1 viewers from anything that might upset them. Who is to say he was wrong?

I did, then and later. Now, like many other things I used to feel so strongly about, I am not so sure.

When I got home, Christine had a house full of Special Branch men, demanding the pictures. This was one murder they did want to investigate, apparently. I gave them the cut report, which they could easily get anyway, and told them the rushes were on their way to London which, fortunately, was true. It was a way out of a difficult moral dilemma. Murder is murder and those who commit it should pay the price, however unjust the law and corrupt the police. The trouble was that, if it got around the townships that the BBC was effectively filming for the cops, we were dead men.

It had been a long day.

It got worse. We were targets of both sides. I lost count of the number of times I was arrested. The cameramen I worked with were regularly shot at and beaten. One had his thumb broken, quite deliberately, by a couple of policemen who had taken him behind a building to be out of sight of the rest of us. One day I was down at the Cape in the coloured township of Athlone where the schools were re-opening after weeks of trouble and boycotts. The pupils who had gone back to one particular school there started a noisy – and illegal – political demonstration. The police moved into the school, closing the gates behind them, trapping the children inside. Within minutes most of the population of Athlone had gathered outside the school, blocking the school gates so that the police themselves were trapped. It was a humiliating situation for them to be in and there was a long and angry standoff until reinforcements arrived to release them. The police wanted to take it out on somebody. They whipped some of the children and then came looking for the press.

I was down the street, in the front room of a friendly coloured family, making a phone call to the BBC in London. Something made me look up just as a policeman outside fired a tear gas canister through the plate-glass window at me. Tear gas is bad enough out on the street, in the open air. In the confines of that small room it was devastating. I threw up, instantly, all over the carpet, and thought I was going to die.

We all knew that sooner or later one of us was going to get killed.

It happened in the middle of what amounted to a full-scale war between the radical 'comrades' and the traditional so-called 'fathers' for control of the huge Crossroads squatter camp in 1985. Hundreds fought on each side, initially armed with knives and pangas, later with guns. Acres of that God-forsaken place were torched in the fighting and much of it began to look like a First World War battlefield. The police made little secret of their support for the 'fathers'. They issued them with guns and carried them around the camp in their armoured Casspirs. A hundred people died and 30,000 were made homeless, if you could call the shacks made of driftwood and angle irons 'home'; poor devils, they did.

The fighting ebbed and flowed through the camp. There were no front lines and there was great difficulty in telling the two sides apart. It was a very dangerous place to be, particularly as, we were told, the police were urging the 'fathers' to attack the foreign media.

George De'ath did not want to be there. He was a lively and handsome young cameraman with a sardonic sense of humour. He used to work for me, from time to time. I had been standing next to him at a demonstration a few months before when he had been shot in the foot. He always used to say he had a charmed life. He took it as a warning and said he was finished with hard news.

I am not sure why he agreed to work for ITN on the Crossroads story. The money was good, of course, and he agreed to go down there on the basis that he would just edit the video packages in the safety of one of Capetown's swankier hotels.

That morning, though, he picked up a camera and went with a black soundman into the squatter camp. Perhaps he was a bit rusty, perhaps he was just unlucky. They got caught by the fighting and hid in one of the shacks. When they thought the coast was clear they tried to escape but walked straight into a gang of men armed with axes and pangas. The soundman made the crucial mistake. 'Comrades,' he said, pushing his fist in the air. These were not the 'comrades'. They slashed at him but he managed to run away. George, weighed down by his camera, had no chance. They hacked at him to bring him down. Then one of them stepped up with a razor-sharp panga and took off the top of his head like a boiled egg. We were told the police had watched it all and not lifted a finger to help him. George lived a few hours. That evening he died and it was best that he did.

We buried him at a pretty church in one of Johannesburg's more gracious suburbs. The priest talked of 'renegades in positions of authority'. Sir David Nicholas, the Editor of ITN, spoke eloquently of television cameramen as the 'point men recording the history of our times'. But eloquence, our trade after all, could not sweeten reality. A fine young man had met a squalid and brutal death. George's girlfriend and his parents seemed the only people who were not crying; they looked hollowed-out with shock. I was used to seeing that look by now. George was the 803rd victim of the township uprising in South Africa. There did not seem to be any neutral ground left for us to stand on.

The government was gunning for us. Everything else had failed. A state of emergency, introduced in July, 1985, across much of the country which gave the police unfettered power to do almost what they liked, had not worked. Locking up thousands of people without trial, including nearly 300 children under 16, had made no difference. Even mobilising the army and flooding the townships with white conscripts could not keep them quiet. Inside the country, the government's power base was cracking. Ultra-right-wing Afrikaners, egged on by proto-Nazis, accused them of selling out and losing control. The outside world, horrified by what they were seeing on their television screens and increasingly sensitive to issues of racism, backed up their demands for change with sanctions. The government looked for a scapegoat. We were ideal.

They were already reviewing the foreign media on the state-controlled television. A government official would appear every night to list all the major world news organisations with a rating for how negative they were being about South Africa. He always seemed to start with us. 'The BBC,' he would say and look down at his notes. He would shake his head as he looked up. 'Nought per cent positive.'

One day in July, 1986, we were called to a meeting to be addressed by President Botha. Whenever I met him he seemed a rather limited man, with a tendency, unfortunate in his position, to lose his temper. He had tiny and resentful eyes, a choleric disposition, and an apparently well-merited reputation as a bully. His wife once told me what a kind man he was to his servants. She even went on television to tell us all he was so sweet he did his own packing, but not many people were convinced.

On this occasion we were all mixed up with state officials of one kind or another over dinner. I had what I thought was a reasonably sophisticated conversation about race with a police brigadier until, late on in the meal and apropos of nothing that had gone before, he solemnly said to me: 'They've got smaller brains, you know.'

'Who have?'

'Blacks, of course. It explains everything.'

Mr Botha's speech was a tirade. He accused the foreign media of promoting and encouraging the violence. He said we paid blacks to throw stones. We had foreknowledge of violent incidents. We were not just unfair, we were criminal.

In a self-pitying passage he said: 'We are paying a very high price for our efforts at reform.' And he wound up by saying: 'I stand for the freedom of the press. But a responsible press. I will not tolerate those who take photos and take television fillums (sic) which they send overseas to besmirch the name of South Africa. That is not freedom of the press.'

The next day he signed into force the most draconian press censorship regulations in the world. It was not just a matter of banning all sensitive news coverage. Overnight it had become a crime for me to be within sight or sound of what was loosely described as 'unrest'. Were I to be in that situation by accident, I had to hand myself over to the police immediately. I could not interview or even quote any opponent of the government. I was forbidden to refer to anything 'subversive' – another word that was not defined but appeared to embrace anything of which the government did not approve. We were not even allowed to speculate on how long the emergency would stay in force. They refused to clarify these sweeping laws into useable guidelines. They would not answer hypothetical questions. We would know we had broken the law when we were arrested. The maximum sentence was ten years in jail.

It was a very beleaguered group that gathered that lunchtime in the garden of the Foreign Correspondents' Association chairman, a donnish and dryly humorous man from *The Times*. There were only a couple of dozen of us at most. The government had been reluctant to let foreign journalists into the country and kept those of us who were there on a tight leash; my work permits seldom seemed to last more than a few weeks. The statement we agreed was short and to the point. 'It's absurd,' we said, 'to hold a small group of journalists responsible for a profound political conflict that has been going on for more than a year, left 800 people dead, and placed a third of the population under emergency rule.'

With the townships' burials and battles off limits, I went on that afternoon to a garden fête. It was being held to raise funds for the ruling National Party, and the Foreign Minister, Pik Botha, was doing the cooking. He was an old antagonist, a combative man who looked like a forties film star gone to seed. He had been charged with the great international public relations campaign that would chart a path out of isolation for South Africa. That strategy was in pieces now, and all that seemed to matter was keeping his own people on side. What he made of it all was hard to tell. In private, he was sophisticated and roughly humorous. In public, he was as bellicose as any of the *Verkrampte Boerevolk*. He was grilling *boerewors*, the farmers' sausage, wearing a ridiculous Robin Hood hat and a wide smile. He seemed pleased to see me.

'You people have had a field day,' he said. 'You wanted drama and unsavoury incidents, and now it is over. It was not television, it was tunnel vision.' He seemed pleased with his aphorism. I made sure half the world heard it.

The first decision we had to make was whether to stay in South Africa and report as best we could, within the terms of the new laws, or to leave altogether and try to cover the story by remote control. The BBC went through its usual process of bureaucratic agonising, but it was obviously best to stay as long as we could, do whatever was possible, pointing out at every opportunity the restrictions under which we were working.

Those restrictions were difficult now that truth was illegal and justice was a matter of opinion. We had to interpret a mass of detailed and sometimes contradictory regulations for ourselves. Always in the back of my mind was the thought that one mistake might mean – in theory, at least – spending much of the rest of my life in a South African jail. Soon we had no fewer than three lawyers sitting with me in the cutting room every day, arguing over each sequence of pictures as they were laid and almost every word of the commentary I was writing to go with them. We had specialised in leaving everything to the last minute. I did not write the script until we had cut the pictures, and I often had less than ten minutes left to do so before the short satellite booking to get the finished report to London. It always worked, but only just, and not without taking years off everybody's life, especially mine. Now, though, it was reporting by legal committee. Each shot and each phrase had to be referred to the thick white book of emergency regulations, published in the *Government Gazette*.

The first real test was 16 June, the anniversary of the 1976 students' uprising in Soweto and the other great symbolic date on black South

Africa's calendar. We could not go there, of course, but we filmed dawn coming up behind the giant township and, over it, I put the voice of the government commentator on the whites' state radio station, which I described as 'the only voice left'. 'Today,' he said, 'blacks are pitted against blacks, even among the self-styled liberators who confuse freedom with power.' We filmed empty supermarkets in downtown Johannesburg. The blacks were too frightened to come to work. The 'comrades' had a brutal way with those who broke their boycotts, everything from forcing housewives to drink washing-up liquid, to beating and even burning to death. The whites were too scared to shop. At many of the intersections, muscular groups of white men made their sub-machine guns very obvious. Some whites gathered in their churches to get together bunches of flowers to send to Soweto as a peace offering. After some discussion my lawyers said this was not subversive and could be shown. The police stopped the worshippers outside the churches and warned them their gesture was forbidden under the emergency regulations. My lawyers pursed their lips and shook their heads. I had to settle for saying: 'The police took certain actions we were not allowed to film and are not allowed to describe.' I was eventually allowed to report that the only way they could deliver their flowers to Soweto was to drop them out of an aeroplane. It was absurd, pure George Orwell. I am glad to say, that night on the BBC, it looked it.

Truth to tell, there were some things about this total press censorship I quite liked. Covering the uprising had been a daily lottery. Whatever the government might think, we did not have foreknowledge of where trouble would happen; still less did we organise it ourselves. Some flashpoints were predictable. Some places were in a constant ferment: in the Eastern Cape, the squatter camps on the Cape flats, the Vaal triangle townships round Sharpeville, and the black areas of the East and West Rand which were now effectively run by radicalised black youth. Some dates, anniversaries of terrible events in the past, made trouble inevitable. The funerals led to violence that would reverberate for months. The trouble was there was so much of it. We had contacts everywhere, but they were not reliable. The government might claim the violence was being orchestrated by ANC terrorist masterminds outside the country. But, from what I had seen, the ANC with Nelson Mandela and the other leaders in jail was the least effective liberation movement in African history. The kids waved the ANC flags and sang ANC songs because they were banned; they were the symbols of resistance and they knew it was the surefire way of antagonising the government and its security forces. There was no masterplan and nobody really knew where the next big incident would happen.

Television lives on pictures. You cannot go along afterwards as a newspaper or radio reporter can and reconstruct what happened from witnesses. You are there or you are not. The foreign networks in South Africa formed three blocs. The BBC was at the centre of one, along with the agency Visnews and the American network NBC. My opposite number at ITN, Peter Sharp, a frighteningly good reporter and, away from the rivalry, good friend, was at the centre of another, with the agency WTN and ABC of America. CBS, the US third network, in those days when Americans bothered about foreign news, operated brilliantly on their own.

At full strength, each of the blocs could probably deploy four or five television news crews across a country as big as a fair slice of Western Europe. We spied on each other, we even bribed travel agents and couriers to tell us what the other side was up to. In this fierce competition, the rivalry between BBC and ITN was by far the most intense. It was a daily duel. Competitively, you lived and died on whether you had the pictures of those who were living and dying for real out in the townships. That combination of professional and personal risk was terribly stressful.

Now, everything suddenly changed. With 'bang bang' – as the more cynical cameramen called it – banned, reporting South Africa called for lateral thinking and some degree of imagination. Church leaders continued to speak out, if rather more guardedly than before, and people like Desmond Tutu (by then Archbishop-elect) and Alan Boesak had become such international figures the government hesitated to move against them. Opposition groups found ways to make their presence felt. The black union confederation flexed its muscles very publicly. The brave white women from Black Sash would stand, motionless, on the main roads into town in silent reproach. And the attempt to suppress all voices except that of the government became increasingly laughable.

Official information came in daily briefings from a former police brigadier, chosen for his presumed telegenic qualities rather than his quick wits. Brigadier Leon Millett got hopelessly tangled when answering questions about the daily death toll, and soon gave up doing so. His mangled English provided light relief in a dark time. 'Which television set are you from?' he inquired of one persistent questioner. When another reporter started to argue with him he said: 'Are you trying to pull the wool over my ears?'

One day I found he had ridden to South Africa's rescue before. A younger Leon Millett had featured in a series of comic books, normally bare-chested and firing his rifle over the mane of a plunging horse, as 'the Rider in Black'. I worked it into one of my reports. 'It was not a speaking role,' I said, 'his words were written down and came out in bubbles.' A cheap shot, but irresistible.

Before he stopped answering questions, I got him into a discussion of what we could and could not report and somehow manoeuvred him into saying the only areas that were really safe were the standard local newspaper fare, weddings and sport. It was a trick, and I was delighted with it because it enabled me to tie in two extraordinary stories that were happening the following day.

The wedding took place in the middle of a treason trial in which 22 black political leaders were potentially facing the death penalty. The trial had been going on for months, but that Wednesday it adjourned at midday. After lunch, 21 of the defendants resumed their accustomed seats in the dock, but the 22nd, an activist with the opposition United Democratic Front called Lazarus Moore, stood at the judge's bench that had been converted into an altar. He wore a smart powder-blue suit with a big white flower in his button hole. His bride was a lovely young woman who had told me, on the way in, that she hoped their wedding would 'soften the government's hearts so he may be released'. She stood alongside her new husband in a well-cut tan suit and straw hat, sobbing quietly, though whether out of joy, or sadness at the circumstances of her betrothal, it was impossible to say. 'Those whom God hath joined, let no man put asunder,' said the priest. The thought that the hangman at Pretoria jail might put them asunder was in the courtroom, but went unsaid. Dancing broke out in the court when the ceremony was over and ribbons were flung over everybody from the gallery. Archbishop Tutu joined in with style. Terry Waite, in South Africa to show Canterbury's solidarity, beamed down from a great height but clearly had no sense of rhythm at all.

Now, to coin a phrase, sport. Windsurfing championships were taking place off the beaches of Port Elizabeth. The previous night, the whites of the city held a referendum on whether they should be opened to all races, and feelings were running high. We had canvassed opinion ourselves. An unshaven and grubby Afrikaner who smelt strongly of drink said he 'didn't want the kaffirs filthying the water'. A middle-aged English secretary of the local golf club said firmly: 'We don't want another Rhodesian affair. We want the beaches closed to blacks for ever, for the purposes of posterity, white posterity.' The diehards won the referendum hands down. President Botha had said again that day that apartheid was over. Not in Port Elizabeth it wasn't.

The mayhem might have been off limits, but there was still a lot to see and say.

Most whites of our acquaintance did not want to hear. Parents' Association events at Simon and Roland's school were becoming increasingly difficult occasions. We had always been the target of patronising lectures about how ignorant we were about South Africa. I used to ask them how much they had seen of the black areas of the country. Most had never even been to Soweto, just ten miles down the road from our smart suburb, still less the tougher townships, the squatter camps or the dreadful resettlement camps. Their only contacts with blacks were their servants, the sales assistants at OK Bazaars, Stuttafords and Clicks, or the waiters at slick restaurants in glitzy Sandton City. Blacks who were anxious to please, with the polite African tendency to say what people want to hear.

I tried to describe what it was really like but was nearly always brushed aside. 'Mah maid says she's very heppy with the way things are. She says only farve per cent of blecks want them to run the country.' Occasionally I would see the maid in question in some demonstration, or banging a dustbin lid in Soweto, and think to myself, If they only knew. But that was the point. They did not want to.

They bought the government line that the whole problem was created by the foreign media, particularly television. It was unfortunate for us that the BBC was the only foreign television station they were familiar with. They continued to be icily polite to us but their children reflected their real views and Simon and Roland had a hard time.

Pridwin was a very English style of prep school, or at least what somebody had imagined an English prep school to have been before England went to the dogs. The buildings at the end of an avenue of jacarandas were blindingly white in the Transvaal sun, under brick-red corrugated-iron roofs. The ruddy-coloured blazers, short trousers and caps had a pre-war look to them, as did the discipline and the manners that were so much a part of the school's ethos. Like many of the other

private schools in Johannesburg, Pridwin had put up a token resistance
to the government's racial guidelines. There were a handful of rich Indian
pupils and one black, who was always placed carefully in the centre of the
group at inter-school choir competitions. The school was run by decent
people and probably wanted to do more; but for most of the parents it
was enough to prove apartheid was finished, and they had played a big
part in getting rid of it.

Simon and Roland had been popular to start with, but as the campaign
against the foreign press grew more and more intense, they began to be
bullied and ostracised. They were constantly told that their dad 'told lies
about South Africa'. It is sad looking back at pictures of their birthday
parties in South Africa. The first has a big gang of happy kids round our
swimming pool; the last, just a couple of loyal friends in our house. There
were two other foreign correspondents' boys in the school, the sons of the
Los Angeles Times reporter, who was to win a Pulitzer Prize that year, and
the bureau chief from *Time* magazine. They suffered the same treatment,
but not quite so badly. The BBC was far better known (and seen by many
worried relatives in the UK) and, for once, this was a disadvantage. It
probably did not help that the boys were top of their class and, though fit
and athletic, were not particularly good at the ball games with which
white South Africa is obsessed.

Christine and I worried a lot about the bullying and kept asking the
boys if we should go to the headmaster. For months they said it would
only make things worse but then, after a particularly bad day, they agreed.

To his and the school's credit, the Pridwin headmaster acted
immediately. While Simon and Roland were having a lesson in French,
which they did instead of Afrikaans, he called their class together. I was
told later he said that the twins' father saw a lot more of what was happening in South Africa than their parents did, that the country was going
through a difficult time and had to change. It was no good trying to
pretend otherwise and terrible that it should be taken out on Simon and
Roland. In the context of the time it was a brave thing for him to do.
Things were better from then on; bearable rather than brilliant, as they
put it.

Perhaps I am being unkind to the English-speaking white community
among whom we lived. There were certainly concerned people amongst
our neighbours who agonised over what was happening in their country.
But I have to say most of them seemed to me to be shallow and selfish and
wilfully ignorant of what was going on around them. Their insensitivity

could be breathtaking. At the height of the state of emergency we were urged to cover a big fund-raising gathering for Operation Hunger, a charity that was feeding a million blacks out in the homelands. It would, our neighbours said, be good news 'for a change'. It proved to be a very grand affair. Out in the garden of a £5 million mansion in northern Johannesburg, a symphony orchestra played soothingly as hundreds of overdressed women tucked into the biggest banquet I have ever seen. Many were already giggly on unlimited Champagne. Their furs trailed into the Stroganoff as they inched along the buffet. Occasionally you could hear scraps of conversation but it always seemed to be about the terrible difficulty of finding anything to wear. When they could eat and drink no more and the fashion photographers from South Africa's glossy magazines had gone, somebody from the charity stood up and said they must not forget what the occasion was for. It was all about hunger, he said. Somewhere, someone belched but had the good grace to apologise. All this in a country that was practically at war with itself, in a state of emergency, with the townships in flames and drought searing the poverty-stricken homelands.

They had a big white cake with a black child's face, what previous generations would have called a golliwog, in the middle and the word 'Hunger' written underneath. I was angry and probably very unfair, but it seemed to sum the whole thing up. When their blacks were hungry they didn't tell them to eat cake, they ate it themselves.

They were worried, though. All around us walls were going up, houses were being turned into fortresses. Broken glass and razor wire were being cemented into place. Most homes in our road had electric security gates. Inside the homes, they created 'core security areas' that sealed off the bedrooms and bathrooms at night. Even the most insipid or ladylike member of our school PTA had a small revolver in her handbag. Their husbands talked of the 'stopping power' of their handguns in the same way that Surrey commuters talk of house prices. The pump-action shotgun, it was generally agreed, was the ideal weapon because it would 'blow the bastards to bits', but there was more paperwork involved in getting one. Everybody was signing up to the freelance commando firms called 'Sandton Sentry' or 'ADT Armed Response' that guaranteed to have a truckload of trigger-happy security guards on the doorstep within moments of a customer pressing a panic button.

Dogs were much in demand, the bigger the better. Blacks, we were constantly told, were afraid of them and if people could not understand why we did not have guns, they were astonished we did not keep a Doberman or two. There was a terrible story, towards the end of our stay, about a couple of Dobermans in a white suburb called Florida on the West Rand who had eaten a black maid. The details were bad enough; she had somehow got caught up in their chains, parts of her body were missing, and the bits the police did find, they had rather they hadn't. What was worse, much worse, was that the owners were swamped with offers to buy them. Such 'proven' guard dogs fetched a high premium.

Every so often a rumour would sweep the boys' school and, no doubt, the other white schools in Johannesburg, that a particular day had been set for the blacks to come and get our children. Extra security guards were hired and the Mercedes and BMWs would be searched going in and out of the wide car park under the plane trees, but there was no reality to it, only an aching fear.

In truth, the great convulsions in the black areas rarely spilt over on to the well-groomed lawns and shady avenues of the northern suburbs. Occasionally there would be a demonstration in the central business district and the police would step in with their whips and guns. But the whites were already in the process of evacuating the city centre for their safer suburbs. Most whites found less and less occasion to go there.

They could do all the shopping they needed in some of the most luxurious shopping centres in the world out in the white residential districts. The emergency brought a huge increase in spending on luxury goods, particularly gold and jewellery. It was a response that was partly rational – their currency was collapsing and it was a very portable form of wealth – but there was something irrational about it, too; a kind of therapy for the spoilt. Most did not want to know what was happening and found the press censorship of their own newspapers a comfort. Not all, though. There was a run on short-wave radios. A shop assistant I asked about this in an electrical store said sales of radios that could receive the BBC World Service were running at ten times the rate of six months earlier. He was not the least bit curious about why. 'I dunno,' he said, 'I don't listen to the radio much.'

It all came to an end in a rather curious way. The emergency regulations were constantly being challenged in the courts. There was a curious faith in a legal system that had been used to inflict so much injustice yet would, occasionally, come up with decisions that checked the government, at least for a time. In May, 1987, the Supreme Court in Natal roused itself to throw out the emergency censorship regulations on a legal technicality. We knew it was only a matter of a few days, maybe only hours, before the government redrafted and reimposed the laws, but now we were legally free to report what we liked. Our lawyers all agreed. We were back to square one.

We did not go looking for trouble, but it was difficult to avoid. In this brief legal window, and probably by coincidence, the students at the University of Capetown staged a political demonstration. The university occupies a prominent site on the lower flanks of Table Mountain, looking north-west across the motorway. At its centre is a broad piazza where the demonstration was supposed to take place. It was banned, of course, and the police chased people away with tear gas. We were up on a rooftop, with a good vantage point, to see the final act of this rather routine drama being played out in what looked like the modern equivalent of a Roman amphitheatre. We were packing up, thinking it was all over, when a white student carrying a bundle of books sauntered dreamily into the middle of the stage. He did not look to be part of the demonstration; in fact, he didn't look to be paying attention to anything at all.

Four policemen attacked him. They all wore gas masks. Three of them had long sjamboks, the fourth had an Alsatian going wild on the end of a leash. The student made no attempt to defend himself or run away. He just stood there and was beaten. It was particularly savage. One police-man, in particular, kept coming back to hit him again, even after he had fallen to his knees. Perhaps it was the setting that added to the theatrically malevolent nature of the event. But it reawakened in everybody's mind what was really going on in South Africa, that afternoon there at UCT, and that night in Britain and elsewhere in the world where our news reports were shown. Later, my spies told me Peter Sharp had also filed something similar. It was like old times.

The blow fell a few days later. Peter and I had been invited to spend the day with the foreign minister, Pik Botha, at his family house outside Pretoria. He was a genial, if occasionally volcanic host, sinking a steady stream of tumblers full of Scotch, which he called his 'stiffeners'. We were getting all the usual stuff about South Africa the bulwark against Communism, about how nobody gave them credit for getting rid of apartheid, how wickedly biased we were against the Afrikaner, but there was a twinkle in his eye. He started to tell us about how he had shot the game whose heads were mounted around his living room. 'That Kudu, there,' he said, 'when I shot him, he sank down to his knees and a tear appeared at the corner of one of those beautiful, brown eyes.' Pik looked sad. 'For a moment, I regretted what I had done and thought I would never kill an animal again.' He looked up at us and his face broke into a smile that was part boy, part wolf. 'It took me thirty seconds to get over it. And the Kudu tasted wonderful on the *braai* that night.'

I noticed Peter looked preoccupied and uncomfortable. When Botha had gone to get himself another 'stiffener', he told me he had been called by the Home Affairs Department to say he was being thrown out of the country. I knew then that I would almost certainly be deported, too. We both needed a 'stiffener'.

I was given ten days to leave the country. It was a very emotional time. The foreign correspondents in Johannesburg were a very tight-knit group who had been under siege for months. Peter and I were key figures amongst them and, of course, kicking out the BBC had a significance far beyond that of any other newspaper or other television organisation. We went to a lot of elegiac parties. Winter was coming on and the afternoons were suffused with the golden sunlight of the short Transvaal autumn.

The Director General of the Home Affairs Department, the most senior civil servant in their equivalent of the Home Office, rang up Christine to say how sorry he was that the decision had been taken. Hardly had we stopped telling each other what a contradictory country South Africa could be than I got a phone call asking me to go to a mysterious meeting in a remote car park out at Krugersdorp in the West Rand. Though it was not spelled out in so many words, the invitation had come from the Information Minister, Stoffel van de Merwe.

I took the most distinguished of my lawyers with me to argue my case. But there was no case to argue. The minister sat in the back of the car and readily acknowledged we had not broken the law as it stood at the time, but that would not make any difference. 'PW' was out of control, he said, and lashing out in all directions. He had seen a short story on the front page of the Capetown evening paper, the *Argus*, saying that, for the first time in a year, BBC and ITN had shown pictures of violence in South Africa, and simply gone wild. The minister painted a picture of a president in the grip of primitive emotions and a government at its wits' end, with apocalyptic consequences for the country as a whole. He was sorry, but there was nothing he could do and he hoped I would understand.

My staid Johannesburg lawyer sat in the front seat with his mouth half open. Working for the BBC had been so steep a learning curve, he looked like he needed oxygen.

The stress of it all was starting to take its toll. I developed a bad case of conjunctivitis and got rather red-eyed and teary. People said how upset I looked but, actually, in many ways I was relieved. The Australian television network, Channel Ten, asked me if I would go into the SABC studio in Johannesburg to record a series of interviews with their stations about my expulsion. They were just one of dozens of television organisations round the world that had been using my reports over the last couple of years when the story had been at the top of everybody's bulletins and their own reporters could not get in.

I was a bit reluctant, especially when they told me it would have to be done at 1 a.m. But they offered a reasonable fee and I found myself, haggard, exhausted, with my eyes streaming, under the lights waiting for the satellite connection to Sydney. I don't know why I felt under pressure but, for some reason, I wanted desperately to get this right. I tried to work out what the first question would be so that I could prepare a pithy, authoritative answer. My reputation, if not the BBC's, depended on my being impressive, I thought. I was still working on the possibilities as I heard the connections being made in my earpiece. 'Through to Australia', 'Through to Sydney', 'Channel Ten, Australia, calling South African Broadcasting, Johannesburg'. I knew my face was being cut up on the monitor in front of the presenter as he was introducing me. I ran for the umpteenth time through the options – perhaps I would be asked for an assessment of the strength of the fractious black opposition, a shrewd analysis of the economic crisis, a view on how the turbulent nature of the State President was skewing policy . . . In my ear, I could hear him introducing me: '. . . and now they're expelling our man there, Michael Buerk.' I was still thinking about that all-important first question. What will it be, what will it be?

'Christ, Mike, have you been on the piss?'

The last day passed in a dream. The family was staying on so the boys could finish their school term – a generous concession agreed without any hesitation at all by the authorities. Everybody came round to say good-bye. I was worried about the boys with all the upset and being the focus of what amounted to worldwide attention. We all gave each other hugs, for the cameras and privately for ourselves. We drove back to Jan Smuts along the same motorway that swept past the secret police headquarters, and the cameramen swung out to get a picture of us with the Joburg city skyline in the background. There was a big lump in my throat the whole way. It had been such an intense four years. I knew nothing in my life would ever be the same.

Everybody was at the airport, too. Probably an illegal gathering, in South African terms, and certainly a breach of the censorship regulations, but the police did nothing. Everybody hugged everybody else, and then before I knew it I was watching the sun flaming into dusk over the Limpopo.

It was drizzling in London, but I did not need rain to tell me it was over.

TWENTY-TWO

IT WAS A SECOND triumphant homecoming and that, for some reason, made it worse. My editors were all there at Heathrow in what was an impressive display of corporate solidarity and, in some cases, personal affection. There were a couple of television crews and a gaggle of stills photographers. It was a strange and not very comfortable feeling to be the story rather than the reporter, to be in the spotlight instead of pointing it, to feel the isolation of the fox rather than the camaraderie of the hounds. The death throes of apartheid had been the focus of world attention for a couple of years. The efforts of the handful of foreign correspondents in South Africa, particularly the two British television reporters, to tell the story despite the violent security clampdown and suffocating censorship had captured the public imagination. Whole pages had been devoted to us in the national papers. Leader columns had seen us as some kind of personification of truth suppressed by evil. Even the cartoonists had fun with our practical problems; the *Daily Mail* front page had me semaphoring my reports back to the BBC; Jak in the *Evening Standard* showed us hammering away on African drums.

It felt ridiculous to be treated as a victim, when hundreds of people had been killed, thousands had been tortured and tens of thousands were in jail without trial. It was invidious to be portrayed as a high-minded campaigner against injustice, rather than a pretty ordinary reporter trying to be fair and truthful. For a time, in the swirl of chat shows and newspaper interviews immediately after my return, I seemed to become a metaphor rather than a person. Views, virtues and vices I did not have were projected on to me by those with axes to grind about Africa and racism and the responsibilities of the First World to the Third. I was unequivocal about apartheid, the more so since I actually knew what I was talking about, which was more than its supporters, and a good many of its detractors, did. I was much more ambiguous about guilt and innocence, about good and evil. I was half living in the recent past and, when pushed to pass judgement, remembered people, not stereotypes; white Afrikaners who were decent and honourable, as well as those who were selfish, stupid and cruel. Black activists who loved the power that violence and murder gave them, as well as the peaceful protestors who bravely stood up to an oppressive regime.

Nobody wanted to hear about ambiguity. The media, my people from whom I suddenly felt so estranged, were – literally – only interested in the black and white. I was lionised or loathed, and did not like either very much. On my first night back in London a big bunch of flowers arrived at my hotel from Neil and Glenys Kinnock. It was a typically kind gesture from the then leader of the Labour Party and his wife, both prominent anti-apartheid campaigners. But it made me feel dishonest and a fraud, caught on the wrong side of all my barriers.

Britain seemed dirty and grey. The streets were full of litter and the people looked miserable. Their lives seemed to have been sucked dry of drama or any real meaning. After the clear colours of the Highveld and the stark emotional landscape of Africa, where the issues were life and death and both the pleasures and the pain so intense, England seemed unutterably dreary. High stakes had turned into small change. In Johannesburg, I used to wonder if I would get through the day without a policeman's bullet in the back or, worse, a blazing tyre round the neck that boiled your brains until your head exploded. Back in the BBC newsroom I had to fill in a 'hazard assessment form', several pages long, if I wanted to climb a ladder for a better view of Princess Diana. I was oppressed by a terrible sense of anti-climax and was missing my family, still back in South Africa. I was probably very irritating, and certainly a nuisance. The foreign desk said I needed space and something to take my mind off things. They sent me as far away as they could, for as long as they could, which was probably a relief all round.

Sri Lanka hangs like a pendant off the mainland of India. It is the original Serendib, island of jewels. The land is green and gold, the air heavy and warm, scented with musk and the faintest smell of corruption. The original Dutch colonists, homesick and marooned amongst vegetarians and people who thought the pork they loved was unclean, said the island looked on the map like a Westphalian ham. Generations have seen it through the prism of their times. These were days of civil war and sudden death and people saw this flawed paradise as a teardrop, beautiful, deadly and sad. It was two hundred years since Bishop Heber wrote of Sri Lanka that: 'every prospect pleases, and only man is vile'; you did not have to be there long to see what he meant.

It was as nasty a war as it gets, as only a conflict between neighbours can be. The long struggle between the minority Tamil Hindus in the north and east of the island against the majority Buddhist Sinhalese was going through one of its bloodier phases. The rebels had bombed a bus station in Colombo, causing a bloodbath in the most crowded part of the capital. The army had stepped up its offensive against the Liberation Tigers of Tamil Eeelam ('precious land') in the north, pushing them across the Jaffna peninsula and back into the old city of Jaffna itself. The Tigers, who all carried a cyanide capsule in a necklace in case they were captured, were too tough and ruthless to be subdued. They were also well supplied by fellow Tamils on the mainland across the Palk Strait, and, tacitly, by the Indian government itself.

The Indian Army was moving towards more open intervention, dropping leaflets and food parcels on Jaffna, ostensibly to deter the growing flood of refugees; 100,000 had already crossed to the mainland. It was an open secret that Indian soldiers were ready to cross the chain of islands that linked the two countries, following in the footsteps of Lord Rama who used them as stepping stones to come and rescue his wife, Sita, from the ten-headed, twenty-armed Demon King of Lanka, in the greatest of all Hindu epics, the *Ramayana*.

The prospect of Indian intervention had revitalised a Sinhalese terror group, the Janatha Vimukthi Peramuna, which had begun its own revolution in the south, a campaign of bombings and political murders aimed at creating a Socialist paradise, free of foreigners and totally cleansed of the hated Tamils. There was no way out except negotiation, but the struggle for power was suffused with ethnic and religious hatred and thousands of lives would be lost before proud men bowed to the inevitable. The situation was familiar to me, even if the surroundings were not.

The BBC has an even higher reputation in the sub-continent than it does in Africa. In the Galle Face Hotel, a grand but shabby old colonial establishment that went in for tiffin and large fans rather than minibars and air conditioning, there were plaques in the lobby, listing its most distinguished visitors. A small one recorded a visit by the Duke of Edinburgh a few years before. It was overshadowed by a larger plaque boasting that Mark Tully of the BBC had stayed there, evidently a far more important endorsement. As Mark's stand-in, I was suitably daunted, but traded shamelessly on his name and the magic three letters. They opened all doors, but the disadvantage was that everybody, on all sides, listened to the BBC, and you were held personally responsible for everything that was broadcast. That responsibility, it was made clear to me more than once, could carry dire consequences.

My main contact was the National Security Minister, Lalith Athulathmudali, a handsome and ruthless young politician who had been President of the Oxford Union and oozed a very oriental kind of dangerous charm. He was running the offensive against the Tamil Tigers and agreed to brief me on the telephone every morning at five o'clock. He was almost always in his bath at his home on the wonderfully named Inner Flower Road at that time and our conversations, a rather serpentine process of flattery and coaxing on one side and calculated indiscretion on the other, were made the more surreal by splashing and spluttering in the background. Once, when I was trying to make sense of the casualty figures from the latest government operation, I asked him what was causing all the noise. 'I am playing with my ducks,' he said. The Indian Air Force had invaded Sri Lankan air space at the time, in order to drop relief supplies around Jaffna city. Lalith was beside himself with anger at this and there were a series of crashes as, I imagined, the minister threw his ducks out of the bath. They were at least as expendable as Tamils, or government soldiers, who were not making much headway and were getting killed in impressive numbers.

Largely thanks to Lalith, I managed to talk myself up to the front line outside Jaffna and went on patrol in a helicopter gunship. We circled high over the star-shaped fort on the lagoon that had sheltered desperate men since the Portuguese had started building it in the early seventeenth century. It was now held by the Tamil Tigers, at bay but undefeated. We stayed high, out of range of the Tigers' weapons, or so we hoped. I looked out over the back of the soldier squatting in the doorway, and below the machine gun he swivelled, warily, back and forth, I could see where the fighting had smashed through the streets leading down to the water.

It was a snatch operation. Back on their side of the front line the helicopters dropped into Tamil villages and seized younger men more or less at random, lining them up with their hands tied behind their backs. Hatred was thick in the air that day. The soldiers pushed their captives around with callous brutality; the young Tamils' backs were stiff with contempt.

It went beyond the war, deeper than the age-old resentment of the Sinhalese that the clever and hard-working Tamils got all the best education and jobs. The Sinhalese, whose swirling alphabet seemed to sum up a decorative and dreamy culture that was part of an older world, felt threatened on every level. They might outnumber the Tamils four to one, but they saw them as an advance guard of untold millions just across the sea, and of historical forces building up to push them out of their paradise.

And then there was religion. In some ways it seemed to underpin the hate, even though Hindus and Buddhists have much in common and both faiths are meant to be fundamentally gentle, peaceful and tolerant. Twenty-nine Buddhist monks had been massacred a few days before. I had gone to see them in their open coffins and then on to a Hindu temple where I watched people put their fingers into flames to cleanse them before touching their foreheads. Religion, it had seemed to me then, can be as morally ambiguous as fire. But, as I watched the soldiers pushing their captives down the muddy street, sodden from a recent storm, both sides radiating suppressed loathing, I wondered how much religion was really to blame. Not for the first time, I asked myself whether any rational man could really hate another for what he believed, or whether religion was often just a badge of 'the other', an outward symbol of something deeper, atavistic, essentially tribal.

I wanted to see what the troops would do with their prisoners, but the helicopters left us behind to make our way back across the peninsula in a military convoy. The Yala monsoon, flowing in on the soft south-east trades, broke out in another heavy rainstorm as we reached the causeway that links Jaffna to the rest of the island. They called it Elephant Pass because, in more peaceful days, that was where the sacred animals would wade across the shallow lagoon. Now it was littered with the detritus of war. It had been the cockpit of the conflict, fought over again and again, and the graveyard of fanatics and reluctant fighters alike.

We crossed on to the vast, low-lying plain they call the Vanni. It is one of the most productive parts of a famously fertile island, growing potatoes, chillies and onions, irrigated from limestone wells. Now its biggest crop was mines. One and a half million had been planted there. The army vehicles stayed carefully in the middle of the road, wary of the mines and even more scared of ambush by the dreaded Tigers. The A9 Highway stretched endlessly south to the central highlands and the great peak of Sri Pada with its fossilised footprint, a metre long. The Sinhalese say it is the footprint of Lord Buddha; the Tamils say it was left by the Hindu god Vishnu as he performed the dance of creation. Local Christians argue amongst themselves. Some say it is the imprint of Adam, serving a thousand-year sentence on one leg for his misdeeds in the Garden of Eden. Others say it was left by Thomas, the doubting apostle, on his way to martyrdom in India. In paradise, they even quarrel over footprints.

Very early on the day I left I rang Lalith, who was in his bath as usual. He told me about a deal being done behind the scenes for the Indian Army to come over as a peacekeeping force. The idea was that they would enforce the ceasefire and disarm the rebels. Lalith was suspicious and sceptical. He thought it would not work and they would end up being hated by both sides. As a hardline Sinhalese Nationalist he was angry about what he saw as an abdication of Sri Lankan sovereignty. We talked about the future for Sri Lanka – and for once he was not confident of a final victory over the Tigers – and for himself. 'I will either be President or be dead,' he said, and his roaring laugh drowned out the sound of more ducks hitting the wall. I never spoke to him again.

He was right on both counts. The Indian operation was a failure. They lost 1,000 soldiers in three years and were withdrawn in 1990. The Tigers were never more than 20,000 strong but they fought the Indian Army and the Sri Lankan Army, both of which had more than 100,000 men in the field, to a standstill. Lalith nearly became President. He broke away from the ruling party and set up his own political organisation which was making huge gains in the election campaign five years later before Lalith was shot in the heart by a lone gunman at an election rally in Kirillapona. The authorities blamed the Tamils and produced a body they said was the assassin's, who they claimed had committed suicide. It seems more likely Lalith was killed on the orders of his former colleague, President Premadasa, whose position and power he threatened. Premadasa himself was killed by a bomb not long afterwards. Politics in Sri Lanka was a murderous business.

I spent the next six weeks in India. It was the hottest time of the year, made worse by moving amongst crowds who seemed to have no notion of personal space, but I loved it. There was colour and life and energy that seemed a match for India's dreadful problems. The poverty was extreme, the organisation chaotic, the climate oppressive, but the teeming millions seemed to me a vivid tribute to human resilience.

I followed Rajiv Gandhi across the northern state of Haryana as he tried to reassert his authority in the state's elections against his political opponents and the Sikh terrorism that lurked on the sidelines. It was raw politics in the world's biggest democracy. I travelled in helicopters and bullock carts, got trampled in a wild anti-government demonstration, and finally watched the poor and the illiterate queue for hours to vote with their thumbs for parties that had symbols, but no names.

I went to Calcutta to make a film about the poorest and most crowded city on earth, where thousands lived in sewer pipes and washed in the gutter. Grotesquely deformed beggars scuttled up and down the pavements outside hotels where it cost a year's average wage to stay the night. I met Mother Teresa and saw a shrunken old woman, focussed to the point of obsession on her way of helping the poor. There were those, even then, who questioned her motives, her austere and narrow methods, and her results. But the force of her character seemed to burst out of her wrinkled old body and wizened face – an extraordinary woman even if she was not a saint.

I doubled back to Bhopal, in central India, to see what was happening around the ruins of the Union Carbide chemical plant that had leaked a poisonous cloud of methyl isocyanate and killed 5,000 people in three days. Those who had died at the time drowned in their own body fluids or were trampled to death as people panicked and tried to run away from a killer they could not see. Four years on, the plant was deserted and rusting away. The walls were now covered in graffiti that mostly said 'Killer Carbide'. In the villages around the poison was still killing people; their lungs were ruined and hundreds were condemned to a life under an oxygen mask. According to local aid workers 30 people a month were still dying directly because of the human and mechanical errors that let a holding tank overheat and burst. It was one of the world's nastiest industrial disasters and the plant was still apparently leaking poisons into the water and the soil. Nonetheless, the area round the site was rapidly being taken over by poor people, careless of the consequences. They washed in and drank the water from a well near the factory that had almost certainly been contaminated. But the monks had declared it holy and the people were building a temple alongside it. India coped with disasters made by man in the way it dealt with disasters made by God. Anger, then fatalistic acceptance, and finally the tide of humanity closed back over the ruins.

Back in Delhi, I was dragged from the massage room in the Oberoi Hotel to cover a fire in a high-rise office block. It was an Indian version of *Towering Inferno*, a film that had just been released. The fire broke out in the middle of the block and was licking its way up the building towards a hundred or so office workers who had taken refuge on the roof. They were far from fatalistic, and way below on the ground we could hear them screaming above the sound of the helicopter which hovered hesitantly overhead. An official near me shouted through a loudhailer that they should keep calm, which was about as useful and effective as the rest of the rescue operation seemed to be.

My crew and I managed to get to the top of a neighbouring tower block just as it seemed the people on the roof were about to have to choose to be burned alive or jump to their deaths. The helicopter had winched half a dozen women to safety but could not do any more. The firemen's ladders did not reach even halfway up the building. I looked across the chasm to the terrified people on the neighbouring roof and thought they were as good as dead.

Suddenly, from nowhere, a gang of office workers came running across our rooftop with an improvised wooden bridge, all sticks and orange boxes bound up with rope and bodged nails. They threw it across the gap and a clerk skipped across and started to organise the people on the other side. For a moment it looked as though it would merely accelerate the disaster as those who had been trapped started to fight each other to get across first. But the clerk somehow managed to impose order and, one by one, they stumbled across the rickety bridge to safety. The last woman across collapsed in my arms. Behind her was the clerk, a hero by anybody's standards, who turned out to be called Nirkagan Singh. 'I am just going home to change my shirt,' he told me, 'and then I must get back to the office. We have a lot of work and my boss will be asking me where I have got to.'

I talked about the quirks and mysteries of India with Mark Tully under the great fan that fluttered the papers on his desk, while his *chai wallah* brought an endless supply of tiny cups of tea. Everywhere I had been in India and said I was from the BBC people had crowded around thinking I was Tully Sahib. Their undisguised disappointment when they found I was not the legend was damaging to my self-esteem. Often people simply assumed I must be Tully and would shake their head, saying things like: 'I thought you would be older and, well, more *distinguished*.'

Mark was a radio man who distrusted television and felt the BBC was in headlong decline. His view of the prelapsarian virtues of the Reithian ideal, and how it was being corrupted by commercial pressure and a spineless management, was unrelievedly gloomy and owed a lot to the distance he was from London. But he embodied much that I admired about the BBC and much that I wanted to emulate.

340

*

I knew, though, that I was at a crossroads in my career. My children were now 13 and had been hoicked around in the wake of my ambitions since they had been born. The time had come for stability in our lives, for the sake of their education and our family life generally. The BBC would have paid for them to go to boarding school but, selfishly perhaps, Christine and I thought that would effectively mean losing them, and rejected the idea. Besides, too many of the reporters and cameramen I worked with had failed marriages and were alienated from their children. I needed to grow up and settle down for a bit. The BBC was pressing me to be a newscaster again. I thought I could always go back to being a foreign correspondent later. I had regrets, of course, particularly sitting under the fan, drinking *chai* and beer with Tully Sahib.

But I had a long time to think about it all. I was sent up into the Himalayas, to the old hill station of Darjeeling, to try to make contact with a shadowy rebel group that was said to be threatening the stability of northern India. The Gurkhas who lived there were angry at new discriminatory laws that made them second-class citizens. Government jobs were to be reserved for those who spoke Bengali, ruling out the Gurkhas, most of whom only spoke Nepali. The ruling brought resentment to a violent head. Riots paralysed Darjeeling and a rebel movement calling itself the Gurkha National Liberation Front began operating in the Himalayan foothills, issuing demands for a separate state of Gorkhaland.

The monsoon broke as we drove up through the tea plantations. Darjeeling spills over a spectacular ledge in the hills, a cascade of interconnecting streets and steps, but it was in the clouds by the time we got there. It only cleared once, briefly, around dawn and I was able to watch the sunrise from Tiger Hill and see, as well as feel, the great loom of Kanchenjunga, third highest mountain in the world, behind the town. It rained almost solidly for the next two weeks as we negotiated with intermediaries to meet the rebels. We stayed in the Hotel Windamere, a relic of the Raj and an Indian version of the kind of English country hotel that has long since vanished. As the rain hosed down the windows and turned the steep streets into rivers, Tibetan maids in starched aprons built up the open fires and served dainty sandwiches. A string quartet played in the dining room while we paddled our Mulligatawny soup. There was cocoa last thing at night, and hot water bottles in our beds. Time had stood still since 1925 and we soon became part of the trance.

I would start every day with a burst of energy, badgering our contacts who were encouraging but vague. When the rain slackened I would splash off down Hill Cart Road and The Mall to the Chowk Bazaar to talk with the traders about the mysteries of tea. I got to be able to tell a golden flowery orange pekoe from mere orange fannings by taste as well as texture. I felt I was in some soaking Lotus Land far removed from the real world. It was strangely seductive but, for the first time in my life, I was homesick.

By the time we finally found our rebels and filmed them, fumbling around in their balaclavas in the dank undergrowth around Darjeeling, I was more than ready to go home. They were wet, in every sense, nothing like the formidable Gurkhas who serve as regular soldiers. They had no ideology beyond their resentment, no strategy, nothing except a few obsolete weapons. I was wasting my time. I was tired and running out of courage for the nasty stuff. I wanted to see my wife and my boys and have a home life and some sort of routine. I put a phone call through to London and told them I would go back to newsreading. I had my reservations but – ridiculously, in my view – the pay would be far better than being a foreign correspondent, risking my life in the wars and rebellions of the rougher corners of the world. The hours were regular, there were perks that went along with being well known, and there would be time to do other things as well if I got bored. Before then, though, there were two things I had to do.

The first was to go back to South Africa to pick up my family and take them on a long holiday. The boys had finished their term by now and the South African authorities were at least kind enough to let me back in to help them pack up and leave. We exchanged the business-class fares back to London for economy tickets that took us to South America, to Rio, up the Amazon, and to La Paz, the highest city in the world, where Roland got altitude sickness and had to be revived on oxygen cylinders that are kept in every hotel reception. We took the boat across Lake Titicaca and the train to Machu Picchu. We quartered the old city of Cuzco and were trapped there by a transport strike. We only got out by hiding on the airport apron and charging up the steps of one of the few planes leaving for Lima. We belted ourselves into the first row of seats and refused to move. Africa had made us resourceful in a crisis.

Back home in England, I had a last task before I swapped my khaki shirt and jeans for the newscaster's suit and tie and became an office worker. I had been asked to do a very personal programme about South

Africa for *Everyman*, a BBC1 documentary series that came out of the BBC's religious department. *Everyman* had a new editor, a woman called Jane Drabble, who had been one of the best producers on *Panorama*. Jane was attractive and clever and I liked her a lot. I was on a story in Paris once which she was also working on and, watching her walk down the street, my crew and I agreed how delightful she was. 'The difference between us,' said the cameraman, a grizzled ex-Navy petty officer, 'is that you like her brain and we like her bottom.'

Jane wanted to move *Everyman* away from specifically religious subjects to the broader ground of morality and wanted her first programme to be one about South Africa unlike any that had been made before. She did not want a current affairs-style documentary, but a series of personal impressions and the kind of insights that are excluded by the disciplines and formulae of news. She teamed me up with an extremely bright and energetic young producer called Stephen Walker. He put the squeeze on me, and everything I had seen and done over the previous four years, for a new and deeper way of explaining what South Africa was like.

He was cheerfully relentless, pushing me to tell the story a different way, not just what had happened but what it had been like to be there. I was reluctant because it went against all my training and most of my instincts. My job had been rigorously to exclude my own thoughts and feelings. I was wedded to the old BBC ethos of detachment, of separating fact and opinion. But, thanks to Stephen's persistence, we found a middle way that gave the whole programme emotional depth without it becoming a polemic.

The things I could remember most clearly were often atmosphere and detail. Of course, I remembered the arbitrary cruelty of apartheid, but I also recalled the eerie consequences of all that large-scale social engineering. The way the city centre of Johannesburg emptied itself every evening as if the inhabitants were escaping some terrible invader. They were, in a sense, fleeing from the police who would arrest them if they stayed in a white area after dark and did not get back to the black townships. When the whites, too, retreated to their verandahs and their pools in the lush northern suburbs, the centre was left to the drug addicts, the dust and the dogs. Little things like the way you could not find a restaurant table on a Thursday, traditionally the maids' day off when white families had to fend for themselves.

We told the story of apartheid through the eyes of a young couple, Bob and Sylvia, who had become friends of mine. Bob was British and white.

Sylvia was a mixed-race coloured girl. I had followed their tangles with the system as they tried to get married and then find some roof under which they both could live, but I had not had the time to put it all together. When I did so for *Everyman* it painted a picture of tyranny by bureaucracy. The cruelty was often courteous. Civil servants would listen to reasoned arguments and passionate appeals, but then turn robotically to the regulations in front of them that made no moral or even common sense. You stepped through the courtroom door into a Kafkaesque wonderland where the attempts to prescribe and proscribe the colour of love and the tint of territory became more and more insane.

I included the murders I had witnessed, including the terrible township butchery that News had refused to broadcast. We had to fight for it against those who felt it was just too dreadful to be shown. But that, in a sense, was the point. On *Everyman* we were able to warn people about what was coming and to set it in the context of my argument that grown ups should, if only occasionally, have the opportunity to see what real violence – not the fictional stuff that's made to look exciting and without serious consequence – can be like. 'You can look away,' I said at the end of my introduction. 'I could not.'

We had expected that whether or not this onscreen killing should be broadcast would be anxiously debated in the highest levels of the BBC. We had reckoned without one of the more idiosyncratic features of the corporation's top management. They seem to be able to concentrate on only one issue at a time. The current concern was not violence but bad language. The boy being cut to pieces was one thing. The top management did not want to hear the word 'fuck'.

To be fair, the programme had a sequence in which 'fuck' was uttered thirteen times. It was part of a play that had been put on at the Market Theatre in central Johannesburg. The theatre seemed somehow to escape the stifling censorship that was clamped down on the news media and put on brave dramas that spoke vividly about what was going on in the townships. The more liberal kind of whites used to go there and say it was the only way they got any sense of what was going on.

I had arranged to film a particularly hard-hitting play in which a black father whose son, Dumisane, had been killed by the police in the townships talks of walking through the white suburbs, looking at their comfortable, ordered and untroubled lives. In a devastating soliloquy he speaks of looking at the neat and precious little white girls in their immaculate playground, and the dreadful urge he has to run amok amongst them with one of their baseball bats: 'to be the monster they want me to be, their own King Kong'. It was a powerful and chilling piece of drama that came to a climax of frustration and rage. 'Fuck you for what you have done to little Dumisane, fuck you for what you are doing to me . . .' The audience in the theatre had been stunned the night I saw it and several people around me were crying. I dislike gratuitous bad language but could not see how anyone could seriously object to it, in this context and with this wider dramatic and journalistic purpose.

Meeting after meeting was called as the issue was referred ever higher up the BBC chain of command. Sometimes I felt I was in a world as Kafkaesque as that of the apartheid bureaucrats, if better intentioned. The central question, settled halfway up the management pyramid, was not whether the word fuck' should be used at all, but how many 'fucks' were permissible. What, in a nutshell, was a fuck too far? Some executives thought we should be rationed to one, others thought half a dozen. Many of those called in to meetings that rambled inconclusively on did not seem to have seen the programme at all, which did not help.

Eventually the decision came to rest with the Managing Director of BBC Television at the time, Bill Cotton, on whose lips, I have to say, that word was no stranger. His initial view was that no programme should ever have more than three 'fucks'. We thought cutting any of them out or, worse, bleeping them would dilute the power of the drama and make us look ridiculous. Eventually, all the 'fucks' were passed, despite pages of minuted reservations going on file and much nervousness on the sixth floor of Television Centre.

When it was broadcast, nobody mentioned the bad language, though there were many who were shocked by the murder. It distilled the most vivid and intense four years of my life in a way that moved me then and still moves me now. It made a big impact when it was shown and was kindly reviewed. Not long after it went out I was the second reporter to win the James Cameron Memorial Award, for coverage of South Africa 'that combined moral vision and professional integrity'. Cameron was a special hero of mine. He was a veteran foreign correspondent in the old style, world-weary, battered and thirsty, but he wrote like an angel. He was funny and urbane, yet nearly all his work had a core of moral seriousness and a basic humanity that elevated it above mere journalism. You would never have found him reading the news.

TWENTY-THREE

'TEN SECONDS TO STUDIO . . . five, four, three, two, one – run titles! On air!' Even the most boring news programme is exciting behind the scenes. The mechanics of live television make every edition seem like a cross between a space mission and a first night. The difference is that hardly anything has been rehearsed, half the programme is not ready, the satellite link to Baghdad has gone down and there is just the hint of a big story on the news agency wires which will mean most of it will have to be junked anyway. The studio director and crew try to find order out of all this chaos. They have a schedule of taped and live reports, of complex computerised graphics and possible interviews, that is sometimes not much more than a wish list. They time what goes out to the split second and pray the next item will be ready as the clock runs down.

The newscaster can hear it all in the moulded earpiece that links him to the control gallery behind the smoked glass wall. Most of the time he does not need to sort out the confusing babble of voices. He is listening to the pitch of them all, checking for the rising note of concern, the first whiff of panic. When it comes, as it does most days, he instinctively concentrates on the director. She is yelling down to the transmission suite, two floors below, where one of the videotape machines will play in the next report – if it is ready in time. It had better be. The interviewee after that has not arrived at the satellite truck and, as things stand, we might have to go to the weather, which would be a very public admission of failure halfway through the programme. Besides, the weatherman has gone to the lavatory and is widely known to have a prostate problem that makes his frequent comfort breaks a lengthy process. 'Is it there yet, TX?' turns from being a mild inquiry to a hiss of desperation. The people in the transmission suite answer with a buzzer – one buzz for 'no', two for 'yes'.

'Is it there yet?' Buzz.

'Is it there yet?' Buzz.

'For Christ's sake, is it there yet?' Buzz.

'What are we going to . . .' Buzz buzz.

'Thank God. Run TX.'

It looks stressful and difficult but newscasting is a doddle. Most of the time it amounts to little more than reading out loud. Anybody can do it.

Anybody frequently does. It is one of the few jobs – off-hand the only other one I can think of is being a junior minister in Her Majesty's government – that requires no talent or training at all. A plausible manner is probably an advantage. One of the great American anchors, a man portentous beyond belief and wealthy beyond imagination, once told me over his fourth dry martini: 'The great thing about this job, son, is sincerity. Once you can fake that, you have got it made.'

It also helps not to have a hare-lip or a wart on the end of your nose though, truth to tell, it is really a matter of familiarity. The British public will get used to anybody who is in their living rooms often enough and, after a time, will actually warm to gargoyle faces or incomprehensible accents (except, of course, a Brummie one) and complain in their thousands if they are taken off the air. It is not just familiarity, it is also trust. The one does not mean a damn. The other is the only thing that really matters.

I was given the *One O'Clock News*, which suited me fine. It meant getting up at six, never my strongest point. But I was home by mid-afternoon and was there when the boys got back from school. I had the weekends off and Christine and I could plan a social life again.

The *One O'Clock News* had replaced a rather eccentric magazine programme called *Pebble Mill at One* that was presented, for no obvious reason, live from the foyer of the BBC headquarters in Birmingham. It is chiefly remembered now for the most delicious unintentional double entendre in live television. The presenter, a splendid Aberdonian called Donny Mcleod, had been talking to the cook Fanny Craddock about making doughnuts. She was hard work and as he turned to end the programme, the relief showed in his face and he relaxed – too early, as it turned out. 'Aye,' he said, 'that's all from *Pebble Mill at One*.' And then, waving airily at the battleaxe beaming proudly behind him, he finished on an upbeat and encouraging note.

'Aye, and I hope all your doughnuts turn out like Fanny's.'

The *One O'Clock News* was a much more dour programme and represented the victory of hard (or, in this case, hardish) news over the floppier current affairs magazines that prevailed in the eighties. Even so, it was popular. In the late eighties, 5.5 million people tuned in every lunchtime, rather more than watch the *Ten O'Clock News* today. To what extent this could be put down to the thirst for information amongst the young families, old age pensioners and the long-term unemployed who

347

constituted most of the audience was not clear. There was more than a suspicion that the high viewing figures might have had something to do with the Australian soap *Neighbours* which followed it and was then at the height of its, totally inexplicable, popularity.

The *One O'Clock News* was the most difficult of the news programmes to present because it went out so early in the news day. Although breakfast television had been running for several years by then, the BBC newsroom was not really a 24-hour operation. It only got going properly at about 10 a.m., after the endless meetings that seem such an essential part of the BBC's culture. At home, most of the day's stories had not yet happened and, if they had, the reporters were more interested in making a big splash on the prestige programmes in the evening which their friends, their peers, and, above all, their bosses were much more likely to see. It was worse abroad. Our American correspondents were still calibrating their hangovers over breakfast out in Virginia when we went out. The timing suited the Far East but little was produced there that was thought suitable for our audience. People who watched news at lunchtime were regarded as somewhat odd and the programme never seemed much of a priority.

As a result, when the countdown ended, the great white clock on the programme titles rolled round to one and the director shouted: 'Stand by to zoom out camera one. Stand by to Quantel. Mix through!' only about a third of the programme was ready. The problem was that, most of the time, it was not the first third.

The editor who produced the programme, and the director who normally put it out, were a study in contrasts. The editor was a burly, ginger-bearded Yorkshireman who regarded soap with suspicion and deodorant as a sign of rampant effeminacy. The director, on the other hand, was theatrical to a point just this side of camp. His hair was dyed an implausible jet black and he moved about surrounded in a cloud of his trademark cologne.

I would finish off writing the headlines and as I went into the studio at three minutes to one, the editor would stop chewing the end of his beard to shout after me, 'Touch and go this one, lad!' The items in the programme were all given a separate page in the programme's running order, which gave the studio crew a totally misleading impression that everything was under control. The introductions I had to read were there because I had written them all in the last hour or so. The main problem was that most of the reports themselves were not yet in. I would launch into the top of the programme and, in my earpiece, I could hear the director calling: 'Have you got page 11? No? Have you got page 13? What! Page 26? Christ! What *have* you got? Page 82? That's the Paris fashions, I can't lead on the Paris fashions!' I learned to read very slowly.

The atmosphere in the control room often became very tense. I would frequently hear a surreal shouting match between the two in the gallery with the director's high-pitched almost squeals of concern as a descant to the editor's gruff bellows of rage at being let down by fate in general and the BBC's newsgathering machine in particular. Neither was particularly helpful for the newscaster who had finally reached the end of his well-crafted peroration and was left staring hopefully into the camera lens for the report he had, so deftly, introduced. After a couple of 'we hope to bring you that report laters' and even the occasional ad lib analysis of the main points of the morning's developments in the Middle East, they would find something to run and the floor manager and I would exchange wan smiles.

At least we did not have to sit in the gallery where the editor's over-powering presence mixed with the director's Eau Sauvage and the general crackling tension to produce an almost feral atmosphere. One spark on a bad day, the vision mixer reckoned, would blow the whole place halfway to Acton.

It was seat-of-the-pants stuff but there were funny moments, most of them unintentional. One day, I managed to transpose two headlines in the most embarrassing way. The first concerned the irascible Tory minister, Nicholas Ridley. The second, unfortunately, was about a tiny and bashful species of snail, so rare that it was facing extinction. It was bad enough when the picture of the snail came up at the same time as I was saying: 'The top Tory who says Europe has gone too far'. It was worse when Mr Ridley himself appeared and I asked: 'Is this the end for the smallest, shyest creature in the undergrowth?' Luckily, hardly anybody seemed to notice. Most politicians and all self-respecting BBC executives were in their favourite restaurants by then, wondering whether to have the salmon mousse for the third day running.

The *One O'Clock News* audience was loyal and sometimes enthusiastic. I used to get at least half a dozen letters every week from mothers which would always start: 'My little girl is your youngest fan.' It seems that as soon as the *One O'Clock News* came on, every toddler in the land would rush to the screen and cover my face with kisses – a slightly alarming thought to have at the back of your mind at the time, I am sure you will agree. I never worked out a satisfactory reply but built up a great file of pictures of children engaged in this aberrant behaviour. I also seemed to hold an irresistible attraction for women at the other end of the age scale. My postbag was full of letters written in a palsied, or at least feeble, hand, professing admiration in sometimes quite forthright terms. I was a bit peeved that I appealed either to females barely old enough to stand up, or those within walking distance of life's greatest mystery, and hardly at all to those in between. That's not entirely true. I have had several proposals of marriage from ladies out of nappies and not half dead, though it was not always possible to vouch for their sanity. I have also received quite a few offers of less formal relationships, a depressing number from men as it happens. At one stage I was apparently a gay icon, whatever that is; I was not keen to find out. For a time I got a regular supply of frilly knickers (always red) in the post with vague, but pressing, instructions on how they could be returned. This caused something of a frisson in the newsroom but the novelty soon wore off.

The really loopy were easy to spot. The envelopes were always brown, the writing was always in block capitals and the notepaper generally had lines on it. Some people found them funny. To me, they were always rather sad.

A lot of the mail was from pedants and bigots. There are thousands of people who police the news for split infinitives or deviant diphthongs. There are others convinced that the BBC is part of a worldwide Jewish conspiracy or intent on handing over England to the blacks/Irish/global capitalism. I used to send them a set letter that read: 'Thank you for your interesting observations on . . . I have placed it in my "irritating prats" file for future reference. Best wishes . . .' The BBC, which is absurdly attentive to everybody who writes in (without ever admitting it has got anything wrong, of course), eventually put a stop to that.

Some people could be woundingly personal. Early on, when I was doing the lunchtime news, I came in one morning and picked up the duty log, which was circulated to all BBC programme departments and summarised all the phone calls to the BBC over the previous 24 hours. Under the *One O'Clock News* was an account of a complaint from a lady in Dorking. It was verbatim and picked out, rather unnecessarily, I thought, in bold italics. '*Why does Michael Buerk speak in that extraordinary way? Is he clenching his buttocks?*'

That was the trouble with newscasting. When you were a reporter or a foreign correspondent you knew whether you were any good or not. There was a broad consensus amongst your peers about who was admirable and who was hopeless, who could get hold of a story and then tell it well, and who could not. It mostly coincided with what the viewers thought of us (with one or two notable exceptions). But whether or not you were a good newscaster seemed entirely subjective. It was based on millions of individual likes and dislikes about personality, age, sex, race, accent – a whole spectrum of prejudices with which we judge people we do not know. It did not bother me too much, which gave me an advantage over other newscasters who could not believe their luck and were determined to cling on to the job at all costs.

I wanted to do it well. I wanted people to like and trust me. But that was as far as it went. The BBC had pressed me into what I thought was pretty much a non-job and if they decided I was no good, I would go back to doing something real again. I suppose it was a defence against the paranoia that overtakes all television presenters, whose careers hang on the fickle public mood or the even more unpredictable mindset of the shoals of BBC executives. I told them, and I told myself, I did not care. However true that was, it worked. The more dismissive I became about newscasting, the more people thought I was just being modest and tried to persuade me it was extraordinarily difficult; that only a handful had the mysterious qualities that would command the respect and affection of the public. The more I said I did not like it much, the more I was begged to carry on. It was all very perverse.

After a year or so on the lunchtime News, the wave of change at the BBC moved me back on to the flagship evening programme, being reshaped along the more austere guidelines of John Birt, who had been brought in from ITV as Deputy Director General and was soon to supplant the man who had hired him and take the top job. It was part of an astonishing change in the technology and the culture of the BBC newsroom that had begun in the years I had been in South Africa. When I left, the floor was covered with linoleum and the air was thick with cigarette smoke. The news was written out by typists on old-fashioned, clattering machines, their fingers black from endless sheets of carbon paper. The journalists were called 'subs'; they were older than me and mostly, I thought in my arrogance, not as bright. They were shabby all the time and half sloshed a lot of it. They only ever seemed to read small papers, and if they did not start at the back it was only because they wanted to remind themselves what women's breasts looked like.

When I came back from Johannesburg everything had changed. The floor was covered in lush carpet, the desks were new and carried flickering green computer screens. The 'subs' were now 'producers' and all looked about nineteen. The men wore collars and ties and all the buttons on their jackets were done up. A surprising number were women, who did not have ties but were otherwise indistinguishable. Both sexes sipped delicately from bottles of Malvern water as they flicked through the *Financial Times*. The other broadsheets were considered intellectually substandard and unreliable. To be seen to pick up a tabloid would have been as fatal to a career as admitting you knew where the bar was. Most of the old BBC Club would, in any case, shortly be turned over to fitness and baby-minding.

The old newsroom had been a little corner of Grub Street in the great broadcasting palace called the Television Centre. The fancy stuff had been left to the current affairs department, a quarter of a mile but a parallel universe away, in Lime Grove. We regarded them as limp-wristed and effete, unconnected to the real world, real issues, or real people, and engaged in what amounted to little more than late-night mutual pleasuring with like-minded politicians and their ilk. They thought we were the benighted foot soldiers of broadcasting who did not really understand anything much and were capable, like some lowly invertebrates, only of responding to outside stimuli. They called us hacks, we called them wankers. The relationship was characterised by little contact and a lot of loathing.

Some of this had changed over the years, along with the BBC's almost religious mission to try to separate fact from opinion which had underpinned it all. *Newsnight* had been established to marry the best of the two cultures, often succeeding, though sometimes it ended up with the worst of them. The problem for the Damians at Lime Grove was that people did not want to watch what they produced. Peak time programmes like *Nationwide* came to the end of their natural lives and their attempts to find a new generation of popular current affairs programmes were disastrous. They became increasingly marginalised, pushed to the edges of the schedules and watched mainly by the sleepless and the sad.

Their solution would be familiar to any science-fiction reader. The cerebral aliens left their doomed home in Lime Grove and invaded the Planet News. They took the place over, promoted each other and changed everything. Lime Grove itself was turned into a low-cost housing development.

The *Nine O'Clock News* that was relaunched at the end of the 1980s was nothing like the programme I had originally presented at the beginning of the decade, still less the one I had started working for as a reporter a decade before that. The editor and his deputy were both called Mark and were both around 30, the first time I had worked for someone younger than me. Like almost everybody on the programme they had been to Oxford. The editor, Mark Thompson, was clearly a high-flyer and would have risen effortlessly to the top in any organisation. He was tall, very clever, and had a combination of earnest geniality and utter ruthlessness that was obviously unstoppable; he is now the BBC Director-General. His deputy was a brain on bandy legs. Mark Damazer was the son of Jewish immigrants and, by common consent, one of the nicest, and easily the cleverest, person any of us had ever met. He came down from Oxford with a starred double first and the programme meetings mainly consisted of an intellectual route-march around the big issues of the day, which he would lead. Actually, he was often the only participant and we were left to listen in to his fierce internal debate as he deconstructed each potential story on the news agenda. It was, in every sense, an education, and living proof of the superiority of reason over instinct. Mind you, instinct would sometimes have been quicker.

The producers were all in the same mould. There really was a Damian, and a Lucien, but not, disappointingly, a Tristram. We had a token prole, nicknamed 'Shagger', though this seemed to be based more on his ambitions than his achievements. He kept his head down but was politely consulted on matters of popular taste about which the others expressed ritual bafflement. The exception was football. Perhaps it was a defence against charges of elitism, but it seemed obligatory to express wild enthusiasm for, and microscopic knowledge of, some tedious football team. It was all very peculiar.

The new *Nine O'Clock News* had two presenters. The other was Martyn Lewis who had been lured away from ITN by a huge salary when BBC News had been going through a showbiz phase a few years earlier. I think the idea was that Martyn would provide the glamour and I, still trailing the prestige of a high-profile foreign correspondent and a bag-load of awards, would provide the journalistic street cred. This was slightly unfair on both of us. Martyn, it is true, had had a glossy career since he was picked out to be the Cow & Gate baby when he was a toddler. At the BBC he was quickly labelled 'the housewives' choice'. But he had been a sharp and hard-working reporter in the North of England for ITN and was nobody's fool. He became a victim of the intellectual snobbery that prevailed at the time. He was not as clever as some of the people on the programme, but then I probably wasn't either. Besides, as I pointed out to one of his detractors: 'If you're so much brighter than him, why are you living in a rabbit hutch in Willesden and he's got a mansion in Kensington?' It was not an easy question to answer.

One of the reasons he was not particularly popular was that he was relentlessly upbeat about everything, including Mrs Thatcher and her government. He saw only the bright side of every subject which could be irritating to normal people and is anathema to journalists. Martyn even went so far as to criticise the BBC and the media in general, for being too negative. He publicly called for more good news to be included in our programmes. There is nothing journalists like less than good news; we shrivel in sunlight.

Martyn was not at all reflective or self-conscious and seemed unaware that for a while he was cordially disliked. At the time, I was going through a phase where I appeared to wink at the end of the programme. It was more of a nervous twitch, or a passing difficulty with my contact lenses, than some prototype Anne Robinson trademark. It did lead to a spate of post-menopausal interest, and a rather cruel little riddle that chattered for weeks across the tops of all our computer monitors. 'What,' it asked, 'is the difference between Michael Buerk and Martyn Lewis?'

You had to wait a couple of minutes for the answer.

'Michael Buerk is the *winker.*'

Martyn and I took it in turns to present a programme that was given a radical new look. It started with a Wagnerian flourish. The opening titles of the programme had been reduced to a momentary 'sting', second for second possibly the most expensive bit of television the BBC had ever produced. It was meant to echo the earliest days of television news, when the primitive programme was preceded by an illustration of Alexandra Palace, radiating gentle airwaves. In the new version, all was darkness, thunder and lightning. The insignias of the SS flashed across the screen as the sound reached an ear-splitting crescendo. It was more like the end of the world than the beginning of a news programme. After seven seconds of *Götterdämmerung* even the most sensational story was something of an anti-climax, and dogs all over the country didn't stop howling until closedown.

They had also decided to follow the fashion of the day and take the programme out of the studio and present it from the newsroom. There is a basic dilemma with this idea. The point of it all is to show that it is the product of a vast and bustling news organisation, where reporters and editors labour frantically to bring you the very latest from all corners of the world. This is a good thing. But if the background is too busy, in fact if anybody is doing anything interesting at all, it is a terrible distraction from what the newscaster is trying to tell you, which is the point of the exercise after all. That is a bad thing.

There are ways round this, quite simple techniques that focus attention on the presenter yet still leave the impression of activity in the background. Unfortunately, months of meetings between some of the most intelligent editorial brains, the most artistic designers and most experienced technical experts the BBC could find failed to come up with any of them. In the end, security men had to come in every night and shoo everybody out of shot, even producers desperately trying to complete their item for the programme, so the newsroom was completely deserted. The *Guardian* reviewer said it looked like a 'Curry's warehouse lit by moonlight'.

The content of the programme was unrelievedly serious. It made even newspapers like *The Times* and the *Independent* look trivial. The Nine concentrated entirely on the most important political and economic issues at home and abroad, however abstruse they might appear and however arid a programme might sometimes result. Often it just seemed to come to a stop. The idea of closing with a warm story, what the trade calls an 'and finally', would have been seen as an unforgivable weakness. It was all very hair shirt or, in the new language of news we were having to acquire, 'high fibre'. The Nine team spoke in a kind of code, about 'semiotics' and 'colour binding', that needed its own vocabulary to understand. It eventually had one. We drew up a *Glossary of Terms* to help newcomers to the programme. In it, viewers became 'punters' and were defined as a 'fast-dwindling group of people whose views, interests and concerns are of absolutely no account'. The Nine team were all 'roundheads' – 'journalists who think a parade for the Queen Mum's birthday isn't news unless a bomb goes off or someone is shot'. When things went wrong there was an 'inquest' – 'a management game involving any number of players and a buck'. It started as a joke, but some people on the Nine, and most of those we dealt with elsewhere in the organisation, needed it to work out what was going on.

To my surprise, the 'high-fibre' *Nine O'Clock News* did not haemorrhage viewers, even though some nights it was, as even its inventors acknowledged, 'a tough watch'. This was partly because we underestimate people's appetite for serious news (we overestimate people's knowledge, but that is a different matter). The editors and the producers on the programme then were very bright indeed, the pick of a graduate training scheme that selected half a dozen or so from thousands of graduate applicants. They were very clever at deconstructing complex issues and leading viewers through them in a simple and logical way. They sometimes missed out the drama and the human interest, but they made difficult issues explicable and accessible. Possibly the other main reason it worked was that news itself suddenly became more serious. No sooner did the *Nine O'Clock News* develop a very unfashionable interest in central European countries few people had heard of, and hardly anybody could find on the map, than the Soviet Empire came crashing down and they were hot news. When the Pacific Rim economies went belly-up, the Nine's viewers knew why. When Japan hit the buffers, when Europe turned right, when antagonism to globalisation burst out on to the streets, when the Balkans blew up, the Nine had been there already. In many cases, the Nine's editors, and certainly the Nine's presenter, were as surprised by these events, or at least the speed with which they happened, as everybody else. There is a lesson there, I think. The flagship BBC News programme should be about what is important, not merely what is interesting. But the important *is* what is interesting – sooner or later, if not always, by definition.

When something big was happening, I found being a newscaster particularly frustrating. It was difficult to be deskbound when the world was changing out there, and you reckoned the whole point of being a journalist was to see it for yourself, at close hand. I always used to say the reporter's job gave you a seat in the front row of history. The newscaster is normally back in the stalls just in front of everybody else. Not always, though. Sometimes you have to ride the breaking wave of news like a surfer, and sometimes you can have it both ways.

I was doing the news the night Pan Am Flight 103 was blown out of the sky over Lockerbie, just before Christmas in 1988. The story broke at two minutes past seven that evening. We got the first call about ten minutes later and from then on the newsroom was a madhouse. The first reports were sketchy. It took about half an hour before we knew for certain an airliner had crashed in the Scottish borders and parts of it had hit the town. We did not know why until much later. It was not clear at first how many people there had been on the plane, whether any had survived, or if there had been casualties in Lockerbie itself. But you did not have to be an expert to know that transatlantic 747s carry hundreds of people and they would be six miles up by the time they crossed the Scottish border. As we broke into the evening's schedule with the first news flash we knew it was a major disaster, whatever else we did not know.

Big stories stutter to start with, and then the news comes in a flood. To begin with, you have to make the most of every scrap of information you have, but it soon becomes a matter of picking out the most important facts in the welter of information to tell the story as directly and clearly as possible, and doing so over and over again. By nine, we had the shape of the story and a close idea of the scale of the casualties. We knew there had been more than 250 passengers on the plane and that it was unlikely, to say the least, that any of them had survived. We also knew there were dead and injured among those on the ground. I talked to people in Lockerbie itself and to reporters who had just arrived. I interviewed firemen and hospital officials about how they were coping with the crash and its casualties. We brought in aviation experts to tell us how it could have happened – the possibility of terrorism was already hovering in the background. As the programme was coming to an end we managed to play in the first pictures from the town, still ablaze after parts of the plane had crashed on to it without any warning.

We had gone on the air with a carefully planned programme in the dustbin and little more than a list of possibilities and a lot of crossed fingers. In some ways, though, they are the easiest programmes to do. People are desperate to know more. Rough edges are barely noticed. And when you run out of new material, summarising what you already know is a virtue, not a fault. As soon as the Nine was over, we had half an hour to get a new programme together. We had pictures now, more eye-witnesses and more of an idea of what was happening. BBC1 was being cleared for Lockerbie and nobody wanted to let *News at Ten* have the story to themselves. Newscasting on those nights is an extraordinary adrenalin rush. You're conscious your thrill comes on the back of other people's tragedies but you are used to the idea that journalism is a morally ambiguous occupation and it is the last thing you think about in the excitement.

After a lot of lobbying late into the night, I talked my way on to the first flight up to Glasgow at six the following morning, hired a car and was in Lockerbie just after breakfast.

I knew the place from my time up in Scotland. I had gone past it on the A74 on countless occasions, and pulled in there once or twice for a break on the long trips to and from the South. The wreckage of the Jumbo was actually spread across much of southern Scotland. Charred bits of the plane were found 90 miles away. But the bulk of it, including the engines, came down on and around Lockerbie with the force of an earthquake. The British Geological Survey said later it had measured 1.6 on the Richter scale. One of the wings, loaded with fuel, had scythed down on to Sherwood Crescent like a gigantic flaming sword. The explosion vaporised houses and the people inside them; no trace of them was ever found. That morning all that was left was a giant crater, 155 feet wide and 191 feet long, still steaming in the early mist. Near a churchyard to the east of the town was the nose of the plane, lying relatively undamaged on its right side in the middle of a field. It was to become the enduring image of the tragedy. The people who got to it first found the emergency light still glowing green. Inside were the two pilots and a stewardess. It is said the stewardess still had a pulse but died a few minutes later. Many of the bodies of the passengers were terribly mangled by the giant forces that were exerted when the plane broke up, but many looked as if they were sleeping. One was still sitting in his airline seat, apparently holding the miniature bottle of red wine he was being served when the bomb went off. On the outskirts of the town we found a field that seemed to be covered with bits of body; the pink of human brains stood out against the dull winter greens and greys.

For the next couple of days I pulled together the BBC's coverage for long reports that took up most of the first half of the *Nine O'Clock News*, and appeared on the other side of the interview for a change at the end of the programme. The suspicions of sabotage were growing all the time we were there. Once the possibility of collision had been ruled out, the extreme violence with which the aircraft had disintegrated pointed only one way. In that town, working amongst the human and mechanical debris, it was impossible not to keep thinking of what that moment of horror had been like and, worse, wonder how long people were conscious before they died. Not for the first time, I found it difficult to see how any human being could do that to innocent people they did not know, and hated whoever had done it with all my heart.

The big, breaking stories made newscasting worthwhile. I was doing the programme the night Nigel Lawson resigned as Chancellor of the

Exchequer, shaking Margaret Thatcher's government to its foundations. She had called him her 'brilliant' Chancellor and he had been running the economy for six and a half years. But his open desire to join the exchange rate mechanism of the European Monetary System worried her. His policy of acting as if Britain was already part of the system, keeping interest rates high so the pound could shadow the Deutschmark, worried her even more. She appointed a mouthy economic guru called Sir Alan Walters as her part-time advisor. He believed, very publicly, that the pound should be left to find its own level and that the EMS was 'half-baked'. Lawson was touchy, Walters was contumacious and Mrs Thatcher was, well, Mrs Thatcher. The situation festered for some weeks. The end should have been predictable but, in fact, came to us as a complete surprise.

At nine o'clock that morning, Lawson had threatened resignation if she did not get rid of Walters, but we did not get wind of it. He finally resigned after Prime Minister's Question Time, when Neil Kinnock taunted her about having 'two Chancellors' and her defence of Lawson was only half-hearted. The news broke mid-evening and threw Westminster, and us, into turmoil. The programme being prepared for that night was torn up and an entirely new one put together in about an hour. It did not just have a detailed analysis of the economic and political issues involved and a history of the most important relationship in that government. It had most of the leading politicians of the land, live, with the shock still on their faces and in their voices. For forty minutes or so I bounced briskly from one to another, in between the reportage and the analysis. It was as if this moment of crisis was being played out entirely on television. The TV critic, Allison Pearson, said that, for a time that evening, it looked as though I was running the country, which was ridiculous, but I certainly felt at the centre of events in a most unusual way. It was easily the most satisfying live broadcasting I have ever done.

These big events always seem to happen on quiet evenings. I was gossiping one night with the programme editor, Eileen Fitt, one of the former Belfast MP Gerry, now Lord, Fitt's many daughters, who had been known collectively in my early days working in Northern Ireland as the 'Missfits'. She is very amusing and hardly anything had happened that day so we were busy picking over old scandals and trying to create new ones.

The first agency newsflash that the Israeli Prime Minister, Yitshak Rabin, had been shot by a gunman in central Tel Aviv put a stop to that.

We scrambled together enough of the breaking news to fill most of the scheduled programme and then, an hour later, went on the air with a special edition. There is an element of luck in all this. You need a brilliant editor, like Eileen, or Mark Damazer who was on the night of the Lawson resignation, to shape it. You need a heavyweight correspondent on the spot who knows exactly what he is talking about and has the contacts to stay ahead of the story and still be there to file and to broadcast whenever you need him. That night we had Jeremy Bowen in Israel, one of the very best. And you need an analyst in the studio with you, to help put it all into context and weave each new bit of information seamlessly into the developing narrative. Brian Hanrahan was there that night and nobody does it better. The result was a programme put together in a matter of minutes that won a Royal Television Society award.

The trouble was that these stories were few and far between. Most stories broke during the day and were already half-digested by the great BBC machine by the time we went on air. Wars, in the Gulf and the Balkans, start in the middle of the night to catch both the enemy, and us, napping.

Too much newscasting was simply routine. I could never persuade myself it was that important. There was some responsibility in being the link between all those correspondents and cameramen across the globe, the humming newsroom at the end of the corridor and the millions of viewers who relied on them for their picture of the world. You were stretched a bit when the whole programme came crashing down around your ears, or on the prayed-for occasions when a big story broke while you were on the air. But it was not much of a job. There was nothing difficult about it. The idea it was stressful was absurd after the years I had spent risking my life every week, and sometimes every day.

The BBC has always been rather nervous of journalist newscasters. It is, in the jargon of the media, a 'producer-led' organisation, which means that the people who run it have often never been on the working side of a camera or microphone in their lives. In the early stages of a broadcasting career being a reporter is infinitely more exciting than being a deskbound producer. Only the latter, though, have much of a chance of making it to the top. There have been a few notable exceptions, but a prevailing characteristic of the senior ranks of the British Broadcasting Corporation is that they are nearly all failed, or at any rate hopeless, broadcasters.

Perhaps as a consequence of this, there has been an anxiety not to give newscasters too much prominence or editorial power. Other channels may build their coverage of news and big events around a single individual who personalises and symbolises the network's credibility. The BBC has always preferred to divide the role up to avoid creating an 'overmighty subject'. At one stage in the early nineties the *Six O'Clock News* had 11 regular presenters. This has put the BBC at a huge disadvantage in marketing its news programmes. In fairness, the superstar newscaster strategy can, and in America occasionally has, created multi-millionaire monsters.

I was about as prominent as a BBC newscaster gets. I may have had the best warpaint but I was always an Indian, never a chief. The management could be strangely nervous in dealing with me and I had fun winding them up from time to time. I rejected all their attempts to send me to a 'style consultant' with immense *hauteur*. They eventually apologised for impugning my taste, if not my virility, though this proved a pyrrhic victory. I lost out on a lot of free clothes.

My best wheeze was to come back from a sailing holiday with a full beard. My tactic was not to mention it and to wait and see what would happen. Sure enough, a growing stream of ever-more-senior managers came into the newsroom, ostensibly about other business but really for a first-hand glimpse of this latest crisis. None spoke to me directly. They went off for meetings but the buck was passed to such good effect that nobody even raised the subject until the middle of the evening.

I took a lofty line about a beard being entirely a matter of personal choice and half believed it. Besides, I was secretly tremendously proud of my new whiskers and felt they deserved a wider audience. Unfortunately, a big story broke late on in the evening and my editor, braver than most, argued that the beard would distract the viewers from what was really important.

I gave in, reasonably gracefully, with ten minutes to go to the programme, but warned them that I had no idea how long it would take me to remove it. Five minutes later, I rang them from the dressing room and told them that, as I had feared, it was proving slow and difficult. The choice, I said, lay between having one half of my face shaved and doing the news in profile, or reducing the full set to a – slightly bloody – goatee. Which would they prefer?

In fact, I had already removed the lot. It was my most successful wind-up. The editors were still pale when we came off air and strangely unable to see the funny side of it all.

*

I did the programme from abroad when there was a big story. From Moscow when the Soviet Union crumbled, from Washington at a crucial point in the presidential election, from Berlin on the night Germany was reunified, and in a rainstorm from Hong Kong the night the colony was handed over to China. In a way they were even more frustrating. I was doing the cosmetics, the presentation, when I wanted to be back doing the main report. I got to interview some of the main participants and often used to disappear with a crew to do part of the story, but it was not the same.

Only once did I manage to combine the roles in a meaningful way. I was in South Africa to front the programme when the country that had been such a vivid part of my life had its first free elections. I spent the day back in Sharpeville, the shabby township in the Vaal triangle whose name reverberated round the world in the apartheid years and where I had watched the beginning of the uprising that led to the system's downfall nearly a decade before. I filmed the survivors of the 1960 massacre cleaning the graves of those who had been killed. It's an African tradition, on days of special importance. Nothing could have been more special than that day. In Sharpeville, perhaps more than anywhere else in South Africa, it had begun in high and dangerous tension. The yellow police armoured personnel carriers prowled past walls daubed with the old Pan-Africanist Congress slogan, 'One Settler, One Bullet'. But then the queues formed as blacks waited patiently for a chance to choose their own government for the first time. Perhaps more than anywhere else in that wonderful country, on that extraordinary day, it was an intensely moving and cathartic experience.

It beat sitting in an overheated studio reading off an autocue, anyway.

I pushed hard to be let out from time to time to do some proper reporting again. The sharp young women who draw up the BBC's rotas, and so really run the place, tutted but eventually agreed. They made it clear this was not freedom. It was parole.

TWENTY-FOUR

DANTE WOULD HAVE RECOGNISED Mogadishu airport in the nineties for what it really was. It looked and felt like the innermost circle of hell, where human nature had been stripped of any pretence of civilisation, a place ruled only by cruelty, violence and greed. The figures that flitted through the ruins, or raced up and down the pitted runway bristling with guns, were like some flashback to prehistory. Man as brute beast, looking to kill and capture and grab whatever was going. They were young men or even boys for the most part, often dwarfed by their prodigious weaponry. The little Cessna we had chartered in Nairobi rolled to a halt and the pilot switched off. 'Welcome to Mogadishu,' he said. 'It's the Old Testament with rocket launchers.'

From all over the airport the battlewagons homed in on us. They were stripped-down jeeps and Land Cruisers. The roofs had been sliced off and the biggest ordnance they could lay their hands on was bolted on to the top. The favourite was a multi-barrelled anti-aircraft gun, but there were 50-millimetre cannons, Stalin's Organ rocket tubes, and even the main armament missiles of a MiG-17, wedged between the front seat of a 4 × 4. They called the battlewagons 'technicals'. They were blow-torched back to bare metal and decorated with slogans, animal horns and even bunches of plastic flowers. The nut-brown, rock-hard and three-quarters-crazed fighters who crammed into them were the clan militias. Somalis are famous for their feuding clans, for the way they will fight anybody, for ever. It is said of them: Nation against nation, tribe against tribe, clan against clan, family against family, me against my brother. The militias who fought over the city were mainly made up of the *moryaan*, tough young nomads drawn from the 242,000 square miles of desiccated sod-all that constitutes the rest of Somalia by the thought of women, loot and killing.

When they were pastoralists, carrying on tortuous feuds over camels and land that went on for generations, it was just a matter of spears and blood money. But Somalia had been flooded with guns by, first the Soviet bloc, and then the West. They were buried in vast underground arsenals all over the country that were now being dug up and the arms passed around to anybody old enough to hold them up and strong enough to pull the trigger. The elders who used to arbitrate and referee the bloodletting had been brushed aside in the storm of violence. Any pretence at law and order, or civil government of any kind, had vanished when the dictator, Siad Barre, fled a few months before.

Mogadishu had been quite a pleasant place, quaint rather than picturesque; 500,000 people, whitewashed houses, an Arab souk, all next to the vivid blue Indian Ocean. The war between the clan armies had turned it into a subtropical Stalingrad. Artillery batteries shelled each other at point-blank range, from street corner to street corner. Tank rounds blew out whole blocks of flimsy houses. The city was constantly shrouded in the smoke and dust from exploding shells. Two warlords from the same *Hawiye* clan were fighting the biggest battles. Ali Mahdi Mohamed and his *Abgal* sub-clan held the north-west of the city; General Mohamed Aideed and his *Habr Gadir* faction had the south-east – two homicidal madmen trying to murder their way to the presidency of a country that no longer existed. Other clan militias tried to control their own territory while launching raids on everybody else.

Ten thousand people were killed in the first few weeks, 20,000 injured. There was no electricity, not much food and hardly anything to drink. Even what passed for hospitals had no water. They had no anaesthetics either, practically no drugs of any kind, in fact. People were crammed in every corner of the filthy wards and laid down in the corridors and doorways, spilling out under the trees. They were a minority. Most casualties died where they fell on the streets. If there was no break in the fighting they were eaten by dogs. If there was a lull they were thrown, a dozen at a time, into the harbour which was seething with sharks.

It was the second time I had been there since this festering armpit of Africa had burst apart. A few months earlier, I had talked my way out of the *Nine O'Clock News* studio to do a series on the state of Africa for Radio Four with a brilliant producer called Sue Davies. We had seen then how people were trying to survive. At night they locked themselves in their rooms with as many guns as they could lay their hands on. They waited for the banging on the door that was likely to be a gang of boys with AK47s and an RPG7 rocket launcher. 'If we don't open up,' they told us, 'they blast the door down. Our wives, children, will be exposed and raped and our belongings taken. So we open up and hand stuff over, trying to keep something back for the next raid. But soon there is nothing left.' People were gathering in bigger and bigger groups, thirty or forty to a house, but even that was no real security against the heavily armed mayhem of the streets.

Sue and I had tried to stay close to the Red Cross, one of the few Western organisations crazy enough to stay there. We had found moving round the city, trying to talk ourselves past the roadblocks and pick our way through the random battles on every other corner, had taken a lot of nerve, a lot of time and a keen sense of geography. A hundred people a day were being killed on the streets. I had tried to act the old Africa hand in front of Sue, but was quietly terrified, and pretending not to be was quite a strain. Sue was Australian and new to Africa. When the rockets went *soof soof soof* over our heads and I worried about what my khaki trousers would look like if I wet myself, she just clucked with irritation that it might be spoiling her recording. She even went up to a gang of young killers, banging away at their enemies-for-the-day down the street, and told them to shut up until we had finished an interview. They did, too.

I have never felt so relieved to get out of anywhere. Sue and I eventually put together a series of programmes about the idea of Western intervention in Africa, to stop its headlong slide into poverty and violence. With most countries we went to, it meant weighing up complex moral, political and economic issues. Not so in Somalia. It was a shithole, fought over by maniacs, and you had to be mad yourself to think of trying to prise them apart. Not long afterwards, the UN tried and failed, and then the boys in their technicals took on the world's great superpower and made swift mincemeat of the American Army, special forces, Blackhawks and all. I was absolutely determined I would never, never go back.

I reminded myself of that as I stepped down off the wing of the plane and looked straight into the crosswires of an anti-aircraft gun, poking over the top of a sawn-off Land Cruiser. The boys were edgy. We had come at the worst possible time, when the militias were expecting their daily supply of *khat*, a drug that comes from the shoots of a bush that grows in the mountains of Ethiopia. Bundles of it were flown into Mogadishu every afternoon in small aircraft piloted by the *khat* cowboys, pretty much the only planes that came to Somalia any more. There was meant to be a truce at the airport between the militias to collect the evening supply – half the city would be chewing itself into a stupor by dusk. But after a few hours without their vegetable amphetamine fix the fighters were tense; there had been murderous battles in recent weeks over the *khat* shipments and trouble, big trouble, was always on the cards. I wondered again why

I had come. The reason was just clambering down off the plane behind me.

Mo Amin had aged in the year since we were blown up in Addis Ababa, which was hardly surprising. He had searched half the world for an artificial arm to replace the one he had lost in the explosion. A laboratory in Warren, Ohio, eventually fitted him with £40,000 worth of NASA technology that could do wonders, but could not make him whole again. It was clever, 'bionic' even. Mo could manoeuvre the mechanical elbow and wrist by flexing the muscles of his upper arm. It was powerful, but clumsy, and there was no miracle to replace his sense of touch. Worse, it ran off two six-volt batteries and was so heavy that Mo developed a pronounced tilt to the left when he wore it. The doctors tried to compensate by building up the heel on his left shoe. In truth, he did not use the new arm that much. Most of the time he went round with an empty sleeve. He even drove one-handed. I can remember several nightmare trips round Nairobi, with Mo, who always insisted on driving, changing gear with his right hand and the big old Peugeot constantly slewing off towards the oncoming traffic.

The main reason Mo wanted the new arm was to be a cameraman again. I kept telling him he had done enough. He was nearly fifty, a rich and successful businessman, and had long ago used up more than nine lives. There was no room in such a physically tough and frequently dangerous business for an old cripple, I told him (subtlety and sensitivity were always lost on Mo). He did not listen. He still saw himself as the macho war cameraman and could not bear to think of himself in any other way. He'd had a camera cleverly adapted so that all the controls could be operated with just the one hand. There was a special brace that went with it. Filming this way wasn't easy, and it certainly wasn't quick, but Mo was a very determined man. He did a few undemanding assignments, covering meetings and press conferences. It was never going to be enough, though. He was desperate to go to a war, to prove something to himself as much as anything. He wanted to go to Somalia, and he wanted me to go with him. I could not find a way to say no; it's a problem of mine.

We were not just in Mogadishu to do some news stories. I was also filming a documentary about war cameramen. It had not been my idea, but I had jumped at it when I was approached by an independent producer, a South African friend-of-a-friend. I had sold it to my boss, Tony Hall, the Director of News and Current Affairs at the BBC, while we were standing at adjacent stalls in the gents at the Grosvenor House Hotel during a break in one of those interminable awards evenings. I had not realised at the time it would mean going back to Mogadishu. But Mo was an obvious subject for the programme and they found the idea of following him – and me – as the one-armed hero fought his way back to the front, irresistible. I was stuck with it both ways.

There was supposed to be a ceasefire in Mogadishu at the time, which meant the gunfire had slackened rather than stopped. Many of the people in the city were starving to death and the UN had brokered a shaky deal between the warlords to allow a freighter carrying 5,000 tons of food into the port. Previous attempts to hand food out had resulted in great bloodshed as the militias slaughtered each other for control of the sacks, the dogs of war fighting to the death over a bone. This was pretty much the last chance, and the tension was high.

Survival in Mogadishu was largely a matter of luck, but you tried to adjust the odds where you could. The city was packed with fighters who had very little left to loot, so we were besieged by heavily armed young men who either wanted to rob us or be our guards. They were all wild-eyed and threatening so it was difficult for us, and maybe for them, to tell which. In the end we hired half a dozen with the cleanest and most vicious-looking guns, making sure they had a couple of rocket-launchers as well as the obligatory AKs. They clambered on to the roofs of the couple of rickety 4×4s we had also hired and we headed off towards the port. I noticed they never seemed to bother to put their weapons on safety; in Mogadishu, where death could come at you for no reason and from any angle, they probably thought there was no point.

The streets leading down to the port were covered in rubble. There were black gaps in the rows of grubby white houses where the shells had landed. This part of the city looked like a giant mouth full of decay. The docks themselves were crushed by the steely heat but streams of men in sodden sarongs still ran up and down the gangplanks carrying the bags of wheat. They were watched by dozens of gunmen from the different factions who eyed each other with mutual loathing and rattled the banana-shaped magazines on their AKs as their fathers would have brandished their spears. The UN had its own guards. Even compassion came at the point of a gun.

We found out from an Irish UN organiser in the middle of it all that the convoy of food would leave in the morning to try to break out of the port and cross the central battleground in the city, where the militias' territories intersected. The warlords had promised safe passage but they had done that before and, each time, the convoy had been shot to pieces. 'What about this time?' I asked him. 'Fuck knows,' he said.

We drove into the centre, along the route the convoy would take the following day. Every wall was pimpled with bullets and half the houses were sliced open by shells. Only the mosque was untouched. The months of gunfire had pollarded the trees that lined the streets.

We stopped the vehicles and climbed out into an eerie quiet, a silence so profound it ached. You could hear the rasping of the harnesses as Mo strapped on his arm, then the brace for his camera, and finally the camera itself. He would not let us help him. His shirt was soaked by the time he'd finished, and the sweat rolled off his nose and down through his goatee beard to leave a trail of speckles in the dust of the street. We walked around in the ruins. The sudden crack of a bullet nearby sent me diving on to a pile of rubble in the gutter. Mo hardly flinched, but he was trussed up like a Christmas turkey and in no condition to dodge bullets. One of our guards kicked an artillery shell case down the pavement and the sound filled the city. A baby cried and we found him round the next street corner. He was stark naked and only just old enough to walk. He was with another boy, not much older. How they had come to be there, in the middle of this deserted battleground, was a mystery. We were trying to coax them into our vehicles to take them to the Red Cross when their mother came running out from where she had been hiding, snatched them up and ran away. A burst of machine-gun fire, close at hand, made us think of other things.

It was nearly dark by the time we left, the sudden nightfall of the tropics that caught us by surprise in that killing suburb. The ride back to where we were staying was a waking nightmare. The gunfire broke out again around us. At one point, we swung right into a side street and the headlights picked out a fighter aiming straight at us, right at me, I thought. I had two seconds of thinking I was dead before we were past him, and I did not stop trembling for an hour.

We had hired a villa in one of the 'quieter' suburbs. The street wall was still riddled with bullets and it was all surrounded by rolls of barbed wire and broken glass. The guards settled down on their haunches in the courtyard, their guns always in reach. Mo and I and Colin Blane, the BBC radio correspondent who had been with us in the Addis explosion, sat around the table in the light of an oil lamp and talked about death.

It was not a maudlin conversation. We were trying to be funny, a gallows kind of humour that disguised our own fears and the affection we had for each other. Mo was talking about what would happen when he died. He assumed he would go to heaven which, fond though I was of him, I thought was an extremely rash assumption. He wondered if I would write his obituary and speak at his funeral. I told him he didn't realise how famous I was. I now commanded large sums for public speaking and my schedule was rather tight, I said. Mo, who had always derided me for my lack of commercial nous, took the point with, for him, good grace. He said he was glad he had taught me something about business and started to negotiate a posthumous discount. He would do a deal with the devil. Come to think of it, that is exactly what he had done, many times. He said he would be watching, even though we would no longer be able to see him. There was sure to be a business lounge in heaven, with first-class viewing facilities. In the corner, the documentary crew was quietly filming it all.

The following day we woke at dawn. The cockroaches scuttled into the shadows but our guards had to be kicked awake after a night chewing *khat*. At the harbour the convoy was already forming up. A row of ramshackle lorries was parked by the gates, each one half buried by a teetering pile of sacks. On top of every cargo was a group of sleepy young gunmen, fingering their weapons and staring out into an uncertain morning. The 'technicals' raced up and down the quayside. Their crews stood on the seats, leaning forward into the wind. They waved imperiously at their allies and made gestures of contemptuous dismissal to their enemies. From time to time you could hear them barking at each other in their guttural language. It seemed to me they were working themselves up for some sort of climactic showdown there in the docks, but the UN man said that was what passed for standard behaviour and normal intercourse between the clan militias.

It took hours to get the trucks and the 'technicals' in some sort of order. Mo and I tried to pick a spot in the convoy that was not too vulnerable but close enough to the front to see what was happening. Mo, for some reason, was wearing shorts and ankle boots and a hat with the brim turned back. He looked for all the world like a cross between Sinbad and Winnie the Pooh. He was in his element again and loving it. But it made me sad to see him trying to climb on to the roof of the jeep we had picked, one-armed, harnessed and burdened. I got in the back, next to the door, instinctively trying to put as much of the vehicle as I could between me and any incoming. I was also best placed to run like buggery if, as the

UN man put it, the 'excrement hit the air-conditioning'. I wondered what I would do if I had to choose between saving myself and trying to help an unwieldy Mo off the roof under the kind of fire the militias could put down. I just did not know any more.

The convoy was an extraordinary sight as it approached the no-man's-land that had once been the city's centre. It was led by a jeep with a huge blue UN flag flying from one wing, and a very nervous Australian at the wheel. Guns poked out in every direction. Hundreds of pairs of nervous eyes scanned the ruins on either side, searching for the ambush that many felt was inevitable.

Every few minutes there was the crack of a gunshot and all the weapons on the convoy would swing round at once. None of the shots seemed to be aimed at us; they were just part of the background noise in Mogadishu. The lorry in front of us jolted over the remains of a barricade across the street and an AK47 on the back ripped off half a magazine by mistake. One round went through the foot of the boy that was holding it. A couple more burst open the sacks under his feet, before the gun bucked and sprayed the houses at the side of the street. They had been blasted so many times it did not make much difference.

We reached the crossing point where the previous convoy had ended in a massacre with just that one, self-inflicted, casualty. The UN men had already dropped back and we stood aside to let the lorries go through into the other militia areas. I did a piece to camera as they went by, talking of 'rays of hope in a city of darkness'. The sun was blazing down, as it happened, but Somalia was a place that made you reach for apocalyptic metaphors. All I could think of was getting out of there which, I dare say, gave my delivery an unusual sense of urgency. A bullet whined overhead halfway through, adding to the drama of it all and adding to my queasiness. As soon as we had finished I was back in the jeep like a rabbit down a hole, but Mo wanted to stay for a while. It was arguably the most dangerous place on earth that day, but he kept saying he wanted 'just one more shot'. After ten minutes of this, I could have cheerfully shot him myself.

We needed to cross the city, to find the places where the people who survived had taken refuge from the violence and were now starving; the people for whom this convoy meant life or death. We hit several roadblocks and at each there was a lot of shouting between our guards and the boys manning them. It sounded to me like competitive bravado and deadly threats. The way they were gesturing with their weapons made it look as though a gun battle was inevitable every time, with us trapped in the middle of course. Somehow, we were always waved through until, eventually, we came to a roadblock that was manned with greater numbers and much more heavily armed. There was no bravado from our guards this time and their body language signalled a keen desire to be somewhere else. Most of the boys on the barricade were very angry, though we could not work out why. Others had been chewing *khat* and were sullen, red-eyed and resentful. It was very tense and, windy as ever, I thought we had had it. Mo suddenly poked his artificial arm out of the window into the faces of the fighters who were shouting at us. However unsatisfactory it might have been as a bionic replacement for a real arm, it was a cosmetic triumph. At first glance, especially if you had spent the past few hours chewing mind-altering drugs, it was indistinguishable from the real thing. Mo slowly rotated the hand through 360 degrees and kept going, round and round. The boys fell back with cartoon expressions of horror. One dropped his rifle, another really did put the back of his hand across his mouth like a ham actor in a melodrama.

It changed everything. Once they had got over the shock, the fighters became boys again, endlessly fascinated by the arm, wanting to see it work, again and again, wanting to try their strength against its fierce, unfeeling grip. It was half an hour before they would let us go with their new toy, but I think it saved our lives.

The suburbs of Mogadishu were packed with the living dead. The children had the diseases of the starving or were just simply wasting away. The adults were walking skeletons, if they were capable of any movement at all. We were taken from one charnel house to another by David Shearer of Save the Children Fund, one of those absurdly brave aid workers who always seemed to turn up in places no sane person would ever want to go to, and even war reporters don't linger. We talked with him of the ethics of Western intervention and, more to the point in Somalia, how it could be done in the midst of heavily armed anarchy. None of us had any solutions. I fell back on my own rubric, my reporter's creed in these situations. *You can only show people what is happening, so they cannot say they did not know.* But it only reframes the old definition of journalism as power without responsibility, the prerogative of the harlot throughout the ages.

I talked for a long time with Mo about this ridiculous trade for the documentary. He was as robust as ever about danger and excitement and how the big stories of war and disaster were the only ones that matter. I was not so sure. I wrestled with doubts, not just about my own courage which was wearing very thin, but on the ambiguities of being a professional misery tourist. The post-facto rationalisations were all very well but they could sound like a Jesuitical excuse. Sometimes I felt it was all puerile sensation-seeking, to feed your own inadequacies and the carbohydrate-rich but emotionally undernourished sofa slugs who engaged with life through their cathode-ray tubes. Mo said I was talking bullshit but I got the sense he wasn't so sure himself any more.

The other war cameramen I featured in the documentary were mostly old friends, or rivals. In the camaraderie of facing sudden death, which is one of the trade's greatest attractions and the only thing about it I miss, it amounts to the same thing. They all seemed to be driven by secret demons, however different their personal style. There was old Bernard Hesketh, the BBC cameraman who looked and sounded like a bank manager, in the days when there were such things and they were the pillars of their communities. I had worked all over the world with Bernard but never seen him without a suit and tie, even in the tropics, and his swept-back silver hair and impeccable manners opened many doors. When he put his camera down he was invariably thought to be the British Ambassador. Yet I remember him in the middle of a mob outside the US Embassy in Nicosia in the seventies, standing on his car, clawing at the boot with bloodied hands, whinnying with rage. The American envoy had just been murdered and the lid of the boot, which had all Bernard's camera equipment inside, was jammed shut. I thought he would go mad with desperation and grief.

Bernard was the model of dignified decency but he would do almost anything to get a story. He would scheme shamelessly to be assigned to the most successful reporters, he would work all day and all night for weeks, and had an unnerving habit of standing up in the middle of incoming gunfire to put his camera on a tripod. 'Steadiness,' he used to say, 'is everything.' (He came through all his assignments without a scratch but was overtaken by a sudden and aggressive cancer just after I interviewed him and died, steady as ever, before the programme went out.)

The two most famous ITN war cameramen were both charming but mad. Nigel Thomson had all the calm rationality of the truly nuts. There was nowhere he would not go; nothing he would not do; and he meant it. He had got bits of a shell in his back while filming the *Mujahedeen* in

Afghanistan but even so had decided he could never be killed. 'I have made a conscious decision on a mathematical basis,' he told me, 'that it is not going to happen to me and therefore there is no problem.' You didn't know whether to give him a medal or a straitjacket, but that's probably the same for most heroes.

Sebastian Rich was a playboy who said war was like sex, from all accounts a judgement he was more qualified than most to make. He was blond and good-looking and played polo in between assignments. He kept going on drink and cocaine until one day in the Shouf mountains outside Beirut he got hit by a grenade that blew his stomach open. He survived and now could not wait to get back to something nasty, or so he said. For him it was simple, childishly so, as he was the first to acknowledge. 'When you've got the shot of the shell going into the tank and the BBC haven't,' he said, 'you've got the toys under the Christmas tree. It's a bigger hit for me than cocaine.'

The war cameramen for the American networks were British, too. Dave Green who did all the tough stuff for CBS specialised in taking calculated risks and, in the first Gulf War, personally occupied Kuwait long before the American Army arrived. Barry Fox joined ABC in Belfast and went on to do a lot of their coverage in Vietnam. To them, it was mostly a question of 'bang bang', the snippet of real violence that would salt the bland diet of news. Like spices in medieval England, it was highly prized and men would go to untold risks, and to the ends of the earth, to get it. Dave Green and Barry Fox were both cynical about their trade. The 'bang bang' was increasingly divorced from its context; it generated excitement, not understanding; worse, the bar was always being raised. The public was being swamped by ever more realistic fictional violence. Factual violence had to be more and more extreme, and so more and more dangerous to get, to make any impact.

I had wanted to do the documentary partly to sort out some of my own confused feelings about covering wars and disasters. I liked all the war cameramen; several were old friends anyway. They were all men's men (except for Sue Lloyd Roberts, the Cheltenham Ladies' College old girl who walks the war zones claiming to be a North London housewife on holiday. She is assuredly a man's woman). They were all tough, brave and vivid people, exciting to be with. But what they did for a living had changed them. There were such contrasts in their lives. The bursts of intensity made normal joys and satisfactions dull and meaningless. Most had terrible problems with relationships and went through long periods of depression. You could admire them but you did not want to be like them. For the first time, I didn't anyway.

I was on duty in the newsroom the day Mo was killed. It was a short item on the programme that night and I had to read it out as if it was just the same as any other news story.

I had seen him only a couple of months before. Christine and I had been passing through Nairobi and went with Mo, his wife Dolly and son Salim to the city's most extraordinary restaurant, the Carnivore. It's a place that does what it says on the tin. You sit at long tables and all around are pits where the carcasses of a dozen different animals are being roasted. As you eat, a succession of sweating cooks brings around a new animal to taste. It starts with everyday beef and pork, but soon you are on to crocodile and hartebeest. We joked that if we sat around long enough we could eat our way through half the endangered species in Africa. We joked a lot that night and shared many memories, wallowing in a kind of unsentimental nostalgia. When we looked back at our times in Ethiopia we did not talk much about the famine, or the explosion that cost him his arm, but about the comradeship on another assignment in the early nineties to film the rebels as they began to get the upper hand. We had driven across the desert from Khartoum, travelling by night as soon as we crossed the border to avoid the government MiGs. Our memories that evening were not of suffering and starvation and violent death but of a wild ride through the bandit-ridden bush and up across the raw Tigrayan Highlands under a fitful moon.

I ribbed him about his MBE. I had written to John Major in Downing Street not long after the explosion suggesting Mo be given an award, and received a kind, personal letter back that was encouraging if necessarily non-committal. Others had weighed in, too, and Mo eventually went to the Palace in his tails and top hat, his left sleeve pinned to the side of his cutaway coat. I suggested that 'Member' of the British Empire was entirely appropriate as the one thing no longer existed and the other was the only bit of him that wasn't three inches shorter than it used to be, riddled with bullets or worked off batteries. Mo had just appeared on *Desert Island Discs* and I had helped him pretend to be a music lover. Music, to him, was the sound of the accountants weeping over his expense claims, but he made a reasonable fist of being enthusiastic about the eight records we had picked for him. But when I saw him straight afterwards he was furious.

'I thought you told me that piece was by Mozart,' he yelled.

'But it was, Mo.'

'Well, who was that bastard Adagio, then?'

At the Carnivore that night he was more relaxed than I had ever known him. The demons that drove him seemed to have quietened down. His many businesses were going well and we got the sense that he was shifting responsibilities on to Salim, who had inherited many of his qualities but not all his faults. We left just before midnight and my last memory of Mo is of him sitting at the end of a trestle table under the velvet African sky, his face lit by a dozen dying fires, at peace with himself at last.

A few weeks later, he climbed on to Ethiopian Airways Flight 961 in Addis Ababa. He had been there for a series of business meetings. It was the regular run down to Nairobi that he had done hundreds of times before. One of Mo's companies published Ethiopian Airlines' in-flight magazine. His seat in first class was free, naturally. Shortly after take-off, three Ethiopian men hi-jacked the plane, claiming they had a bomb. They demanded to be taken to Australia and would not listen when the captain said he had not got enough fuel to go a twentieth of the way. Mo was seen taking notes. He stood up and began negotiating with the hi-jackers; he had, after all, got a lifetime's experience of talking to the crazed and dangerous. Mo clearly thought they were bluffing and appeared in the main cabin of the aircraft which by then was full of hysterical people screaming and praying at the tops of their voices. He asked all the men to stand up and help him overpower them, but nobody would.

The plane ran out of fuel over the Indian Ocean and crashed off a beach in the Comoros Islands. A few got out alive, but 122 passengers and crew were killed. Mo was standing up when the plane hit the sea, probably still talking to the hi-jackers. He was flung against the bulkhead and it broke his neck.

A family of South Africans on the beach filmed the plane as it came down. Mo died, as he had lived, on camera.

The ironies were unbearable. To have sought out so much danger and survived, and then to be killed by a million-to-one chance, a story he wasn't covering, was hard to take. Nobody could believe he was dead. We all thought the great survivor would come hobbling up through the surf with another world exclusive. Not this time.

They laid him out in front of his weeping womenfolk in the big hall of his house in the ritzy Nairobi surburb of Lavington. His broken body was covered in a black and gold cloth. His face was left exposed, grey but untouched. When he used to talk about his impoverished childhood he would say he had not been born on a bed of roses. He died on one. His deathbed was awash with red flowers.

We buried him in the Moslem cemetery in Nairobi. The funeral was chaotic. He was carried there on a torrent of people – friends, enemies, and hundreds of people who just wanted to see the famous photographer laid to rest. We put him under a zambrow tree and I gave the eulogy. For free. If he really was watching, he would have said I had learned nothing from him over all those years.

I made a half-hour film tribute to Mo for BBC2 and had great difficulty not breaking down in the edit room as we put the sequences together and I wrote the commentary. The worst moment was when we edited in the documentary footage of us joking about his funeral back in Mogadishu. It had not been used in the original programme and the rushes had been lost, but we found them by chance in an attic in West London. They were like whispers from beyond the grave.

It was odd, really. We were complete opposites in almost every way. He could be a monster, cruel, ruthless and uncaring. But he was warm and funny, too, and curiously vulnerable. I suppose it is the things we shared that made him so important to me, the danger, the petty triumphs and disappointments of television journalism – and so much joint experience of others' pain. I miss him still.

TWENTY-FIVE

BY THE TIME Mo died, a lot of my work was outside news. I was principal newscaster on the main evening programme but I was still feeling it was not a job for a grown man, most of the time at least. I was forever plotting and scheming to get away on some news assignment or other, but the BBC bureaucracy wanted its money's worth. They were paying me the inflated salary of a presenter; war correspondents are worth much less. Besides, BBC News is a Byzantine organisation and the major stories, the ones I was interested in, were already being fought over by competing baronies. When the British Prime Minister meets the American President in Washington over a potential Middle Eastern war, for instance, more blood seems to be spilled inside the BBC than is likely to be shed out in the desert. The political editor and jealous rivals within his department are fighting over the right to report the event for the flagship television programme; it's a political story, surely? The diplomatic editor and his staff are absolutely certain that politics abroad equals diplomacy; the story is theirs by right, it's only a matter of deciding which of them will do it. The Washington bureau can't believe what they are hearing from London. America is their territory and they are more protective about it than the Pentagon. The BBC management was never very good at resolving these turf wars and a footloose newscaster just made matters worse.

The obvious finesse was to concentrate on Africa; stories I had become well known for and where I stood some chance of pulling rank. Early on, I had managed to get away to South Africa to film a *Panorama* programme about Nelson Mandela and the expectations he raised ahead of majority rule. It had been an extraordinary feeling to come face to face with a man who had so overshadowed my years there but whose appearance, personality and thinking had been hidden from us. We followed him back and forth across the country. He was the most impressive public figure I have ever met. It was not just his strength of character and his dignity, attractive though they were. It is as if he was somehow sanctified by his suffering, and lack of resentment. His time behind bars had kept him pure. No politician who has had to fight for power, and then exercise it, can possibly avoid the taint of compromise, the grubby residue of a hundred backstairs deals. Mandela was above all that, thanks to his tormentors. He was human, with human weaknesses. He could be autocratic, unfeeling, even cruel. Aides who crossed him risked a devastating dressing down. You knew, though, you were in the presence of a great man.

You also knew the burden of people's expectation was enormous and contradictory. The white family who lived next door to him in his temporary home in the previously whites-only Johannesburg suburb of Houghton were decent and relatively broadminded people. But they were convinced that South Africa's survival depended on the privileges and prosperity of whites like themselves being left untouched. They had a vast house, his 'n' her Mercedes and a yacht, and thought their taxes should be cut.

We tracked down black women in the Kliptown section of Soweto who had heard him speak in the fifties before his long imprisonment. Kliptown was still a place of open drains and a daily shitwagon. They expected him to provide electricity and water for the 90 per cent of blacks in South Africa without either.

'How long will it be?' I asked.

'Oh, two months,' they replied. 'In two months everything will be so different. You'll see.'

Mandela carried the weight of all those impossible, irreconcilable hopes and fears. This was not a question of a promised land; it looked touch and go if it could be held together at all as it turned the corner into democracy. Mandela inspired a suspension of disbelief, though, even in cynics like me. If anybody could lift the country through that transition, he could. And he did.

I did not always want to be retracing my steps, much as I loved Africa and however strongly I felt I was a news animal at heart. I was increasingly doing programmes outside news. The BBC2 environmental magazine programme *Nature*, that I was doing live from Bristol every Tuesday, was a change of pace and good fun into the bargain. The programme attacked the issues in an exciting, and often racy, way. I was particularly pleased with the start of one edition about Japanese opposition to the moratorium on whaling, which was driven by their love of whale meat. We found a wonderful shot of a whale leaping out of the water for my headline: 'The whale – the world wants it forever, the Japanese want it for lunch'. I would never have got away with that in News.

Nature was an ambitious programme. It was always done live and the big studio in Bristol was packed with props and demonstrations that I had to find my way between as the cameras swooped in and out and Andy the director told risqué jokes in my left ear.

Sometimes it was too adventurous. For a programme on the controversial fur trade, they had the bright idea of draping a live racoon around my shoulders in the opening sequence. The animal seemed quite benign during rehearsals but, with only three minutes to go before the start of the programme, suddenly became resentful and bit a large chunk out of my right ear.

My first thought was revenge. Unfortunately my kick missed it entirely and it trotted over to the corner of the studio and smirked at me for the rest of the programme. The wound was excruciatingly painful and, rather more importantly as far as the programme was concerned, extremely unsightly. The BBC nurse did what she could but I still had to go on air with my hand clamped over my ear like some camp crooner. For the rest of the time I tried to stay in profile and not worry about the blood dripping down my shirt.

Even when I was not being attacked by the props, I found *Nature* quite a challenge. It was always a hair-raisingly complicated programme, a kind of split-second gavotte through tricky demonstrations and testing interviews. I had no time to worry about all the things that could go horribly wrong, which was just as well. There was no desk to hide behind.

There was always a party afterwards and the '*Nature* Nights Out' became something of a legend. It was after one of these that I found myself, without quite knowing how, back at my hotel room.

The Glenroy was a family-run hotel and the better rooms, the ones with en-suite bathrooms, were down the street from the main building in an annexe. It was there that I stripped off – former foreign correspondents travel light and sneer at the very idea of pyjamas – shakily removed my contact lenses, drank a large glass of water against the morning's hangover and settled down to what little of the night remained. The water was a mistake.

Within an hour, I was awake again, muzzily trying to work out the geography of the room in the dark and, in particular, which door led to the bathroom. I felt my way to the nearest, pushed through it and fumbled for the light switch. Just as I found it, the door slammed shut behind me. I flicked the switch and, after a moment blinded by the light, found myself in the lobby.

My door was locked shut and so were all the others. In any case, the annexe seemed to be full of middle-aged ladies on a computer course who were likely to misinterpret the motives of a naked man banging on their door at two in the morning. The night porter was the only hope, but he was down the street in the main building.

I knew it had to be a dream. Being caught like that, bollock naked in a public place, is the classic Freudian metaphor for insecurity. I had been having dreams like that all my life. I pinched myself, and nothing happened. I pinched myself again. It hurt. I was still there in the hotel lobby, still without a stitch on, hyperventilating with panic. My first instinct was a lapsarian urge to cover myself, with anything, at any cost. I cast around and, halfway up the stairs, finally found a door that would open. Inside was the hot-water tank wrapped in lagging that would make a perfectly serviceable kilt if only I could get it off. I tried. God, how I tried. I tore with my bare hands at the copper bands that held the insulation in place until my fingers bled, but I just couldn't shift it.

I had more luck with the beaten-up sofa I found on the landing. Half-crazed with desperation by now, I wrenched at the cushion covers with my bleeding hands and managed to rip two of them off. They were not much bigger than a couple of fig leaves, but they were all I had. With only those two torn and bloody scraps of cloth, I shuffled to the front door and out on to the street.

It was only a hundred yards or so but it seemed to take all night. I froze for several minutes hoping, like lizards do, that if I did not move I could not be seen. There was so much traffic for the middle of the night. It did not occur to me then that many of the cars had turned round to have another look.

I started to move, trying to dart from shadow to shadow in a kind of prancing crouch. A shrill wind whipped under the cushion covers and made them crack like whips. The barracking got louder. Some of the remarks I did manage to catch were personal and rather wounding.

After what seemed like hours of this, I thought: Sod it. I drew myself up and marched to the front door of the Glenroy like a guardsman.

The front door was locked. Worse, the doorbell was high up, level with my right ear, and I had both hands fully employed trying to keep the cushion covers in place in the gusts of wind. With inspiration born of desperation, I wedged my private parts and the scrap of cloth that just covered them against the door knob, and with my free hand reached up for the doorbell.

It was another eternity before the night porter came to the door, incidentally dislodging the one thing that stood between the world and my modesty. 'It's a long story,' I stammered.

He seemed unmoved.

'And I don't want to hear it, sir,' he replied, before leading me with quiet dignity back to my room. I thought I had seen it all, his back seemed to say, but this takes the effing biscuit.

The environment was a fashionable issue at the time and *Nature* attracted a lot of big-name interviewees. As a news reporter, I had bumped into Mrs Thatcher on several occasions. I could not call any of these encounters an interview as such, I merely held the microphone while she lectured me, and the world in general, about her current concerns.

This time, I told myself, it would be different. She had agreed to do a sit-down, 15-minute interview with us in Downing Street. I spent weeks beforehand watching old tapes of great political interviewers like Sir Robin Day and John Freeman. I boned up on government policy about all the main environmental issues and the holes picked in them by the government's critics. With a couple of *Nature*'s brightest producers, I mapped out a line of questioning that set little traps and tried to anticipate how she would defend some of her government's more controversial decisions.

As I waited in the back room of No.10 I felt every inch the grand inquisitor. I had no personal or political animus against Mrs Thatcher, rather I saw I myself discharging some sacred journalistic duty in holding the Prime Minister to account, stripping government policy bare and showing its fudges and its contradictions. I felt smug and confident as I waited for her to arrive.

Nearly an hour after the appointed time, with still no sign of Mrs Thatcher, I was feeling less sure and also uneasily aware that I might have peaked. We could hear the hair dryer in the room down the corridor and the chuntering of a civil servant who was briefing her as the finishing touches were being applied to her make-up.

I tried a little small talk when she finally arrived and settled herself in her chair, but she ignored me. I drew breath to ask the opening question, but she cut right across it. I did not manage to get another word in for 7 minutes and 39 seconds – believe me, I have timed it. Actually, that is not quite true. I managed to get two words in – I think they were 'but' and 'er' – but she swept over both like an avalanche. I was merely a spectator at a curious performance. It was as if she wanted to unload all the facts and ideas she had picked up from her briefing before she forgot them. Once she had done so, she pursed her lips, rearranged her hands more decorously in her lap and appeared suddenly to realise I was in the room. The interview was not going according to plan.

To be honest, I never really recovered from the opening *blitzkrieg*. After she had exhausted her ammunition, I scored a couple of minor points over her exaggerated claims to have reduced beach pollution, but they were not knock-out blows and even they seemed to drift out of reach, like turds on an ebbing tide. When it was over, she stood up briskly, patronised me for ten seconds, and whirled out. I was left with a sense of failure and an overpowering smell of setting lotion.

Prince Charles, something of an enthusiast on environmental matters, also agreed to give us an interview, which would have been a coup for the programme if he had remembered to turn up.

Interviewing royalty used to be, and probably still is, a big deal for the BBC that sends the massed management ranks into a tizzy. Instead of the usual down-at-heel couple of technicians in their patched jeans and scuffed Doc Martens, they send along a whole outside broadcast unit, sweating in their wedding suits and half strangled by their unaccustomed collars and ties. At the appointed day and time, I arrived in the quadrangle of St James's Palace at the head of what looked for all the world like the advance guard of an invading army. The Prince's aides received us with something less than their customary aplomb. I caught the odd nervous glance but thought no more about it than that His Royal Highness might have got out of bed the wrong side and would need careful handling. The legendary efficiency of the royal household could be counted on to smooth any wrinkles.

We had been standing out in the yard for half an hour when the Prince's private secretary emerged. His hands wrestled with each other and contradicted his rather fixed smile. 'I'm frightfully sorry,' he said, 'but I'm afraid there's been a bit of a Horlicks. The Prince should have been here but, umm, he's in Turkey, sketchin'.'

Our attempts to interview his father were more successful, at least to the extent that he kept the appointment. The Duke of Edinburgh is titular head of the Worldwide Fund for Nature and had agreed to a long interview to publicise the fund's activities and its latest campaign to save the natural world. We went up to Balmoral with some trepidation. The Duke has a well-merited reputation for being testy and none of us fancied being on the end of one of his famously dyspeptic tirades. In the event, he could not have been nicer. He was forthright and controversial in the interview, and quite charming over tea and cakes in the castle's sun-dappled courtyard afterwards. I became quite a fan.

It did not last. The next time I met him, I was handing out gold Duke of Edinburgh awards at the Palace, along with several other B-list celebs, on his behalf. The Duke himself moved amongst us like the Holy Ghost while all this was going on. When he came into the room where I was dishing out the medals to the winners from Northern Ireland we all fell into the pre-emptive cringe which subjects seem instinctively to adopt towards royalty. He barked at a couple of the youngsters then strode up to me, invading my personal space and pushing his face right into mine.

'Know anything about it?' It was more of a snarl than a question.

I explained that I was too old to have done the scheme myself but I had done some research and so knew a bit about it.

'Well, that's more than you know about anything else then, isn't it?'

With that he turned on his heel and was halfway down the corridor before the words 'fuck you' had begun to make their way from my still deferential brain to my vocal cords. They never did get uttered. By the end of the day I had thought of far wittier responses but they were just as useless.

Nature did some superb spin-off documentaries. With Amanda Theunissen, an old friend from my Bristol days, I looked at the terrible consequences of uncontrolled and uncaring industrial development in Poland. The timing was perfect. Communism was collapsing and doors that had been closed to Western journalists for half a century were – if not actually being thrown open – at least being left unguarded. We pushed our way into the giant Nova Huta steelworks outside Krakow to film it in all its ramshackle and deadly decay. We scoured Silesia for evidence of the consequences of terrible pollution and found it. In Zabrze we found an orphanage packed with malformed children. A generation was riddled with genetic mutations, an horrific human legacy of the past. *The Poisoned Inheritance* won me the Science Writer of the Year award which I particularly appreciated, having made such a cock-up of my science 'A' levels.

I went to Bangladesh with Grant Mansfield, a fellow reporter who was in the process of vaulting into the senior management ranks of television, if not at one bound, certainly at no more than two. We uncovered a natural phenomenon that was ruining millions of lives, yet could so easily be countered. The monsoon rains wash the iodine out of the soil. You don't need much – a teaspoonful over a lifetime – but the lack of it leads to the vastly enlarged thyroid glands called goitres. The condition causes cretinism in the newborn and hampers and stigmatises tens of millions of Bangladeshis trying to get by in one of the world's poorest and most disaster-prone countries. It could be stopped, quite simply, by putting iodine in salt. There seemed to be unaccountable difficulties in doing this. Nobody regarded it as a priority. What salt was being produced with iodine was slightly more expensive and the great mass of the poor would not buy it. The aid industry could have alleviated untold suffering for a relatively small investment but had not done so.

The issues in both documentaries, and a third one I did amongst the burning oilfields at the end of the first Gulf War, were clear cut. It made a change. The magazine programme also tackled environmental issues on home ground. There were enough careless polluters to keep us going, but the people who irritated me most were the protest groups and particularly the more messianic of the campaigners. They often seemed to act as if every issue was a simple question of good and evil. They were good, of course. Their current target, indeed practically all commercial enterprises and public bodies, by definition, were evil. You rarely got the sense from them that most of these arguments were finely balanced – jobs and the economic prosperity that sustained a society with leisure to worry about things like the environment on one hand; that threatened patch of wetland, or the Alamo of the Natterjack Toad, on the other. I did not mind their beards but I found their two-dimensional mindset rather tiresome.

Nature was a programme of its time. It was fun while it lasted and it started several brilliant careers, but it was never going to run for more than a few seasons.

Two other programmes I did while moonlighting from news turned into long-running hits. They could not have been more different. One was an unapologetically cerebral radio discussion programme, the other was a peaktime television show that chased ambulances and audiences with populist panache. It was called *999*.

TWENTY-SIX

IT IS THE LITTLE things that often make the difference between life and death. In India Roffey's case, it was a patch of mud on the back seat of her dad's car. There were a lot of big things, too. The extraordinary courage of a passer-by, a fireman and a nurse; the inch-perfect skills of the emergency services; luck on such a scale that you did not have to be too religious to think in terms of a miracle. But if it had not been for the mud, she would have died in an instant on that December night on the Old Crane Marsh Road.

India Roffey's story was one of the first to be broadcast on *999*, which became a hugely successful BBC television series I presented throughout the nineties. It was one of the best of them, a good example of what made the programme so strong and so popular.

India Roffey was five at the time. That evening her father had picked her up after a day's fishing with one of his friends. His gear had left mud on the back seat of the car nearest the kerb, so India went round to the other side, and is alive today.

It was a dark and wintry night, but it is still difficult to work out how the accident happened. Their car met a lorry carrying a huge container, coming the other way down the Old Crane Marsh Road in Staffordshire. As they drew level, the container slid sideways and crushed India and her father under seven and a half tons of metal. Colin Gregory had been in a car just behind. When he got there he found one end of the massive steel box was still on the lorry, the other had smashed the driver's side of the car so flat he was convinced everybody inside must be dead. But they weren't.

India's father had been battered down into the tiniest of spaces, hard up against the wheel, with his legs trapped under the steering column. He was screaming in pain and fear and it was some time before Colin realised he was shouting about his little girl in the back of the car. Colin reached behind the seat and, down in the floor well, his hand brushed against a small, limp arm. Christ, he thought, she's dead.

Colin stayed there with India's father. Once or twice he glanced up at the giant container balanced precariously over them. If that goes, he thought, we're all dead. It was several minutes before he felt behind the seat again. He imagined he felt a slight movement. Then a tiny hand squeezed his fingers.

385

It seemed a lifetime before the rescuers arrived. It always does. The firemen swarmed under the container. Colin refused to leave. The little girl would not let him go. She did not say anything but she clung fiercely to his hand.

Peter Reid was sitting down to dinner when the call came through. He was Staffordshire's Chief Fire Officer, but he hated being stuck behind a desk. He had a lifetime of spoilt meals behind him. He and his wife were used to it.

He had his own reasons for going there that night. The office had told him a child was trapped and it brought back bad memories. Only a month before he had been called away from a Sunday lunchtime drink to a road crash that had trapped two children. One had lived, the other little boy died from terrible internal injuries. Peter Reid had carried him to the ambulance; seven years old and not a mark on him. He was a sensitive man who had seen a lot of tragedy but had never got used to it. Death had been much on his mind and that night, more than ever before, he wanted to keep it at bay – to 'beat the Reaper', as he put it.

It was a sight he has taken into retirement, which he will remember for the rest of his life. A great jumble of metal was blocking the lane, lit by emergency lights and blue flashes from the rescue vehicles. He could not see how anybody in the car could have survived. Even the uprights of the doors, which can withstand a lot of pressure, had been telescoped almost flat, and the great box seemed to be resting on the top of the driver's seat. The bulk of the container was hanging over the road, 'floating free' as the firemen say. It was obviously unstable and likely to move at any time. If it did, when it did, anybody underneath would be killed.

Peter and his men ruled out using a crane, because the container could easily move sideways as the load was taken up, which would certainly be fatal for India and her father. They decided to raise it from underneath with air bags and portable power rams. It was still very dangerous and it was not just the lives of the casualties that would be at stake. Several of their own colleagues would die if they got it wrong. Including Peter Reid.

He decided to run the operation from inside the wreckage, the only position where he could see the whole situation and monitor the casualties. He was a burly man, but he was used to tight situations. He took his helmet off as he went. There wasn't room for it and, besides, if the container fell it would be about as much protection as a parasol. He took over from Colin Gregory, who was reluctant to go.

In his 29 years as a fireman Peter Reid had never been in a situation where he could only see the casualty's hand. His first impression was how tiny it was, how warm, how eager to clasp his own. It was going to be a long night before they could get India out. He tried to remember what his own daughter, long since grown up, had liked to talk about at that age.

The first thing he did was let her feel his hands and his face, as he told her who he was. It was more than reassurance, he wanted her to have a bond with her rescuers, an emotional lifeline to the outside world.

She was calm, self-possessed and even funny. She thought his strong Scottish accent was French, which made him laugh. She said she was not in pain but very cramped and crushed. She kept asking how long it would be before they got her out. Peter Reid wished he knew.

He talked about his dogs, the German Shepherds and the Labrador puppies he and his wife used to walk for the Guide Dogs for the Blind, and how one of them, called Zara, had been turned down by the charity and ended up staying with them. He talked about his favourite colours, about the ducks on his pond, about poetry.

There were two rescue operations going on simultaneously. Getting her father out was a straightforward cutting operation – if the container didn't move and kill them all, of course. But they would have to lift the whole container to rescue India, which was much more difficult and much more dangerous. Peter Reid was doing his best, but the noise was deafening and India was starting to get distressed. She needed more tender loving care than just a gruff elderly fireman could provide, he thought. He slipped out from under the container to look for some and found Sister Kathryn Clayton.

Sister Clayton and two doctors formed the flying squad team from the Staffordshire Royal Infirmary. There wasn't much medical help they could provide until the casualties were released but it wasn't medical help Peter Reid was looking for; he wanted a mother figure for India. Sister Clayton knew the danger but did not hesitate.

Peter Reid introduced her as 'a nice nurse who's come to say hello'. He held the girl's hand and passed it over his rough face, and the nurse's smooth one. If only we could see *her* face, the sister thought, we would have a better idea of how she is and how she is coping.

It took an hour to get her father out. He had bad back and leg injuries but would live. Now they could all concentrate on the little girl. Sister Clayton knew she had to stop India losing consciousness and try to keep her mind off what was going on. She started to tell her the story of Cinderella, which kept her attention. She got India to respond to bits of the story. When Cinderella went to the ball, for instance, she asked India if she had been to any parties recently. She spun the story out as long as she could and tried to think of another.

To the rescuers who could see them it was an extraordinary sight. The tiny arm sticking out of the wreckage. The nurse on her knees talking about Cinderella and the Ugly Sisters. Peter Reid and another fireman huddled over her as if they were trying to shield her with their bodies from the vast metal container hanging over them all. Then it moved.

Afterwards, they thought it was just the structure of the container adjusting to the different strains as the rams took up the load. But, at the time, they thought it was starting to slip and they were going to die. Peter Reid took the difficult decision to ask Sister Clayton to leave. It was hard enough to justify the danger to his firemen; he couldn't risk a woman's life any longer.

They all felt there was not much time left. India was getting more and more distressed. They stopped using the deafening compressed-air saw and used ordinary hacksaws instead. They cut their way round the front seat, replacing the hacksaw blades as they snapped off in their hands. Then Fireman Peter Burton, an ex-marine, pushed himself right inside the car, across the driver's seat, to try to free it from the other side. It was an extraordinarily dangerous thing to do, but it worked. They felt the seat move, just slightly. A few seconds later – and to this day nobody who was there quite knows how – India appeared and seemed to shoot out into Peter Reid's arms. When he carried her out, they all cheered and nearly everybody, hardened firemen and policemen as well as the bystanders down the road, had tears in their eyes. It had been almost unbearably tense all along and was almost unbearably emotional now it was over.

Sister Clayton thought the little girl took it like a queen, smiling and waving to her rescuers as she was carried to the ambulance. The firemen did not seem to want to let her out of their sight. One of the fire engines, loaded down with men, set off in pursuit; others followed. India was carried off to hospital in a convoy of emergency vehicles. They stayed with her while she was examined – a roomful of men still kitted up and grimy from working in the wreckage. They had done so much to save her, they did not want to let her go.

India only had superficial injuries. Sister Kathryn Clayton and Colin Gregory were awarded the Queen's Commendation for Brave Conduct. Peter Reid and four of his men were officially recognised for what they did that night. But, as he said, his greatest satisfaction was 'beating the Reaper'.

India's story was the very essence of *999*. It was not just that it was a 'dramatic story of a real life rescue', as the programme titles claimed, after the signature *Pa-Pa-Pam* of its opening. It was a gripping account of how ordinary people coped with extraordinary situations. At a time of crisis, often at terrible risk, how men and women just like you and me found within themselves qualities that made a difference and saved lives. It was a programme that unashamedly celebrated what was good and brave, even noble, about human nature. To some people in the BBC that was one of the problems with it.

The idea for *999* was lifted from American television. Peter Salmon, my boss on *Nature*, had been promoted to run the features department at BBC Bristol and was keen to develop new ideas for popular, factual programmes. He had the disarmingly simple brainwave of sending one of his producers to New York with instructions to lock himself in a hotel room for a week, watch as much television as he could, and come back with new formats. He did. One was called *Gladiators* which was deemed 'too ITV' and later appeared there. The other was called *Rescue 911* – that's the emergency number in the United States. It was fronted by William Shatner, Captain Kirk from the *Star Trek* series, and majored on news footage and amateur pictures taken at spectacular accidents in America. It was extremely successful there but considered too cheap and trashy by the elevated standards of the BBC in 1992. Peter and his sidekick, Andy Batten Foster, thought it could be modified for British viewers, and for television executives that craved big audiences but didn't want to be ashamed of the programmes that drew them. Andy was a former Radio One DJ with the sort of red hair that looked as though his finger was permanently stuck in an electric socket. He was a creative and delightfully easy-going man given to telling awful jokes at inappropriate moments. I liked both him and Peter a lot, which is why I agreed to do *999* when all my instincts were telling me to steer clear of it. I was a serious journalist, after all, or at any rate I took myself extremely seriously. I saw myself as the heir to James Cameron, not some kind of Limey Captain Kirk fronting a downmarket programme about road crashes. I was armour-plated in snootiness, but no match for Peter and Andy.

Most of the BBC hierarchy were against it, too. These were the early days of John Birt's reign at the BBC when ambitious television executives devilled for the cold approbation of a Director General who preferred structure and analysis to drama and excitement. The people who tried to stop *999* at birth did so for one of two reasons. Some thought that, however much it was adapted, it was far too tabloid and exploitative an idea for the BBC to stomach. The idea of reconstructing dramatic rescues was somehow intruding on private pain and grief. They felt it would be crossing some elusive boundary of taste, difficult to define but obvious to all right-thinking BBC committee persons. The only other reconstructed reality on the BBC at the time was *Crimewatch UK* and they were under strict instructions *not* to make it exciting in any way. It was not, they were warned over and over again, *entertainment.* It is only a decade ago but, looking at today's television, that kind of high-minded fastidiousness now seems almost Victorian.

The other opposition came from my colleagues, the news and current affairs people, whose power was growing in John Birt's BBC. This was a programme full of decent individuals and good news. True newspeople wrinkle their lips at the very idea. We know that only bad news is real news; good news is public relations or, as we were already coming to describe it, spin.

I had a lot of sympathy with both these arguments, but my biggest worry was that it could so easily be totally, irredeemably, naff.

We made a pilot programme with three expensively reconstructed rescue stories. They set the formula for the series to come, sometimes using actors, sometimes the real people who had been involved in the rescue. In any case, they were present during the filming and we only interviewed them afterwards when what they had been watching had brought the original events vividly to life. Because the idea had been criticised for being exploitative, everybody was treated with an extraordinary degree of sensitivity – especially by the rather offhand standards of most television programmes. Because it had been accused of being cheap, they spent a lot of money on it. They hired good directors and went to extreme lengths to copy the exact circumstances of the original rescue. The production values were very high. Each of the programmes in the first series cost £250,000.

To make *999* seem more of a public service television programme we bridged the rescue stories with safety and first-aid information. I developed a challenging, at times downright hectoring, tone in introducing this stuff, invariably ending by pointing a metaphorical finger – even sometimes a real one – at the viewer and demanding: 'Would you know what to do?'

To start with, this was frankly a fig leaf to soothe the consciences of prissy BBC executives and deflect the rather more predatory attentions of the lawyers from CBS, the American broadcasters of *Rescue 911*. But the safety information developed a life, and a following, of its own. Viewers who had engaged with the excitement and suspense of the reconstructions got locked into the increasingly sophisticated ways of showing how to cope with emergencies of that kind. It provided a kind of resolution after the emotional roller-coaster of the drama. More than that, it seemed to give people some sort of permission to watch what were often dark and grimly realistic films. It also gave parents a reason to let their older children watch and they became the programme's biggest enthusiasts.

The BBC decided *999* could only go out after the nine o'clock watershed, in fact after the *Nine O'Clock News* itself which, more often than not, I was also presenting. The audience for the first programme was 8 million which, even in those days, was strikingly high. The second programme got 13 million and Jonathan Powell, the Controller of BBC1 at the time, was seen dancing down the sixth-floor corridors of the Television Centre, yelling, 'It's a hit!'

The big issue at the end of the first series was whether all the stories had to have happy endings. In fact, several had already been shown that had mixed consequences for those involved. The very first reconstruction was of a gas explosion at a block of flats in Putney, South-west London, that buried two Czech-born sisters. One had been pulled out alive after firemen heard her tapping with a brick deep under the rubble. But the other was killed, along with several other people in the flats at the time. I was struck by how people were swept along by the suspense of the stories, and argued strongly that we ought to deal with rescues that failed or else the element of suspense would be lost.

I was completely wrong. The happy, or at least not unrelievedly tragic, ending was essential to the programme's success. It seems they operated like fairy tales for adults. The important thing about a fairy tale is that children can engage with many of their deepest fears within the safe framework of a story they know will end happily ever after. So it was with *999*. The stories might be gruesome, and it was the ethos of the programme not to gloss over the brutal realities of events of this kind, but viewers could go on that journey with us knowing there was something positive to be drawn from it. You did not need to be a psychologist to see it, just a bit brighter than me.

999 did not rely on footage shot at the time of the rescue, but made good use of it when it was available. One of the most emotional stories the programme did was about a five-year-old boy called Gavin Hall who was running up a hill on Cannock Chase one springtime Sunday morning when the earth simply swallowed him. Afterwards, they decided that heavy rains had been to blame. He fell down a hole only 18 inches wide into a chasm that seemed bottomless, or at any rate nobody was ever able to find out how deep it went. Gavin would never have been heard of again if his head had not been trapped in a crevice which held him swinging with his feet hanging over a drop that was at least several hundred metres deep.

It took five and a half hours to get him out, and there was not a moment in all that time that most of the rescuers weren't thinking they would end up recovering a corpse. When he finally popped up out of the hole like a champagne cork and was held head-high above the crowd, half the rescuers were cheering, the other half were in tears. The moment was captured by a local cameraman; the emotions of that extraordinary scene could never have been reconstructed, even by *999*.

The programme treated those who had been through these situations with extreme sensitivity and a great deal of care. The actors who played their parts had a much tougher time. They were chosen for their physical similarity to the people they were playing, rather than their distinguished list of credits with the Royal Shakespeare Company. They were mostly inexperienced and generally not very successful; in fact, if they were recognisable from some other role we could not use them. They were subjected to endless ordeals. One lot were submerged in a gasometer for three days by a director looking for an especially high degree of realism. The (genuine) firemen agreed they were in far worse condition at the end than the people they had originally rescued.

They tended to be the acting roles from hell. They were dropped over cliffs, buried in mud, strapped to stretchers and pushed through narrow tunnels in pot holes, hundreds of feet underground. They were normally either drenched in fake blood, or smothered in bandages, and their lines were often reduced to a series of low groans. One lot of actors were accidentally trapped for hours under some cliffs in the Bristol Channel by the racing tide. There were genuine tears of gratitude and relief in their eyes when the Sea King helicopter (and film crew) finally arrived to take them off in the middle of a stormy night. By common consent, it was the most realistic *999* reconstruction, with the most convincing acting performances.

Because a lot of the filming was, by the nature of things, dangerous, the BBC went to extreme lengths to ensure everybody's safety. To somebody who had spent a lot of time in war zones without the BBC seeming to be unduly concerned, it was astonishing to see the endless forms and checks that had to be gone through, the safety experts that had to be on hand, the routines that had to be followed.

They only failed once. It was a story about a parachutist whose main 'chute had failed to open, and the reserve had got tangled, but he had somehow survived. The BBC had hired 'Tip' Tipping, one of the best-known stuntmen, and most experienced parachutists, in the country. The idea was to film him as he jumped. He would try to open his first parachute, appear as if he was in difficulties, and then open the reserve. To this day nobody knows why, but Tip did not manage to open either. He went straight into the ground and was killed instantly.

The tragic irony of a stuntman being killed while reconstructing a story about a parachutist's lucky escape wasn't lost on anybody and cast the programme into gloom for months. *999*'s safety procedures were examined with nit-picking rigour, but no fault was found and the BBC representatives were not even called to give evidence at the inquest. It seems to have been a million-to-one accident, which was no consolation at all.

Most of the time, the programme saved lives. The safety information that started as a fig-leaf proved hugely popular. When we published a brochure of lifesaving advice at its cost price – £2.50 – we did not expect to sell many. It ended up selling 75,000 copies, four times the previous record for a BBC Education brochure, and had to be reprinted again and again. When we set up first-aid courses with the safety organisations, 1.5 million people rang up, clamouring to get on them.

We lost count of the number who told us they had used their *999* knowledge, often saving lives. Half a dozen people found themselves in situations similar to those we had reconstructed, and said that at the crucial moment, when they were upside down in a car that had driven into a river, for instance, they heard my voice telling them what to do. My role as a disembodied saviour of accident victims was rather spooky, but oddly pleasing.

My own biggest nightmare was that I would somehow become embroiled in one of these situations myself. I would wake up in the middle of the night dreaming I was at the scene of an accident and the entire crowd turned round and pointed at me, saying, 'He'll know what to do!' I did a couple of courses but the nightmares did not go away.

One day I was stuck in a queue of traffic near the Television Centre in West London when it actually happened. A remarkably verminous-looking bag lady collapsed on the pavement only a few yards from my car. A crowd gathered around her and someone spotted me. I was practically dragged from behind the wheel and pushed over to her. She stank so high you had to hold your nose even to look at her, but the crowd wanted me to give her the kiss of life. Now, I am as much of a Samaritan as the next man, but I would have needed to have been forced at gunpoint to touch her with a pair of rubber gloves. The idea of giving her the kiss of life almost made me pass out. I was gibbering out a load of excuses when my silent prayers were answered. A young policeman arrived and gently told me my car was blocking the traffic. At that particular moment, I could have kissed *him* with considerable enthusiasm. The bag lady seemed to stage a miraculous recovery as I edged away. I was pleased for her and relieved. She would have been on my conscience if she had died.

I wasn't cut out to be a hero.

Some rescues we featured were so extraordinary they went beyond heroism and seemed almost supernatural. A walker called Roger Green fell badly while climbing a lonely part of Scafell Pike in the Lake District back in 1990. He was very seriously injured; he had broken bones and severe internal bleeding. There was nobody around to help and he sent his family off, mainly because he did not want them to see him die.

Suddenly, that lonely part of Scafell Pike was swarming with people with just the right skills to save his life. Two surgeons appeared out of nowhere with the specialist expertise to deal with his internal injuries; a fell runner who loped up was the ideal person to go for help. When it arrived, they all melted away without leaving their names. The more impressionable of our viewers were convinced Roger Green had been saved by angels. The cynics on the programme thought it more likely they wanted to escape any legal consequences if their efforts had failed to keep him alive. Most likely they were just modest heroes, content with the anonymous satisfaction of a life saved in difficult circumstances.

The programme was enormously successful, pulling in big audiences all through the nineties and spawning several offshoots. By the time it finished in 2002, there had been 16 different series over 11 years. *999 Lifesavers* was a shorter and more sanitised version of the programme that went out earlier in the evening and was aimed at a younger audience. It ran in tandem with the main programme for many years. There were a number of one-off *999 Specials*, single stories so spectacular (and so expensive) they could not be kept within the confines of the normal format. We also did a series of programmes about rescues abroad. I went off with a round-the-world ticket to set up stories in Minnesota, Las Vegas and Seattle. Then we crossed the Pacific to film the fireman in New Zealand who walked through the flames of a blazing fuel tanker to rescue a little girl trapped underneath. On the way back we did the story of the doctor who did a life-saving operation with a coat hanger on a British Airways 747 en route from Hong Kong.

Many other countries had *999* lookalikes and sometimes we swapped stories with them. It did not always work, often because their production values were not as high as ours, sometimes because they had a more robust view of what was appropriate for a peak-time mass television audience. The French version, called in the grandiose Gallic style *The March of the Heroes*, once featured a farmer's wife giving the kiss of life on her kitchen floor to a pet pig that had managed to chew through an electricity cable. It made arresting television but was thought to be a bit strong for British tastes. They trumped it a few months later with an extraordinary tale of a couple stuck in a light aircraft that could not land because the hydraulic fluid in the undercarriage had leaked away. One of them climbed out on the wing and replaced the missing fluid with his own urine. Heroic, certainly, resourceful, without doubt, but the story (known affectionately in the *999* office as *Wingtip Willy*) never quite made it across the Channel.

999 was proud of the gritty realism of its reconstructions, but some of the detail could be too much, even for us. The film that we made with the working title *Two Pole Man* was not the first we did to feature a driver who had been skewered by a road barrier but it was easily the most excruciating, for him and for us. We told the story of how Mark Hayes had been in a lorry that somehow veered off the M53 towards a boundary fence. He tried to wrestle it back on to the road but, instead, hit the fence end-on. Two of the horizontal poles smashed into the cab. One went through Mark's chest, just below his breast bone. The other went into his groin, out through the left side of his back, through the seat he was sitting on and three or four feet into the engine compartment behind the cab. It should have killed him but it didn't.

We showed how the firemen had fought to free him, and how he had a strange out-of-body experience, looking down on the whole scene from the hillside. We showed the intricate operation to get him out and the surgery that saved his life and repaired his dreadful wounds. We reported the end of the story, the baby born to Mark and his wife two years later and named after the ambulance man who had kept him alive.

We did not mention one of the real heroes of that night, the fireman who spent hours lying full length across the wreckage, holding Mark's half-severed scrotum off the red-hot metal. Some heroes remained unsung – even on *999*.

In a rather different way, and right at the other end of the broadcasting spectrum, the Moral Maze is not for the squeamish either. The high-minded and intellectually elevated Radio Four programme that debates the moral issues behind the news stories of the day can sometimes sound like a bear pit. The people who are invited on to it are chosen for their ability to put forward and defend their point of view. They are assumed to be able to look after themselves. Sometimes, in the clash of argument, no quarter is asked and none given. My job as chairman is to hold the ring, to keep people to the point, to prevent bullying or outright unfairness, and to move on quickly if any of the participants actually starts whimpering.

People are surprised it comes from BBC religion. But that is because they see religion in terms of the sepia gentility of latter-day Anglicanism rather than the brisk rigour of the Holy Inquisition. The religion department is not staffed by dreamy vicars but by bold (and sometimes rather fearsome) women and alpha males who are not content with pleasuring the dwindling devout of Middle England with *Songs of Praise* and Thought for the Day. They could certainly give the hard cases in the newsroom lessons in ruthlessness.

They dreamed up the idea for the Moral Maze in 1990. The first I heard of it was an invitation to lunch which turned out to be like a lion's den with croutons. I was surrounded by forceful people and their big idea was what was really on the menu. It sounded wacky to me. Something like a parliamentary committee, they said, only about morality. You and a panel, specially picked to represent a broad range of views in a forthright way, would call expert witnesses each week and cross-examine them on the rights and wrongs of the news story of the moment.

My first thought was that I did not really want to do programmes for a lot of half-soaked Bible-bashers. But they were actually alarmingly direct and extremely forceful. Their boss was the Reverend Ernest Rea, whose name had put me in mind of the worst kind of narrow-minded, self-righteous Ulster Presbyterian. He had indeed been a minister on the Shankhill Road in Belfast, but turned out to be worldly, passionate and wickedly amusing. My objections were decisively swept aside. They had settled on me for the job because of my years in South Africa reporting on apartheid – a long-running news story which was as much a moral issue as a political one. My own lack of religious conviction did not matter at all; in fact, it seemed to be a positive advantage. The more I said that it was impossible for me to reconcile my own experiences with the idea of an omnipotent and benevolent deity, the keener they seemed to get.

In the end I agreed, with two provisos – there must be as few vicars as possible and no politicians. As I left I noticed what an astonishingly large number of empty bottles were left on the table.

It did not take many programmes for the Moral Maze to develop its distinctive tone. From the start, it was designed as a Highest Common Factor programme, for intelligent and interested people. If you couldn't keep up, tough. The airwaves are full of reassuringly uncomplicated pap for brain-dead couch potatoes. We only got worried once, when an early programme about religion and morality disappeared up its own fundament into an ethereal dispute about neo-Aristotelianism, but that was an exception.

From the start, it was a programme which tended to say the unsayable. It trampled over the comfortable limits set by the BBC's soft left consensus. It spat in the eye of political correctness. It was quarrelsome and quirky, always intense, sometimes funny. Often there'd seem to be more blood on the floor of studio B12 than in any of *999*'s accidents. In a BBC that was ever keener to push at the boundaries of taste and increasingly reluctant to push at the boundaries of thought, it stood out like a noisy stepchild. We only got away with it because it was unashamedly intellectual. It also helped that it came from religion; it would not have lasted five minutes if it had been done by current affairs. And the key to its success as a programme, and its survival to become a BBC institution, is that it is broadcast live. By the time you have thought 'you can't say that', it's been said.

The Moral Maze was no respecter of reputations; it took on professors and politicians, bullies and braggarts, everyone with powerful opinions from Don Cupitt to Michael Winner. Some emerged triumphant, some were bruised and bloodied by the experience. We rarely felt guilty because, with one exception, they could all fight their corner.

The exception was an extremely fetching young lady called Linzi Drew. She had come along as a witness in an edition about pornography. She had the job title of 'Editor' of *Penthouse*, though it was difficult to see her as hands-on, at any rate in an editorial sense. A lot of her certainly appeared in the magazine but she seemed to be more of a doer than a thinker. I am not sure that she quite realised what sort of programme she was on, and she was obviously relying on sex appeal to win the argument. The long blonde hair, cleavage like a crevasse and sprayed-on leopard-skin pedal pushers made a deep impression on me but not, alas, on the panel.

Edward Pearce was the northern, Methodist kind of intellectual, with a formidably well-stocked mind and a fearlessly abrasive personal style. He had already stopped one arrogant witness in his tracks with a withering: 'That's not morality, Sir Alfred, that's *hygiene*.' Now he turned all his guns on Ms Drew.

It may have been the previous witnesses, a woman whose life had been ruined by her husband's addiction to pornography, and Ray Wyre who ran a unit treating sex criminals in Birmingham. It may have been that he never actually looked at her. When Edward was feeling particularly didactic his eyelids would flutter behind his outstretched palms like an earnest cleric telling the Holy Ghost to go back and wipe its feet. Whatever the reason, he went for her with cold and deliberate fury. It was no contest, of course. It was like an intellectual version of Tom and Jerry. Ms Drew was picked up, smashed off every wall, trampled into the carpet, dusted down and whacked all round the furniture a second time. She simpered a few trite phrases when she could get a word in, but they were buried under a mountain of scorn. I tried, chivalrously, to protect her but was blown away myself by another squall of righteous invective. By the time Edward had finished with her the whole weight of human weakness and folly was resting on her shapely shoulders. She seemed bowed down by it as she slunk out of the studio. The Radio Four listeners loved the whole thing. If it had been television, he would have been lynched.

Without any question, the stars of the Moral Maze's first decade were Rabbi Nice and Dr Rude. Rabbi Hugo Gryn was much more than nice. Dr David Starkey was, and is, devastatingly rude on occasions but disarmingly human and charming when he chooses. In their different ways they were both larger than life.

Rabbi Hugo Gryn was possibly the most delightful man I have ever met: warm, witty and wise. He was full of wonderful stories – so wonderful you never minded hearing them several times. One of his favourites was about the man from Berehovo, his childhood home in the foothills of the Carpathian mountains, who arrived at the gates of heaven. The guardian angel asks him to describe his life. 'Well,' says the man, 'I was born in the Austro-Hungarian Empire, I was educated in Czechoslovakia and started work in Hungary. Then I worked in Germany for a while, but I have spent most of my life in the Soviet Union.'

The guardian angel was impressed. 'Gosh, you moved around a lot,' he said.

'Oh, no,' said the man. 'I never left Berehovo.'

Hugo had an idyllic childhood, despite the political turmoil in that part of central Europe. He was only 13 when the Jews of Berehovo, including Hugo and his family, were rounded up in the town's brick factory and sent to Auschwitz.

It was a Moral Maze tradition to gather for dinner the evening before the programme. I remember the night when Hugo told us about arriving at Auschwitz. It was a terrible story that made an especially deep impression on me because I had recently been there on a filming trip and could picture it all so clearly. He told us how the doors of the cattle trucks had been pulled back and somebody had shouted, '*Macht euch fertig!*' (Get yourself ready.) There were prisoners in white-and-blue striped pyjamas on the platform and one had muttered to him in Polish: 'You are nineteen and you're a mechanic. You are nineteen and you have a trade.' Hugo didn't know what he meant but decided to do as he said.

'*Wie alt bist du?*' (How old are you?) Hugo remembered the SS officer at the head of the queue had a monocle over his left eye.

He stammered that he was nineteen. The officer asked him for his occupation.

'*Tishler und Zimmermann,*' (carpenter and joiner) he replied.

'All right, you will go to work,' said the officer.

Hugo and his father Geza were sent off to the right. His two younger brothers, Gabby and Clem, were sent to the left. The last he ever saw of them they were crying as they were led off to the gas chambers.

Hugo and his father survived Auschwitz. They were moved to a slave camp in the forests of Upper Silesia called Lieberose ('lovely rose') and lived through that as well. The two survived the infamous death march to Sachsenhausen and were both still alive when they were finally liberated by American troops in May, 1945. Hugo weighed less than five stone. He and his father both had typhoid. A few days later his father died.

The thing about Hugo was that all that suffering, loss and grief – the death of his father at the moment of their freedom drove him berserk, he said – did not lead to bitterness and hatred, but to hope.

It is true he never forgave. He held all Germans responsible and used to tell how the civilians came out to spit on them when they were on the death march. He was also determined never to forget. One of the witnesses on a programme that examined racism in Britain was a deeply unattractive man from the British National Party, the BNP. He started to deny the holocaust had ever occurred, or at least had not happened on the scale that had been reported. Hugo, warm, funny Hugo, went icy cold.

'Look me in the eyes and say that.' He couldn't and didn't. It was an electric moment.

Hugo's dreadful experiences could ruin programmes; an early edition about the moral purpose of prison had become slightly bogged down in a discussion about how 'slopping out' was demeaning when Hugo said, half-musingly: 'Of course, when I was in Auschwitz . . .' The momentum of the programme instantly drained away. Set against the enormity of what the Jews call the *shoah* (catastrophe) it did not seem that important any more.

Sometimes his recollections made the programme. A Maze about murder was going nowhere when Hugo started to confess that he was a murderer himself. He was on a work detail from the Lieberose camp when he and several others set on a cruel Ukrainian guard and beat him to death with wooden staves. He was glad about it then, he said.

'And do you know what? I still am.'

The dreadful experiences of his lifetime, how he had overcome them and used them, gave his world view an authenticity and a resonance few others could match. He did not just talk about morality and moral authority, he embodied it. His wisdom was warmly laced with humanity. He was extraordinarily kind and only intolerant of bigotry. To be frank, he wasn't terribly keen on traffic wardens, white van drivers and people with body odour either but the only thing he could not stand was intolerance. He was an emotional safety net for the programme. Some witnesses might get the intellectual equivalent of bright lights and baseball bats but you knew nothing bad, or truly unkind, could happen with Hugo there.

He had his faults, of course. He was much given to an appalling French beret and black trench coat, which made him look like a superannuated onion seller when he came bounding into the studio for the programme. He was, on occasions, a truly dreadful driver and, after that well-lubricated dinner that always goes along with the Maze, I was not always sure that he could be totally confident about the breathalyser. He was stopped from time to time, but policemen found Hugo instantly fascinating and he was never, I think, tested.

Those meals stay vividly in my memory. Hugo was such good company. On the odd occasion the Maze meal would be in a Turkish restaurant called Efes, where a belly dancer would perform in the basement. I wanted to go down and watch but most of the others didn't. A lofty lady academic, normally a good sport, snorted with politically correct disdain, a couple of BBC colleagues were, perhaps, overtired by that time of the evening, and Dr Starkey's tastes lay in a completely different direction. Hugo came along, though, and put a fiver into her costume the same as the rest of us. He loved life and everything that went with it.

Hugo got prostate cancer first, and thought he had beaten it. On our drives back from the Maze meal he would talk openly of his fear and of trying to find a foothold in his faith on which to fight it. Then a separate strain of cancer appeared in his brain. The disease, and the steroids and radiotherapy with which it was treated, sent him into swift decline. He made one last appearance on the Maze, looking terrible and having to he helped every inch of the way down those long Broadcasting House corridors. When the red light came on, he was the old Hugo, warm – always warm – funny and sharp. Afterwards they helped him away and I never saw him again.

I often feel he's still there when we gather in B12, sitting close on my right as he always used to, his spiritual bottom wriggling with impatience at some bit of bigotry, ghostly hands waving with that central European expressiveness. Sometimes, I even feel a nudge and a voice sounding like a bottle of bourbon and a carton of Lucky Strikes, saying: 'Michael, you can't let him get away with this.'

I suppose you could say he loved the limelight. He liked being on the radio, being heard by millions and being talked about. Who wouldn't? But he was a humble man in the sense that he treated everybody with respect and gave them his time and attention. When he died, I said I felt he was my special friend and only then fully realised how many thousands of people felt they were Hugo's special friend, too.

Dr David Starkey was an entirely different kettle of *fruits de mer*. He is fond of French expressions and used to describe himself as the programme's *goût de merde*, the speck of shit that the finest chefs in southwest France say is essential for the perfect *cassoulet*.

When he first appeared on the Moral Maze, as a witness in a programme about the Royal Family, he was a relatively impecunious historian at the London School of Economics, frustrated and angry. He had not written a big book and had largely lost out in the venomous world of academic politics. He was pretty venomous himself on air, delivering a clipped and devastating indictment of Diana, Princess of Wales, with all the authority of one of the world's great experts on the court of Henry VIII. He was waspish and clever, a show-off who did not seem to care who he upset. We loved him. Soon he was on the panel and his life changed for ever.

Freud would have regarded him as a text-book case. His mother was a clever and domineering Quaker who scrubbed floors for a living in Kendal, Cumbria. She devoted her life to David, blotting out his father who worked his way up to be a foreman in a washing machine factory.

David was born with two club feet and later had polio. He was an outsider at school, at least to begin with, but defended himself with his tongue. He was the unchallenged king of the Kendal Grammar School debating society – so intelligent, well-read and ruthless he never lost a debate. He went to Cambridge, became an academic and led a flamboyantly rackety life on the gay scenes in London and Manchester while his academic career blossomed and then stagnated.

For years he was the right-wing libertarian on the Maze. He had a top-down view of history, that it had been shaped by kings and queens and that the clearest example of the power of the court was in communist states. He tended to wipe the floor with the woollier kind of leftist. Environmentalists and street-marching foes of global capitalism had him licking his lips in a positively vulpine way; we would joke about keeping the St John Ambulance on standby outside the studio. His special snack was the odd unsuspecting and well-meaning cleric. David is not a believer but knows his Bible backwards and seems to have read more theology than most archbishops. He would revel in tying the poor witness up before he cut them off at the knees, looking around as if soaking up the approval of an imaginary audience and whinnying at his own cleverness. He had no sense of restraint and would sometimes get completely carried away. He would bounce up and down on his seat, wattled like the proverbial turkey cock, and become abusive. George Austin, then Archdeacon of York, was on the programme defending Prince Charles in a way that David interpreted as oleaginous and patronising. 'Doesn't he genuinely want to make you vomit?' he trilled. 'His fatness, his smugness, his absurdity!'

His spats, especially when they were a more even contest, could be very funny. He had a long-running feud with the columnist and fellow historian Paul Johnson. On a programme ironically entitled 'What happened to love and peace?' they both lost their tempers.

Paul Johnson: 'You are a silly little man!'

David Starkey: 'The only things about me that are smaller than you are my nose and my liver.'

It was my job to keep some sort of control over all this. It was not always easy, and with David it could be almost impossible. Trying to stop him with body language was pointless. The standard civilities were sometimes swept aside. I often had to resort to 'Shut up, David.' When even that did not work, either the producer or I had to physically get our fingers round his neck. He was in full flow on one programme and the clock was running out. I had tried everything to stop him but he was in full rant and I had to try to cut across him, talking very loud and very firmly. He whirled round on me and yelled 'Fuck you!' across the table. Live. On Radio Four, of all places. He was full of apologies later. He could be very winning when he was contrite.

The *Daily Mail* called him 'the rudest man in Britain'. David was delighted. 'That's worth a hundred thousand a year to me,' he said. It was, as he has acknowledged since, a considerable underestimate. His Moral Maze fame led to other broadcasting appearances, to a £2 million contract with Channel Four for history programmes, to best-selling books about Tudor monarchs. He is wafted around in a chauffeur-driven Jaguar these days, and owns two properties now in a pleasant street in North London. One houses a magnificent collection of paintings; the other he and his young partner, James, use as an office.

It was easy, on occasions, to loathe David but impossible, generally, not to like him. Normally he is an extremely charming man, and as clinical about his own faults as those of others. He has a weakness for posturing, but a lot of us have that problem and he, at least, is honest about it. He seems mellower these days, a little more portly, his silver hair a little longer, his walk (not that he does much walking now) even more of a Regency strut. Say what you like about him, he was never dull.

The Moral Maze is a live and often quite dangerous broadcast, a lot different from other, more carefully choreographed, debate programmes like Any Questions and *Question Time* where I often get the sinking feeling I know exactly what is going to be said as soon as I hear the cast list. By its very nature, some editions work brilliantly, some misfire. We have only had two complete failures.

One was the hundredth anniversary edition. The impressionist Rory Bremner was one of the witnesses and he immediately started to imitate all the panel members. He was as forensically American as Janet Daley, as flutingly northern as Edward Pearce, as orotund as David Starkey, and had even better rabbinical homilies than Hugo Gryn. It was a side-splitting performance – for us. It was a disaster for the audience. Rory's impressions were simply too good. You could not make head nor tail of who was really speaking; it collapsed into chaos.

The other great failure was the Moral Maze's translation to the screen, a saga that says a lot about what is wrong with television these days. The Maze was such a success that it was inevitable that someone would try it on television. When the BBC approached us we were all (apart from David Starkey) a bit wary, but we knew exactly what had to be done. The essence of the programme was the interplay of the arguments, the cockpit of ideas. Knowing a bit more about television than the others, I explained this to the earnest young men and women who came to see us. 'We want the minimum of fuss,' I said. 'It's just the faces and the interchange. Why don't you stage it around a table which is in a bowl of light, but the surroundings are in total darkness? That way you can move the cameras around freely without it being a distraction. It's like a particularly argumentative dinner party, without the dinner. And it has to be live.' They seemed to take it in and appeared to agree. They went off muttering words like 'simple', 'uncluttered', 'faces and ideas', 'live'.

When we got to the first programme we found the BBC had hired the Granada studio in Manchester, the biggest in the North of England. They had constructed what looked like an Aztec temple, set up for human sacrifice. The panellists and I sat in a row on a dais facing a runway that came curving up towards us from the wings. The witnesses had to walk up it, an agonisingly long way, before being allowed to sit on a scarlet sacrificial chair, chosen presumably so the blood would not show.

Everything was wrong. The set was designed so that the panellists could barely talk to each other, let alone have the close, face-to-face exchanges that make the radio programme. The witnesses looked, and felt, as if they were on trial for their lives. It was all dreadfully over-produced. Teams of earnest young researchers and producers tried to drill everybody to take the parts, and almost speak the lines, that they had prepared for them. It was crass and dull, and all spontaneity was relentlessly squeezed out of it. The programme was recorded and then edited out of all recognition. They were so terrified of the unexpected they made it utterly predictable; so frightened of failure, they guaranteed it.

There was only one light moment in the whole depressing series. Back at the hotel one night the wonderful Conservative MP and diarist Alan Clark, who had appeared as a witness, made a characteristically chivalrous attempt to seduce Janet Daley. It may have been a reflex action for the old roué, and Janet said she politely declined. But she was quite breathless about it for months.

Towards the end of the nineties the cold blast of change started whistling through the corridors of Radio Four. A new Controller was appointed and he started to shake the channel up. James Boyle had come down from Scotland where, perhaps unfairly, he had been regarded as such a hatchetman for the Director General he was known as 'McBirt'. He deployed the full Birtist armoury on Radio Four – consultants and focus groups, the lot. One focus group was set up to look at programmes for nine o'clock in the morning, the slot occupied on Thursdays by the Moral Maze. They were asked whether they wanted conflict at that time in the morning, so soon after the Today programme which could often be abrasive. Not surprisingly, they said they did not. James Boyle himself turned out to be an extremely pleasant and persuasive man, even though he was as clearly wrong about the Maze as he was in most of the other changes he imposed on Radio Four, to the distress and anger of its loyal audience.

He certainly had guts. He came down to face the Maze in its studio lair and the argument became extremely heated. It did not seem to matter that the Moral Maze often had a higher audience than any other programme in that slot. It also did not matter that it was one of the most talked-about programmes on the network. The focus group had spoken and it would be moved to the evening whatever we, or anybody else, had to say. There were three compensations. The first was that we could now have the dinner after the programme and not the night before. It was more relaxing even though the lack of hangovers did somewhat reduce the programme's characteristic note of ill-temper. The second was that the programme would be repeated later in the week, so the overall audience would broadly be the same. The third was that I would get one of the programmes that replaced it in the slot (an interview programme called The Choice).

We have been on Wednesday evenings ever since. The panellists have changed and new stars have been created to replace the old. We have a particularly vintage crop now, with the all the passion and forensic skills of the programme at its best, brusque and even brutal as well. It continues to be a corner of the BBC where the unsayable gets said, where arguments have to be strong and well thought out to survive, where if you can't keep up, well, tough.

The producer is as mischievous and turbulent as the programme. David Coomes has produced it from the beginning. He is a tall man, with improbably luxuriant grey hair, and gives an entirely misleading impression of dignified dependability. He comes from a family of Plymouth Brethren, which probably explains his complicated relationship with the religion that shaped him. He strives for balance without blandness, for heat *and* light. He knows to within an inch where the boundaries of acceptability lie and often pushes the programme right up to them. He seems to revel in taking risks which, these days, makes him a very unusual BBC producer indeed. David can be very hands-on. When one dreadful witness threatened to ruin a programme by boring us all into stupefaction he danced into the studio with a placard that he held up over her head (where thankfully she could not see it). It read: 'Who is going to go for this bitch?'

When Professor Steven Rose, the distinguished biologist, used the word 'fuck', he used it so specifically and so much in context David did not mind. But, just in case, he came into the studio with another big placard that read 'NO MORE FUCKS'. The witness under cross-examination at the time, as unused to David's ways as to the spirit of the programme, was temporarily struck dumb.

David takes a lot of risks but he makes a lot of effort to be fair and his judgement is good. His career has only been under threat once, and then it was not really his fault. It was at the end of a long and boozy Christmas lunch for the BBC religion producers in a crowded restaurant in Manchester. There had been discussion about the love of money being the root of all evil and David, challenging as always, had suggested that if enough cash were offered even the most respectable of the lady religious producers would dance naked round the restaurant twice. He waved his wallet around to illustrate what was an entirely theoretical point and it was snatched off him. The conversation moved on and he thought no more about it.

Twenty minutes later, the door of the Ladies swung open to reveal one of the better endowed women religious producers. She was not dressed for a carol service; in fact she was not dressed at all. All she had on was a pair of socks. She ran round the restaurant twice, a performance that was greatly appreciated by those who could still focus. Then, yelling, 'This one's on me,' she ran round a third time.

The newspapers had wonderful fun with it all. Even *The Times* ran most of a page on it. The story had everything: BBC religion, the producer of – ho, ho – the Moral Maze, the socks and the extra lap, two delightful touches. The full weight of the BBC's disciplinary machinery was deployed. Reprimands were issued, notes were put on files, tutting could be heard from on high. It was close for a while but both survived.

The BBC is a much more conformist organisation than it used to be. Sometimes you feel that there is an internal campaign against the eccentric and the unconventional, those whose views don't quite fit the prevailing fashion. I liked it when it was a tolerant and worldly place. It is good to know there is still room for the odd maverick producer and the odd risky programme.

TWENTY-SEVEN

IF YOU CLING on long enough in television, you get to be famous. Most of the time it has little to do with talent. It is longevity and familiarity; you appear so often in so many people's homes you become part of the nation's mental furniture. It seemed to me that I reached that critical mass after I had been presenting the BBC's main evening news for about six years. 'Don't I know you from somewhere?' became 'You're Michael Buerk, aren't you?' I enjoyed it, and not just because the second question is much easier to answer.

Fame is fun. For every late train trip to Manchester being abused by drunks, there are dozens of occasions when you are treated with far greater deference than you deserve. You get paid a lot more than you are worth, you are invited to loads of smart parties packed with other self-regarding semi-celebs, you get flattered beyond reason for your genius in just being there.

There are a few drawbacks, but they are minor. It is true that an adventurous private life can suddenly become very public. You certainly have to work hard to keep in touch with old friends who think there may be no room for them in what they imagine to be your glossy existence. The worst thing is that it is difficult, unless you spend your entire time under a duvet of self-admiration, not to realise, even if only from time to time, that it is all spurious. You are not famous because you can do something, like play the violin with a spiky haircut. You are not celebrated for your achievements. You are famous merely because you are *recognisable*. It is a worthless kind of celebrity, however much you get paid.

I am not complaining. Fame brought opportunities to do programmes I probably would not have had a chance of doing otherwise. I filmed documentary series about religion, *Soul of Britain, Future Watch* and *Hand of God*, despite being a badly informed sceptic. I presented a big BBC1 series on the scandalous history of tobacco, called *Tobacco Wars*, and my only real qualification was being a weak-willed ex-smoker. I got to front big events for the BBC though well-oiled gravitas was not really my speciality. I presented the key period of the millennium night programme, which could well turn out to be the most chaotic night in a thousand years of broadcasting. I did the royal wedding of Prince Edward and Sophie Rhys-Jones with Sue Barker. I think we probably had more fun than they did. The BBC got me to do the 1999 solar eclipse. I thought there was something vaguely familiar about the scientific expert they had roped in for me to talk to down in Cornwall as the great shadow raced in from the Atlantic. It was halfway through a very long morning when he told me we had been at school together and I had once tried to push his head down a toilet. I said he must be used to sudden darkness then, and we were both caught sniggering when the programme switched back to us.

Television presenting is largely a matter of bluff and it is easy to get caught out. I was filming a big drama documentary for BBC1 about Sir Christopher Wren with a delightful arts producer, inevitably called Julian. We were lining up a shot on the steps of St Paul's and I was feeling under pressure to establish some cultural credibility. 'Look at that,' I said, pointing airily across the river. 'There, down there, that ghastly old factory. Do you think if this were Paris or Rome they would let that dreadful industrial monstrosity ruin such a splendid stretch of the river?' I had worked myself into a state of high indignation.

Julian's jaw had dropped with what, at first, I thought was new respect.

'You do know,' he said, 'that's the Tate Modern?'

News was what I really loved; covering it, not presenting it. There is nothing quite so exciting as heading for the airport with a cameraman you like and respect at the start of an assignment you know is not going to be easy. I have been lucky that, on the occasions over the last twenty years when I have been able to get away and do that, I have worked with the best cameraman around. Cliff Bestall is a rugged South African who used to teach fine arts at the University of Capetown. He is an award-winning documentary maker in his own right, so I try not to notice when he uses posh words like *chiaroscuro* which I do not understand (I looked it up; it means light and shade). We think the same way about stories, work well together on the road and share the same weakness for red wine at the end of the day.

My occasional filming trips with Cliff reminded me of why I had really become a journalist. I liked being famous and the trappings that went with it. The novelty wears off but it is surprising how used you get to being treated as something special and how reluctant you can be to give that status up. The money was not bad either, but after the boys left university, that was less of an issue.

I should really have stopped newscasting when the BBC moved the main evening programme back from nine o'clock to ten. I did not agree with it (or, at any rate, would not have agreed had I been consulted). I was against the idea for reasons of sentiment and personal convenience. The BBC news had always been at – or very near – nine, going right back to the thirties. The nine o'clock radio news had been the central shared broadcasting experience of the British people throughout the Second World War. It seemed a shame to me to throw away that almost genetic link with the BBC's past in an opportunistic grab for our biggest opponent's timeslot and identity.

Besides, it meant I got home later. The first glass of wine did not slip down my throat until 11.15, which is as close to hardship as pampered newscasters get. But I had no great issue of principle over it. The BBC's public argument that ten was a better slot for news was eyewash – the move was being made to clear the way for hour-long drama programmes to start on the dot of the nine o'clock watershed – but ten o'clock was almost as good. I stayed on precisely because I did not want it to look as though I was leaving in a huff. I was also keen for the new programme to be seen to have some continuity with the old one and its central purpose: to be a mainstream news programme for grown-ups.

Grown-ups did not seem to be in fashion and, everywhere, news on television was going through another slow-motion revolution. A lot of thought seemed to be going into making it thoughtless. It seemed to be getting both thick and thin.

Part of me says it is not important. 'It's only television.' News bulletins have the lifetime of a terminally ill mayfly and there are so many other sources of information these days, does it matter?

Well, yes, it does. The majority of people get most of their news about the world from television. It can enable us to see more, know more, wonder more than the mass of humanity has ever done before. It can also be a reductionist monster that squashes the complexity of life into two physical dimensions and a single emotional one.

To be pompous about it, unpolluted sources of important information are essential for a working democracy and a civilised society. Television cannot tell us how to think, but it does set an intellectual, cultural and political agenda for public, and private, life. More, it helps us construct our moral framework, not so much because it influences our ideas about right and wrong (though it does), but because it seems to show us what is generally acceptable.

This is not a swipe against the BBC. The corporation is probably our best hope of getting through the media revolution and having worthwhile programmes at the end of it. Besides, there is something unedifying about

411

veteran broadcasters bellowing, Lear-like, into the winds of change and mourning some long-lost golden age. I have trawled through stuff we did in the so-called golden age and it was a salutary experience; a lot of it is embarrassing tripe. In my experience the people now running the bits of the BBC that I work for are at least as good as their predecessors and, often, a great deal better. But even the BBC cannot be immune from changes in society. Pressures from all sides are growing. In particular, there is a trend towards what one media academic has described as a new public discourse: 'one which privileges experience over knowledge, emotion over reason and popular opinion over expert advice'.

The first thing that worries me about television news is that there may be a lot of it, but most of it is coming from one place. If you are a broadcast journalist the BBC is the only game in town. ITN has been chopped down by the greed and managerial incompetence of the ITV companies that own it. Sky News, though vigorous, efficient and sometimes brilliant at what it does, is still a marginal operation on a channel few people bother to watch.

The wilful destruction of ITN is one of Britain's great cultural disasters of recent times. For its size and reach, it was far and away the finest television news organisation on earth in its heyday. I know, I worked against it over the decade or so when its income matched its ambitions. It was sharp and irreverent, it took risks, talked sense, and its best reporters scooped everybody, including me from time to time. Even when they didn't, they made you sweat just wondering what they were up to. Their programmes, especially *News at Ten*, were lively without being trivial, serious but rarely patronising. I thought a lot about joining ITN but when I was keen they were not, and when they wanted me I was going through one of my better times at the BBC. I am very glad now that I stayed where I was.

ITN has mutilated itself to keep its contract to supply news to ITV. It got rid of 200 people and chopped its annual budget from £45 million to £36 million. It is now not much more than half what the regulator, the Independent Television Commission, said 12 years ago was necessary to produce an acceptable news service. To add insult to injury, it was even stripped of its name; it is ITV News now. ITN RIP. It went downhill at frightening speed, sometimes producing a diet of celebrity pap and tabloid crime that would have embarrassed a local station in Cincinnati.

The BBC spends nearly ten times as much on its much wider range of news services and is now said to have the largest newsgathering operation in the world. I am very proud that it does. But it is not good for any organisation to have such a dominant role in its marketplace, especially the BBC. Complacency can be an art form within such a vast bureaucracy, run by armies of middle managers (cynics say BBC management is like musical chairs except that when the music stops, they put another chair *in*). It is too easy for the non-commercial BBC to measure itself by its own yardsticks. It needs strong competition to give it a kick up the backside, preferably on a daily basis.

The television news revolution that helped push ITN over the edge started, as most revolutions do, in the United States a decade before. The people who used to run the great network news operations there had the uppity self-righteousness of most American journalists. They took themselves terrible seriously and had more money than they knew what to do with. They kept lavishly staffed foreign bureaux everywhere and swamped every big international story. I frequently found myself with my one BBC crew working alongside an American network that was fielding eight. We were poor cousins and knew it.

In the mid-eighties that all changed. The American television networks were taken over by tougher, less indulgent owners. Audiences, and advertising income, were in decline. It was a crisis as much of confidence as anything else.

They responded by marketing news like chocolate. First, they called in the focus groups who told them their customers did not like anything abstract or unfamiliar. The market research established that people wanted news to be 'relevant' and exciting and (this was inferred rather than spelled out) not too intellectually troubling. The networks closed down nearly all their overseas operations. Foreign news disappeared from their news programmes, which soon largely consisted of crime stories and health scares. The grizzled veterans of Vietnam and the Middle East hung up their trench coats and were replaced by more attractive presenters, more attractively presented; packaging, after all, was the point.

Maybe this is one reason why a lot of Americans seem to be so ignorant, and so unconcerned, about what is happening in the rest of the world. If television is, even partly, responsible for that detachment, then the failure of its news programmes has consequences for us all.

In the early nineties, the BBC, or at any rate its news and current affairs departments, were heading smartly in the other direction. The arrival of

John Birt led to a new era of seriousness. He clearly thought the BBC's journalists were ill-disciplined, mentally lazy and self-indulgent. He brought the whole operation under strict central control. The agenda of nearly all the programmes became much heavier.

Birt was keen on a rather arid style of analysis. His journalism was no longer about discovery. His method, famously, was to decide what the story was first and then go and find people and events to stand it up. The programmes became relentlessly worthy. There was no room for humour or human interest; flair of any kind seemed to be frowned upon. Sometimes, coming to the end of a particularly uncompromising edition of the Birtist *Nine O'Clock News*, I would sign off wondering if anybody out there was left alive. The viewers stayed with us, though, and for much of the nineties we produced a news programme a great deal more serious than *The Times* and the *Daily Telegraph* for an audience nearly double the circulation of the *Sun*.

When Birt left, news lost its pre-eminent and protected position within the BBC. It was to be judged on the same basis as any other television programme. Its style and content were to be brought up to date. We were told we were dinosaurs facing extinction. Audiences for news programmes were falling. This was particularly true of people in so-called multi-channel homes, who now had a wide range of satellite or cable programmes to choose from. Even worse, the young, the 18–24-year-olds, were switching off. The writing was on the video wall.

It was a strong case, and much of it was true. Besides, the BBC is full of competitive and ambitious people, good at sniffing the wind. This was the future and if you questioned the assertions, or the assumptions, you might not be part of it.

If you looked closely at the figures they told a slightly different story. News audiences had fallen but they had for every other kind of programme; the arrival of so many more channels made that inevitable. The interesting thing was that news had not done worse than the other programmes. It had actually done *better*. Over the period they were looking at, the main evening news had lost 7 per cent of its audience. But the other peak-time programmes on BBC1 had lost an average of more than 10 per cent. We were certainly doing disproportionately badly in multi-channel homes. But the people buying Sky satellite dishes at the time were, typically, sports fans living on council estates. The core audience for serious news programmes was being slow to join this broadcasting revolution precisely because the new channels did not have the programmes they liked.

I was never sure why we bothered so much about the 18–24-year-olds. Advertisers like them because they are free-spending and easier to influence than other age groups, but the point of the BBC is that it does not have to bother about what advertisers want. Besides, people that age have much more exciting things to do than watch television news. Trying to work out what they want, and getting them to stay still long enough to give it to them, struck me as a pointless exercise best left to others. By definition, serious news is aimed at mature people. Making the news childish seemed to me to be the wrong response.

Nobody suggested that in so many words, of course, particularly at the BBC. The new thinking at all the networks came clothed in its own euphemisms. There was much talk of 'relevance', of 'broadening the agenda', finding 'new ways of telling stories'. It would have been churlish to object to any of these things. In the widest sense, they were long overdue. But it was difficult to escape the idea they were also a code for shifting the news downmarket, for a kind of news-lite.

It was difficult to argue against 'relevance', or even its snappy but essentially meaningless subtitle 'news you can use'. Of course we should be reporting news that touches the everyday lives of our viewers. But 'relevance' could be a blunt instrument. It could be used to exclude anything difficult, or abstract, or far away, and the forces that shape our existence are often all three. It can also be a selfish yardstick. It assumes we are only interested in ourselves and are not concerned about others.

'Broadening the agenda' was fine, in principle. What is news anyway but the collective choices of lots of half-ignorant journalists? The agenda had been stuck in tramlines for years, particularly television news programmes which only had room to do eight or nine reports properly each night. We banged away endlessly at some stories while hugely important issues, places and people never got mentioned at all. The problem was that 'broadening the agenda' could also be an excuse to run trivia. The new, wider definition of news embraced the cult of celebrity with enthusiasm. Even soap operas and television stars were news now, producing a kind of mindless media howl-round. The question was no longer 'Does it matter?' but 'Is this what people are talking about?' By that standard, a fading pop star who falls off his quad bike is a much bigger story than Zimbabwe leaving the Commonwealth, or the struggles over a new constitution for Europe.

It was right to experiment with new ways of telling stories. Perhaps news programmes had become formulaic. The problem was that all the networks, even the BBC, seemed to concentrate more on cosmetics than content. A Channel Five newscaster who sat on the edge of her desk, rather than behind it, was regarded as somehow groundbreaking. The fact that the programme's content at the beginning was often juvenile, and hardly anybody bothered to watch, did not seem to matter.

What the BBC said it was looking for was sensible enough. It wanted to find a better way to engage the viewers – to attract their attention, explain why they should be interested in the story at all, and then lead them through it, step by step. The answer they came up with was to change the role of the reporter. He or she would no longer be just a dispassionate observer who gathers up the most telling images of the day, crafts them into an edited news report with a commentary that describes what has happened and why it is important. Instead, the reporter would be more of a live performer, telling us, rather than showing us, what has happened. The personality of the reporter and his or her ability to look natural in unnatural situations were now as important as the traditional television journalist's skills. The BBC even imported a performance coach from the United States called Carla Haggis to show the corporation's journalists how it should be done. I was not amongst those selected for retraining so she did not get an opportunity to exercise her talents on me. But, judging by her effect on others, her main advice seems to have been that you should get between the viewer and the story, walk energetically towards the camera, and wave your arms about a lot.

All news programmes are now spattered with choreographed mini-interviews with their own reporters. It can work well. Somebody like the BBC's political editor, Andrew Marr, can bring a dull story to life with vivid conversational language and apparently spontaneous humour. It is as if we had just stopped him halfway down Whitehall and said: 'Come on, Andrew, what's really happening?' Unfortunately there are few reporters as talented as Marr, or as well qualified to make impromptu judgements about the stories they are covering. Some of these so-called 'two-ways' are done simply to show the range of our technological reach, or because 'going live' looks good. It is difficult for the reporters to avoid glib oversimplification.

They are also beyond immediate editorial control and the consequences of getting it wrong can be seismic. One impromptu conversation on the Today programme about the government's case for going to war against Iraq brought the BBC to its knees and cost the corporation its Chairman and its Director General.

The more insidious threat is how this is displacing authentic reporting across all the networks. The reporter caught in the middle of a big story now can be under such pressure that it makes it difficult to find time to discover what is actually going on. There are sometimes dozens of programmes and channels who want a part of him or, more often these days, her. BBC1 has four main news programmes, *Breakfast, One, Six* and *Ten*. Radio Four has five. BBC2 has *Newsnight*. The corporation has two round-the-clock television news channels, BBC News 24 and BBC World, and the radio news and sport network Radio Five. Then there is the World Service on radio, BBC Online, not to mention BBC Scotland and BBC Wales, both of whom see it as part of their national remit to cover events beyond their borders.

It is little wonder that stories are sometimes reported by men and women who may be in the right country but, because they spend their days and nights on some hotel roof with a camera and a satellite link, may have no more first-hand knowledge about what is going on than you do. They call them 'dish monkeys' in the trade; the women are called 'dish bitches'.

Those who are considered particularly good at this sort of thing graduate inside to deploy their new skills in front of a video wall in the warmth of a studio. They deliver miniature lectures as whizzo electronic graphics whirl behind them. There are some television pictures mixed in. Their organisation's cameraman was probably too busy shooting two-ways on the hotel roof to take them, but there are lots of freelances and everybody seems to have a video camera these days.

These techniques can work extremely well. Sometimes you get led by the hand through a complex story and know more about it, and what it means, than you might have done any other way. Sometimes a 'dish bitch' brings a connection, an immediacy, a real-time update, that makes the story more vivid and more understandable.

What worries me is when these essentially stagey devices become a substitute for the reporter's real job. To my mind, that is not waving her arms about in a studio or on a hotel roof, it is going out there with her cameraman – they're still mostly men – and seeing for herself, bringing back the pictorial evidence of what she has seen and telling us what it means from the basis of her direct experience. That is the way to get closest to the truth, and to produce the most authentic journalism.

Many of these changes are being driven by the rise of the round-the-clock television news channels. I am not a great enthusiast, but I do admire those who appear on them. I have tried it myself from time to time and it is hard work, by journalists' standards. You have to be clever and quick to handle breaking news on the hoof for hour after hour. It is even more of a strain trying to create excitement and interest when nothing much is happening which, in the nature of things, is most of the time.

The snag with the news channels is that nobody watches them, in broadcasting terms anyway. Last time I checked, BBC News 24 had an average spot audience of around 37,000, roughly the circulation, and about a third the actual readership, of the local weekly paper in the Midlands where I started in journalism. According to the official figures, News 24 broadcast 472 hours in 2003 when nobody at all was watching (mostly late at night). Sky News figures are not much different. ITV's version does even worse. It is the same for CNN's domestic audience in the United States and most of the other versions in the developed world.

Proponents of the news channels say this is an old-fashioned way of looking at audiences. What matters is not how many are watching at any one time, but how many tune in for more than a couple of minutes over a whole week. This adds up to millions and is particularly helpful for BBC News 24 which is broadcast on BBC1 after closedown and can count in the insomniacs, shift workers and drunks who feel the need for television in the small hours.

The main reason that all the big networks now have these news channels is because they fit in with a widely shared vision of how television is going to develop. Digital broadcasting makes it possible to have large numbers of channels. The argument, and it is a convincing one, is that this will lead to a high degree of specialisation. It has already happened; there are channels just for sport or old films, channels specialising in history, or lifestyle programmes, and, of course, news. The television theorists say specialist channels will multiply and the 'mixed economy' networks, like BBC1 and ITV, will either adapt or die. The logic of this theory is that they will become just mass audience entertainment channels. If you want any news at all, you will have to switch to a news channel that is broadcasting it all the time.

This may well be inevitable and, to the extent that it offers the viewer more choice, may be a good thing. But there are big drawbacks, too, and profound implications for television news in general and the BBC in particular.

The first problem is money. Decent television is expensive and there is only so much money to go round. The more television there is, the cheaper it will have to be. That is certainly true of 24-hour television news. BBC News 24 is a low-budget operation but still costs the licence payer upwards of £50 million a year. That, though, is not the only issue. The real difficulty, to my mind, is that its very nature tends to promote the kind of journalism I distrust, and squeeze out the thoughtful, well, crafted first-hand reporting I admire.

The news channel is driven by the tyranny of *now*. Though the BBC, in particular, has a culture of double-checking news before it is broadcast, the pressure to get it out first is strong, and embarrassing mistakes have been made. Sometimes it has been a relief that few people have been watching.

On all news channels, what's just happened is automatically more important than what went on earlier in the day, at least when it first breaks. A lot of the time nothing much is going on anyway and the channel keeps going by repetition and padding, hoping for something new. Something entirely trivial can be treated with the same sense of breathless urgency as a truly momentous event. The priority, in either case, is to get something, anything, on the air. The space has to be filled, often by putting the reporter, who ought to be going there to find out about it, in front of the camera in his office. We may have to feed the information to him so that he can regurgitate it, but that is 24-hour television.

The BBC is well run and big enough to be able to handle these competing demands pretty well, most of the time. But all newsrooms live in a state of perpetual crisis, and tend to give priority to the next outlet. More often than not that is 24-hour news, because it is always on the air. There are synergies, of course, and it is an advantage to have the newsroom operating all night, but there are big opportunity costs as well; 24-hour news soaks up a lot of talented people and scarce resources that might otherwise be available to the programmes people watch.

Those of us who raise these questions are told that, whether we like it or not, this is the future. Viewers are impatient and do not want to wait until six or ten o'clock for their news. They want a quick update so they can get on with their busy lives.

I think the future is more complicated than that, more threatening to the existing way of doing things but also more exciting in the possibilities it opens up. The key is the way the television will merge with the computer. BBC Online news is one of the corporation's quiet successes.

It is far and away the best online news site in the world and is constantly receiving international awards that recognise it as such. It is already streaming audio and video reports that are available at the click of a mouse. It is not difficult to see a future in which the viewer can edit his own news programme, and it is not far away. He won't even have to wait the 15 minutes it takes for the news channel's headlines to come rolling round. At any moment of the day or night he will be able to log on to his television/PC and bring up a constantly updated menu of video reports. He can choose what he wants to see and click on that piece about the riot in Trafalgar Square, that item about David Beckham's latest haircut, and the funny story about the crocodile that escaped in Watford. But, just as important, he can completely ignore what he does not think he will be interested in. The Chancellor's statement about the Euro – too dull. Human rights in China? Aids in Africa? Depressing and nothing to do with me. Public transport crisis? When isn't there one? Anyway, I haven't time to watch.

It will stand the old idea of public service broadcasting on its head. That was based on us knowing best what is good for you. Obviously, we made the news as interesting as we could, but the great thing about a conventional linear programme is that the viewers absorb a lot of stuff they would not have chosen to see, through inertia. Now the power will shift decisively to the consumer. What is more, the broadcasters will be able to see, second by second if they want, what sells and what does not. It will take a very brave and confident public service broadcasting organisation to persist with covering serious issues that only get a few 'hits', when other kinds of lighter stories are getting millions.

Maybe only the BBC can do it. It has so many advantages, after all. It has an assured income from a poll tax of nearly £3 billion a year. It has one of the three most recognisable brand names on the planet. Every bright graduate wants to work there. The people who run it are mostly decent, intelligent and high-minded. Many of the people who work for it, especially in news, are the best in the world at their jobs. No other broadcasting organisation can come up with a list of big-name journalists of such distinction. No competitor manages to win more than a fraction of the international awards the BBC walks off with every year.

The BBC wants to do it all. It wants to experiment with news-lite and keep its reputation for news-heavy. It wants News 24 and *Panorama*, the Today programme and *Vacuous Conversations With Celebrity Airheads*. (I made that up, but you weren't sure, were you?) Some people might be concerned that the one is edging out the other, but it could just be the swinging pendulum of broadcast fashion. In any case, doing it all is a way of getting around the increasingly difficult conundrum of what the BBC is for.

The corporation's existential dilemma is clear to see but horribly difficult to resolve. If we pay a poll tax for programmes they must, broadly speaking, be in the community's interest and not merely duplicate those already supplied by the market. But, because everybody has to pay, the BBC feels it cannot be exclusively elitist, and when its networks' share of the audience slips below 50 per cent it has, historically, started to worry. This means it tends to deal in slippery concepts like 'quality' and 'distinctiveness', or even the clumsy and not very illuminating Birtist slogan 'extending choice'. These characteristics are easy to spot in Radio Four or, I would say, the *Ten O'Clock News*, but it is more difficult in some other parts of the television and radio schedules.

Sooner or later, people are going to ask why the BBC should have a total monopoly of publicly funded broadcasting. Why should we be taxed for programmes advertisers are happy to make? Why should we not privatise Radio One and Two, and BBC1 and 2 for that matter? Why, come to think of it, should the bits we do want to fund from taxation not be put out to tender?

I think that the BBC's size and genetic sense of purpose is the best guarantee that what we value is protected from political pressure, technological change and dumb fashion. I will continue to think that for as long as the BBC keeps serious news on at peak time for a mainstream audience. It is as good a yardstick of public service broadcasting as you can get.

TWENTY-EIGHT

THE MOST BEAUTIFUL young woman in Africa took two hours to make me coffee. The coffee ceremony in the highlands of Ethiopia is an elaborate ritual of friendship and respect and cannot be hurried. She had already strewn newly cut grasses on the packed mud floor of her *tukul* to bring the smells and freshness of nature into her home. There was incense on a little charcoal burner placed between us and the room was filled with its sharp sweetness.

She sat on a tiny stool fanning a bigger charcoal stove into life. First, she roasted the coffee beans in a pan and I remembered how I was supposed to waft it towards me, sniff deeply and say the customary *beetam teeruno!* ('how delightful'). She ground the beans up in a pestle and put them to boil in a cracked and blackened *jebenya* (coffee pot) perched precariously on the coals. I was offered a tray of popcorn and bread, and a dish of cracked wheat, as she rinsed the little china cups she kept for best.

I had to drink three cups for the ceremony to be properly performed, each half filled with sugar. The first, the *abol*, was for refreshment, the second, the *tabuna*, for enjoyment, but the third was the one that mattered. The *bereka* is the blessing, the seal of Ethiopian hospitality and the high point of a coffee tradition that goes back a thousand years.

The girl was called Birhan and must have been around 21. I know her age pretty precisely because I saw her when she was a baby. You probably did, too, if you were alive on 13 July 1985. Birhan was the dying baby in a short video of suffering Ethiopian children, cut to the Cars' song 'Drive' and shown at the climax of the great Live Aid concert. The vast crowd in the stadium at Philadelphia went totally silent and were still; most seemed to be crying. So, I dare say, were the half a billion people watching on television all over the world.

There seemed little doubt she was dying. Her father had taken her at the height of the famine to the nuns who ran a clinic in Makele. A Canadian television crew, following up my first reports, actually filmed the nuns saying there was no hope for her. A sister lifted the rags that covered her emaciated body, stroked her deathly pale face, and gently pronounced her death sentence. 'There's no hope for this child. She is too far gone. She will die.' The nuns had seen a lot of death by then and were not often wrong. Her father had even helped dig a grave for her, with the help of the nuns' shovels. But, as he picked her up for, as he thought, the last time, he felt a fluttering in the chest under his fingers.

Birhan did not die. The nuns, of course, say it was a miracle. Her father is convinced of it. 'God smiled and the sun shone on me,' he said. He is a man of extraordinary dignity and sweetness and when he talks of his favourite child his face is transfigured with love. Birhan and her father not only survived the famine but they lived through the *Derg*'s infamous resettlement operation. They were flown in the unpressurised cargo hold of a Soviet Antonov 'plane down from the mountains to the sweltering and diseased lowlands, along with hundreds of thousands of others. Many of them died but he did not and he returned to his homeland in the highlands, walking for two and a half months with Birhan on his back. They survived the wars and she had been educated, thanks to the support of a Canadian reporter, a friend of mine. I had found her and her father, nearly twenty years after the famine, at their home at Quiha. She was trying to decide what to do with her life, whether to train as a nurse or an agricultural development worker. She wanted something that would do good and repay the debt she felt she owed to God, fate and my Canadian friend. She was beautiful because of what she represented; the triumph of life over death, the human capacity for selflessness, a glimpse of what might be possible with luck and a little help of the right kind, even in the country that is such a byword for misfortune and despair. She really did not have to look so beautiful as well. That was just our luck.

I spent a lot of time in Ethiopia in the months before the twentieth anniversary of the famine, putting together a big programme for the BBC. We wanted to tell the story of what happened then and try to find out why the fate of those poor people, at that moment, so captured the attention and sympathy of the rich world. We wanted to see what had really changed in the twenty years since the terrible hunger and the worldwide campaign to save its victims.

There is no monument at Korem for the thousands who died. The plain outside the little town stretches pleasantly away to the surrounding mountains and all there is to be seen is a couple of flocks of goats being driven by ragged children carrying long sticks, taller than themselves. We drove across what was the famine camp towards a circular church in the distance, and only realised when the ground got bumpy that we were driving over the dead. There was no room then in the graveyard for all the bodies but they were buried as close as possible to the old church and its little grove of trees. You had to look hard, but you could see slight humps in the land, radiating out from the church, like ripples after you have thrown a pebble into a pond. Otherwise, all that is left of the famine is the collective memory of the millions who survived because, for once, the rest of the world felt inspired to save them.

We tracked down the orphans of the famine. I had made a film about them early in 1985. There were thousands of them up in Makele then, so many that it took them fifteen minutes to file out into the field where they were being gathered. I asked a rhetorical question at the time about what was going to happen to so many parentless children in a society that had lost all capacity to cope. Twenty years on, I found them as adults. Many had, in fact, been given more opportunities than they would have had if their lives had not been overtaken by disaster. The big orphanages were run by some outstanding people and backed by a German religious charity. One orphan had become a teacher, another a computer operator.

When they heard who I was, they wanted to see the television reports from those days. It was a mistake. They sat transfixed by what was happening on the screen, and by the nightmares it recalled for them. Their faces were full of pain and many put their hands over their eyes and ears to try to shut it out.

One of them was called Girmai, a thick-set young man with a friendly, open face. His story was a terrible one but not unusual for those desperate times. He had been in one of the camps with his mother and one of his sisters. The rest of his family had died. His mother was sick, he told me, and she had sent him to look for some water. When he got back, his mother was dead. Nobody could tell him what had happened to his sister and he never saw her again. He still does not know if she is alive or dead.

He talked a lot about how grateful he was for the help from abroad, which saved him and gave him the chance of a better life. He described his time in the orphanage and the comradeship of those who had shared such dreadful experiences. He had married another orphan and while we were in the town they had their first child. They named him Michael and it all became very emotional.

The hunger was back when I was last there, all across the mountains of northern Ethiopia. People were not dying, or at least not in large numbers. A complex warning system is now in place and the big international donors finally responded, but it was touch and go for months. The wars are largely over and there is now a government which, for all its faults, is not the *Derg* and does at least seem to care. Just enough food got where it was needed, just in time. The ration had to be cut from 15 kilos of grain a month, which is supposed to be the bare minimum, to 12.5 kilos. If you are as experienced at starving as the Ethiopians you can survive on that, as long as you lie down for most of the time. Watching them queue in their thousands for hours for their bag of foreign food, seeing them hanging on the wire mesh fences that surround the relief depots, you have to wonder what we are doing there. We were feeding 14 million people in Ethiopia at the time, almost twice as many as went hungry in the great famine of twenty years before. It was a bad year but, even in an average one, we have to feed 6 million and the trend is relentlessly upward.

We seem embarrassed to let them die but incapable of helping them to escape this slide into dependence and international beggary. Ethiopia is already the largest recipient of relief aid per head in the world, but gets less development aid than any of the needy countries. All we seem to be able to do is to keep more and more people barely alive. The population is soaring and the fertility of the land is falling, despite extraordinary efforts being made in some places to terrace the mountains and capture the fickle rains. There is a neat but chilling symmetry here; the population is growing at almost exactly the same rate as the topsoil is being washed off the hillsides, nearly three per cent a year. It is a Malthusian nightmare already. You do not have to extrapolate the figures to realise that it is unsustainable but, if you do, it becomes truly frightening.

I went to see Mengistu's successor in the government buildings behind Haile Selassie's royal palace. Meles Zenawi is a clever man who did an Open University MBA course as soon as he came to power. 'The worst thing is to die,' he told me. 'The worst thing after that is to beg.' He and his ministers are reconstructed Marxists who, I think, genuinely want the peasants to have a better life, but want them to stay peasants. His strategy is to keep them on land they are not allowed to own and that has already been divided so much that many live on so-called 'starvation plots' of little more than an acre. He told me he that he had five years to produce a decisive improvement. He did not spell out the consequences if he and the world community fail to do so, but he has the eyes of a man who has looked into an abyss.

It was not just Ethiopia. Since I finally left the *Ten O'Clock News* desk, a decade and more after I had originally planned, I have been back on the road again; a reporter once more. I have travelled a lot and this book has given me a wonderful excuse to retrace my steps and see what happened to those places, and those people, whom I encountered in my correspondent days.

I have spent a lot of time in South Africa, which will always be special to me. Its largely bloodless transition from apartheid to multi-racial democracy still seems a miracle. The black people's ability to forgive is even more remarkable than the whites' capacity to adjust. I went down to Kenton on Sea in the Eastern Cape, a little holiday town with one of the most beautiful beaches on the Indian Ocean. When I used to go there in the eighties it was strictly for whites, and the only blacks who were allowed on its pale golden sands sold ice creams. Now it is for everybody. An Indian family sat around an elaborate picnic, next to a white couple with their sandwiches. A group of black boys played energetic and noisy football on the harder sand close to the water's edge. It was such a contrast, I climbed up the hill behind the beach to take a picture.

I was still so taken with it, and the glimpse it had given me of a rainbow nation at peace with itself at last, that I wanted to share it all with the white taxi driver who was taking me back to Port Elizabeth. He heard me out without expression and then asked me if I had been told what had recently happened on the beaches there. A white mother and her two young daughters had been abducted at gunpoint by a gang of young black men, he said. They were raped and murdered and their bodies were found in a culvert a few days later. Just when you think you have made your mind up about South Africa reality smacks you, and your glib judgements, over the head. Write it off as a racial tyranny heading for a bloodbath and up steps Nelson Mandela and a decade of compromise and resolution. Acclaim it a paradise and it suddenly goes dark.

Violence is only one of the epidemics threatening South Africa. All the races there have a culture of violence and the country is so awash with guns that a teacher in Soweto told me it was easier for her pupils to get a pistol than a pen. The murder rate is the highest in the world. There are around 21,000 murders a year in South Africa; in the United Kingdom, which has a larger population, the figure is fewer than 1,000. What is really worrying is that many of the killings are entirely gratuitous. People are shot after they have handed over their car keys, or given the burglars all their valuables. It seems to be about power. The gun gives people who have been powerless for generations the ultimate control over life and death. The temptation to use it seems to be overwhelming. Power also seems to be behind the extraordinarily high incidence of rape in South Africa. There are more than 50,000 cases a year, again the highest in the world. The police reckon only 1 in 36 rapes is ever reported. If true, that would mean a woman is raped in South Africa every 26 seconds.

It is a dangerous country now, paradoxically more dangerous than it was at the height of the township uprisings. The last time I was in the rich northern suburbs of Johannesburg where I used to live, the Hertz man gave me a lecture on defensive driving, South African-style. 'Don't stop at red lights after dark,' he said. 'Don't do your seatbelt up because the hi-jackers will think you are going for a gun when you try to release it. And never, never look them in the eye.'

'What should I do?' I asked.

'Just pray, man,' he said. 'Just pray.'

I was in South Africa reporting on the country's other epidemic, Aids. South Africa has more people living with the HIV virus than any other country in the world. The statistics are extrapolated guesswork, and the predictions based on them are probably even less reliable but, if they turn out to be only half right, the future verges on the apocalyptic. Approaching 20 per cent of adults are thought to have the disease. According to the country's Medical Research Council, it threatens to kill 800,000 South Africans a year by the end of the decade. By then, 3 million children may have been robbed of their parents.

I went down to the Avalon cemetery in Soweto, where I used to stand in clouds of tear gas watching them bury kids killed by soldiers in the riots of the apartheid years. It is the biggest cemetery in Africa but Aids had nearly filled it. There were 180 funerals a weekend and the authorities were so short of space they were talking of burying people in old mineshafts.

Nelson Mandela's successor, Thabo Mbeki, seemed to be in denial at the time. His attitude was reflected in an extraordinary 114-page document produced for the national executive committee of the ruling African National Congress. Parts of it, leaked to the local press, seemed almost hysterical in its sensitivity to the idea that Aids was reinforcing white stereotypes of black African behaviour.

'Yes, we are sex-crazy! Yes, we are diseased! Yes, we spread the deadly HI virus through our uncontrolled heterosexual sex! Yes, we, the men, abuse women and the girl-child with gay abandon! Yes, among us, rape is endemic because of our culture! Yes, we do believe that sleeping with young virgins will cure us of Aids!'

The author was believed to be a prominent ANC leader called Peter Mokaba, who publicly denied the very existence of HIV and described the anti-retroviral drugs used to treat it as 'poison'. He died shortly afterwards at the age of 43. His doctor said he had suffered from 'pneumonia, linked to a respiratory problem', but it was almost certainly Aids.

The South African government has now authorised the use of anti-retroviral drugs that are being provided cheaply by the pharmaceutical companies with the help of the Americans. Whether it can stem the spread of the disease in South Africa is uncertain.

Neighbouring countries are in an even worse situation. The prevalence rate amongst adults in Botswana is thought to be nearly 40 per cent, and if you go to Gaberone, as I have just done, you can see the human wreckage of Aids piled up in the Princess Marina Hospital. Hundreds of people in the final stages of the disease start queuing for the HIV/Aids clinic well before dawn. Botswana is prosperous and well run, by African standards. The countries around are neither and the infection rates appear to be almost as high.

Not long ago I met an African nurse called Asmara who I had known in the famine camps of the north during the eighties. Her husband had already died of Aids. Now she had the disease. She did not know, and could not bear to find out, whether her little son who was playing outside was infected too. As I left, she grabbed my hands and just said: 'Africa. Why Africa?' She died a month later.

Some of the countries I used to cover have taken one step forward, some two steps back. The wars in Angola and Mozambique have stopped, but Zimbabwe, the beautiful country, has been comprehensively ruined by Mugabe, and Congo is in anarchy with its rich resources plundered by foreign armies. Africa, the majority of it anyway, is sliding away from the conditions and the expectations of the rest of humanity as surely as if it were adrift and heading for the Antarctic. The World Bank defines 'absolute poverty' as having to live on less than $1 a day. Nearly half a billion Africans now fall into that category. During the nineties their numbers increased by 74 million – more than the entire population of the United Kingdom.

Though many make good careers in the industry of aid, and the more idealistic politicians in the rich world try to put Africa's problems on the agenda, people barely pretend to have solutions any more.

*

Some of the other trouble spots I used to patrol are off the front pages and glad of it. Peace, or at least a ceasefire for negotiations, has stopped most of the killing in Northern Ireland, in Sri Lanka and El Salvador. Cyprus is still divided despite decades of effort to broker a federal reunion. Argentina has rid itself of a military dictatorship but run into economic meltdown. The Middle East remains complex and intractable; still the flashpoint that could kill us all.

In Britain, many of the steps along my personal road have changed beyond recognition. Bromsgrove is a satellite township of Birmingham now, not the overgrown country village Eric Belk knew and I can still remember. Birmingham is, as always, energetically tearing down the old and rebuilding. This time, thankfully, what they are pulling down is the gimcrack ugliness of the sixties not the glories of the Chamberlain years. Bristol has grown, too, and managed to become simultaneously posher and rougher. Cardiff seems to have totally reinvented itself, and the brothel and hoodlum district the *South Wales Echo* used to call Butetown, and foreigners knew as Tiger Bay, is now fancy hotels and slick shops. The Taff no longer flows black with coal dust and the new Cardiff Bay is for yuppies, not drunken lascars from the coaling ships.

Scotland has its own Parliament but seems to me to be even chippier about England and the English than ever. As a good many organisations in Britain are still largely run by Scots this remains as much of a mystery as it always was. They are still subsidised by the English (the state spends £6,246 a year on every Scot, £5,012 on every English person). The oil has started to run out.

Even Manchester seems to have improved. Last time I went I managed to get through the whole trip without a single shudder. I had lunch in a rather good fish restaurant looking out on Albert Square. Chips were available, but not insisted upon. I distinctly saw two people smile and it wasn't raining very hard. Maybe I have been doing Manchester an injustice all these years.

I try to take Christine along when I am travelling now. I always wanted to show her the places I got to over the years and sharing experiences nearly always makes them more fun. Besides, as a fully paid-up coward these days, if it is unsuitable for a woman (a gutsy woman at that) it is definitely unsuitable for me. We have the time and the freedom now. The boys have long since grown into men and, as I write this, have just celebrated their thirtieth birthday. Roland is far better at the sort of job I do than I ever was; Simon works ridiculously hard for one of the major oil companies. We are very proud of both of them. And I have another family now.

The ferry for Nanaimo leaves from Horseshoe Bay, just a little north-west of the city of Vancouver. It is not a long way. You hardly lose sight of the wooded coastal mountains of mainland British Columbia before the long green hump of Vancouver Island looms on the horizon. But I was in a hurry that day. I had waited fifty-seven years and now I was impatient and, if I am honest, a little fearful.

Vancouver Island is a place the size of Holland. The west is wild and rainsoaked, a spectacular coastline of stone beaches littered with logs. The east is flatter and calmer. It lies in the rainshadow and has the mildest climate in Canada. The eastern coast highway as it heads north from Nanaimo is rather dull, and even tawdry. Parkville is a particularly drab place which tries to give itself some distinction by staging the world sandcastle competition every July. It was April and I was never any good at sandcastles anyway. We hurried on, past Rathtrevor Beach where the tide that funnels up and down the Strait of Georgia goes out more than a kilometre, past French Creek with the channel narrowing and the island-studded coastline clear against the mountains of the mainland beyond. We stopped by the great piles of shells at one of the oyster factories on Fanny Bay. A dozen women dressed by the hygiene regulations bayoneted their bivalves with the casual precision of long practice. Vancouver Island oysters are the size and texture of a *tournedos* steak. They make the mincing little Brittany *belons* that I have always been rather fond of look like congealed snot. We bought a white plastic pail stacked with them, but just one was as sustaining as a Big Mac and we were soon back on the highway.

We found the man we were looking for at the Royal Canadian Mounted Police station in Courtenay, one of three sister towns set in the farming landscape of the Comox Valley. He was the station sergeant there. Sergeant Gary Buerk. My brother, the Mountie.

It was a strange first meeting. The other policemen and women obviously knew who I was and were surreptitiously comparing the two of us. I suppose we were doing the same thing. He is ten years younger than me, a trim man with a moustache and steady grey eyes. As Christine put it, rather insensitively, I thought, 'Very like you really but, you know, handsome.'

We did not stop at the station. He buckled on his gun, picked up his bullet-proof vest and ushered us out to his prowl car. It seemed a bit over the top for a blameless little town in the far west of law-abiding Canada that seemed to be largely populated by tree-huggers and rednecks. It was the rules, apparently, and in his last posting, as an undercover agent in the big city of Vancouver, he might well have made a few enemies.

This was something of a dream job towards the end of his career. He had certainly earned it. He'd spent a long time in the far north as the resident Mountie on Southampton Island in the frozen mouth of Hudson's Bay. That was why I had not met him a few years earlier when I saw his brother Greg, who never moved from Vancouver and owns two garages there.

Gary now lives a spacious life in a community that looks pleasant and easygoing. He and his wife Judy, their son David and daughter Cathy, have a big Canadian house in the rather more genteel neighbouring town of Comox. We went there for lunch. It could have been uncomfortable. It should have been difficult. In the end it was neither. Comparing notes about our father was like talking of two different men. To me, he was the bigamist, serial liar and ne'er-do-well who deserted my mother and totally rejected me. To Gary, he was a warm and dependable father at the centre of a loving home that, while rarely prosperous, was always secure. Their mother, Fern, was clearly an admirable woman, warm and strong. But that does not fully explain the change in my father from the flash phoney my mother married to the loyal family man he seems to have become. A man who, even when he was hard up, would scrape together enough money for a babysitter so he could take his wife for a picnic in the park. A man who withdrew his children from Sunday School because he hated the idea of not being able to go on family outings with them.

There was a time when I might have been hurt by the thought of the kind of father I had missed. It is a bit late for that in your fifties. Instead, I tried to make some sense of it but did not get very far.

Gary and Greg did not know I even existed until after our father died. It was obvious he had forbidden Fern to tell them, for she took the first opportunity she had, even before the funeral. There were a lot of things Gary still did not know. It was a shock to him that his father had been a bigamist and that his other family had been so thoroughly erased from his life. Gary took it well. He has a pleasantly dry sense of humour. 'My,' he said at one point, 'what a lot of detective work you've done.' I suppose I pulled a few punches because I liked him so much, but not many. It was clear that his fondness for our father was so strong that nothing I said about him would alter it, and I was glad.

It was equally clear that nothing he could say would really change my view of our father, which was a shame. I know now he was a better man than I imagined or, at least, was capable of being better. But that does not really help very much, and might even make it worse. It makes the rejection a matter of choice rather than character, after all. Still, I have two fine brothers instead of the father I never knew.

After lunch we persuaded Gary to put on the ceremonial uniform of the Mounties, so that we could take a picture. The famous red coat came out of the cupboard, along with the dark blue jodhpurs and the hat in its special press to keep the wide brim flat. He looked quite splendid in the full fig, a Canadian icon.

I have the picture in front of me now. I can't help thinking that if things had been different I might have been a Mountie, living in a forest island on the far side of the world.

But I took a different road.

INDEX

state of emergency 319
township uprising 308–29,
344
Transkei 245–6
Uitenhague 311
upsurge in violence 426–8
use of Ethiopian famine reports
300
Western Cape 242–3
white, definition of 240
white fears and black sensuality
233–4
white ignorance 325
white insensitivity 326–7
white security precautions
327–8
Windsurfing championships
324–5
South America 342
South Today (BBC South
programme) 111, 112–4
South Wales Argus 62, 69, 76, 79
South Wales Echo 66–8, 69–82
Southampton 114, 115
Southampton General Hospital
139–40, 140–3
Southern Evening Echo 115, 140
Soviet Union, collapse of 356,
362
Spandau Ballet 301
Sport Aid 291, 305
Springbok rugby team 194
Sri Lanka 334–8, 429
Sri Pad, Sri Lanka 337–8
Stanley (BBC soundman) 152,
154, 156
Starkey, Dr David 402–4, 405
Starr, Jack 190
starvation, effects of 284

Status Quo 301, 304
Stewart, Peter 125
Sting 301
Stockport 83
Stoddart, Ted 157
Stoke Brush Works 57–8
Style Council 301
sub-editors 69
Sullivan, Michael 187–8
Sun, the 86–7, 298
Sunday Times 69
Sylvia (South African friend)
343–4

Talbot, Richard 99–100
Tamil Tigers 336–7, 338
Tanzania 224, 268
Tavern, Birmingham, bombing of
163–5
Taylor, Lindsay 11, 18
Teasdale, Ralph 29
Ted (*Bromsgrove Weekly Messenger*
reporter) 56
Television Centre 126, 151
television news, competition
9–10
television, takeover of newspapers
role 87
Teresa, Mother 339
Thatcher, Margaret 209, 212,
255, 302, 359
and Angola 263, 264–5
debt to SNP 185
Nature interview 381–2
and the Ngema tribe 235
and North Sea oil revenue
173
Theunissen, Amanda 383
Thompson, Mark 353